LOT'S DAUGHTERS

lot's daughters

sex, redemption,

and women's quest

for authority

Robert M. Polhemus

STANFORD UNIVERITY PRESS
STANFORD, CALIFORNIA

Stanford University Press
Stanford, California

Printed in the United States of America on acid-free, archival-quality paper

Library of Congress Cataloging-in-Publication Data

Polhemus, Robert M.
Lot's daughter's : sex, redemption, and women's quest for authority /
Robert M. Polhemus
p. cm.
Includes bibliographical references and index.
ISBN 0-8047-5051-3 (cloth : alk. paper)—
1. Fathers and daughters.   2. Lot (Biblical figure).   3. Oedipus complex.
4. Man-woman relationships.   5. Feminism.   I. Title.
HQ755.86.P64   2005
306.874'2—dc22   2004019649

Original Printing 2005

Last figure below indicates year of this printing:
14   13   12   11   10   09   08   07   06   05

Designed by James P. Brommer
Typeset in 11/14.5 Minion

Contents

Part II
Generating and Representing Modern Daughters of Lot

Part III
Lot's Daughters at the Millennium:
Potomac Testaments

Figures and Plates

A section of color plates of Lot and his daughters
in Renaissance art appears in Chapter 4.

for carol

Preface

Look about and you see the rise of daughters in the world—daughters who have more opportunities to increase their freedom and power. The concerns and interests of daughters and fathers, the education and erotic experience of boys and girls, and the vocational ambitions of men and women are converging as never before. The gender gap narrows and gender roles blur. It might be the biggest story of our lifetime. And yet this process has produced and does produce turmoil and psychological confusion as well as promise.

My subject is the crucial development of father-daughter, older men–younger women relations in history, psychology, and art, and, specifically, in the creative experience of figures important in the shaping of modern culture. That huge story features women's continuing quest for authority, especially in the last two centuries. I tell it mainly through a wide-ranging series of portraits analyzing and dramatizing the remarkable life and work of famous men and women who, in their diverse ways, have made the world care more deeply about the destiny of daughters. I start off with a world-historical biblical family and those prophets, saints, painters, and writers who first interpreted them and represented them for posterity. My gallery then goes on to include Luther, Calvin, and Shakespeare; and then the nineteenth-century novelists Jane Austen, Mary Shelley, and the Brontë sisters—pioneers in giving brilliant, passionate daughters a voice. Continuing through the ages, I discuss the comic subverter of patriarchy Lewis Carroll and also the major father figure of psychoanalysis and modern mind-reading, Sigmund Freud. Then follows my array of influential twentieth-century celebrities: Shirley Temple, Woody Allen and Mia Farrow, Carolivia Herron, Bill Clinton, his wife Hillary Rodham Clinton, their daughter Chelsea, and Monica Lewinsky. All of them play big parts in ongoing human drama of what I call the "Lot complex"—mutual attraction between young females and older males.

In light of the Lot complex, I intend my studies of these figures to show them clearly and in a new perspective. And I mean this book to have a broad appeal. One of my goals is to make it vital and engaging for anyone who has an interest in any or several of its diverse cast of characters—whether or not you care at all about psychological theories or Bible history. The chapters make a collective whole, but individually, they can stand—and be read—on their own. You can, for example, read and learn about the miracle of the amazing Brontë family without knowing anything about Martin Luther. You can see why Shirley Temple really matters without poring over Scripture or discover the visionary power of Renaissance painters of Lot's daughters without thinking about Woody Allen. You can see what Freud and Clinton were up to without comparing them to Shakespeare (even though setting these subjects next to each other turns out to be remarkably revealing).

I hope *Lot's Daughters* is a work on the side of the angels, telling of women's progress and men's progress too. It is, however, liable, for one basic reason, to be disturbing and controversial: its major premise is that a disreputable Bible story of father-daughter incest (Genesis 19) offers an effective means and model for understanding the history of gender and familial relations not only in the past but right now. This book begins with the power and reality of incestuous attraction and what humanity does about it. But that word "incest" can give you the creeps, and so I worry about being misunderstood. I feel a silly urge to write *Reader, I'm not "soft" on incest; I never lusted after my daughters; our relations are good; I'm a nice grandfather, etc., etc.* Still, like novelist Carolivia Herron, I believe that the dark Lot family narrative, with its unavoidable, cosmic disaster, its irrepressible sexual sin, its pressure to sublimate erotic familial desires, and its potential for redemption, goes on living in us because it holds repressed secrets of the past and epic possibilities for the future. I mean to show how and why what happens in this scandalous myth comes down through the ages, roils people's imaginations, gets modified, and helps explain contemporary life—why, for example, father-daughter relations have been getting more and more critical attention and why, in a time of raised feminist consciousness, older men and younger women keep taking up with each other seriously and show no signs of stopping.

But there's no denying the Lot story *is* shocking, does describe offensive behavior, does probe shameful erotic secrets, and does make readers face troubling moral and psychological issues that emerge out of the old chaos of sex lives. People like and need to gild the past—but there was no golden age for girls. If the history of civilization features women rising, the Lot text shows how long that climb has been. It describes, for instance, a benevolent Old Testament patriarch, by the standards of his times a moral man, not bad man. Nevertheless, when a mob threatens his home, he offers his own daughters up to the vicious men as sex objects for their diversion. It tells of a wife and mother obliterated and then replaced as her husband's mate by their willful daughters. It makes the girls the active, incestuous seducers. It sexualizes the relationship of fathers and daughters and sets forth as one absolute basis and strain of human culture and history the potentially eroticized father-daughter tie. It suggests that there is, for some reason, a potential erotic component in father-daughter relationships not paralleled in mother-son relationships and that civil culture must face that problem.

Obviously such material sets up resistance. You might resent being told that you somehow share the sleazy heritage of Lot's cave. Daughters and fathers and middle-aged men and young women may not like to read that they have repressed erotic complexes or that their lives are the result of the way other people lived out such complexes in the past. They may be uneasy about reflecting on the way they use each other's love and regard to get what they want. Those coming up like to feel strong and independent —that they make it on their own—and so women, long kept down, may resent the idea that their achievement relies on help from older males with sublimated crushes on them. Daughters may not want to admit that they adored their fathers, longed to be like them, and looked down on their mothers. Older men may not like the self-image of running out on wives, nor do they want to admit that they see younger women first as symbols of their own youth and power (which they desperately want to hang onto) rather than as unique people. Fathers don't want to talk much about how they love their daughters madly and need to displace inchoate longings towards them in positive, moral acts of responsibility and help. And fathers and daughters—older men and younger women— may be queasy about the kinds of bonding between them that alienate and demeans aging wives and mothers. There is something off-putting about saying that in some important way, daughters want to be like their fathers but sons do not want to be like their mothers. These, however, are key facts of social life worth exploring.

My overall argument is that the consequence of the Lot's-daughters myth, as it plays out in the Bible and in history, art, and real life carries hope—the hope and the narrative direction that my subtitle to *Lot's Daughters* traces: *Sex, Redemption, and Women's Quest for Authority.* The scriptural text begins with the fact of sexual possibilities and incestuous desire as a biological and cultural *given* of history, but then its heritage moves towards modes of moral redemption and the long quest for female empowerment. That is my narrative, but let me end this Preface with an incident that captures both the communal, enduring nature of the Lot's-daughters pattern and the rich particularity, struggle, and changing implications alive in it:

In Bill Clinton's autobiography, there's a snapshot of the president with his teenage daughter Chelsea. They're at the funeral of a dear family friend who was suddenly cut down in the prime of life. The girl stands very straight, looking somber and grown-up in her sensible coat and dark glasses. Her tall father has turned to her, bowed his head, and laid it on her shoulder. It is a gesture of paternal intimacy. He wants and obviously expects the support and sympathy of a strong young woman, and she looks likes she's there to give it to him. She looks like a person who could be in charge. The gesture is anything but improper, but it's not without its unconscious erotic tinge. Hundreds of pages earlier, Clinton describes getting together with Chelsea's mother: "Hilary sat . . . and I sat beside her talking. Before long, I leaned over and put my head on her shoulder. It was our first date."[1] The intimate gesture of alliance with the daughter uncannily repeats and amplifies the former act of affectionate supplication towards his ambitious, forceful wife-to-be. It is the extended meaning and the human potential of that picture—*everything old is new again*—that I wish to wish explore and bring to life.

Acknowledgments

It has taken me more than ten years to think through, write, and finish *Lot's Daughters*. I want to express my profound gratitude to the many people who have helped me in its making—more than I can name.

For their reading, encouragement, useful, wise, and generous critiques of large and small portions of this work, I thank, in alphabetical order: Elaine Auyoung, Shirley Temple Black, Megan Bradley, Bliss Carnochan, Terry Castle, Debbie Chung, Mary Jean Corbett, George Dekker, Simone Di Piero, Dorothy Driver, Page duBois, Arnie Eisen, Martin Evans, Jay Fliegelman, Renee Fox, Denise Gigante, John Glavin, Sara Hackenberg, Judith Hibbard, Nick Jenkins, Gerhard Joseph, James Kincaid, Don Lamm, Seth Lerer, Anne Mellor, Helena Michie, Diane Middlebrook, Franco Moretti, Stephen Orgel, Mack Polhemus, Norris Pope, Arnold Rampersad, David Riggs, Hilary Schor, Carol Shloss, James Simpson, Jennifer Summit, Nora Sweeny, Elizabeth Tallent, Helen Tartar, Domino Torres, Blakey Vermuehle, Elizabeth Vezzani, Alex Woloch, and Bill Wyman.

For support in the early stages of planning this book, I am greatly indebted to the Stanford Literature and Psychoanalysis Reading Group and specifically to Rick and Barbara Almond, Norm Dishotsky, and Diane Middlebrook. I also would like to thank the students in the "Lot's Daughters" English 368 graduate seminar in 1997 for their insights and helpful intellectual probing. To directors John Jordan and Murray Baumgarten, and the ongoing University of California Dickens Universe Project in Victorian Studies, I owe a great deal of thanks for giving me the opportunity to present first many of the ideas in this book here and abroad.

I've received generous institutional support for my work. A fellowship at the Stanford Humanities Center allowed me to write a good part of the early draft of the book. I've also had financial support for this project from the Stanford English Department and from the School of Humanities and Sciences thanks to Deans

Keith Baker, Iain Johnstone, and Sharon Long. I owe a huge debt of gratitude to my Department—faculty, students, and the entire staff. In particular I doubt if this book would have seen daylight without the support and help of two extraordinary, generous, dedicated, and brilliant administrators of the department (and good friends), Dagmar Logie and Alyce Boster.

I owe much to the people at Stanford University Press. It was the former Humanities Acquisitions Editor Helen Tartar's interest and persistence at the beginning of my project and then the enthusiastic support of Mike Keller, Norris Pope, Geoffrey Burn, Alan Harvey, Judith Hibbard, Lowell Britson, Rob Ehle, Jim Brommer, and David Jackson. I'm especially grateful for the wisdom, good sense, tact, and exactitude of the gifted Judith Hibbard who has aided me greatly in preparing the book for publication. I would also like to thank Nicholas Koenig for indexing the book and Anne Friedman for her proofreading.

I'm grateful for the efficiency and ingenuity of Helen Blythe and Ryan Johnson in arranging for artistic representations of Lot's daughters in this text.

And I particularly wish to thank Elaine Auyoung and Renee Fox for their intelligence, patience, good humor, diligence, energy, and their perceptive judgment as superb research assistants and unofficial, but very engaged editors.

The great kindness and faith of dear friends old and new and of family have helped me complete this work, but for how much the example of their lives has meant to me in getting this project done, I want to single out the courage of George Dekker, Diane Middlebrook, my sister Marian Woessner, my sister-in-law Nancy Polhemus, and my brother Joe Polhemus.

I am blessed to know and understand about proper, sweet love between the generations through my children, Camilla, Mack, Josiah, and Andromeda, whom I cherish and whose lives I esteem and honor. They are wonderful teachers about the possibilities and beauty of friendship and sympathy between children and parents.

My greatest debt is to Carol Loeb Shloss, the distinguished biographer of modernism's daughters, whom I met on a Joyce conference panel discussing fathers and daughters. Her work, love, support, vision, and faith have made this book possible. I dedicate it to her.

                                                                    RMP

. . . they came forward to raise the father and daughter
from the ground.

—Dickens, *A Tale of Two Cities*

Chapter 1

Introduction

THE LOT COMPLEX

Now follows the text about Lot and his daughters. It perplexes both
the Jews and our own people, and causes them to ask many questions.
Our fathers generally passed it over, either because they were hindered
by other endeavors or because God so directed it.

—Martin Luther[1]

I.
Back to the Source

Let me begin by reviewing the shocking old story that haunts modern life
and literature and has worked to make us what we are.

To seek his own good and avoid family strife, an ambitious young
owner of herds heeds the advice of his wise uncle, a heaven-blessed nomad
leader, that they part. The nephew heads for fertile country and moves into
a rich city. God-fearing, well-meaning, but worldly—a compromiser—he
dwells and prospers with his wife and daughters among wicked men in a
thriving but doomed community. Meanwhile, the aged uncle is visited by
divine messengers who tell him, first, that his barren old wife will miraculously conceive a child, and, second, that God means to destroy the bad city
where his nephew dwells. The uncle, however, thinking of his relative,
pleads and bargains with God to spare the place.

Two angels, posing as men, do come to observe the nephew's city, notorious for its evil ways. He rushes to welcome them, bowing and scraping,
and presses them to take shelter, knowing that the men of the town, wild
for "strange flesh," will try to ravish the visitors.

He is right. A violent horde masses around his house. The townsmen demand that he give up the two strangers so that they can know and use them. Frantic, terrified, believing his sacred duty to God requires him to defend his guests, he improvises a desperate plan. Wheedling, he calls the men "brothers" and tells them if they leave his two guests alone, he'll give them his own daughters to use sexually. Caught up in choosing what he sees as the lesser of evils, he opts to sacrifice his own female flesh and blood, and he chooses, for God's sake, the safety of his visitors and his sacred duty of hospitality over the life of his girls.

But the townsmen scream that he has no right at all to tell them what to do; they mean to break into his house, do what they want—rob, rape, or kill whomever they like. Then they maul him and try to force entrance. At this point, the two archangels reveal their power, rescue their host, pull him inside, and blind the men of the crowd, leaving them outside, stunned and groping to get in. God, the angels say, has now passed judgment and will obliterate the place. They tell the man to take his family and get out right away. He tries to rouse his prospective sons-in-law, but they laugh, doubt his story, and think him ridiculous. In the morning, the two divine visitors tell the man again to hurry up and take his wife and daughters and flee. The man delays, but the angels grab him and the three women and whisk them out of the city. The voice of the Lord tells them to escape for their lives, head for the hills, and under no circumstances look back.

Soon God unleashes a rain of fire that burns up their former home, the people in it, and all the surrounding cities and land. The man and his daughters are spared, but his wife disobeys the command, look backs at the searing destruction, and then hardens into a pillar of salt—a bitter monument of death. She becomes a part of the suddenly arid, dead landscape— female flesh turned into a geological fossil.

Perspective switches momentarily to the righteous uncle. This patriarch—safe and removed—gazes out from high ground, watching the whole plain and its cities go up in smoke. His survival casts irony over all that follows. The nephew and his daughters have no idea that anyone else survives the holocaust.

Surrounded by ruin and horror, the man and the two girls, desperate refugees, flee to the mountains where they find a cave to live in. In flat contrast to their final hours in the city, when, in a panic, their father treated them as sex objects to trade, the young women now become decisive, action-taking subjects; it's their father who becomes a thing to manipulate. The daughters look to the future. Thinking the rest of humanity has been obliterated, the elder conspires with the younger to save the race. Their father is old, she says, and there are no other men left to mate with. It's up to them to begin repopulating the world by seducing him—to "preserve the seed of our father," she says.

But that means incest. Together, it seems, they must take responsibility for species survival by breaking the law and mating with their sire. The situation between father and daughters is completely reversed from what it was in town. Then he sought to dispose of their sexuality to preserve life. Now, they seek to control and manage his sexuality for what they determine to be the general good, no matter what he thinks or wills. The plotting older daughter assumes that the incest taboo is so powerful that their father would not rationally choose to have sex with them. Therefore they must overwhelm his inhibitions. On successive evenings, they ply him with wine, get him drunk, and then each—the older on the first night, the younger on the second—lies down naked in the cave with the oblivious man. They both get pregnant by him and have sons from whom two peoples spring (people destined to be scorned by the uncle's seed). That's the tale. After two nights of drunkenness and venery, nothing more is ever heard of the father, nor, after they give birth, of his daughters.

The story, of course, is scriptural—mainly from Genesis 19.[2] The man is Lot, that morally equivocal, bumbling, God-struck, put-upon, incestuous founding father—the patriarch, so to speak, in the closet (more precisely, in the cave). The uncle is Abraham, whose wife becomes the post-menopausal mother, Sarah; the petrified, nameless woman of salt is Lot's wife; the city is Sodom; the crowd of men are Sodomites; the punishment—like the punishment of Hell—is fire and brimstone; the once-fertile land is the land of the Dead Sea (also known as the Sea of Lot); and the conspiring, incestuous girls are Lot's daughters, whose respective issues are the Moabites and the Ammonites—nations alien to Israel. But scriptural history makes the elder daughter the mother of Moab, and thus the ancestor of the virtuous Moabite daughter Ruth, whose canonized Book of Ruth shows how the sexual relationship between a father-figure and a younger woman can be redeemed, legitimized, and blessed. From Ruth eventually descends the great poet-king David, the wise Solomon, the House of David, and, hence, in the Christian Bible, the genealogy, family, and holy figure of Jesus Christ, the incarnated Word. Thus the scandalous Lot family may be seen not only as figures representing the disreputable history of heathen, marginal peoples—outsiders, *others*—and the repressed incestuous history of human civilization and its origins, but also as the indispensable generating agents of female subjectivity, the integration of peoples, catholic sensibility, moral redemption, and even of Holy Scripture itself.[3]

II.
Defining the Lot Complex and Disovering its History

Stories as well as people have their biographies, and it's the vibrant life of the Lot's daughters narrative I want to tell. In it, I find the origins of what I call the "Lot complex," a dynamic configuration of wishes, sexual fantasies, fears, and symbolic imagery that has worked to form generational relationships and structure personality, gender identity, religious faith, and social organization.[4] By the term "complex," I mean a convergence and drastic condensation in human psychology of personal and social experience, images, drives, motives, and impulses that can be seen both to form and represent a pattern. A "complex"—as I use and define the term—is constituted out of the interaction between members of different generations and the history of adult-child relationships. As an organized and organizing group of ideas, memories, and powerful unconscious feelings, a complex serves to shape the psyche—its emotions, attitudes, and behavior. I don't claim that the Lot complex is universal, but I do argue that, given the similarity of certain historical, psychological, and biological conditions, it is general and prevalent, and I contend that in modern times especially, the evolving Lot story permeates imaginative life.

The Lot complex, as I read it in nineteenth- and twentieth-century culture, features the drive or compulsion to preserve, adapt, and/or expropriate the traditional paternal power to sustain, regenerate, define, represent, and transmit life and civilization—the patriarchal seed of culture in history. It thus plays a central part in the high drama of the change in the status of women and the liberation of female aspirations. Future-oriented, *Lot* expresses the agonizing demand to sacrifice the past, as you can read in Jesus's famous command, "Remember Lot's wife" (Luke 17:32)—the succinct biblical verse that popularized Lot and the Lot complex in the minds of millions.[5] "Remember Lot's wife," an oxymoronic command, means you must give up the past with its memories to which you are wed—the past which has mothered you—and make yourself ready, under any circumstances, to give birth to the future. "Remember Lot's wife" is an injunction to look to the past so that you will *not* look to the past, but forward. It offers a logical contradiction, a "double bind"—*always remember to forget*—and makes the ability to accept and live with that contradiction the key to the preservation and flourishing of humanity.

In Lot the father-daughter relationship becomes indispensable in the making and preservation of culture, but *Lot*, with its image of young females conspiring to take power and act also contains the seeds for transforming that patriarchal culture. The Lot story includes wish-fulfilling symbolic projections, unconscious longings, resentments, fears, rationalizing defense mechanisms, conflicts, and transgressions *of both fathers and daughters—of both women and men.*

It's a perplexing myth whose meanings have always been contested. Why is this incest canonized in Scripture? What impact has it had on human consciousness? How does it work on people? Did Lot and his daughters do right or wrong? Readers from the beginning have wondered about it and differed. Full of ambivalence and irony, the problematic Lot-Scripture often gets repressed in religious history, but, like the repressed, it always returns—old wine in new vessels.

What you can see figured in Lot are desires that shake the world: the desire for immortality through progeny; the desire to continue life under any conditions; the desire for sexual pleasure without guilt or responsibility; the desire of women to control the action of men to whom they traditionally have been subject and take an active role in determining fate and history; the desire of men to preserve themselves, conquer time, remain potent, and keep on wooing the future.

My subject, therefore, turns out to be a very large one, but my approach and the structure of this book are quite simple. In Part I, Chapters 2–5, I identify and lay out the rich heritage of this biblical narrative of incest, with its major historical and cultural implications.[6] In Part II, I look closely at some important, representative modern daughters of Lot—both real and fictional—and the male figures whose relationships with them generate conceptions of the way we live now and might in the future. There, in Chapters 6–11, I discuss the lives and significant Lot stories of Jane Austen, Mary Shelley, Charlotte and Emily Brontë, Lewis Carroll and William Stead, Sigmund Freud and his "Dora," Shirley Temple, and Woody Allen and Mia Farrow. In Part III, the concluding section, I end with two recent, substantial Lot's-daughters narratives set in the modern Mecca of power, Washington, D.C. These Potomac testaments, one by the African-American writer Carolivia Herron and one featuring Bill Clinton, Monica Lewinsky, Linda Tripp, and Chelsea and Hillary Clinton, make clear the full power—personal, political, and global power—that the evolving Lot complex still holds in the imagination of the world at the turn of the century.

Overall my main aims are (1) to stress the comparatively underestimated importance of father-daughter, older male–younger female relationships in history, particularly in the last two centuries of developing female ambition and progress for women;[7] (2) to explore, as a test case, the complex ways that an important literary text from the past goes on living in social history and popular culture by showing how the effects and aesthetic processes of Lot over time can and do work on the human imagination—how, that is, a specific, written narrative can fuse indelibly into unfolding history, individual lives, and works of art; and (3) to make clear the historical reasons and ideas that would cause James Joyce, one of the true anthropological geniuses of the twentieth century, to end his last book with the voice of the dying mother merging into and becoming the regenerating voice of the daughter. In light of gender history and social flux, remembering Lot's daughters as well as Lot's wife becomes an urgent matter, but such remembrance of things past keeps on taking new meanings and forms.

III.
A Grid Through Which
to View the World

The patterns, figures, and imagery of Lot have such explanatory power for reading the history of human relationships that—especially for times and texts concerned with women's subjectivity, the emergence of once marginalized people, and the nuances of social and familial power-shifts—they can form a useful grid through which to view the world. And the Lot complex can help redress and clarify the pervasive influence of the Oedipus complex and myth with its inherent narrative biases stressing male desire and action. Like Oedipus (with which it clearly has much in common), Lot brings together diverse ancient legends and living impulses.[8] Oedipus features unwitting patricide and the intercourse of son and mother; Lot features the divinely ordained death of the wife and mother and the intercourse of father and daughters. Lot offers key male fantasy projections, as does Oedipus,[9] but the Lot complex shows how these adult male projections (for instance, the power of disposal over young women, fulfillment through children, a supply of youthful sexual partners into old age, a successful drive to outlive one's contemporaries) form and determine the representation of the *younger* generation's voices, experience, and desires, as Oedipus arguably does not. It also presumes to figure crucially and explicitly both rational and unconscious *female* wishes, fears, and drives; and it stresses the arbitrary death and metamorphosis of the mother, the traumatic impact of her loss and absence, and the meaning of her replacement by the daughters. The Lot text represents the terrible sacrifices, compromises, and self-deceptions necessary for survival, which the offering up of the daughters, the panic of the wife-mother, the stupefying of the father, his blind rut, and the desperate strategy and fertility of the daughterwives shockingly trope.

A narrative lives when people can read it so as to find in it their particular sense of life, their passions, and their secrets both represented and reformed. And what turns a narrative into a complex is the relevance for living human beings of its broad-based, lasting analogical power—its felt quality of distilling for many over a long time a paradigm of experience that directly or indirectly shapes their minds and the minds of those they touch. It continues somehow to be like what human beings know and see happening. A story becomes a kind of map and code by which men and women can read and organize the chaotic turbulence and psychology of their relationships, activities, inner conflicts, and longings. A "complex" is, then, a complex narrative that, in one way or another, has sunk deeply into people over the years.

Lot fills that bill. The potential meaning of this text is rich and provocative. But a complex has a complicated history. It both endures and changes. If it is to continue to make sense and show how minds and societies are structured, it must and will be rediscovered, refashioned, and relived. I mean, in Part I, to stress that point in three related ways: first, by making clear in this introduction what I, writing at the beginning of the third millennium CE, find most generally relevant now in the Lot text and complex; next, in the second chapter, by setting out, as a preview and overall pattern, defining images and instances of modern Lot's daughters as they evolved in the last two centuries; and then, in the three following chapters, by looking briefly at the history of Lot-Scripture interpretation from the beginning and at some of its most revealing manifestations in art and literature before the modern era.

IV.
Features of the Lot Complex
in Modern Life

To make clear what's at stake in this book, let me set down the main features of the Lot complex touching modern life that I see coming out of the *Lot* text—thirteen ways of looking at Lot and his daughters.

1. *Sex for pleasure versus sex to preserve seed: the tension between the desire to use sex for immediate, sensual gratification and the desire to use sex only for the regeneration of life and the sake of the future.* The Lot complex features the drive to control, displace, and suppress sexuality: Sodom is destroyed; the cities of the plain are burned; the children of incest turn out to be the outcast neighboring tribes of Israel, not the children of Abraham and God; all sex without the purpose of progeny is for the time being eliminated. Allegorically, the story of Lot moves from the lawless pursuit of sex as polymorphous pleasure (the men of Sodom) to what seems the regrettable but necessary practice of genital sex for the sake of procreation. And yet there is a subversive undercurrent here that shows how people are attracted to, and held wallowing in, the tides of transgressive sex. *Lot*, notoriously set in Sodom and Gomorrah and then in the incestuous cave, immortalizes the forbidden backward look that can be read as nostalgia for a world of sexual pleasure in and for itself; the text offers the diversity and power of erotic appetite and even suggests that amoral, sexual besotment and the suspension of reason and law are sometimes absolutely necessary for survival.

The obvious fissure in the myth, as it has conventionally been interpreted, is that God blasts the cities of the plain for sexual sin, but then human salvation, for the survivors, apparently depends on the three refugees from a world damned by immoral sexual behavior, breaking the incest laws and using drink and tabooed sex to renew life. Incinerated and petrified, the repressed returns.

2. *Progeny—preservation of seed—as the primary responsibility of humanity.* One meaning of Lot might be: for the sake of children (whose lives are an imaginative projection beyond the self) all is allowed, all is required. Children make the future: no children, no future; no hope for the children, no hope for the future. Faith, then, becomes invested in the child.

3. *The primacy of the father-daughter relationship.* Lot provides a corrective to the Oedipus complex's nominally skewed stress on the primacy of son and mother roles. In it, what signifies most is not the son's drive to replace the father and possess or control maternity, but the father's desire to implant his seed, countenance, and symbolic being in and on the living flesh of the future. As for woman in the myth, she lives by defining her desire and function in relation to man as father. Generalizing, you might say that power relations between the sexes until very recent times would best be symbolized, not by a mother-son relationship, nor a husband-wife relationship, but by a father-daughter relationship.

4. *The existence and force of incestuous impulses—both conscious and unconscious.* Though *Lot* may be the sole example of specific parent-child incest in the Bible, God supposedly recreates and incarnates Himself through his "daughter" Mary. The model of the Christian Holy Family is incestuous. Taken together, the pregnancy of Lot's daughters by their father and the pregnancy of the Holy Virgin Mary through God symbolize the psychological contradictions of the Lot complex and represent the conflicted feelings about the nature of incestuous desire that develops and drives history. Collectively, humanity is an incest-surviving species. The Lot complex exposes much that is sordid in domestic history and troublesome in personal and social psychology. Lot's scheme to placate the lust of the Sodomites by offering them his girls only makes sense if, at least instinctively, he himself thinks of them as sexually attractive. Nevertheless, civil order and society depend on the existence, control, and benevolent use of incestuous affections—*on the sublimation of incestuous desire into positive concern for the long-term survival and well-being of other family members.*

5. *The power of projection.* People think about, wish for, and sometimes ruthlessly do forbidden things, but they don't like to feel guilty, and so they

often project their wishes and their responsibility onto others (it's not me but God who wills the destruction of my vicious foes and my stony, bitter, old spouse; it's not me but these naughty, crazy girls who get me drinking and coax me into bed; it's not me, but the good of society and my victimization that makes me seduce and use an older man for my purposes). The logic of the unconscious mind reveals itself as the (projected) discourse and behavior of others. The daughter's talk of sexual seduction can be heard as the expression of Lot's (the aging male's) desire. The older generation—meaning both men and women—has overwhelming power to project and inculcate desires, motives, fantasies, thoughts, actions, and expression onto and within the younger generation. Momentous examples in history would be the projection and displacement of sexual desire by mature, aging father figures onto young women and the displacement of this desire by men into fields of power and influence. (The decisions that have determined the running of the modern world have for the most part been made by older men whose physical power has peaked and is declining—men who often try to project their tangled wills upon society.)

Even childhood traumas and memories are defined by the actions, wishes, expectations, and suggestions of the older generation. There is no going back to the beginnings of individual development in childhood without taking into account adult projections. Recollected images, psychic memories, early "object relations," the private material of one's unconscious, that which is most personal to the self, are conditioned by the drives of elders, by their use of language, by their powers of suggestion, by their examples as role models, by the narratives through which they organize their lives, by the emphasis they put on words and things, and by the child-rearing arrangements they make.

In light of Lot and his daughters, you can see easily how an adult projects disingenuously back into childhood *his or her own desires and claims that it's not he or she who controls the inner dialogue, but the child.* But just because, in the Lot complex, the desires of the father are projected upon the daughters, it doesn't follow that the daughter's desire for the father—for his seed, for some imagined paternal essence, for his perceived power—is inauthentic.

6. *The drive for female agency; the development of female subjectivity in order to establish and sustain civil culture.* By projecting upon the daughters the moral onus for incest, the Scripture ironically allows them to be-

come conspiratorial, socially responsible agents. Women move from sacrificial objects to reasoning subjects. From chattel, they become paradigmatic figures out to save the world. They identify with the divine command and purpose to look forward, not back, and their plotting together to use the father shapes history. They seek to intoxicate and obliterate the "rational" male will that would leave them without a future. They can be seen moving to replace the rivalries of sons and brothers with sisterly cooperation. Daughterhood might become a sisterhood moving to recreate social life. It might even come to reanimate the lives and minds of the abandoned older women.

7. *A subversive, evolutionary—even potentially revolutionary—pattern.* In the Lot myth, the objects of libidinous desire, the objects that power seems able to dispose of at will, themselves become empowered. The angels, objects of the Sodomites' aggressive libido, take power over the men of Sodom; the daughters take power over the father; the powerlessness of progeny becomes the power of progeny to determine the future; the slighted parental obligation becomes the primary obligation; the rigid, lifeless mate-and-mother becomes the quickened, life-giving mother doubled; the displaced, disgraced, incestuous refugees, children of Sodom and Gomorrah, become the ancestors of David and Jesus. Those who feel excluded can reinterpret matters so that they find themselves included in scripts that change ideas about who it is who "belongs." The Lot complex can incorporate and express feminine resentments of injustices and oppression and can even figure imaginatively the problems of historical, international, personal, and communal disparagement and exclusions of peoples.

8. *The drive to be part of eternal being and a supernatural reality.* Lot complexes incorporate and refashion in modern life religious longings and the drive for permanence. Lot shows the search for faith and the ambiguous human relationship towards the sacred to be alive and determining, though protean and ambiguous. Put-upon Lot, especially plucked from Sodom to be saved, converses with supernatural beings, and even his eldest daughter identifies her thinking with the righteous purposes of immortality. Life is to be regenerated not by miracle, but by women using their spirits and bodies to carry out naturally what they see as the will of God.

The inclusion of the Lot family in a sacred canon points up the need to turn compromising—even squalid—experience into something lasting, something part of a larger plan, something that can be inscribed and preserved. A drive exists to immortalize family and sexual relationships in the symbolic order—in language, articulation, and scriptural lessons.

9. *Specific symbolism and the challenge of understanding it as that which orients, actuates, represents, and translates human experience, making communication flow, psychology deepen, and interpretation of meaning reverberate forever.* "Pillar of salt," "fire and brimstone," "cave," "wine," and "seed" stand out here. "Pillar" and "cave," for example, may represent the primacy of genital physiognomy (or heterosexuality) in history; "fire and brimstone" may represent hell, the beginnings of earth formation, and/or the historical furor about homosexuality; "wine" may stand for the power of intoxication in human affairs; "seed" may be understood to germinate metaphorically and metonymically in any number of ways. You might see that bitter "pillar" (sometimes translated as "statue") as the hard fate through history of the female past childbearing age or as an example of the way traditional patriarchal vision sees everything in phallic terms. In subjective mental life, the symbolism of image and word are not distinct, and together they fuse with physical reality and matter. Along with fire and brimstone, the potent image of Lot's wife turned to the pillar of salt, a signifier of world-historical proportions, is what has stuck most vividly in the world's memory of this chapter. The point is that the life-bearing woman loses life and is turned into something else—*some thing*—and people are left to try to find the meaning of that thing: they *literally* and *symbolically* must try to find the point: "*Remember Lot's wife.*"

10. *The power of ambivalence and contradiction to define, dominate, and control personal and communal life.* The Lot-Scripture says the law of the fathers must sometimes be broken to preserve the law of the fathers. It says the life force may depend upon drunkenness and blind sexual arousal, and it says that drink and sex corrupt family life and family values. It says both "this passage is relevant, this is the seed from which we spring," and also "these are not our people—be glad and learn from their bad example." It gives you the point of view of those caught in an apocalyptic crisis and forced to cope as best they can; and it gives you the point of view of the God-blessed, safe progenitor of a chosen people removed from the turmoil, looking down on the cataclysm, and thus showing, with his being and perspective, the dubious plans and acts of the refugee survivors to save the species to be deluded and misconceived. It can both say and mean "this father is weak and despicable," and "this victimized husband-and-father is

good enough—man, beset by human iniquities and terrible acts of God, trying to survive as best he can." It says "these desperate daughters are concupiscent sinners" and "these victimized, resourceful young women are brave and wise in breaking the law to preserve life." It says young women want to rescue the father and also be rid of him once and for all.

Most important—crucial in modern history—the complex Lot pattern can figure as a human success story in which the conjunction of fathers and daughters, of older men and younger women, develops historically for the benefit of society and cultural progress, *and/or* it can figure as the anachronistic preservation and misuse of an obscenely despotic power—erotic viciousness, incestuous bad faith, and irresponsible oppression.

11. *Split personality, schizoid being, pluralistic identity as characteristic of female representations.* The daughter made binary is a striking fact. *Lot* gives you not one, but two girls. Mother, mate, sister, daughter—the female role in the Lot chapter is she who must live and act in concert with another. This repetition and division is a complex male projection (women are relative creatures; a man's object of biological desire is replicated, like one breast becoming an image of two, or like the vision of the female genitalia as a splitting; the patriarchal story of the two copulating girls enacts a fantasy of a continual supply of stimulating but undemanding young mates to draw forth the man's seed, etc., etc.); but it can also be a female projection representing drives for being another self, for a sister's support in challenging prevailing law, for gender union in taking decision-making power away from the man, and for a transcendence of time-doomed individuality and fertility, which the fate of Lot's wife brings home.

Imagine the scene of Lot's seduction. You have the two daughters. Attention focuses on the girl who lies with the father, but try to imagine the other daughter. What does she do? She removes herself from sexual encounter. She distances herself from the present action, but psychologically, she may repeat an experience she's had before. Her father is lying with a family member. She is an emotional voyeur hanging somewhere around the cave. She may repeat a "primal scene." It may seem as if her mother (in the substitute guise of her sister) is again alive, but she, the other daughter, is back in pre-pubescent childhood. The mother and the opportunity for a recouped childhood are returned to her—that is, the conditions of such, through fantasy and analogy, are re-invoked for her. Momentarily she is a pure girl beyond the fray, contemplating the wild passion of physical being

—like an awakened child or like Abraham looking on the terrible force of nature. The Lot complex includes the grandiose idea that the daughter might control the sexual life of the father, and that she both participates in it and is exterior to it—free of it. One daughter is engaged in incest with the parent, but one is not. The binarism shows how the Lot story can be seen to represent the fulfillment of contradictory wishes—for example, *I outstrip and replace my mother* and I *retrieve the time of my mother's life, when she was alive and cared for me.* The myth of Lot's daughters expresses a deep desire to *be* the mother, to *regenerate* her, to recreate a world in which the self-as-mother lives and lies with the father, but it also expresses the desire to be the self-as-child-witness, preserving security in virgin regression, never having to grow up. Behind the incest in Lot may lie a fantastic symbolic logic expressing a twisted passion for the surety of the past—an idealized, projected normalcy in the midst of actual disaster and miserable deprivation.

12. *The emergence in Lot of the "anti-hero"—man as the foolish, flawed, victimized survivor in a violent world where conventional heroism often means a sea of blood and the reign of death.* Lot has something oddly comic about him, and he, with his ineptness in the face of violence, may draw a sneaking sympathy. Or maybe his final unawareness hides the guilty denial of a man contemptible for the weakness of his flesh and paternal irresponsibility. He may do the best he can, but that isn't good enough. He needs help. If patriarchy depends on him, maybe patriarchy's days are numbered. This equivocal image of manhood for centuries would lie mostly dormant, but if you look now at figures like Lewis Carroll's White Knight, James Joyce's Leopold Bloom and HCE, Franz Kafka's protagonists, Samuel Beckett's talking heads, and Woody Allen's self-portrayed "heroes," you can see why moderns might feel they have more in common with Lot than with Abraham. In twentieth-century psyches, Lot awoke from his slumber, an ancient schlemiel inextricably joined to the fate of young women.

13. *Human life as defined by personal trauma and the crises of history.* The Lot chapter presents the threat of violence and death—from God, nature, and men—as the determining fact of life. If *Lot* is about the preservation of the seed of life, of the possibility of civilization, it shows that desperate measures are unavoidable in their pursuit. The Lot complex stresses expulsion and exile in every sense—exile, the ineluctable human experience, from womb to tomb. It assumes that experience devastates physical

and moral security: you live under historical necessity, and you will surely be called upon to make agonizing, questionable choices and take imperfect, distasteful, and even morally improper actions in the wake of inevitable disasters, one of which is the metamorphosis and loss of some mother-pillar of being.

V.
Why the Subject Can
Make You Nervous

When people think about the Lot episode of the Bible, with all the tabooed sex, cosmic violence, and ambiguities, it has always made them edgy, and why not? It has been, off and on, a school and hunting ground for both puritanical and pornographic imaginations. It brings up the hottest topics imaginable: flagrant incest, fire and brimstone, divine judgment and wrath, holocaust, a rationalization for ultimate violence, a world-shaking calamity of nature, religious faith, Sodom and Gomorrah, moral condemnation, creation myths, ethnic history, the threat of human extinction, blatant evil, human nature in a horrible light, sexual deviance, sexual harassment, a city of buggers lusting after angels, a man who offers his daughters to Sodomites, alcohol abuse, girls pregnant by their own father, good people who do bad things, issues about women's reproductive functions, pressing questions of blame and guilt, and the never-to-be-forgotten woman who, unable not to look back when her home and land turn into a colossal furnace, gets instantly soldered into the landscape. No wonder that with so much bad behavior, so many dilemmas, and so much meaning condensed in its three pages, the Lot-Scripture could give you a complex.

Appendix

1   And there came two angels to Sodom at even; and Lot sat in the gate of
     Sodom: and Lot seeing *them* rose up to meet them; and he bowed himself
     with his face toward the ground;

2   and he said, Behold now, my lords, turn in, I pray you, into your servant's
     house, and tarry all night, and wash your feet, and ye shall rise up early, and
     go on your ways. And they said, Nay; but we will abide in the street all night.

3   And he pressed upon them greatly; and they turned in unto him, and
     entered into his house; and he made them a feast, and did bake unleavened
     bread, and they did eat.

4   But before they lay down, the men of the city, *even* the men of Sodom,
     compassed the house round, both old and young, all the people from every
     quarter:

5   and they called unto Lot, and said unto him, Where *are* the men which came
     in to thee this night? bring them out unto us, that we may know them.

6   And Lot went out at the door unto them, and shut the door after him,

7   and said, I pray you, brethren, do not so wickedly.

8   Behold now, I have two daughters which have not known man; let me, I pray
     you, bring them out unto you, and do ye to them as *is* good in your eyes:
     only unto those men do nothing; for therefore came they under the shadow
     of my roof.

9   And they said, Stand back. And they said *again*, This one *fellow* came in to
    sojourn, and he will needs be a judge: now will we deal worse with thee than
    with them. And they pressed sore upon the man, *even* Lot, and came near to
    break the door.

10 But the men put forth their hand, and pulled Lot into the house to them,
    and shut the door.

11 And they smote the men that *were* at the door of the house with blindness,
    both small and great: so that they wearied themselves to find the door.

12 And the men said unto Lot, Hast thou here any besides? sons-in-law, and thy
    sons, and thy daughters, and whatsoever thou hast in the city, bring *them* out
    of this place:

13 for we will destroy this place, because the cry of them is waxen great before
    the face of the Lord; and the Lord hath sent us to destroy it.

14 And Lot went out, and spake unto his sons-in-law, which married his
    daughters, and said, Up, get you out of this place; for the Lord will destroy
    this city. But he seemed as one that mocked unto his sons-in-law.

15 And when the morning arose, then the angels hastened Lot, saying, Arise,
    take thy wife, and thy two daughters, which are here; lest thou be consumed
    in the iniquity of the city.

16 And while he lingered, the men laid hold upon his hand, and upon the hand
    of his wife, and upon the hand of his two daughters; the Lord being merciful
    unto him: and they brought him forth, and set him without the city.

17 And it came to pass, when they had brought them forth abroad, that he said,
    Escape for thy life; look not behind thee, neither stay thou in all the plain;
    escape to the mountain, lest thou be consumed.

18 And Lot said unto them, Oh, not so, my Lord:

19 behold now, thy servant hath found grace in thy sight, and thou hast
    magnified thy mercy, which thou hast shewed unto me in saving my life;
    and I cannot escape to the mountain, lest some evil take me, and I die:

20 behold now, this city *is* near to flee unto, and it *is* a little one: O, let me
    escape thither, (*is* it not a little one?) and my soul shall live.

21 And he said unto him, See, I have accepted thee concerning this thing also,
    that I will not overthrow this city, for the which thou hast spoken.

22 Haste thee, escape thither; for I cannot do any thing till thou be come
    thither. Therefore the name of the city was called Zo'ar.

23 The sun was risen upon the earth when Lot entered Zo'ar.

24 Then the Lord rained upon Sodom and upon Gomorrah brimstone and fire
    from the Lord out of heaven;

25 and he overthrew those cities, and all the plain, and all the inhabitants of the
    cities, and that which grew upon the ground.

26 But his wife looked back from behind him, and she became a pillar of salt.

27 And Abraham gat up early in the morning to the place where he stood before the Lord:

28 and he looked toward Sodom and Gomorrah, and toward all the land of the plain, and beheld, and, lo, the smoke of the country went up as the smoke of a furnace.

29 And it came to pass, when God destroyed the cities of the plain, that God remembered Abraham, and sent Lot out of the midst of the overthrow, when he overthrew the cities in the which Lot dwelt.

30 And Lot went up out of Zo'ar, and dwelt in the mountain, and his two daughters with him; for he feared to dwell in Zo'ar: and he dwelt in a cave, he and his two daughters.

31 And the firstborn said unto the younger, Our father *is* old and *there is* not a man in the earth to come in unto us after the manner of all the earth:

32 come, let us make our father drink wine, and we will lie with him, that we may preserve seed of our father.

33 And they made their father drink wine that night: and the firstborn went in, and lay with her father; and he perceived not when she lay down, nor when she arose.

34 And it came to pass on the morrow, that the firstborn said unto the younger, Behold, I lay yesternight with my father: let us make him drink wine this night also; and go thou in, *and* lie with him, that we may preserve the seed of our father.

35 And they made their father drink wine that night also: and the younger arose, and lay with him; and he perceived not when she lay down, nor when she arose.

36 Thus were both the daughters of Lot with child by their father.

37 And the firstborn bare a son, and called his name Moab: the same *is* the father of the Moabites unto this day.

38 And the younger, she also bare a son, and called his name Ben-am'mi: the same *is* the father of the children of Ammon unto this day.

part i

The Heritage of
Lot and His Daughters

Chapter 2

Telling Examples

dadad's lottiest daughterpearl

—James Joyce, *Finnegans Wake*

T wo overlapping experiences, one literary and one involving a real child custody case, first brought me to see and want to investigate the living force of the Lot story and complex.

I.
'Finnegans Wake'
and the Lot Story

The literary experience came from reading and teaching James Joyce's *Finnegans Wake* (1939), that astonishing, pun-mad, unfathomable, absurdly magnificent, secular Bible and tower-of-Babel novel set in the night world of sleep. From the first page to the last, Joyce used the lore of Lot and his daughters as a key motif in his representation of humanity.[1] The recurrent Lot references sent me back to the Genesis text. On the face of it, choosing to focus on Lot and a disreputable episode of incest seemed odd for one who before had adapted for his time Ulysses, the classic hero of the *Odyssey*. But if Joyce, surely one of the greatest writers of the modern era, found antiquity's Lot story important and featured it in his most ambitious work, then it must be worth trying to understand how and why it could become so relevant for modern life.[2]

In the *Wake*, published on the eve of World War II and a new holocaust, Joyce set out to show that any human being is a weird, individual collective—a biological, linguistic fusion of unique psychology, natural matter, thousands of years of history, countless lives, any number of languages, and the residue of all sorts of books, myths, dirty jokes, and sacred writings. Lot drove Joyce's creativity in *Finnegans Wake* because he felt its power. How could he not? He lived out the last quarter of his life increasingly preoccupied with the condition of his beloved daughter Lucia (diagnosed as schizophrenic), with his own susceptibility to drink and blindness, and with the inevitable aging process in himself and his wife Nora. Like Lot, he faced the coming of international and personal darkness, worrying about what he would leave behind and whether he could finish his "Book of the Night." He had the growing sense of himself as an aging, absurd, doomed refugee trying to preserve himself in a quixotic scripture of comic faith.

The *Wake* represents a change in Joyce's muse from his sensual wife to his talented, brilliant, mentally disturbed daughter.[3] Her powers of expression and wit and her physical grace (she was a promising dancer) touched and moved him. So did her sexual vulnerability to young men, her faithful interest and help in his work, and her love for him. And, in the last decade of his life, so did her fragile, deteriorating mind and the painful ordeals of her medical treatment and institutionalization. The daughter's talents, plight, and poignant life inspired him to think through and finish his last book.

The name "Lot" resounds throughout the *Wake* in such phrases as "blotto after divers tots of hell fire" (39.33), "the Old Sots' Hole" (41.32), and "dadad's lottiest daughterpearl" (561.15).[4] He even imagined a version of the salty metamorphosis of Lot's wife as the conclusion of his life's work, transforming the Lot family incest into the most famous passage of the book, the Anna Livia Plurabelle monologue on death and regeneration in which the voice of the passing, dying wife and mother flows into the voice of the daughter.

Yes, you're changing, sonhusband, and you're turning, I can feel you, for a daughterwife from the hills again. . . . And she is coming. Swimming in my hindmoist. . . . Just a whisk brisk sly spry spink spank sprint of a thing. . . . Salterella come to her own. . . . Now a younger's there. . . . For she'll be sweet for you as I was sweet when I came down out of me mother. . . . But I'm loothing them that's here and all I lothe [one spelling of the name "Lot" in the Middle Ages]. Loonely in me loneness. . . . it's sad and old it's sad and weary I go back to you, my cold father, my cold mad father, my cold mad feary father. . . . Yes. Carry me along, taddy, like you done through the toy fair! . . . A gull. Gulls. ["girls" as well as "birds"] Far calls. Coming, far! ["far" is the Danish word for "father"] End here. Us then. Finn, again! Take. Bussoftlhee, mememormee! (627–628)

One chapter in the *Wake* (2.3), featuring the children of its "typical" family at their homework, presents the comments of the daughter as manic footnotes at the bottom of the page. Joyce, thinking of his own daughter as kept down and craving her own form of expression, literally represents the utterance of history's daughter figures as a series of wildly worded footnotes that express rebellious female will and sexual desire (Joyce's lines here also, of course, project male desire and fantasy). Focusing on *Lot* might offer a way to bring daughters and their history up out of footnote status and give voice to a repressed subject that you need to know to understand human life: namely, the power, development, and moral ambivalence of incestuous feelings and their sublimations.

II.
A Story in Family Court

While I was teaching *Finnegans Wake,* I also observed a bitter child custody case involving a six-year-old girl. In her first year, her parents separated and ended their marriage. In court, the judge said that "fathers have rights too," and the girl was ordered to spend one week with the mother and then one week with the father until school age, when she was to live with permanently with the mother. Both parents remarried soon after the divorce. According to the mother, the split custody was very hard on the girl: she hated what she called "the back and forth." When she began first grade, she seemed glad to settle in with her mother and stepfather. But the father retained visitation rights after school twice a week, and one afternoon, according to the mother, the girl came back frantic, wailing: "I gotta love my dad. I gotta love him. Daddy said you wrecked our happy home."

The father, losing custody of the daughter, decided to go back to court, and in the hearing it came out that during those two afternoons a week, he made tape-recordings of the child, which he then edited. On one she recited by rote, in a dead voice, "Dad. I love you so much and—uh—so and so. Oh. I don't remember." The transcript went on:

FATHER: "Tell Daddy now. Daddy's your daddy. Daddy's your daddy so—"
    [waits]
DAUGHTER: "I got to tell Daddy whatever."
FATHER: "That's right."
DAUGHTER: "Nah. Uh uh." [silence] "Sorry, I messed up."

That little transcription can stand for a whole strain of domestic history. As in the Joyce text, it was hard for the daughter to find and make known an authentic voice. The court-appointed psychologist said the father had tried to project onto and through the girl his own words, hopes, and plans.

Sometimes the girl wanted to be like her dad, she said. But when she finally got to express her wishes to the court, she chose to live with her mother.

In short, this case and its language showed me that the Lot text is neither buried in the past, nor academic; it's the stuff of common strife and life.

III.
How a Myth Lives and the
Why(s) of Lot's Daughters Now

That juxtaposition of the Lot material in *Finnegans Wake* with the little girl's complicated feelings and words brought home the interplay of written text and individual life—their fusion in the historical, social, and personal stream of consciousness. Looking at Lot in both Joyce's epic and a real girl's experience, you could see not only how paternal wishes could be projected onto daughters, but also how the facts, forms, and nature of such projections would flow and change over time. Different fathers from different times have a different "seed" that various daughters might want to "preserve." And different daughters' drives to identify with, and yet still somehow be free of, fathers and their power could bring into play different tensions and feelings of rivalry and sympathy with the mother that would change social history.

Eras find and adapt the myths they need. In the popular imagination, the story of Lot's daughters (unlike Lot's wife) had remained a relatively obscure, marginal piece of lore until in the twentieth century Freud (obliquely and by implication—see Chapter 9) and Joyce (explicitly, but in obscure language) made it central to their comprehensive dreams of humanity and its future. When you look at it Joyce's way, it's easy to see developing variations on the myth over time that can and do reveal Lot's daughters at the core of modern life and consciousness.

If ambitious daughters were successfully to push for more education, look for a broader scope of action, seek fulfillment through new vocational opportunities, want higher cultural status and greater autonomy, they would have to become both closer to men and more independent from them. To open up the world they would need to attract the favor and mentoring good will from men, but then also they would have to find ways to control and distance them. The danger was that in wanting to take for themselves the strength and knowledge of men, daughters might be corrupted in various ways by male desire.

As for fathers, if, dreaming the dream of secular progress, they wanted to live on into the future by somehow making the world more civilized and a better place for their progeny, they would need to enter into the lives of daughters (as earlier men had not) and work to raise them up to be all that women could be—could be, but, for many reasons, had not often become. The danger here was that identifying more closely with girls and their lives and coming to value them more highly than previous generations, men with their power might turn them into precious creations to be manipulated and possessed—soulful icons of faith and trophy fetishes of erotic and moral beauty. Modern history, therefore, has meant both new, tighter bonding and new forms of conflict between fathers and daughters—between women and a diffusive, diffusing patriarchy.

Overall, the main point of the story of Lot's daughters in the last two centuries is the history of growing female authority. But that history is a tangled one. I want to begin with a dozen telling examples from fiction and life that make clear—and stand for—the prevalence of Lot complexes, their mixed motives, and the directions in which they continue to move the world. Together, chronologically, they preview the overall narrative of this book and the significance of the specific figures and subjects I discuss in Parts II and III.

1.

THE DAUGHTER AS AUTHOR:
HER DEDICATION TO THE FATHER

The motherless Frances Burney (1752–1840), one of the very first respected female English novelists, dedicates her novel *The Wanderer* to her beloved father, whom she credits for her success. Here she refers to her early writing as if it were a guilty teenager's masturbatory bad habit.[5]

[A]t the age of adolescence, I struggled against the propensity which, even in childhood, even from the moment I could hold a pen, had impelled me into its toils; and on my fifteenth birth-day, I made so resolute a conquest over an inclination at which I blushed, and that I had always kept secret, that I committed to flames whatever, up to that moment, I had committed to paper. . . .

The passion, however, though resisted, was not annihilated: . . . and, in defiance of every self-effort, Evelina struggled herself into life [*Evelina*, her first novel, made her famous]. . . . And your fortunate daughter . . . may still hope to retain . . . the power of interesting [your] affections . . . dearest Sir!

. . . Will the public be offended, if here, as in private, I conclude . . . with a prayer for my dearest Father's benediction and preservation.[6]

This woman, driven and empowered to write by him, in her loving literary dedication to him, identifies her project with the father and the preservation of what she understands him to represent. For her, he is the main audience, the reason for her art, and she, the author, is his creation—as her fulsome verse dedication to her father at the start of *Evelina* shows so clearly):

> Oh author of my being!—far more dear
> To me than light, than nourishment, or rest
>
> · · ·
>
> Could my weak pow'rs thy num'rous virtues trace,
> By filial love each fear should be repress'd;
>
> · · ·
>
> Oh! of my life at once the source and joy!
> If e'er thy eyes these feeble lines survey,
> Let not their folly their intent destroy;
> Accept the tribute—but forget the lay.[7]

Here, on the face of it, is a success story. The daughter's talents bloom, and, nurtured by the father, she speaks with the voice of authority. He's the male muse of her vocation. But if, in double-entendre wordplay, you were to take the dedicatory last word "lay" as an obscene pun, it would epitomize a nasty reason for repressive censorship about the history of human origins and, further, one strand of sublimation at work in the developing Lot story (including—and featuring—literary daughters inspired to write by their fathers).

2.
THE GIRLCHILD
AS REDEEMER

In *Silas Marner* (1861), a novel in which the figure of a little girl makes possible the moral regeneration and faith of an aging man, and through him, of a community, George Eliot writes:

In old days there were angels who came and took men by the hand and led them away from the city of destruction. We see no white-winged angels now. But yet men are led away from threatening destruction: a hand is put into theirs, which leads them forth gently towards a calm and bright land, so that they look no more backward; and the hand may be a little child's.[8]

Those words make explicit the important modern intellectual and emotional linkage that binds Lot's daughters to what I call *faith in the child*. Children can save you from the depravity of the past. Girls, in their innocence, can be the agents and angels of what's everlasting and immortal.

Notice that the lines refer directly to the sordid events of Sodom and Genesis 19, but they present a crucial new version of Lot in which lawless sex and violence totally disappear. A new faith and a transmutation of the myth emerge here: *believe in the idea of daughters as preservers of the seed of culture and humanity, but clean up the story by making them little girls and thus desexualizing them.* One great, developing version of Lot and his daughters in modern times reverses the lyric "Thank Heaven for Little Girls" to proclaim it, in essence, *thank little girls for heaven.*

3.
THE DAUGHTER
AS SYMBOL AND SEED

In Nathaniel Hawthorne's *The Scarlet Letter* (1850), the classic American novel about the dark force of sex in a puritanical culture, "little Pearl," the bastard love-child of Hester Prynne and the Reverend Arthur Dimmesdale, *does* lead her father away from "moral destruction."[9] At key moments in the novel the girl insists that her father stand up in public with her and let their relationship be seen. When the minister stops hiding his paternity and ac-knowledges his daughter—when they hold hands on the scaffold and she kisses him before the people of New England—he does find salvation, and she finds her life in the world. "Pearl kissed his lips. A spell was broken" (173). The novel insists on stressing the bonding of the father and daugh-ter—the father must acknowledge the daughter—as a moral necessity for faith and redemption. The daughter not only preserves the seed of her fa-ther, she becomes the very seed of faith and hope for the future.

But Hawthorne makes her also the seed and symbol of adultery. No part of *The Scarlet Letter*'s vision has been more influential than its focus on the tension between sex as the means of progeny and sex as disgraceful behavior—the very basis and heritage of the Lot-Scripture. At the begin-ning of life in the New World lies old sin. Hawthorne calls little Pearl a "liv-ing hieroglyphic" and makes her a figure in whom you can read both the lawless origin of life and the need to control and transcend the intoxication of sex (140). When the novel begins, he shows you Hester "with the infant at her bosom" standing like "the image of Divine Maternity": "Here there was the taint of deepest sin in the most sacred quality of human life" (41). Hawthorne, then, starts with that problematic tie between the sex act and nativity—between, that is (to make shockingly clear the jarring historical disjunction that afflicts people about the processes of regeneration), *fuck-ing* and *babies*.

The conception of "little Pearl, herself a symbol" (106), is the heart of the novel. Children, on whom people project their hopes and desires for spiritual rebirth and the justification of their lives, are, in fact, the products of wild appetite. Mysteriously life has its beginning in lust, and the most se-rious responsibilities of humanity—the repopulating of the world and the nurture of children—depend on rutting. A child is, in one sense, a big headline crying that sex drives life, but, of course, the sensual hunger that makes the child cannot raise the child. Hence the many conflicting emo-tions and attitudes surrounding children and sex. The flickering Pearl— sometimes "demon offspring" (176), sometimes pure upholder of good and honest behavior—conveys the contradictory sentiments hovering around girls in modern culture. What Hawthorne so brilliantly represents through "little Pearl" is a cultural penchant to see daughters as symbols rather than people and to project onto them the incoherent fears and longings of their parents and their society.

The Scarlet Letter, as a modern Lot story, makes the daughter's desire prevail over the mother's: Dimmesdale, in effect, chooses the daughter's kiss over the mother's. Hester Prynne had planned to leave the community, make a new start, and live openly with Arthur and Pearl. The daughter, though, seeks the paternal identity and recognition that is a child's due, but her choice reinforces the communal allegiance to the ethic her parents have violated. The father elects to regenerate himself for his God through Pearl.

Arthur, however, like Lot, disappears following the embrace of the daughter. The strong mother and Pearl remain, but the future belongs to the girl. Hawthorne portrays early Puritan America as a harsh patriarchal world that needs a woman's touch. Hester, an ostracized but admirable character, in the end becomes a counselor—a proto-therapist—to unhappy women, assuring them, "in Heaven's own time, a new truth would be revealed, in order to establish the whole relation between man and woman on a surer ground of mutual happiness" (177). One implication is that Pearl, who, according to the narrator, grows up to flourish elsewhere, might both *be* and *sow* the seed of such feminine agency.

4.
. THE OLD WIVES' TALE AND THE BIOGRAPHICAL IMPERATIVE

Two years before he started to write *Great Expectations* in 1860, Charles Dickens (1812–1870), the best-known novelist of the nineteenth century and the famed laureate of domestic virtue, publicly and shockingly announced his separation from his wife Catherine, who had born him ten children. He had begun a long, secret liaison with 18-year-old Ellen Ternan, a girl younger than his oldest daughter. That affair, had it been known, would have amazed and dismayed his audience, but, in retrospect, it figures. Dickens had a Lot complex that shaped his outlook, his relations with women, and his hugely influential fiction.

A sanitized Lot theme featuring the benevolent embrace of daughterly figures by men and of paternal figures by very young women appealed to him, and he used it again and again. He seems at a young age to have transferred the focus of his love for a female from his mother to his sister, and that pattern of change—from an older woman to a girlish figure—shapes his vision and desire. In his life and novels, sister figures, pretty, innocent young girls, and sets of sisters supplant or replace aging wives and mothers. Dickens's gratitude for the help, love, and inspiration he got from his sister, his sisters-in-law, and, later, his daughters has much to do with the sentimental way he develops the sweet young things of his novels. He often imagines them shunting aside foolish or irresponsible older women and taking over the job of bucking up men, saving what's good about them, and regenerating the world.[10]

Relating an artist's life and work is a notoriously tricky thing to do and must always be hypothetical. Still, thinking about how, why, and what autobiographical signs appear in an artist's work helps you see what generates it, how it functions, what needs it fulfills, how it touches and moves people, and why they might care about it at all. Whatever disparagers of biographical criticism and probings into personal psychology may say, a biographical imperative surely drives most narrative art in modern times. The events and urgencies of life can show how imagination develops and grapples to preserve and extend human consciousness. Artists may have love affairs and/or they may write about having love affairs, but both the love and the story come out of real, fusing mental processes.

In *David Copperfield*, Dickens coins the revealing Lottish term *"child-wife,"* the pet name for David's first wife Dora. The concept of the "child-wife" is central in his work and important in modern social and psychological history.[11] The strange term can suggest, among other things, desire for secure family structure, for a wedding of generations in peace and domestic harmony, for a happy and lasting childhood to counteract the traumas and defeats of the early years, and for regressive coziness and safety. It can also mean treating women as children and male fetishizing of youth.

Dickens did have a Lot complex, but a complex, like the rest of inner and outer life, can change over the years. And if you're a writer, your changing psychology drives your art. For a long time, he was able to compartmentalize his real-life marriage and sex life from his fantasies about ideal young females.[12] That changed, however, with the breakdown of his marriage. In *Great Expectations*, sexual anxiety, guilt, and fantastic images of transgenerational relations suddenly blaze out. Dickens's midlife crisis helped inspire him to create one of his most disturbing and memorable characters, Miss Havisham, and, in the burning of Miss Havisham, one of the most powerful symbolic scenes in all his work.

In October 1857, Dickens, without first informing Catherine, had the door blocked up between his dressing room and what had been the marital bedroom, creating two separate bedrooms. He shut his old wife out.[13] Catherine, devastated and frantically jealous, quarreled with him day and night until, a couple of days later at 2:00 a.m. in the morning, he left his Tavistock house half-crazy and walked "in a daze" thirty miles to his other home, Gad's Hill—spooked to battiness by a woman who wouldn't let go. Dickens transposed and used details of what he went through with Catherine when Pip, in *Great Expectations*, visits Miss Havisham, his supposed benefactor and his beloved Estella's "Mother by adoption."[14] The next time Pip sees her, Miss Havisham burns up. The image of the burning of the desiccated bride, who lives in a corrupt past of erotic obsession, symbolizes both a personal conjugal catastrophe and a male cover-up of historic proportions. Out of his own marital predicament, it seems, Dickens imagined one of the most memorable deaths by fire since Lot's wife.

I looked into the room where I had left [Miss Havisham]. . . . I saw a great flaming light spring up. In the same moment, I saw her running at me, shrieking, with a whirl of fire blazing all about her, and soaring at least as many feet above her head as she was high.

I had a double-caped great-coat on, and over my arm another thick coat. That I got them off, closed with her, threw her down, and got them over her; that I dragged the great cloth from the table for the same purpose, and with it dragged down the heap of rottenness in the midst, and all the ugly things that sheltered there; that we were on the ground struggling like desperate enemies, and that the closer I covered her, the more wildly she shrieked and tried to free herself; that this occurred I knew through the result, but not through anything I felt, or thought, or knew I did. I knew nothing until I knew that we were on the floor by the great table, and that patches of tinder yet alight were floating in the smoky air, which, a moment ago, had been her faded bridal dress.

Then, I looked round and saw the disturbed beetles and spiders running away over the floor, and the servants coming in with breathless cries. . . . I still held her forcibly down with all my strength, like a prisoner who might escape; and I doubt if I even knew who she was, or why we had struggled . . . until I saw the patches of tinder that had been her garments . . . falling in a black shower around us.

She was insensible. . . . I unreasonably fancied (I think I did) that if let her go, the fire would break out again and consume her. . . .

. . . At about six o'clock of the morning . . . I leaned over her and touched her lips with mine, just as they said, not stopping for being touched, "Take the pencil and write under my name, 'I forgive her.'" (414–415)

Is it banal and simplistic to say Dickens burned up Miss Havisham because Catherine's existence had come to threaten his freedom and sap his potency? Not if you see that, though that's only one of a number of meanings here, the fiery passage projects a disingenuous hostility towards aging women.[15] In this one memorable embrace between a man and a woman in all Dickens's fiction, Pip and Miss Havisham struggle and lie together in fire and nakedness—clothes burned off—and Dickens's choice of imagery hints at gross sexuality. What comes through in a Lot reading of Havisham is a feverish fear of age—of a cloying old lady and the debilitating effect she might have on a man and his future—including his hope for a rejuvenating love. Stated baldly, that's not a pretty vision, but it's a powerful one: the burning of Miss Havisham uncovers the inherent ruthlessness preserved in the Lot story.

Dickens cast his own wife in the role of Lot's wife and, middle-aged, found himself joined with a daughter-like figure in the erotic darkness of dissimulation. This change was an emotional necessity for him. But it shook him and fired up his imagination. If you focus on the displacements and aggressive fantasies in the scene—guilt shifted to the ugly, old witch-bride seared to death, innocent suffering for a man behaving heroically, crippling injury to his vital male extremities, nudity joined with putrid decadence, and the cremated trappings of marriage—it's not hard to see the symbolic angst of men feeling trapped by the menace of age and the grotesqueries of tedious matrimonial roles and longing for a chance at new alliances. And thus it becomes easier to see how prominently that unsavory theme, in various forms, runs through the stuff and texts of modern life.

The dirty little secret code in the fate of Lot's wife ciphers conflicted male feelings about sex life. *All* stories, as Dickens's burning embrace implies, are cover stories. People may want to be free to have sex with new partners, but they also may want to get away from the humiliations of bad sex with oh-so-familiar mates and obligatory erotic performance. Suppose Dickens at times found sex ugly and demeaning. Suppose he resented having to sleep with his wife, possibly because he couldn't help himself from having sex with her, possibly because he couldn't perform with her, or— very likely—for both reasons at one time or another. In both the abandonment of a petrified Lot's wife and in Dickens's vision of the hot, morbid clutch of Havisham and Pip, I sense narrative not only covering the desire for new love, but screening confused male anxieties about their conjugal duties to old mates. The involuntary bout of agonizing, sensational, blistering nakedness both stirs and then unmans the male, leaving him dazed, weak, wounded, almost impotent—almost a child. But it leaves the woman dying and repentant. Pip goes on to Estella and Dickens to Nelly.

When Pip goes through the fire with the old lady and leaves her for good, I see Dickens displacing the crisis of his own failed marriage and excusing himself as a new Lot: leave the old bride behind and look to a new flame for inspiration. It's a morally suspect story, but a passionate one, and it presents a vision for understanding modern social history, an underrated, widely influential feature of which has been a sacrificial old wives' tale.

5.
EROTIC PEDAGOGY:
DON'T GO TOO FAR

One of the great subjects of modern Lot stories is pedagogical: what girls and men have—and need—to learn from each another. Henry James, in *What Maisie Knew*, his remarkable novel about a much put-upon girl of divorced parents, explores in depth the sentimental education that grows out of Maisie Farange's relationship with her beloved stepfather, Sir Claude. James imagines them moving through a symbolic pedagogy that has two allegorical parts, "French literature—and sacred history."[16] The terms can stand for the Lot-complex contents of the novel's teaching and knowledge. The adjective "French" held erotic connotation for the Victorians (as in "French kiss" or "French letters"), France being, in the popular English imagination, the land of exile from sexual restraint. "French literature" is shorthand for sex education, and "sacred history" really becomes the inquiry into the search for a credible faith in the modern world.[17]

Maisie, her schooling neglected by her irresponsible parents, wonders who'll give her lessons. Sir Claude, the child's good-natured Adonis of a stepfather, and Mrs. Beale, her ex- governess who marries Maisie's father, are brought together by their concern for the girl. But they themselves soon fall into adultery. They tell Maisie they plan to enroll her in "courses" on the most important subjects, "French literature—and sacred history." "All alone?" asks Maisie. "Oh no; I'll attend them with you," says Sir Claude. He, unlike his wife or Mrs. Beale, really does care about the well-being of the girl. "They'll teach me a lot I don't know" (118). These two, the man and the girl, make an odd, but important couple in modern Lot history. She hungers for love and knowledge, and he becomes her favorite teacher—she adores him. In fact, it's obvious—though critics hardly mention it—that James makes this wonderful girl moving into adolescence desire him as a teacher-father-lover. And that's what gives the book its psychological daring and candor.

James, writing about the power of Maisie to regenerate morality in a decadent world, uses seed imagery suggesting Lot's cave and daughters. The girl, he says, flourishes "to a degree, at the cost of many conventions and proprieties, even decencies, really keeping the torch of virtue alive in an air tending infinitely to smother it; really in short making confusion worse confounded by drawing some stray fragrance of an ideal across the scent of selfishness, by sowing on barren strands, through the mere fact of presence, the seed of the moral life" (Preface, 25–26). The sowing of this moral seed is the result of the pedagogical intercourse between Sir Claude and Maisie, and it produces, according to James, "something sacred."

What Maisie Knew, a harbinger of the twentieth-century age of divorce, describes a daughter's struggle to learn what she needs to know to survive selfish parents and keep hope and faith alive. Before Sir Claude involves himself in her education, she is the pitiful object of child abuse. In the first chapter James shows the little girl "handled, pulled hither and thither and kissed" by her father and his friends: "Some of these gentlemen . . . holding her on knees violently jolted, pinched the calves of her legs till she shrieked—her shriek was much admired—and reproached them with being toothpicks. The word stuck in her mind and contributed to her feeling from this time that she was deficient in something that would meet the general desire" (39–40). Bad early lessons for Maisie pop out of that passage: that she is an object, that girls are cute bundles of fresh flesh, little things for men's fun and patronization; that she's inadequate because physically she doesn't meet some aesthetic standard; that her feelings don't matter; that her purpose is to fulfill some "general desire" (which a patriarchal pun might uncover as *the general sire*).

It's a needy little victim Sir Claude finds, and, somehow, this idle womanizer turns out to be just the right mentor for her. Informally and formally, he teaches her that, rather than an agent of divorce—the identity her mother and father had foisted on her—she positively brings people together. He shows her that she is worthy of kindness, concern, and friendship, that her affection for a man can be requited, that there can be camaraderie, communication, and moments of equality—even intimacy—across the generation and gender channels: "He was liable in talking with her to take the tone of her being also a man of the world" (84). He teaches her that she is a fine, admirable person just as she is, that she deserves good treatment, and—the sweetest kind of lesson—that he whom she adores finds her lovable. Not least, he teaches her how to have fun and what a good education ought somehow to include—namely, the possibilities of sheer joy.

He also teaches her practical lessons about sex. Through the information she gathers from Sir Claude—for instance that even while talking seriously to her, he can't help looking with a venereal eye at strangers ("she seemed . . . to see him . . . as he stood there and with a kind of absent gaze —absent that is, from *her* affairs—followed the fine stride and shining limbs of a young fishwife who had just waded out of the sea" [184])—she begins to learn the power, if not the name, of sex. Some mysterious force drives the adults she sees, but can't be spoken directly about—at least she doesn't yet know the way in which it could be expressed. James's girl, like any child, must grow up in a world battered by the two whirling tornadoes of sexuality and greed. Sex and money, the proverbial staples of French literature, determine the conditions of her life, but not only can she not grasp them clearly, the adults around her cannot speak of these matters except in the mystifying idiom of translation.

But let me invoke James's French connection to stand for the verbal form of sexuality. If the narrative of Maisie's childhood is in part a sentimental journey through a world of sexual double entendre, then France, motherland of double entendre, where Sir Claude takes the thirteenish Maisie, is the crucial stopover on her not-so-grand educational tour. Trying to protect her from her parents and also fulfill the plans of both his mistress, Mrs. Beale, and Maisie's moral nanny, Mrs. Wix, Sir Claude takes the girl out of England to the channel city of Boulogne. In other words, he takes her—symbolically, this fact is key—just to the edge of France. There, writes James, taking Maisie's point of view, "once or twice . . . on the sands, he looked at her for a minute with eyes that seemed to propose to her to come straight off with him to Paris" (252). Maisie soon after propositions him with the offer to abandon Mrs. Wix, her tutor in conventional morality, and live with him alone if he agrees to leave his mistress, Mrs. Beale. She begs him to run off with her to the heart of France, Paris, "the *real* thing, the thing that . . . one does . . . abroad" (182). Looking at the Paris train, she says, "I wish we could go. Won't you take me?" (253) When, tempted but doubtful, Sir Claude talks to a porter about departure times and tickets, James moves to French and Maisie's astonishing precocity:

> "*Monsieur veut-il que je les prenne?*" the man said.
> Sir Claude turned back to her. "*Veux-tu bien qu'il en prenne?*"
> It was the most extraordinary thing in the world: in the intensity of her excitement she not only by illumination understood all their French, but fell into it with an active perfection. She addressed herself straight to the porter. "*Prenny, prenny. Oh prenny!*" (254)

Taught by Sir Claude, she speaks literally, for a moment, as a subject of French literature. The passionate cry "prenny" from this exploited, neglected, love-hungry child rings out as both deeply moving and disturbing, and just as moving is Sir Claude's hesitant, tacit renunciation of her "*prenny*" and the new sense of responsibility it signifies in his character. What follows is her reiterated desire to be with him only and *his refusal to take her any farther in France.* And since she can't have Sir Claude on her own terms, she leaves him and returns to England. James gives her at the last the voice to express her mind ("I love Sir Claude—I love *him*" [264]), the authenticity to know what she wants, and, when she can't get it, the will to act in what she sees as her own best interests—"'Good-bye,' said Maisie to Sir Claude" (266).

But the world of *What Maisie Knew* is really a modern Sodom and Gomorrah, and even a good course in French and French literature by itself won't free you from its corruption and doom. There must be sacred history, and what Maisie embodies, conveys, and teaches *is* a new faith. In erotic pedagogy, the student is always a teacher and education a mutual process. One key to the novel is the narrator's remark, "I am not sure that Maisie had not even a dim discernment of the queer law of her own that made her educate . . . those elders with whom she was concerned" (212). *French* brings Maisie to the articulation of desire that's necessary for selfhood and any sort of authentic future freedom, but Sir Claude is portrayed as learning a redeeming sense of the "sacred" from the feeling that Maisie's love arouses in him. *If the moral seed is to germinate, she must know her own desire, but he must learn the moral necessity of bracketing the pubescent child off from the potential, natural flow of erotic desire and teach her the painful lesson of erotic discipline.*

On the last page, Maisie appears as a revisionary daughter refiguring Lot's wife.

[S]he put out her hand to her stepfather. He took it and held it a moment, and their eyes met as the eyes of those who have done for each other what they can. "Good-bye," he repeated.

"Good-bye." And Maisie followed Mrs. Wix.

They caught the steamer. . . . Mrs. Wix had courage to revert. "I didn't look back, did you?"

"Yes. He wasn't there" said Maisie.

"Not on the balcony?"

. . . "He wasn't there" she simply said again.

Mrs. Wix was also silent a while. "He went to *her*," she finally observed.

"Oh I know," the child replied.

Mrs. Wix gave a sidelong look. She still had room for wonder at what Maisie knew. (266)

James has Maisie look back, learn, and remove herself from the modern land of sexual license with its new Sodom and new caves. She subsumes and revises the fate of Lot's wife and thus redeems her. The lesson she learns is that to preserve the moral seed, she must reject the sterile, selfish desires of the older generation. Sir Claude teaches her to take care of herself because she matters. So in Maisie James reverses the old myth. She looks back, but leaves. Lot's wife redeemed becomes the individualized, valorized daughter, the moralized seed—moralized remarkably, for the sake of civilization and its discontents, by Sir Claude. The point about the "lot" that Sir Claude didn't know—the revision of Lot—is that people might come to learn that preservation of *the daughter's* seed may just be the main point of civilization.

6.

THE INCESTUOUS TRANSFER:
SUBLIMATING DAUGHTERS

In an article from late in his career, Sigmund Freud remarks, "Every analyst has come across certain women who cling with especial intensity and tenacity to the bond with their father and to the wish in which it culminates of having a child by him."[18] In fact, such a relationship of intense desire between the younger woman and the older man was present at the creation of psychoanalysis. "The Case of Anna O.," the first case-history in *Studies in Hysteria* by Freud and his older colleague Joseph Breuer, marks a seminal clinical experience in the development of all subsequent psychoanalytic thought and work. After the death of her beloved father, "Anna" (Bertha Papenheim), a 19-year-old patient of Breuer's whom he was treating for hysteria, found relief in hypnosis, free-association expression, and the transference of feelings for her father onto her doctor. Her treatment helped make a path to the discovery of the Freudian unconscious and thus to the whole Freudian "climate" in which we still live. In his edition of *Studies in Hysteria*, James Strachey notes, "At this point (so Freud once told the present editor) there is a hiatus in the text. What he had in mind and went on to describe was the occurrence which marked the end of Anna O's treatment. . . . [I]t is enough to say here that, when the treatment had apparently reached a successful end, the patient suddenly made manifest to Breuer the presence of a strong unanalyzed positive transference of an unmistakably sexual nature."[19] Peter Gay comments:

Behind these technical terms lies a dramatic story: after Breuer had said good-bye to his patient, about to go off on a trip with his wife who had become jealous of her husband's interesting patient, he was suddenly called back that very evening to discover that she was in the throes of a hysterical pregnancy, claiming to be carrying Breuer's child.[20]

The seed of Freud's theory came alive in his verbal and intellectual intercourse with a number of other "hysterical" young women—young enough to be Freud's daughters. Set next to the experience of one "Anna" that of another:

Anna Freud, the youngest of Sigmund and Martha Freud's six children, was born in Vienna in 1895, the year to which her father attributed his discovery of the meaning of dreams, the key to his creation—psychoanalysis. To Anna Freud's reckoning, she and psychoanalysis were twins who started out competing for their father's attention.

By the time Anna Freud was thirty and a practicing psychoanalyst as well as a lecturer . . . on her specialty, child analysis, she and her twin were no longer rivals. They were merged. In 1936, for his eightieth birthday, she gave her father a book she had written, *The Ego and the Mechanisms of Defense*, which marked a reconfiguration of their lives: she was then the inheritor of her twin, the mother of psychoanalysis; the one to whom primary responsibility for its spirit, its future, was passed.[21]

Anna preserved his intellectual seed. The daughter figure in modern culture is a mother of much that is called "Freud"—and much that is called psychology.

7.

THE PAST REANIMATED

In *Ulysses*, that most famous novel of twentieth-century modernism, James Joyce introduces the middle-aging, compromising, mind-wandering Jew, Leopold Bloom, and sets him thinking idly one Dublin morning about a Zionist project to cultivate fruit in a re-blooming Palestine:

No, not like that. A barren land, bare waste. Vulcanic lake, the dead sea: no fish, weedless, sunk deep in the earth. No wind could lift those waves, grey metal, poisonous foggy waters. Brimstone they called it raining down: the cities of the plain: Sodom, Gomorrah, Edom. All dead names. A dead sea in a dead land, grey and old. Old now. It bore the oldest, the first race. . . . It lay there now. Now it could bear no more. Dead: an old woman's; the grey sunken cunt of the world.

Desolation.

Grey horror seared his flesh. . . . Cold oils slid along his veins, chilling his blood; age crusting him with a salt cloak. Well, I am here now. . . . Be near her ample bedwarmed flesh. Yes, yes.

Quick warm sunlight came running from Berkeley road, swiftly, in slim sandals, along the brightening footpath. Runs, she runs to meet me, a girl with gold hair on the wind.[22]

Through Bloom, father of a teenage daughter, Joyce is rendering the drive for rejuvenation that often animates conscious and unconscious life. Here he is showing how and why, in the midst of mundane life, the sensual imagination can give form to the Lot complex through its ancient history.

8.

THE DAUGHTER'S AMBIVALENCE

In "A Sketch of the Past" from *Moments of Being*, Virginia Woolf writes late in her life about her "immensely important relationship" to her famous father, Leslie Stephen, towards whom, "rage alternated with love."[23] "[He] obsessed me for years," she says:

Yes, certainly I felt his presence; and had many a shock of acute pleasure when he fixed his very small, very blue eyes upon me and somehow made me feel that we two were in league together. There was something we had in common. "What have you got hold of?" he would say, looking over my shoulder at the book I was reading; and how proud, priggishly, I was, if he gave his little amused surprised snort, when he found me reading some book that no child of my age could understand. I was a snob no doubt, and read partly to make him think me a very clever little brat. And I remember his pleasure, how he stopped writing and got up and was very gentle and pleased, when I came into the study with a book I had done. . . . I was often on his side, even when he was exploding. . . . For some reason . . . while noting my mother's half laughing deprecation . . . I shared his mood not hers. You are right, you are right, I kept repeating. (111–112)

[W]hen Nessa [her sister] and I inherited the rule of the house [after the premature death of their mother], I knew nothing of the sociable father. . . . [I]t was the tyrant father—the exacting, the violent, the histrionic, the demonstrative, the self-centered, the self pitying, the deaf, the appealing, the alternatively loved and hated father—that dominated me then. It was like being shut up in the same cage with a wild beast. Suppose I, at fifteen, was a nervous, gibbering, little monkey, always spitting or cracking a nut and shying the shells about, and mopping and mowing, and leaping into dark corners and then swinging in rapture across the cage, he was the pacing, dangerous, morose lion; a lion who was sulky and angry and injured; and suddenly ferocious, and then very humble, and then majestic; and then lying dusty and fly pestered in a corner of the cage. (116)

In the relationship of bookish father and daughter, obviously—whatever else was going on—the seed of literature and a drive for authority through authorship were preserved, and they would germinate. But Woolf's critical assessment of the father and the use she makes of it in her art show not only how much she wanted to come to terms with her father, but also how much she wanted to get out of his cage.

9.
DEBAUCHING LOT'S DAUGHTERS AND THE "POWER OF ARTICULATE ART"

Vladimir Nabokov, making fun of Freud, remarks, "Let the credulous and the vulgar continue to believe that all mental woes can be cured by a daily application of old Greek myths to their private parts."[24] But, in *Lolita*, that witty putdown doesn't keep him from applying the Hebrew myth of Lot to the private parts of his middle-aged anti-hero Humbert Humbert and his pubescent heroine Lolita. It's surely no accident that you can find the letters, name, and unmistakable trace of Lot in both "Lolita," the chippie off the old block, and her mother, Char*lot*te Haze (the name reads like wordplay on the aftermath of the cities-of-the-plain burning). And there's a Lot plot in the book. Charlotte, like an avatar of Lot's wife, perishes instantaneously, and that leaves Humbert free to journey with the girl and live in dark cohabitation. Later Lolita spends time on an "utterly lush" ranch where boys, girls, and men make pornographic movies and do all sorts of freaky sex things, but afterwards she learns that the ranch "had burned to the ground, *nothing* remained, just a *charred* heap of rubbish" (279; emphasis mine)—like Sodom and Gomorrah. Calling his testimony "Lolita, or the Confession of a White Widowed Male" (5), Humbert writes of a time when he has become both legal guardian and sex partner of the girl: "I read and reread a book with the unintentionally biblical title *Know Your Own Daughter*" (176).

In *Lolita* the Victorian and modern ideological bag that was supposed to hold the sacred figure of the innocent girlchild—the little angel-in-the-house unspoiled by sex—turns out to be full of brimstone. What if the strategy to preserve the seed of civilization by loving and idealizing that girlchild with all her potential for goodness, instead of bringing redemption, can actually promote erotic fixation on girls and lead straight back to cities-of-the-plain lasciviousness and the sacrifice of daughters? What if the pure daughter turns out to be a seductive nymphet with sisters everywhere and the worldly, delightful father figure turns out to be a marauder of little dames far more prevalent than anyone had noticed?

That was the outrage of *Lolita*: in essence, a modern form of blasphemy. It brought home not only the sexual vulnerability of pubescent girls, but also their sexual precocity. And, even more disturbing, *Lolita*, a great novel about a terrible love, certainly did expose, in the responses it evoked, a huge, prurient fascination with the whole subject of juvenile sex and girls as erotic objects. Says Humbert,

Of course, in my old-fashioned, old-world way, I, Jean-Jacques Humbert, had taken for granted, when I first met her, that she was as unravished as the stereotypical notion of a "normal child" had been since the lamented end of the Ancient World B.C. . . . The whole point is that the old link between the adult world and the child world has been completely severed nowadays by new customs and new laws. (126)

Humbert tells readers, "Lolita, with an incestuous thrill, I had grown to regard as *my* child" (82). The nymphet and her lover blew away the girl-as-redeemer cover story sanitizing *Lot*. *Lolita* drove home the anarchic force of tabooed erotic life in that myth—the dangers of incestuous impulses and the wildly unpredictable consequences and dangers of intergenerational intercourse.

What actually was going on between older men and girls? Here are four passages from the novel showing the eruption of a salacious modern Lot story that would have many consequences:

"Look here, Lo. . . . For all practical purposes I am your father. I have a feeling of great tenderness for you. In your mother's absence I am responsible for your welfare. We are not rich, and while we travel, we shall be obliged—we shall be thrown a good deal together. Two people sharing one room, inevitably enter into a kind—how shall I say—a kind—"

"The word is incest," said Lo. (121)

I am going to tell you something very strange: it was she who seduced me. (134)

However, I shall not bore my learned readers with a detailed account of Lolita's presumption. Suffice to say that not a trace of modesty did I perceive in this beautiful hardly formed young girl whom modern co-education, juvenile mores, the campfire racket and so forth had utterly and hopelessly depraved. (135)

Had I been a painter . . . and commissioned . . . to redecorate, . . . this is what I might have thought up . . . : There would have been an arbor in flame-flower. There would have been nature studies—a tiger pursuing a bird of paradise, a choking snake sheathing whole the flayed trunk of a shoat. There would have been a sultan, his face expressing great agony (belied, as it were, by his molding caress), helping a callypygean slave child to climb a column of onyx. There would have been those luminous globules of gonadal glow that travel up the opalescent sides of juke boxes. . . . There would have been poplars, apples, a suburban Sunday. There would have been a fire opal dissolving within a ripple-ringed pool, a last throb, a last dab of color, stinging red, smarting pink, a sigh, a wincing child. (136–137)

No wonder the controversial book had trouble finding a publisher in the baby-booming America of the 1950s (or why the Adrian Lyne's *Lolita* film of the late 1990s had even more trouble getting distributed). *Lolita* made its sinful, fixated version of the Lot complex too graphic, disturbingly seductive, and plausible.

Nabokov's mock foreword by an imaginary psychiatrist, John Ray, Jr., Ph.D., presents ironically (but not *only* ironically) a defense of the novel on the basis of its implied social message and civic effect: "Viewed simply as a novel, 'Lolita' deals with situations and emotions that would remain exasperatingly vague to the reader had their expression been etiolated by means of platitudinous evasions." "Dr. Ray" continues, describing one path of recent Lot complex history:

> As a case history, "Lolita" will become, no doubt, a classic in psychiatric circles. As a work of art, it transcends its expiatory aspects; and still more important to us than scientific significance and literary worth, is the ethical impact the book should have on the serious reader; for in this poignant personal study there lurks a general lesson; the wayward child, the egotistic mother, the panting maniac—these are not only vivid characters in a unique story: they warn us of dangerous trends; they point out potent evils. "Lolita" should make all of us—parents, social workers, educators—apply ourselves with still greater vigilance and vision to the task of bringing up a better generation in a safer world." (7–8)

Nabokov might mock, but somehow *Lolita*, which treats matter-of-factly cross-generational sex, *did* work to fulfill that call for vigilance. The novel's outrageous nympholepsy and its brilliant, perverted narrator (De Toqueville and Molière meet the Marquis de Sade) did stimulate and sanction the public discourse on sexual child abuse, daughterly victimization, and incest that flooded the last part of the twentieth century.

Near the end, a remorseful Humbert says, "I see nothing for the treatment of my misery but the melancholy and very local palliative of articulate art" (285). The power of that articulate art, even in the revulsion it caused, showed the way and need for an agonizing reappraisal of *Lot* and the need for other voices, other stories to emerge. And they have. Men had been the principal myth-makers and creators of cultural imagery, but after "hurricane" *Lolita* and the feminist explosion of the late 1960s hit, women found new, urgent means of expression. Incestuous dads, seductive uncles, child-abusing stepfathers, and other lecherous older males would slither their slimy ways with girls through the pages of Toni Morrison, Jane Smiley, Dorothy Allison, Kathryn Harrison, Edna O'Brien, Paula Vogel, Carolivia Herron, and innumerable other writers.

Nabokov, like Freud and Joyce, is one of the great patriarchs of modernism, and it's important to see that all three of them turned at crucial times in their careers to *Lot* and the daughter figure and away from paternal myths of triumphant power. They lived to see the devastation of civil and moral order by the unprecedented deadly violence of the last century. In Nabokov's *Lolita*, the American daughter is vulgar and amoral, but she's also smart, daring, and full of inchoate longing. Phony old world charm and deadly male madness kill her, but still Nabokov layers into his prose hints that the daughters of a new people in an outlandish culture might somehow preserve seeds of humanity.

10.
THE BLACK GHOST OF LOT'S DAUGHTER:
SURVIVING THE CAVE

In *Beloved* (1987), Toni Morrison's celebrated novel about the effects of slavery, the ghost-daughter Beloved, hungering for her mother Sethe's life and attention, seeks to move the problematic father figure Paul D out of Sethe's bed and out of the house. She also is driven to experience the sweet sensuality of life and the fulfillment of desire that the horrors of American slavery and racism have murdered. Seducing Paul D, she says,

"I want you to touch me on the inside part. . . . And you have to call me my name."

As long as his eyes were locked . . . he was safe. If he trembled like Lot's wife and felt some womanish need to see the nature of the sin behind him; feel a sympathy, perhaps, for the cursing cursed, or want to hold it in his arms out of respect for the connection between them, he too would be lost.

"Call me my name."

"No."

"Please call it. I'll go if you call it."

"Beloved." He said it, but she did not go. She moved closer. . . . What he knew was that when he reached the inside part he was saying, "Red heart. Red heart," over and over again.[25]

Later he thinks, "[H]e had come to be a rag doll—picked up and put back down anywhere any time by a girl young enough to be his daughter. Fucking her when he was convinced he didn't want to" (126).

The sexual behavior, compulsions, and modes of survival of denigrated, alienated people individually and collectively, mark one point of the developing focus in the Lot story and show the broad social implications for ethnic history that the Lot complex can hold.[26] Redeeming the ghost of incest becomes an important theme in the struggle for the subjugated to become free not only in *Beloved*, but in many texts featuring the daughters of the exploited and enslaved. The passionate trauma of the sexual cave is inseparable from the passionate trauma of a race's captive existence in a land where a white populace has seen itself as a chosen people (see Chapter 12).

11.
OUTING INCEST:
LIGHTING UP THE CAVE

On the first page of a polemical, controversial book, *Virginia Woolf: The Impact of Childhood Sexual Abuse on Her Life and Work*,[27] Louise DeSalvo writes, "Virginia Woolf was a sexually abused child; she was an incest survivor." She goes on, "Virginia . . . was raised in a household in which incest, sexual violence, and abusive behavior were a common, rather than a singular or rare occurrence, a family in which there is evidence that virtually all were involved in either incest or violence or both, a family in which each parent had lived through childhood trauma."

De Salvo dedicates her book to another feminist critic: "For Jane Marcus who taught me how to read Virginia Woolf in a new way." A newly empowered generation of communicating, networking women stresses the victimization of daughters in history through "homosocial" motives, abusive projections, and incestuous impulses of fathers" and brothers—that is, "patriarchal culture."

12.
DECONSTRUCTING LOT

In a 1993 newspaper column, "The 'Real' Lessons of Sodom and Gomorrah,"[28] Joyce Lore-Lawson explicitly takes on Genesis 19 to attack discrimination against gays and what she sees as the prejudices of Christian fundamentalists:

I'd like . . . to focus people's attention on the seldom-mentioned details concerning that Biblical standby, "Sodom and Gomorrah."

. . . Obviously, the story contains a powerful lesson . . . but just what is that lesson? . . .

As the story goes, two angels come to Sodom and are invited by Lot to spend the night at his house. When all the men of Sodom come to his door and ask Lot to send out the two visitors, Lot begs them to leave his guests alone. Then, he adds: "Behold, I have two daughters who have not known man; let me bring them out to you and do to them as you please." (Genesis 18:8)

I blinked with disbelief.

What kind of man would offer his two virgin daughters to a howling mob, to do with as they pleased? Surely, this was a person who should be destroyed in the fire and brimstone that God was planning to rain down on the evil cities, right? Even today, in these wicked times, such a man would be punished, or at least have his children taken away from him, right?

Well, the angels come to the rescue and blind the mob who are trying to batter the door down. They then tell Lot to get away and not look back. Lot's wife does, however, and is turned into a pillar of salt for this infraction.

Let's get this straight—Lot offers his daughters to be gang-raped with no consequence to himself, and his wife is killed for not following instructions?

I was beginning to see a lesson, all right.

But the story gets better.

Afraid to live in any city, Lot hides out in a cave with the daughters and then has sex with them to "preserve offspring." (Genesis 19:32) True, it was the girls' idea. They got him drunk two nights in a row so that he didn't know what he was doing and the two sons engendered went on to found the tribes of the Moabites and the Ammonites. Lot presumably lives happily ever after.

. . . So, it appears that there are five other lessons to be learned from this story, besides the one that the righteously indignant perpetually harangue us with:

1. Not following directions is very bad, especially if you're a woman.

2. Pandering is OK.

3. Offering your daughters to rapists in order to protect strangers is OK, too.

4. Incest is also OK, and even to be encouraged, especially if your wife messed up, and you need to preserve the gene pool.

5. Drunkenness is a good excuse for committing incest. . . .

All in all, however, it seems to me that a person should die of shame, rather than hold up this story.

There is enough in the Lot chapter of the Bible to offend and keep on disturbing not only this writer, but—consciously or unconsciously—just about anyone; that's what makes it both an enduring narrative and a "complex." The material is so emotionally loaded that most people who hear it—or versions of it—come up with their own slant on it, as I do. Behind Lore-Larsen's righteous anger, you can read the reenactment of one main feature of *Lot* and its modern history: the daughter becomes the woman assuming authority. Beneath the scathing tone and the ironic "lessons," there lies the conviction that the story somehow still lives and matters; that it demands and is getting editing and revision; and that its "true" meanings, having somehow been distorted, or repressed, need to be refigured and laid out.

I share this sentiment with Lore-Larsen—and with such writers as George Eliot, James Joyce, and Carolivia Herron, for example, whose fiction features and is inspired by a Lot complex. Like it or not, stories about older males and younger females, about victimized people, about people living morally equivocal lives, about family crisis as the defining crux of the human condition, about female agency, about the fluid nature of subjectivity and psychological projections have all become central to the modern imagination. Lots and Lot's daughters are all around. And tracing their ancestry down from its source can let you see how it is they can be named and recognized as such.

Chapter 3

Faithful Interpretations

LOT AND HIS DAUGHTERS FROM
THE BIBLE TO THE REFORMATION

What is the history of Lot's daughters and why should we care? It is important to see that this mysterious story was considered sacred to humanity and the making of human nature. But how could the incest of early human history and the impulses to which it alludes be redeemed, moralized, and made part of a sustaining faith in life? To show how Lot and his daughters became a part of modernity, I mean in this and the following two chapters to give an overview of the ways their part of the Scripture was understood and represented from biblical times up through the Renaissance and beyond.[1] Much is at stake in interpreting Genesis 19, but the stakes change. The record of how people saw the Sodom–Lot-Scripture and what they thought it meant helps to show what matters for different times, groups, and individuals. In any given period, a text—even and especially a sacred text—is the history of its interpretation.

I.
Biblical Mystery

Without getting lost in a maze of exegesis, I want to bring out some of the highlights in various theological interpretations of the Lot family that have had a lasting impact on consciousness. Two remarks about Lot and his daughters sum up the whole religious tradition of ambivalent response to the Sodom-Lot passages: "An almost universal consensus cast neither a complete censure nor a complete acquittal upon Lot and his daughters for the incestuous act"[2] and "There is much that is uncertain about this curious episode."[3] Reactions to it clarify how reading continually recreates the past and how that past regenerates and creates the language and vision of the present.

Reading Lot at the beginning of the twenty-first century, it's hard not to fix on homosexuality in Sodom and Gomorrah, the awful fate of Lot's wife, and the father-daughter incest, but that was not necessarily true for the prophets and early exegetes poring over the Torah. J. A. Loader, in his study of Sodom and Gomorrah in the earliest Jewish and Christian traditions, writes that the "*function* of this text is to argue that God punishes wickedness, but that he respects individual innocence in the midst of mass guilt" (46). Massive, collective guilt is punished, "but not at the price of justice. So God is vindicated in the face of doubt about his righteousness when he intervenes in the affairs of humans" (47). For different people over time, God may change, remain, withdraw, not exist, disappear, or come back, but what sticks out from the beginning of the Lot story is a faith in "individual innocence" amidst horrendous immorality and crisis, and a hope of identifying with the righteous power of the life force.

Most commentators on Genesis 19 find it strange and puzzling.[4] Its effect is to disrupt complacency and scandalize conventional wisdom. Mystery has always surrounded it—mystery meaning the touch of the sacred as well as the enigmatic. The early Christian father Origen writes:

For if someone, for example, points out to us the stories of Lot's daughters and their apparently unlawful intercourse with their father . . . what else can we answer than that [there] are certain mysteries and types of spiritual matters, but that we do not know of what sort they are?[5]

Mystery, the awful, unknowable, uncontrollable content at the core of the social and individual human being, confronts those who think seriously about the Lot text and the image of women in it. Sodom-Lot—its symbolic essence, the questions it raises—cries out with the need for what it resists: a higher authority to put it in perspective.[6] And that desire is as alive now as it was two thousand years ago.

II.
Fusing Early Perspectives

The scholars of the Talmud (Horayoth 72–76) and Midrash Genesis Rabbah (228–229) disagree sharply about the meaning of the father-daughter incest and how much moral blame it deserves. According to one recent synopsis of the traditional views about the cities of the plain and their obliteration, "The transgression of Sodom's inhabitants mainly consist in sexual debauchery, human hubris, and violation of (the law of) hospitality"; "Sodom and Gomorrah were characterized by . . . sins of fornication, and by the reversal of the order of nature."[7] That consensus took time to form. As for the Lot-and-his-daughters part of the story, there was never a general consensus about its meaning.[8] These figures taxed the ingenuity of interpreters, some of whom wanted to ignore them and some of whom, like the voyeuristic Elders gazing on Susannah, were excited by naked girls and incest. The behavior of the daughters, it seems, always had a surreptitious, mind-grabbing power. Men are repelled by the story, says a rabbi in the Midrash, but, says another, women are attracted to it. And another asserts, "There is not a Sabbath on which people do not read the passage dealing with Lot."[9]

Genesis 18–19 seems to be one integrated narrative composed by an author from about the seventh century BCE, and that means that Sodom, sin, sex, destruction, Lot, his wife and daughters, incest, generation and regeneration, doubt, faith, and the rest of the components of the story ran together in a single mind. That unity matters because it set the precedent and pattern for their continuing, complex fusion in consciousness—remembering Lot's wife implies remembering Lot's daughters too; thinking of Lot means thinking of Abraham; visions of sex in Sodom run together with visions of sex in the cave. The fusion persists and upsets people and they try to repress it. As an ancient canonized text, the history of Lot is inseparable from faith and theology, but the equivocal narrative as a whole, "the ambivalence of the biblical text itself" (Loader, 135), challenged the ingenuity of theologians whose trade was to uphold an omnipotent, infallible God, comprehend Scripture, propound moral lessons, further the interests of their faith, and convey their own ideas of divine wisdom.

This problem text called for commentary and sermonizing, and it got them. The various matter layered into it appears to reflect traditions and legends about an old catastrophe in the Dead Sea Plain, the compromised origins of the alien people to the east of Israel, the virtue and kindness of Abraham and his relations with Lot, Lot's settlement and alien existence in a corrupt city, the difference between how families of "chosen" and non-chosen peoples survive and reproduce, and the awful living presence, just power, and the possible, if unfathomable, mercy of the Everlasting. Though it does form a complex whole, many commentators (most notably, Jesus) chose to pick out parts on which to focus, preach, and allegorize, and left out what didn't fit easily into their schemes. In the Hebrew Old Testament itself, Deuteronomy stresses "the innate wickedness of Israel's enemies" (Loader, 72), the differentiation of Abraham's progeny from Lot's, and the exclusion of Lot's Moabite and Ammonite descendants from the Jewish congregation (because of their shameful, incestuous origins). More significantly the major Hebrew prophets Isaiah, Ezekiel, and Jeremiah use the wicked example of Sodom to warn about the sinfulness of Jerusalem, Israel, and their fellow Jews. Sodom, not Lot (a hard figure to pin down), offered moral visionaries a great opportunity because its evil and doom made such easy subjects to preach about.

"Behold," says Ezekiel to Jerusalem, "this was the iniquity of thy sister Sodom, pride, fullness of bread, and abundance of idleness was in her and in her daughters, neither did she strengthen the hand of the poor and needy" (Ezekiel 49). The sexual misconduct of Sodom is always implicit, but it gets little special attention in the Old Testament. For the prophets, the sin is primarily social, economic, and political in nature, and what that heritage presages for the history of Lot—why it matters right down to the present—is that when the sexual and psychological aspects of the story came to be emphasized, they could and would still be felt to have broad public implications.

III.
Commentary on Divine Vengeance
and Its Refugees

Jewish tradition emphasizes social cruelty as a main reason for Sodom's destruction. Any brief characterization of the extensive commentary in early Jewish writings (Apocrypha, Pseudepigrapha, the works of Philo, Flavius Josephus, and the huge mass of rabbinical literature—Talmud, Targum,

Midrash) is bound to be crude and oversimplified, but this Talmudic passage sums up the dominant view of cities-of-the-plain immorality:

The inhabitants of Sodom are cruel cheaters, exploiters of strangers, grasping, money-crazy, and unkind. They are terrible to the poor. A poor man came to Sodom and was denied food, until a daughter of Lot met him and fed him. When the people of the city saw Lot's daughter giving him bread . . . they carried her before the judges, who condemned her to death by burning, and this punishment was inflicted on her. . . .

For such acts were Sodom and her sister cities destroyed by fire from Heaven, and only Lot and his family spared through God's love for his servant Abraham.[10]

Notice how this description stresses the vicious treatment of the young woman and builds sympathy for her, this other daughter of Lot, who here combines her father's charity with the burning fate of her mother. The vignette gets at what usually remains latent in the text but what comes out with a vengeance in twentieth-century Lot complexes: bad men victimizing young females. They even do it as a matter of policy—*so girls need protection*. Note also how this rabbinical story works to deflect moral blame from Lot (for the panicky offer of his daughters) back onto the misogynist Sodomites. But it ends with the soothing piety of faith in Abraham and the subordination of the Lot family to orthodoxy.

It's worth quoting an allied text: "God had no choice but to intervene. God heard the cries of the girl Peletit [there are other names of the girl in other rabbinical traditions] who had taken bread in a jug to a poor man. She was found out, whereupon she was smeared with honey and put on the top of a wall, thus attracting bees that devoured her."[11] In other words, in Sodom and in the biblical text, a combination of public cruelty and erotic sadism exists that would almost inevitably make the drive to extend female agency and power a matter of life and death.

One key feature from the early Jewish reading of Lot is the interplay with other parts of the Bible and the dialectical meaning that results. For example, the girl offered to the crowd of wicked men, then raped and killed in Judges 19 puts Lot's offer of his daughters in a scary new perspective.[12] And obviously the "Noah's Flood" chapters, with the provocation of God's deadly ire, His devastation of the whole world, the saving of Noah and family, Noah's later drunken, naked presence before his sons, and God's curse on Ham for uncovering his father's nakedness, cast light on the apocalyptic Lot chapter and mythic fantasies of destruction (note the salvation of Lot's family, his wife's disobedience, his drunken, naked presence with his daughters, and the ostracizing of their progeny). Next to *Noah*, the problematic prominence of women in Lot stands out.

The dialectical tradition within the Bible continues, of course, in the New Testament, as this passage from the late book, Peter II, bringing together the flood and the fire-and-brimstone and assessing both Noah and Lot favorably goes to show:

5   [God] spared not the old world but saved Noah the eighth person, a preacher of righteousness, bringing in the flood upon the world of the ungodly;

6   And turning the cities of Sodom and Gomorrah into ashes condemned them with an overthrow making them an ensample unto those that after should live ungodly;

7   And delivered just Lot, vexed with the filthy conversation of the wicked.

Early Christian tradition, stressing miraculous new beginnings, the necessary destruction of old ways, and the seeds of greater catholicism, is, in general, more approving of Lot and his daughters than the Jewish tradition, but about those three there was no true orthodox reading. One Midrash passage typifies the split reaction to Lot family incest and reveals the latent prurience that would color commentary through the ages:

C. R. Hinema bar Pappa said, "In the beginning of the conception of Moab, it was not for the sake of fornication but for the sake of heaven. . . . D. R. Simon said, "In the beginning of the conception of Moab, it was not for the sake of heaven but for the sake of fornication." . . . Said R. Levi, "If the beginning of the conception was for the sake of heaven, so too in the end it was for the sake of fornication."

Various rabbis and the monks who read the Jewish commentators sometimes could not help projecting their own erotic speculations onto the episode: for example, *the Scripture must be wrong and Lot knew what he was doing; you can't have sex and not know it; who got on top of whom and how did it work? where and how did they get the wine for sexual seduction?* Augustine (surely one of the most important thinkers for the history of sexuality in the Western world), after calmly balancing the good motives of the daughters with their mistaken procedure, suddenly bursts out, "Had the daughters learned in Sodom some vile art which enabled them to intoxicate their father, so that in his ignorance he might sin, or rather be sinned against?"[13] It may be literally true, as one recent critic says, that "in the biblical account of Lot and his Daughters there is no hint of eroticism,"[14] but, more to the point, it is also true that erotic thoughts keep seeping into the minds of those who read the account or contemplate its meaning.

IV.

Biblical Women:
Fertility Rites/Rights in the Dead Sea Area

Myths and sacred literature are summations, allegories, and symbolic constructs of the history of formative human experience, but their various parts and images also form different versions and judgments of that experience. The canonical Book of Ruth, featuring Ruth's alliance with her Jewish mother-in-law and her fruitful marriage to old Boaz, looks like a revision and redemption of the Lot-Scripture and its incest—or a cover-up. From another point of view, the spirit that shows up in much of early Jewish commentary tends either to alienate Lot from righteousness or to make him a figure of no consequence (except for his escape from fire and brimstone, which reflects God's grace and blessings on Abraham). In the Bible itself, however, the tenor and upshot of Ruth contradict the tendency to dismiss Lot's importance. Its implications move Lot's daughters from the margins to the center of human life and faith.

Within the artfully structured Sodom-Lot unit itself, the Abraham chapter (Genesis 18), featuring the heavenly visitation announcing God's plans to destroy the evil city and Abraham's plea to spare it, is carefully balanced by the Lot chapter, with its similar scenes, verbal formulas, and rhythms. The two parts compare and contrast the two patriarchs, their familial relations and their need for "preservation of seed." It is important in understanding the history of gender right down to the present to see that the juxtaposition of Abraham's wife Sarah in Genesis 18 with Lot's wife and daughters in Genesis 19 is crucial in developing the significance of the Lot paradigm and complex through the ages. Here are the verses when Sarah learns from the Lord, about to destroy Sodom, that she will conceive:

10 . . . and lo, Sarah thy wife shall have a son. And Sarah heard it in the tent door where she was behind him.

11 Now Abraham and Sarah were old and well stricken in age; and it ceased to be with Sarah after the manner of women.

12   Therefore Sarah laughed within herself, saying, After I am waxed old shall I
     have pleasure, my lord being old also?

13   And the Lord said unto Abraham, Wherefore did Sarah laugh, saying Shall I
     of a surety bear a child, which am old?

14   Is any thing too hard for the Lord? At the time appointed I will return unto
     thee, according to the time of life, and Sarah shall have a son.

What is this annunciation by divine power on the way to annihilate a
land and countless people doing here? This miracle of exhausted loins, which
later produces Isaac and holds inestimable importance for Judaism and all
of history, could be called not the parting, but the restarting of the Red Sea.
And my remark, bad taste or not, has a very serious point. At the heart of
the text, beneath the sins of Sodom, the Lord's vengeance, and the travails of
Lot, you can find complex issues about women, their fertility, and the desperate need of people threatened with extinction to beget progeny.

Lot's wife set over against Sarah can bring out the historical dilemma
of aging women, as one fantastic bit of traditional lore about her fate clearly
shows. Her "menstrual blood was said to glow periodically from the remains of the pillar."[15] Supposedly, this image is based on the geology of the
Dead Sea region where white masses and spires of mineral-salt had been
stained red by oxidation. It turns Lot's wife to physical matter, fusing her
into the land, and the poetic thought is revealing: the earth is a woman and
the barren earth is a barren woman whose blood is petrified.

In "Sodoma," a poem found among the writings of the third-century
CE Christian author Tertullian, the poet describes Lot's wife as changed to
"brittle salt, herself her tomb" and illuminates her in an amazingly resonant image: "Still is she said / To live, and 'mid her corporal change, dis-
charge / With wonted blood her sex's monthly dues."[16] To begin to unpack
that vision in the context of Sarah's news, the suicidal backward look at
Sodom, and the daughters' dilemma and action is not only to uncover
sources of psychological and sociological complexes, but to open up the
underground flow of women's history and, eventually, feminism.

Put Sarah's initial doubt about God's words, knowing she lacks a menstrual flow, together with the preposterous menses of the salt block—literally, blood out of a stone—and you sense tremendous anxiety about reproduction, fertility, and woman's functional identity as a child-bearer.
Symbolically, it's possible to interpret menstrual blood coming out of the
inanimate pillar as the seed-preserving daughters (new fertility). Then the

image would mean the life and fate of the mother and her daughters are actually dependent and inseparable, but it would take nearly two millennia for that reading to prevail. A woman's essence and immortality in the tradition of such a vision, then, is part of an anonymous, endless process that passes on "a moonflower and bloodvein" of generation: though Lot's wife doesn't even have a name, the biological flow of menstruation never ceases.[17]

But such thinking about an absolutely essential female role can also mean the petrifaction of a woman's blood and being. You can also read this pseudo-Tertullian verse to show that the true condition of representative woman appears as a figure who cannot give up the image of her breeding self because she has no other real value for the tribe. One possible meaning of the backward gaze is surely a wife's desperate nostalgia for a time of maternity—acknowledged social purpose and value. To remember Lot's wife is to remember the hard lot of women in history.

One enduring, implicit question of the Sodom-Lot text could be put like this: *Who owns and controls the fertility rights of the Dead Sea region?* Sarah, after her initial skepticism in which, implicitly, she flirts with the disobedient decision to reject sexual intercourse as wrong at her time of life, is finally willing to leave everything up to God (and her husband's special relationship to God). She needn't decide or plan—God can trump the laws of nature and make her an aging vessel for "the magic of birth." As for Lot's wife, for whatever reason she cannot obey God's command to move on without looking back, and so in the new world she preserves no seed. The daughters, however, plan out and take responsibility for getting pregnant. They decide as individuals to face what they deem the necessity of incest because to them, in crisis, having children looks like an urgent duty, and they don't feel they can rely on faith, miracles, or the agency of others to survive.[18]

Orthodox Judeo-Christian tradition generally blesses Sarah, but downplays Lot's daughters, either judging them to be well-meaning sisters acting in error, or, more rarely, condemning them for lechery. Complex history, though, would eventually lose tranquil faith in supernatural solutions and rediscover the psychological and cultural turmoil figured by Lot's daughters. The Midrash sets down a revealing discussion among rabbis that shows both an underlying male fascination with female sexual thinking and behavior in general, and, in particular, with the sexual behavior, independence, and responsibility of these two young women: "Said R. Eleazar [casting implicit doubt on their virtue], 'A woman never gets pregnant from the first act of sexual relation.' . . . They raised an objection from the following statement: 'Thus were both daughters of Lot with child by their father.' . . . Said R. Tanhuma, 'They exercised great self-control and removed their own virginity and so became pregnant by the first act of sexual relations.'" (228)[19] This registers the planting of a world-historical seed: you can't leave hard choices about having to do wrong things for the larger good up to a supernatural male God or patriarchs. You can't leave control of your sexual body up to men. In a sense, in terms of reproduction and bringing new human life into the world, the command to remember Lot's wife and, regardless of the past, move resolutely, if painfully, into the future, could be seen to be fulfilled by Lot's daughters more faithfully even than by Sarah.

V.
Christ the Teacher and What His "Lot's Wife" Means

Jesus's focus on the story, "Remember Lot's wife" (Luke 17:32), makes that bleached pillar and statue the ultimate dead white female for study: *Do as I say, believe me, have faith in me, follow the new-found truth and ethic I'm expounding, or that can happen to you.* She becomes the type for the moral warning that seems to come from every would-be savior of humanity, every sage, every charismatic leader, every system of belief, every faith. She can teach moral lessons, it seems, to and for every school. For Christ's followers, the wife of Lot becomes the prime figure reminding them that if they want to avoid a hellish fate, they must avoid any nostalgia for their corrupt, pre-Christian lives and look sharply to the future, no matter how hard the present.[20]

Jesus here speaks as an allegorical symbolist—the most charismatic of all typological readers and teachers—as he subsumes the sacred Scripture of the past into his message. He takes an odd, troubling text and shapes it into a pillar of his faith. And by emphasizing Lot's wife, not Lot or his daughters, Jesus makes it easy for his followers to bury or skim lightly over the father-daughter incest. But Christ's speech here eventually made it inevitable, by etching Lot's wife in the world's memory, that various people, sooner or later, would remember Lot's daughters and the incestuous act.

For the faithful who believe in the divinity or the moral authority of the

Bible, that incest can present a very big problem. If you take it (and leave it) as literal, Scripture might seem either to condone incest or to reveal in it the fundamental chaos and absurdity of life on earth. For early biblical scholars, the way to preserve faith was to move from the literal to the allegorical, to see how that incest can be read to represent, symbolize, and fit God's larger moral plan. And this is not a question of fussing about a dead academic subject. Human culture and the positive history of intimacy, family, and society has depended upon the movement from literal incestuous behavior to the spiritualizing and symbolizing of emotional attraction and love among family members. And, in particular, it also happened that in the twentieth century the very nature of people's early life and history as individuals would become a matter of controversy about whether little children's incestuous dreams and feelings were literally true or symbolic forms of allegory. Biblical exegetes prepared the way for fights to come.

The Judeo-Christian interpretive tradition that grew up around the study of the Bible is the "typological" method, and it holds sways for teachers, ideologues, and true believers of all times (including contemporary literary critics—Marxist, Freudian, feminist, post-colonialist, Catholic, neo-materialist, group-identified, etc.—though most would deny it). The Apostle Paul defines the point of such scriptural reading succinctly: "Now all these things happened unto them for ensamples: and they are written for our admonition" (Corinthians 1, 11:11). You "explain" and preserve old texts in "modern," symbolic terms. You read and study writings of the past allegorically to find and clarify general truths, learn about the present, support your faith and intellectual judgment, illuminate historical developments now and in the future, and prove what you've decided to prove. Contradictions, impieties, and embarrassing facts can be explained away; dead words and obscure events can be made vital; divine purpose can be found in cosmic desperation and anger. For example, Philo, the Alexandrian interpreter of the Torah, a good Jew and a contemporary of Jesus who profoundly influenced the early major Christian thinkers (Irenaeus, Tertullian, Origen, Jerome, and Augustine) and the whole history of Christian scholarship, allegorizes Lot as "Mind," and his two daughters as "Counsel" and "Consent." No lover of feminine logic, he even offers this sexist gem as a reading of the meaning of Sodomites and Lot's offer of his daughters:

The wickedness of the men of Sodom was pederasty, which allegorically means that impure people threaten those who are self-controlled. As for Lot's abandoning his daughters to the lust of the mob, its deeper meaning is that the feminine thoughts within us, that is, the thoughts of the passions, should be abandoned in favour of the masculine thoughts. (Loader, 92)

Thus typology, perfuming the past, can mean never having to say you're sorry—sorry for the horror that is ineluctably part of your heritage and identity. Such patronizing of the feminine, of course, makes an easy target and reveals one big cause of the modern Lot-and-daughters history and complex. That feminine thoughts mean erotic passion and should be given up for "masculine thoughts," which Philo presumes are more spiritual and abstract, looks zany in this context of sensual, physical male thinking and action (the Sodom mob is nothing if not male, and of course it's the father who has the wild idea of the Sodomites slaking their lust with the girls). But the logical contradiction is actually less simple and more important than it seems. If the daughters = feminine thoughts = passionate, erotic thoughts, then why are the daughters saved and why is it that those feminine thoughts lead to reproduction and progeny? Survival must somehow depend on such thoughts.

Philo, like so many thinkers in the Greco-Judeo-Christian tradition of idealism, harps on the superiority of spirituality and the weakness of the flesh. Yet the transmission of life and the future—the very existence of these fathers and messiahs of immortal wisdom to come—depends on those daughters, on those "feminine thoughts," on the sexual impulse and women's bodies. The Lot story thus focuses perfectly the enigma of a great cultural heritage that struggles with, deplores, and can't escape or explain satisfactorily the lawlessness of sex, the tyranny of the body, and the utter dependence of spirit on the reproductive flesh of women.

VI.
Christian Allegories

Christians following Philo heavily allegorize Lot, his wife, and his daughters. Irenaeus sees Lot as Christ and Lot's wife as the fickle Bride of Christ; he even interprets Lot's incest with his daughters as "a sign of the fructifying insemination (*vitale semen*) of the divine Word in the body of history" (Gallagher). He's out to protect the sacred text he believes in, even when it looks perverse, so he speculates on the idea of the daughters as the two testaments of the Bible—the idea, that is, of the daughters as inscribed and holy truth. Lot's daughters, he says, are two synagogues, and from such a notion you can see how a will to conceive of daughters as holy could and would float down streams of (un)consciousness to modernity.

Origen, though he sympathizes with Irenaeus's motives, doubts that Lot stands for Christ or the daughters for Scripture. Deeply engaged with the text, he stresses its mystery and its range. His literal reading of Lot's daughters has been immensely influential:

[I]t appears that scripture justifies them in a certain way; for one sees that the daughters of Lot had a certain knowledge of the end of the world which would come by fire, but, as that of little girls, their knowledge is incomplete and imperfect. They did not know that near the country of Sodom ravaged by fire, there was still much space intact in the world. They had heard it said that at the end of time the earth and all things would be destroyed by the power of fire. They saw the fire, they saw the sulphur flames, they saw the total devastation. They saw also that their mother had not been saved. Thus they imagined that something had happened which resembled that which they knew about the epoch of Noah, and that they and their father remained alone in order to assure a human race. The desire to perpetuate the human race came to them, and they thought that the new age should begin with them. Thus, knowing well that it is a great fault to surprise their father, and to unite with him, it appeared to them nevertheless that it would be a very great impiety to destroy by their chastity, as they believed it, the hope of continuing the human race. That is why they decided—which as I look at it, the importance of the hope the guilt of which is diminished by the motive—to dispel the grief of their father and to soften his rigor by the wine.[21]

Though that view of the daughters' behavior shapes the thinking of Augustine and Martin Luther, the two most important theologians to treat the subject, nothing casts more light on the shape and history of the modern Lot syndrome than the simile Origen slips into his exposition, "*as that of little girls.*" The Christian father, in typical fashion, patronizes female understanding, but I want to suggest how the movement of mind that can compare Lot's daughters to "little girls" opens the way to the future identification of the daughters, especially in the Victorian imagination, with little girls and their supposed innocence and purity—and thus to a possible purging of sex from the Lot complex. The drift of Origen's thought works to absolve the daughters and the father of immoral sexual desire (the civic-minded girls err, but they mean well; the good man Lot, giving in to the lesser sin of gluttony—here, as so often, defined by the ingestion of that mind-altering, conscience-dulling drug, alcohol—loses the capacity to distinguish reality).

Origen famously condemned sexual desire, and he regarded aging wives who liked it as sinners gazing back at Sodom. The ascetics of early Christianity found plenty of ammunition in Genesis 19 for war against the senses. The very prominence of women and their sexual being in the Lot story gave the male priests, in love with their mysterious vocation and the righteous power of their developing Church, a chance to denigrate the judgment and responsibility of women, and to decry sensual desire and natural sexual life.

VII.
Augustine and the
Stress on Sex

Augustine (354–430), who brooded on the conflict between his passionate early sex life and his Christian mission, found in Sodom-Lot and Christ's word on Lot's wife the perfect rationale for his thought and career. His reading of the Lot matter had enormous influence in the moral history and the making of the Lot complex. He not only interpreted the story, he lived it. In *The City of God*, he mentions Lot "whose wife, by looking back on the way and being straightway turned to salt, provided a solemn and sacred warning that no man who has set his foot on the path of salvation ought to yearn again for what he has left behind."[22] His *Confession* tells us that, like Lot, following God's wishes, he left his mother and abandoned his wife. Jesus Christ, he knew, told him he did right ("Remember Lot's wife"). For the greater good, you can leave a woman behind, move on from your old sexual partner, and obey the summons of immortality. You can and should follow a new calling if it will save you.

Augustine's force shaped the meaning of the Sodom-Lot tradition for 1,500 years. The social and political aspects were "superseded by the sexual aspect, resulting in the creation of common words such as 'sodomy' in which only the sexual aspect of the tradition is remembered" (Loader, 140). Homosexual behavior is the only evil of the Sodomites Augustine mentions, and after him the social cruelty and oppression of Sodom, at the center of Jewish tradition, fade away into moral outrage about sex and sodomy. You have, in other words, a typical instance of the reduction of sin to sexual misconduct.

Augustine's tack on Sodom-Lot sets a mighty precedent: blame sex. When he thinks of the hostility of Israel's neighbors and the problems they cause for the Jews, he mentions that "all the enemies of God's people, troubling them from the beginning with their devilishness, were produced in the coupling of Lot with his daughters."[23] So, of course, was the singer of the psalms, David, but Augustine, like so many who would come after, wants to root political enmity and social problems in bad, deviant sexual behavior. It seems much easier for aggressive men to inveigh against sex and forbidden sexual practices than against pride, ire, and greed. People seeking and wielding authority on earth through institutions live with, use, and depend upon righteous anger, ambition, moral pride, and covetousness. Naturally, it is much easier for them to rail against obsessive sexual desire than against the desire for power and authority.

Coherent Christian authority is Augustine's goal, and to uphold it more easily, he breaks Genesis 19 into sections for explication. In *The City of God*, he reiterates the message of Christ to remember Lot's wife (and, implicitly, to forget the daughters). From this work, you would know nothing of Lot's progeny, and it sets an example for those who wished to bury the rest of the story.

In his *Reply to Faustus the Manichaean*, Augustine *does* treat the end of the Lot chapter, but he carefully distinguishes between Lot's flight from Sodom (in which he "was a type of the body of Christ . . . among the ungodly and wicked") and his drunken intercourse with the daughters. At the cave with the girls, he falls into guilt and sin—not of incest, but of drunkenness. That distinction was important in Christian tradition. The commentators after Augustine tended to seize upon the drunkenness of Lot to avoid—or fudge—the moral ambivalence of the incest passage. They want to assume the high ground of the moral surety on which the propagation of faith finally depends.[24] Augustine, himself, absolves the daughters of guilty motives, but pronounces the judgment of orthodoxy, "It would have been better for them never to have become mothers, than to have become mothers by their own father" (Kind, 54).

In one passage, however, the future saint shows himself to be a true father of a familiar strain of male paranoia—*men sin because women tempt them by playing on their better nature*: "What can have made Lot consent to receive from his daughters all the cups of wine . . . ? Did they feign excessive grief, and did he resort to this consolation in their loneliness, and in the loss of their mother, thinking they were drinking too, while they only pretended to drink?" Augustine, who left his beloved mother Monica on the far shore, and who knew the pleasures of sex with females, the necessary rationale of casting them aside, and their desperate grief, cannot help imagining the psychology of the bibulous seduction and, in effect, projecting himself into the story.

As a result, he does end up sanctioning the prurient focus on the scene of incest by certain Christians down through the centuries. Nicholas de Lyra, for instance, picking up on Augustine, says that the daughters mixed a love philtre into the wine and gave it to their father (see Kind, 72). Some Christian readers, in one developing tradition, blamed Lot and made him into a drunken, lecherous old sinner. That way, they didn't have to bother about any moral ambiguity in the text. Jerome (347–420), using Jewish sources, cast doubt on Lot's ignorance of what was happening: "the Hebrews represent it as practically incredible, because in the nature of things it is not possible for anyone to have intercourse without knowing it" (Kind, 56). Hrabanus Maurus writes of Lot's eldest daughter, "The fact that she lay on top is incredible, and also that the nature of things does not hold that one can have sex without knowing it." He goes on to speculate, "When Lot went to bed with his daughters, it was not that this was a freeing from Sodom, but rather the forming of another" (Kind, 73). That harsh reading contains a seed that, after germinating for hundreds of years, would grow into the whole revisionist scrutiny of family life in the twentieth century.

VII.
Luther and the Reformation
of the Lot Family

The emotionally charged Lot-Scripture carried the seeds of conflict from medieval times into modernity. During the Reformation, radically different interpretations of the story emerged, and these point to contradictions developing around family life and generational relations. Are the father, wife, and daughters contemptible, or are they more to be pitied than censored? Are we like them? In the first half of the sixteenth century, the two most influential men of the Protestant Reformation, Martin Luther and John Calvin, each found something basic to their religious vision and themselves in the Lot family.

Luther makes clear both the power and the living history of Lot in his long commentary on it. By the end he has turned the biblical chapter into his own Lot complex; no commentator before him had been more sympathetic to the daughters and wife, nor identified so fully with Lot's dilemma. You can see why. This ex-monk married and had children. He defied Rome as the Sodom of his era, and, amid the upheaval, he denounced the all-male priesthood, the Pope, the corruption in the Church, and the official Roman Catholic ban on marriage and families for the clergy. A godly, deeply flawed man, Luther barely survived the tremendous schismatic apocalypse of the Christian faith that he did so much to spark. He became deeply invested in the Lot story, and he projected his own passions into it.

His long discussion of Genesis 19 begins with a thoughtful meditation on the awful, humbling reality of God's wrath and the destruction of Sodom. Luther here preaches the necessity of fearing God if righteousness and decency are to endure. You can sense that, as he sees conflict, war, violence, and ecclesiastical cataclysm raging around him, his concern for the Lots' plight in the cities-of-the-plain holocaust comes right out of his time. And when I call this family "the Lots," giving them a tinge of middle-class, modernish identity, I'm only following the direction that Luther stakes out in the rest of his discussion. It's almost as if his commentary turns into a novel of family crisis, and that "novel" and its "characters" shape the outlook and desire of Luther. This excommunicated priest, having unexpectedly and in the midst of religious conflagration become a family man himself, is very protective of the Bible's first firestorm refugee family.

Luther wanted to uphold the truth and authority of the Scripture, and he condemns biblical exegetes who, he thinks, go against the letter and spirit of the sacred text by denying the virtue and pious intentions of Lot's daughters or by minimizing their awful situation. Of course you can find the conventional sexism of his era in his exegesis (e.g., "women are rather weak by nature"), but what matters more is to consider how his writing and its force here could and did work to promote the dignity of familial life and ultimately the status of women. He's definitely the foe of the anti-feminism among clerics that Lot's wife and daughters often provoked. Surprisingly he shows himself here as a pioneer of the sentimental imagination and even as an author of the modern "family romance." He writes of the daughters and their father and mother with new sympathy:

Above all, then, Moses must be defended against the suspicion of lying. Hence we declare that it is certain and beyond doubt that Lot and his daughters were in extreme fear and distress, not only because of the sad spectacle—that they saw such a great multitude of human beings suddenly perish—but also because of the misfortune in their family—that Lot had lost his very dear wife and that his daughters had lost their very lovely mother. If anybody is not crushed by this misfortune, he has a heart that is harder than adamant.[25]

Such ideas usher in fresh modes of thinking and begin to make family affections and domestic emotional history the center of moral life. In that passage you can see how and why the novel will rise. Luther is *psychologizing* here, turning the Scripture into the literature of moral sentiment; virtue lies in a feeling heart that can identify with these figures. Raising the whole subject of female independence of mind, he goes on to say of the daughters, "Thus they devise this plan, not because they are stirred up by lust but because of their extraordinary compassion for the entire human race." Their reasoning may be specious, but, he says, "it is nothing but genuine concern for preserving the human race that troubles the saintly girls" (310). He is finding a way to include these figures and bring them closer us, rather than shun them. "The father is saintly, and the girls are saintly; but both sin, yet not because of malice and lust" (310).

"Lot," he says, "had lost his very dear wife and . . . his daughters had lost their very lovely mother." That daring statement (nobody before or after Jesus, until Luther, had many good words for Lot's wife) is pregnant with the future emotional history of inner conflicts—with individual complexes. *Think of the inner life of these refugees*, Luther is saying.[26] Whatever he intended, he shows how the Scripture can be read not only as religious and moral symbolism, but as a symbolic psychological text.

In Luther's reading of Lot, the mother is present in her absence, a figure that inescapably becomes part of father-daughter interactions. He intuits that what obsesses them is the loss of a beloved being who made the wrong decision. He patronizes, but excuses the daughters, and in doing so he rationalizes the motives of young women who look at the disaster of a mother's life and desperately seek to transcend it. Sin, time, natural human emotions, and superhuman force break up the loving family unit, which, for the sake of preservation, the members must consign to the past, but which they cannot help wanting to recreate. The young women, to make the future, think they must use the father to reproduce life. But Luther tries to rehabilitate and honor Lot's wife: "But so far as Lot's wife is concerned, this example is instruction . . . rather than condemnation of the woman, who, I fully believe, was saintly and was saved" (299–300). The rabbis and the papists who condemn her, says Luther, are the ones "looking back" (299), and he asserts that "the saintly woman is compelled to suffer this punishment—in order that it may reach all succeeding generations. Thus this pillar is truly a spice and the salt of wisdom" (300).

Salt and spice and everything nice—that's what sacrificial mothers are made of. Luther points the way towards a revisionary future for Lot's wife and the history of expendable women. The fate of this woman bothers him, and he can't easily let go of her memory. He more and more identifies in his commentary with what it seems almost fitting by the end to call his *characters*: "From our own sentiments we shall readily gauge how hard it was for the saintly man Lot on such an occasion and because of such a sin to lose his very dear wife, with whom he lived for so many years and who had followed him so dutifully during so prolonged an exile" (301).

Luther turns the chapter into a narrative of hope and redemption—a story with an ending in which he obviously projects himself. He can confront the incest and incestuous relations when they are desexualized and shorn of erotic motive, and he enters the minds of the girls:

If no man is left besides our father, we shall have offspring from our father. But he is an old man and will be ashamed of the deed. Therefore it will be necessary to make him drunk, in order that he may forget the present misfortune and in order that his senile body may be inflamed by wine. He will never do this when he is sober. (311)

"His senile body": telltale words—not the language of girls but of an aging man drawn to the scene in wonder. "When carnal people . . . read things like this, they think of their own desires and suppose that these girls were crazed by lust" (307). Luther, therefore, to exculpate *himself*, is at pains to defend the virtue of both the daughters and the father, and in his rationalization of Lot's supposed ignorance of the incest, he highlights matters that in our time seem to stand out: the troubling question of memory, its function and repression in the relations between parents and children, and the murky, vexed role of sexual impulses in intergenerational relationships:

Lot was undoubtedly aware of having had intercourse with his daughters, since coition is a shaking of the entire body and an excitation of soul and body. But why does Moses state that Lot was not aware of it? . . . [I]n order to point out that Lot had been absorbed in the height of excitement and for this reason does not remember afterwards what he did. . . . He is intoxicated in a twofold way: his body with wine and his heart with care. (300–309)

The incest provokes Luther's curiosity and keeps driving him to imagine the inner life of the participants: "But by what thoughts shall we suppose that Lot himself was tortured after he had learned that his daughters had been impregnated by him?" Most previous commentators distanced themselves from these figures, but the Reformer feels their pain and guilt. The cynical speculation of Nicholas of Lyra "that Lot sat in a tent under a fig tree and that both Lot and his daughters lived at ease in Abraham's home" disgusts him: "On the contrary, it's more likely they died" (313).

But then he imagines his own happy ending—an inspired projection. Abraham, as authoritative churchman, comes to the rescue. "Lot," says Luther, "heard numerous comforting discourses from Abraham" (312). He looks at the Scripture and sees the tainted progeny of Lot and the legitimate progeny of Abraham coming together: "But how . . . glorious it is that Ruth, the ancestress of Christ, was a Moabite!" The last page of Luther's commentary is extraordinary—pure fiction. Here you can see how the Lot story changes into Luther's very own, positive Lot complex. He is discussing the names the daughters gave their sons, Moab and Benami: "It seems likely to me that these names were given to the sons as a result of the comforting addresses with which Abraham encouraged the women; for we shall not doubt that they had need of unceasing comfort and that Abraham, as the chief bishop, diligently did his duty in this situation:

"My daughters," he said, "you have indeed committed a grievous sin; but do not despair on this account. God sees your hearts." Then he added . . . : "It is not that you should fear that God will pass on your sin to your sons. He will bless your sons as a part of His people; He will not cast them aside."

Look what happens here. Luther wholeheartedly identifies with the good patriarch, and his revision practically turns Abraham, the obedient founding father who puts God before his son Isaac, into a merciful father of daughters—Lot's daughters. And Abraham's progeny and Lot's daughters' progeny become the same. The father-daughter relationship becomes central; the Reformation moralist finds faith, hope, and charity in the relationship of the older man and the younger women. Physical incest, having played a role in "genesis," gives way to the spiritual fertility of the "good" patriarch and the women he calls "daughters." Luther projects a scenario in which a wise leader of the faith comes into, and reforms, the spirit and life of daughter figures, and the union preserves his seed forever —a wish-fulfillment of lasting power and a millennial moment indeed! For fathers, for a very long time, something like the metamorphosis in Luther of Lot to Abraham served as a proper model for the working-through of a Lot complex.

"I believe," said Luther, "that Lot is a divine miracle and that in him God wanted to reveal His wisdom and power" (261). One big reason for Luther's sympathy and his attempt to rehabilitate the Lot family is that for him, whether consciously or not, Lot's movement out of Sodom and into the tricky, treacherous, sin-ridden survival country of his life and kin had typological meaning: it's an allegory signifying the movement of true faith from the male, unwed clerisy of the Roman Church (Sodom and its men) to a Reformed, Protestant faith with clerics enmeshed in familial life and its paradigms.

For modern readers, the most repugnant act of Lot is his offer of his virgin, betrothed girls to the Sodomites. Yet though Luther calls it "execrable" (258), even here he defends the father with a telling bit of sophistry. "Yet so far as the account before us is concerned, I excuse Lot and think that he adopted this plan without sinning. He did not plan to expose his daughters to danger, for he knew that they were not desired by the frenzied men; but he hoped that this would be a way to soften their wrath. Therefore this speech should be regarded as a hyperbole" (259). What's at stake for Luther here is making clear the contrast between the well-intentioned, if mistaken, Lot family's regard for sex as a means of somehow preserving God's seed, with the men of Sodom's debased regard of sex as the trivial pursuit of pleasure and power. You can sense in Luther's reading an idea that conjoins the Sodomites with a woman-disparaging, family-denigrating priesthood: "They make no reply to his proposal concerning his daughters. Instead, as frenzied men are wont to do, they spurn women, as though they wanted to say that the ravishing of girls is an everyday sport" (256–257).

Luther, frantically projecting, even tries to rationalize Lot's offer as a proof of faith in God:

What if he, a man full of faith in God, was firmly convinced that God would dispel all danger of harm to his daughters and that at the same time there was hope of rescuing his guests? Surely you will not condemn a heart that looks to the goodness and omnipotence of God when danger is very close at hand. (260)

IX.
Calvin's Condemnation

But Jean Calvin *would.* Relentlessly skeptical about human nature, Calvin, Luther's fellow Christian Reformer and doctrinal antagonist, condemns Lot and detests his daughters. He finds in them and their story stark evidence for the worthlessness of good intentions and the hopelessness of humanity operating without God's mysterious grace. In his brief, disgusted commentary on the Lot chapter, he abuses these sinners with his special new Protestant brand of moral absolutism that would go on to roil and frame family conflicts and complexes for the next five centuries. He has no patience with Luther's plea of extenuating circumstances. The daughters knew, says Calvin, that "they were committing a great crime. For why is it that they made their father drunk, except that they conjectured sufficiently that they would not be able to induce him nor to make him consent to it? . . . Thus they are not in the least excusable of being prostitutes to such a villainy."[27] He has total contempt for the daughters, which he expresses in remarkable terms:

[T]hey were not as much driven to such an evil deed by the ardor of their lechery as by a foolish desire to have descendants. It was however a blinding madness to reject the modesty and the shame which nature itself teaches us and to abolish all difference between honesty and villainy as in the manner of brute beasts. (305)

He won't allow them the slightest justification. They are like calculating prostitutes, like lecherous villains, like shameless breeder-beasts, and what sticks out is how perfect an occasion Calvin finds the Lot chapter for expressing an ideological misogyny and a fear and loathing of sexuality that would have huge, if various and unpredictable, social and psychological consequences. In one swoop he collapses the distinction that shaped the traditional interpretation of the Lot chapter, which distinguishes between sex for illicit pleasure (Sodom) and sex for progeny (Lot's daughters). Sex is just plain bad: "a foolish desire to have descendants." The immediate occasion for those astounding words is of course the two particular acts of incest based on a mistaken premise (no other men), but the language of disdain for the way of all flesh goes to the heart of Calvinist repression and the momentous drive to substitute for the desire for sensual pleasure, sex, and fertility, a desire for authoritarian righteousness. As Luther might have put it, Calvin, in his judgment of Lot's daughters, had "a heart harder than adamant" (so, about Jews and about killing rebel peasants, did Luther), and such hearts hammer out the inner and outer life and history of others.

Even Calvin, however, seems unconsciously to be pulled into the story and driven to project his own fiction that refutes the innocence of the daughters' motives and turns them into literary characters with inner drives. He picks up on the old speculation about how the girls got the wine to seduce Lot and goes off into an astonishing fantasy about why they really chose the father. They must have had servants along, he says, "because otherwise they were able with great difficulty to have given wine in a cave if it had not been carried there with other previsions." They mated with their sire, he asserts, even though there were male servants available: "it is . . . probable . . . because they did not wish to marry servants, they said there was no one living whom they were able to have for a husband." Behind the mean-spirited misogyny here lies a vision of ambitious daughters aspiring to the status and social position of the patriarch and disdaining class subservience. Calvin's fantasy does gets at latent class implications in the complexity of Lot. Lot's girls are for him, in effect, class-conscious snobs, the incestuous gold-diggers of 1935 (BC), but his reading of selfish motive is one key to understanding the history of older men–younger women relationships.

Calvin is easier on the father, though he depicts his lechery and drunkenness. He makes Lot an instrument of God's teaching. Saved as the only just man in Sodom, Lot then gives way to vice. Calvin argues that Lot's drunkenness makes him oblivious to his incestuous acts. Therefore this "holy patriarch" offers a lesson in temperance.[28]

X.
Escaping Scripture

What stands out in both Luther and Calvin and, despite their split over Lot's daughters, joins them is the strong impulse to make this Bible story the stuff of the imagination. Each turns it into a personal vision of the divine cosmos that threatens to burn up the flesh. One shows the potential for humanity's development out of the fearful circumstances of forbidden sex acts, family dependencies, trauma, and the threat of species death; the other sees the fatal, immoral bias of human desire and familial interaction—and thus the absolute need for an external authority's saving grace in family life. With variation, those are the two ways that most secular artists have rendered the text and that most people have indirectly perceived its meaning. When Luther and Calvin wrote, graphic artists and makers of literature were turning to Lot. In the Middle Ages, the Reformation, and the Renaissance the issues raised by Lot and the relative gauging of sympathy and antipathy for its figures by various interpreters would help define the historical movement of a whole culture.

Lot becomes increasingly prominent in secular literature and art in the fourteenth, fifteenth, and sixteenth centuries CE, though in some cases the incestuous end of the chapter gets omitted. When it is featured, attitudes vary towards the father and daughters. Sometimes they serve as types for the sins of lechery and gluttony, sometimes as types of error, occasionally even as types of self-sacrifice, but the fact of incest is the sensational impetus behind their appearance in literary and artistic works and the baited hook for a growing audience.

When the Lot family moves beyond the margins of the Bible, biblical exegesis, and biblical illustrations into other narrative traditions and onto the canvases of ambitious painters, taking different forms—when Hebraic and Christian lore can mix with the lore of the classical world and the dilemmas of Sodom-Lot can be seen and felt to transcend the province of the priesthood (no matter how important that clerical territory is)—then it is ready to dissolve into complexes and permeate the psychology of human desire.

Chapter 4

A Family Museum

VISIONS OF LOT AND HIS DAUGHTERS

T o show how the mind's eye has imagined Lot and his daughters, I want to look at a few important paintings engendered by their story. I mean my reading of these pictures to illustrate how the biblical text, its figuring, its potential impact on general and individual consciousness, and the interplay of that influence with the flow of culture and history, shape the way we think, live, see, and create. Art and expression reflect and formally shape reality in a potentially endless process. The pictures are shown in a section of color plates in this chapter.

Let me begin with an image that suggests the tension between the sacred and profane that characterizes the scriptural passage and much of the art it inspired: the well-known "Destruction of Sodom" illustration from the *Nuremberg Chronicle* (Plate I). This woodcut shows Lot's wife both as a pillar and as a bust of a youngish, naïve-looking woman's head. Beneath the piety and credulous simplicity of the scene, the rude viewer can read starkly one bawdy allegorical meaning of the Lot myth down through history: that old wife's tale somehow turns into a pretty face and a hard cock.

I.
Albrecht Dürer and the
First Great Lot Painting

When Albrecht Dürer completed the first great Lot painting around 1498, millennial doctrines, apocalyptic fervor, religious schism, and the threat of violence and war were spreading through Europe. The Genesis 19 chapter featuring refugees from a fire-and-brimstone holocaust seemed highly relevant (a fitting image for sixteenth-century history to come, the picture could just as easily stand as an emblem for the twentieth century). What Dürer did—and what subsequent painters often would do—was to fuse the two parts of the Lot story that the religious commentators had usually tried to keep separate: namely, the "flight from Sodom" and "the drunken Lot" (the bibulous incest of Lot and his daughters). Huge explosions of flames and smoke seem both to rain down and shoot up, devastating Sodom and, in the background, Gomorrah, and turning the sea into a deadly cauldron with ships burning and salty aridity spreading; the wife-mother back on the rocky landscape in the middle distance has already turned to a little ashy statue of death; Lot and his daughters, well-dressed refugees bearing the remnants of prosperity, plod forward on the illuminated path to the future, resolutely not looking back. But in the moment of flight, Dürer previews incest—and even potential salvation. Already the daughters' gowned bellies seem to swell; a rocky cave appears oddly in the grassy ground they move through; and iconographic symbols of sex, fertility, and the incestuous fate to come surround these figures of survival—for example, the calabash on Lot's head and the cucumber in it (a calabash is a liquid-holding vessel; a gourd, in Renaissance iconography, stood as a symbol for the Resurrection), his long staff and exposed thigh, the wine flask on his back, the younger daughter's red dress.[1] The elder daughter even carries keys and, prominently, a jewel case, whose sexual meaning Freud would famously, if redundantly, unlock four centuries later in his Dora analysis.

The trappings intimate the rest of the story and they also imply that worldly goods and order may be snatched away in a moment. You may have to flee the wrath of God instantly, even though you're not dressed for the occasion. Dürer's *Lot* also recalls the old theme of the expulsion from paradise—Adam and Eve as refugees cast out into the human fate of sexuality, death, and regeneration. What matters about this running together of past, present, and future is that it suggests how the discreet events of the Lot text and chronology can meld into individual consciousness and form a whole Lot psychology—a complex. The mind, in its meditation or its emotions, is like this painting; it holds material from different times in one space, and to the viewer that space's time is all in the present. You can find in the picture representations that bring home the menace of knowing that the world and self are subject to a morbid "final solution," that the beloved in your life will dwindle and fade away, and that the demands of survival and the world to come may bring futility and the potential loss of dignity, respectability, and personal will—that all you might be left with are your children. Durer's art can help focus the particular meanings that the ancient text might carry.

At the turn of *our* millennium, to see the Dürer *Lot*, you have to find in Washington's National Gallery a Dürer painting of the Virgin Mary. Then, when you walk behind that Madonna, on the reverse, almost hidden—easy to miss—you see *Lot and His Daughters* (Plate II). Nothing about the picture is more telling than Dürer's juxtaposition of these two compositions on opposite sides of a single piece of wood, for it almost forces you to see that somehow these are comparable phenomena—literally, *part of the same structure*. The Virgin Mary bore the seed of God the father, but Lot's daughters, in preserving the seed of Lot, preserved the seed of David and, as Luther surmised, helped to preserve seed that would become divinity.

The best-known thing in Genesis 19 is the fire and brimstone, and Renaissance artists, representing the Scripture, personalized the vast catastrophe. Memorably, with the magnificent rage of fire and the burgeoning pillars of smoke and flame, Dürer ties the Lot, father-daughter theme to cataclysmic public events and apocalyptic punishment. The fire-and-brimstone theme predominates, but the painter in turn ties it to particular people. The figures in the foreground escaping destruction call forth sympathy. (The look and effect of the life-killing devastation engulfing the green natural setting seems eerily like a still image of a nuclear bomb's blast wave.) The only way to escape extinction is to obey God as best you know how, turn to the immediate family, and do anything to preserve a future. Public-personal, political-psychological—*it's all one picture*. Dürer's view is Luther's view: *look what these people have to go through without even being allowed to look back at it from their own perspective*. The relationship and endurance of daughters and father are part of a whole social fabric, and the picture shows that they must live and interact with one another in a world whose providence immediately and suddenly features terror, fear, the necessity of imperfect choices, and divine retribution for error and sin. Look and you see that destruction, hellfire, and damnation hover directly over the daughters and father here. Such images would help to mold psyches and families.

Luther calls Lot a "pious old man" and the daughters "saintly,"[2] and Dürer makes them responsible-looking, almost stolid bourgeois figures. The three all have their eyes lowered modestly and focused on the next steps of a prescribed path. In the crisis, there is nothing sinister or libidinous about them. Lot and the daughters look like innocent, if incongruous evacuees from this almighty assault on the polity, but they don't appear tragic. Already, the elder daughter holds the distaff of the mother, and though the girls follow their father, they now occupy the center of the picture. It's their countenances, not the father's, that you see clearly, and the elder appears to be in deep thought. The daughters are assuming prominence in Dürer, and they don't look immoral. Lot has a heavy, but not a commanding, presence. There is even something comic about him: the stout, affluent burgher marching out as a pilgrim into John-the-Baptist territory with his polished staff, his short, little black-stocking legs, his cassock billowing over his thigh and rear (a variant of the "slung-leg" motif that, according to Anne Lowenthal in her commentary on Joachim Wtewael's *Lot* paintings and Renaissance iconography in general, symbolizes intercourse[3]), his golden headdress bearing the calabash gourd and the symbolic cucumber—a distinctly unprepossessing, middle-class founding father. "Judged the only good man in Sodom," says Lowenthal, "Lot made a pilgrimage to salvation; thus the staff and the . . . flask. The cucumber and gourd also allude to Lot as a precursor of Christ, since they are symbols of the Resurrection." "Wine," she states, "is synonymous with intoxication, lust, and pleasure, and accords with the incestuous union, but it also is a component of the Eucharist and a reminder of Lot's typological role." Still fat Lot looks an unlikely figure of salvation. Dürer shows agency passing to the daughters. He has put them at the heart of a work that visualizes fabulous fires of damnation, the end of civilization, mother turned to dead matter, and intimations of paternal incest, yet still holds implications of salvation. The ambivalent meaning of the picture—and of the unfolding history of Lot complexes—might best come clear if you could see oscillating together the two sides of the wood Dürer painted: Lot's daughters, Virgin Mary; Lot's daughters, Virgin Mary: somehow they're always in touch with each other.

II.
Lucas van Leyden and the Intoxication of Sexual Fantasy

What biblical commentators had often tried to keep asunder—the flight from the burning, apocalyptic Sodom and Lot's drunken intercourse with

his daughters—two masterpiece *Lot and His Daughters* of the first half of
the sixteenth century memorably join. One is attributed to Lucas van Leyden; the other is by Albrecht Altdorfer. Like Dürer they both collapse time,
but they foreground the incest.

The Leyden painting just shatters chronology (Plate III). It is a fantastic
work, by which I mean that it not only offers fantastic images, but that it
also portrays the way fantasy and imagination operate in any given moment
of inner life. Here, the escape from Sodom, the blast from the skies, and the
vinous love-making all take place in the same broad vision. The effect is
haunting because everything is happening at once—the linear time sequence disappears. For example, you can see all together the punishing fire
and brimstone pouring down out of a dark sky from a sun-like engine of
God; Sodomites still alive and moving in the distant town square; Lot and
his daughters on the bridge leaving the city with the wife turning back; and
before the bright red tent, Lot, the amorous father, caressing one daughter
while the other pours the wine. It's as if you were in the mind and memory
of Lot or one of the girls, and images of passing thoughts and visual impressions were set out side by side. For a viewer nowadays it feels as if subsequent frames from a moving picture, *Being Lot's Daughter*, were frozen in
a collage. Another way of thinking about this mind-jangling work is to remember that in theological tradition all time is contained in the mind of
God, so that especially in this instance of God's direct intervention in the
world, the simultaneity might reflect the divine view. But if you explain the
picture by supposing the artist to be representing the mind of God, then
God's thinking is dominated by a sad, incestuous orgy, so for modern viewers, it's more like a visualized psychodrama of the unconscious.

The painting owes much to Dürer and his influence, as the rocky path
on the viewer's left, the small dark image of Lot's wife on the bridge, the
broken ships in the sea, Sodom as a harbor town, and the sumptuous limn-
ing of the fire assault all go to show. But the moral atmosphere of the painting and its emotional force are very different. In Dürer, as in the Bible, there
is nothing overtly erotic about Lot and the daughters. The Leyden picture,
however, reeks of sexual sin and decadence. Specifically, the artist seems to
have used a piece of Jewish lore that Luther refutes, asserting that Lot "sat
in a tent under a fig tree and that both Lot and his daughters lived at ease"
with Abraham (Luther, 313). The painter is now exploiting the erotic potential of the subject with this display of suggestive shapes and intimacies.

Note especially the father's flesh-seeking hands, his bizarre "slung-leg" (that symbol of sex), and the dominant red tent of the coming intercourse with its dark, slit, widening vertical opening—a blatant vaginal symbol to go with the toppling, burning phallic towers of Sodom in the background. Lot the seduced in Scripture has become a seducer; he looks almost youthful pawing his stiff daughter before the semi-pornographic tent into which he looks prepared to creep, like a sheik of Araby. This historic picture has in fact, turned Dürer's middle-aged, upright, city-father Lot into a creepy sultan of incest, an identity that has stuck around ever since.

What you see here is the making of art out of a longing to imagine and vicariously know incest and the tabooed erotics that the Bible mentions but does not dwell on. Sexual curiosity drives this creation and many subsequent renderings of Lot and Lot material—what was incest like for Lot? for the daughters? How did they do it and how did it feel? The limits of the Bible as a field for interpretation expand greatly in the sixteenth century, as different people claim Scripture as their own. The rendering of Lot's embrace of the shy, inert, almost rigid daughter—she looks unhappy and scared—brings to the Lot theme (for the first time, as far as I know) explicit intimations of the daughters' sexual victimization. This representation of Lot makes him a patriarchal lecher, and this image of an incestuous father exploiting terrified daughters would feed and come to haunt popular consciousness. Still, the greatest merit of the picture may lie in its original power in making external and visible in original ways inner fantasies, conflicts, unconscious relationships, obsessions, and taboos: Lot psychology.

Take the fusion of the Sodom-Lot chapter in the Leyden painting. The father-daughter relationship is set against the disastrous failure of civic life. They are joined. Fire, the besieging of cities, forced evacuation, and the trauma of losing your home mean the breakdown of families and wild, lawless life—the ironic return to Sodom. The path and sight line that leads from the imminent death in the city, across the bridge, winding around then through the rock and into the camp of Lot and his daughters ends in the darkness and dead wood to the right of the couple—Sodom again. The artist produces on the top left of the main tent an odd crown shape with an insignia—gold snaky lightning streaks on white—that repeats in miniature the fiery flashes over Sodom, and he indicates therefore that the same burning fate awaits the figures before the tent and for the same reasons. The fire in Sodom on the right is matched with the fire in the camp to the upper left of the tent. "It's better to marry than to burn," says Paul, but if you're burned out, it's hard to find and hold onto the sanctity of marriage and keep hellfire out of the soul.

If you concentrate on the most highly colored features of the canvas— those bright globules above Sodom shooting off from the instrument of God's punishment and that enticing big red tent ready to be entered—it's possible to view the picture (and thus the Lot narrative and its meaning) as a huge allegory of humanity's psychological thralldom to sex and the relentless, twisted forces of erotic desire. Sodom and the Lot family are parts of the same whole; the social is the self. Sodom-Lot shows you that, without godly authority, life and the world are given over to sexual pursuit, sexual misbehavior, and a sexual symbolism that transforms everything, even good intentions, into strange plots of libido. The picture finds a way to replicate the sentiments of Augustine and Calvin (among others) about the Lot episode; that is, it shows you what they fear about sex. Sex leads to this scene—the world in ruins and survivors trying forlornly to gratify appetite, locked into the futility of a purely sensuous, quickly doomed existence in a dream world. Everything in the picture, and in Genesis 19 according to this vision, both feeds and reflects an obsession with illicit sex and the disguised, devastating shapes and forms of its concupiscent force. Sex fells the topless towers of Ilium and Sodom; it mauls a daughter; it corrupts the just patriarch; it empowers a girl to pour the incestuous wine that eventually turns into the eucharistic blood of her crucified progeny (with rivers of blood to follow). It makes you hallucinate. And yet the lovely red tent dazzles and invites.

This painting illustrates the case I want to make in this book. A biblical myth of immense primal interest imposes itself upon history, religion, art and individual psychology, and people in turn impose their history, experience, personal mindsets, and imaginative skills on the biblical text. That interplay and its consequences can help you see and give form to the disturbing, evolving social fabric. This picture features the importance of fantasy and makes *Lot* inseparable from fantasy. People, even if they don't know the Bible, still, in one way or another, do "remember Lot's wife," but that memory will be both personal and living—a matter for the present time.

Look at that odd bridge and you see Lot's wife behind and separated from Lot and his daughters; poised above the water, they are in suspended animation. This is fantastic: the only way that Lot and his daughters can be in two (or more) places at once, as they are here, is through the powers of the imagination that relive, revisualize, *re-present* the selves of the past. The wife, set over the salt water that will encrust her, gazes back at the heavenly bombardment, and yet, since the incest scene is already taking place, she should already have been turned to salt. Her form, then, is someone's fantasy; yet it's there—it exists. You can see also a puzzling, jagged shape of dead wood in the foreground to the right of Lot that looks suspiciously like a small, sculpted wooden statue of his wife with its little head still gazing back at the holocaust. And now look at that faint human shape in the doorway of the tent to the left of the red one—who can that figure be, since in the Bible, the three refugees are alone? It's fantasy again; I see it also as Lot's wife—enter the tent with the father and you find your mother. Lot's perished wife is living all over this place of quirky shapes and mysterious phenomena.

But what if my highly subjective reading of the Leyden *Lot and His Daughters* is fanciful and wrong—my own fantasy? That's just the point. The subjectivity of my views shows how Lot becomes a part of both collective and personal psychology. Lot in this picture and time, is becoming both the object and shaper of imagination in the present tense and the subjective case. Leyden paints a picture of Sodom-Lot, but he is painting his era, his social and psychological vision. He uses a definite subject and text to imagine the world. The conjunction of subjective vision and the episode in Scripture is the enduring, living Lot complex.

III.
Albrecht Altdorfer and the Sinful Way of All Flesh

For many viewers, the most extraordinary painting of Lot and his daughters is the flamboyant piece by Albrecht Altdorfer (Plate IV).[4] It deserves close attention, bearing as it does Lot's bad seed into modernity and crucially setting the unsavory story and its incestuous imagery in a larger pattern of redemption and progress. Two small crosses in the picture claim the subject for the Christian tradition: Altdorfer has limned a little rood among pearls on the elder daughter's head, and, in the transparency of the wine in the goblet, he has imagined and subtly painted a cross in the reflections of light.[5] These small symbols may look like mere gestures towards orthodoxy, but they imply more. They signify that from the evil in representations of the past can come eventual good, and, moreover, that the full immorality of the origins and the early stories of humanity can and must be transubstantiated, through the metaphorical sweep and force of scripture, art, and history, into the living seed of virtue and continual regeneration.

The power of the painting comes from its refusal to sentimentalize lust and the naked ruses of human survival. The picture appears to accept and dramatize the ugly force and huge moral tax on which communal salvation depends. It's a wicked, wonderful creation—a disturbing, semi-pornographic, eerie, and brilliant picture set on the verge of a literal and figurative hell. The diffused, implicit sin of the Leyden *Lot* is here made flagrant, and the evil is focused blatantly in the poses and expressions of the three figures and in the amazing fire consuming the cities of the plain. Lot fiddles while the world burns.

To say that Altdorfer portrays the potential danger and immorality in the Lot story and syndrome understates the case. If you could have one picture worth a million words in condemning father-daughter incest and making June-January eroticism look repulsive, yet fascinating, this is it—this is what gives the Lot complex a bad name and makes people nervous when I mention it. Altdorfer gave form to what it is that people would most fear and resent about patriarchy, paternal abuse, and trans-generation "love": dirty old men and dirty-minded and/or victimized girls—is there a satyr in every father and a slut in every daughter waiting for the right (wrong) occasion to break out? The two foreground figures can make even Calvin's sinners seem innocuous. The painting, however, is far from simple. It not only looks like modern feminism's worst nightmare, it makes graphic several reasons—some of them contradictory—why feminism in all its complexity would develop and prosper. It surely puts in doubt the reason the father's seed should be preserved at all unless it can be mutated.

Altdorfer has taken the daughters and Lot out of the biblical text and set them free to fire imaginations. He paints them stark naked, a remarkable thing to do, and the effect is shocking: something like, *since the idea of their incest titillates, let's lay that very idea bare and see what it really looks like—make visible the unmediated way of all flesh.* The picture pushes you to focus on the age difference of the foreground figures (Susannah and the Elders became a popular subject in the same era) and to see how weird and

Visualizing the Renaissance
of Lot and His Daughters

PLATE 1. Illustration from Hartmann Schedel, Liber Chronicarum, Nuremberg, 1493. Courtesy of Department of Special Collections, Stanford University Libraries.

PLATE II. Albrecht Dürer, *Lot and His Daughters* (reverse), Samual H. Kress Collection, Image © 2004 Board of Trustees, National Gallery of Art, Washington.

PLATE III. Lucas van Leyden, (attr.) *Lot and His Daughters*, Louvre, Paris, France.
Réunion des Musées Nationaux / Art Resource, NY.

PLATE IV. Albrecht Altdorfer, *Lot und seine Töchter*, Kunsthistorisches Museum, Wien oder KHM, Wien.

PLATE V. Guido Reni, *Lot and His Daughters Leaving Sodom*, National Gallery, London.

PLATE VI. Peter Paul Rubens, Flemish, 1577–1640, *The Departure of Lot and His Family from Sodom*, about 1613–1615, oil on canvas, 86¾ x 96 inches, SN218. Bequest of John Ringling. Collection of The John and Mable Ringling Museum of Art, the State Art Museum of Florida.

PLATE VII. Jacob Jordaens,
Flemish, 1593–1678, *Boaz*,
1641, oil on canvas, 76½ x
30¾ inches, SN987. Museum
purchase. Collection of The
John and Mable Ringling
Museum of Art, the State Art
Museum of Florida.

PLATE VIII. Jacob Jordaens, Flemish, 1593–1678, *Ruth and Naomi*, 1641, oil on canvas, 76½ x 30¾ inches, SN988. Museum purchase. Collection of The John and Mable Ringling Museum of Art, the State Art Museum of Florida.

wrong sex across generations can look—not to mention actual incest. Knobby, wrinkled old Lot with yellowing skin holds and dandles his lovely, white-skinned daughter with her "cute," firm breasts, her voluptuous belly, and her impossibly long legs. Her young, smooth face contrasts sharply with his wizened, satyr-like leer. His nasty old mouth twists coarsely in grotesque, seductive lechery, while her pretty red lips smile slyly with the dismal, manipulative precocity of a young whore. Altdorfer seems to have painted the elder daughter to represent the powerful appeal of nubile young flesh for aging men. Thus the pornographic effect of the girl's image for viewers reinforces one theme of the picture: the widespread existence of such Lottish desire.

Ethically, the most troubling thing about the scene may be the depicted pleasure of the incestuous figures. They appear to like what they're doing. To see sinners delighting in their iniquity can, for many reasons, drive nominally moral people wild and turn them into angry, prurient puritans. In this frame, unlike the Leyden picture, both Lot and the embraced daughter look happy. According to their smiles, they both appear to be getting what they want. He is possessing beautiful youth sexually, the horrors and losses of the past for the moment obliterated. Her plot is working, and, self-satisfied, she appears to be enjoying it. In the general conflagration, the trappings of luxury still surround them; she holds the glittering, half-filled goblet of wine, sparkling by the light of the inferno, and wears a gold necklace with a rough ruby pendant, while he rests on green, silken bedding; a shapely flask stands at her feet. Her astoundingly lewd pose with her rear nestling onto his sex, her showy beauty and sexuality displayed to the gaze of the onlooker by the father, and her pleased demeanor obviously affront moral order and decorum: "Oh Daddy—yes!—a little lower." I choose that sleazy verbal snigger in order to stress without critical euphemism the kind of sex and the incestuous outrage the picture sets before you.

This art works in a complex, contradictory fashion. One moral justification presumably would be something like this: *see how even the supposedly saved can be lured into evil and the hellfire that looms outside the cave; avoid this debauched, damnable behavior and anything like it.* But of course, intentionally or not, the picture is made—the elder daughter is painted and placed—so as to elicit the precise spirit of male desire that Altdorfer's Lot embodies. One reason this painter and others turned to the subject was as a pretext to paint attractive female nudes.[6] The painting figures its own reception. It may represent not only Lot and his daughters but the lustful prurience and hypocrisy of its viewers.

Some viewers, that is. Different women and men, for instance, may be bent on seeing it in their own lights across a gender gap, and the aesthetic skill, daring immediacy, and unconventionality of the picture mean that it will engage the individual imaginations of its audience both intensely and variously. It also represents and organizes people's nebulous fears and—possibly—the chaos of their desires. Everything seems out of control. The fire looks to be at about the same stage as the fire in Dürer's work when the well-clad figures are retreating with dignity, and yet here the incest is already being consummated. Sexual misbehavior and punishment for that misbehavior seem to be occurring simultaneously. From one point of view taking in her frontal pose, the elder daughter is merely a patriarchal display object, testimony and trophy of his continuing vitality. From another, the duped father has become the gross means to new progeny bespeaking amoral female agency and influence in the propagation of life. From a third, the scene might mean the deserved end of a bad world. A Protestant view might find that the daughter of Lot is the Roman Catholic Whore of Babylon, and the crimson of the fleshy ruby stone hanging round her neck (sex imagery) may brand her as a scarlet woman.

You can infer the legitimacy of the view that has the family burning up here in general disaster and private lust. Drink, sex, unforeseen circumstances, catastrophes, and mysterious fate wreck families. One fear the work surely brings home is of the patriarch's narcissism and sensual irresponsibility, but another is the wanton ambition and free sexuality of the daughter and her willing participation, even identification, in the father's desire. These fears—and covert wishes—would live and make *Lot* live.

For many, the most compelling figure here may be the other daughter. No Lot's wife appears in the painting. Where in the middle distance of the Leyden and Dürer pictures you find her, in Altdorfer you see the second daughter waiting outside the cave. Look back to the holocaust and you see not the petrified mother figure, but an enigmatic nude girl, alone, set between apocalyptic flames and incest—between burning rocks and an obscene hard place—a family orgy before her in which she is expected to take part. The Lot plot in the Bible is (ostensibly) a woman's plot to preserve maternity, but even the memory of motherliness seems absent from this Altdorfer scene. What happens when the mother is gone? Does it mean that what preserving motherhood boils down to is a confused virgin waiting to be impregnated by the natural desire her body can arouse in a fuddled old man? Is this where we came from and periodically return—holocaust, lecherous lust, sick fantasies in gorgeous color, desperate measures for survival, the stimulus of intoxication, the cruelty of incest? Or is such art, with its continuing metaphorical life and its absorption in culture, the way to bundle up, control, and purge the fears of natural cataclysms, sexual impulses, and the curse of motherlessness? The painting pushes you to say "yes" and "yes" to both questions.

The sight lines of the picture pull you sooner or later away from incongruous faces of the old man (he looks like Woody Allen in his later years—see Chapter 11) and the elder girl to look back at the younger daughter. The drawing of her raised left arm is a stroke of genius. One interpretation says that she's combing her hair, siren-like, a seductress eager for her chance. But the shape of the arm and position of the hand surely do not suggest primping, but anxiety and/or the head-clutching, inchoate gesture of coming trauma. The younger daughter has nothing of the sensual lust of the elder. She is virginity caught between the corruption of the past and the necessity of creating new life.

Look at what's being portrayed here—the puissant, engulfing fire, the loose-haired girl set before it, and the irrepressible act of incest—and imagine the emotional life it might suggest: *I have been chosen. The main thing I know is that I mustn't look back at the fiery burning, but when I look ahead in the cave, my father and sister are doing what they all did in Sodom and Gomorrah. Can I do it? I think I can—I think I can. I'm ready to be fertilized. Will he want me? Will it work? I don't know what is going on. I want to scream.* And this figure in its framed setting of the open cave mouth does somehow convey that sense of desperate angst and helplessness that you find in *The Scream*, Edvard Munch's famous icon of twentieth-century despair. Altdorfer's girl is a mother of that screamer.

Even more important, she is also, as an Israelite virgin about to be impregnated by her father for the supposed regeneration of mankind, an ancestor and metaphorical sister of the Virgin Mary. This younger daughter, her image, and her avatars, make the Lot complex and the importance of my subject: *the girl on the outside, in crisis, looking in, sexually vulnerable and precocious, desiring something she's been told the father can give her—some precious seed.* In the picture, nothing is protecting this naked girl. Cut off from the agency and power of her relatives, for the moment excluded, but, in an infernal daze, she's ready to offer herself up for the sake of the future. As a virgin in this picture containing two crosses honoring Christian orthodoxy and signifying the possibility of salvation, she literally relates to the Virgin redeemer who bore God, the Son, from God, the Father—her Father.

Let me return to the wine and the reflection of the cross in the elder daughter's glass, which offers a key not only for a Christian interpretation of the picture, but for faith in the historical redemption of father-daughter, older men–younger women relationships. Through the long history of peoples, faith, imagination, and the potency of symbolic thought, the wine that seduces Lot turns into the blood of Jesus, which becomes the wine of communion. "I am the true vine," said Christ, and, passing the wine cup, proclaimed, "This is the blood of the New Testament, which is shed for many." The wine is thus a symbol of the human ability to make one thing stand for another and specific actions and figures part of a much larger picture—life as a whole process of flow and transformation that uses the past to transcend the past. As the wine of lechery could be transmuted into the symbol of salvation, so the incest of Lot and his daughters might be redeemed by new modes of bonding between fathers and daughters for the future benefit of both.

IV.
Guido Reni and the
Redemption of Lot's Daughters

After Altdorfer, at the end of the sixteenth century and then on into the first half of the seventeenth century, Lot, with its sensational, titillating subject matter now opened up, became a popular theme for painting and drawing. It was taken up by Hendrick Goltzius, Joachim Wtewael, Simon Vouet, Orazio and Artemisia Gentileschi (father and daughter, significantly, are both credited with a painting on the subject), Guido Reni, Rubens, Jordaens, Rembrandt, Bernardo Cavallino, and Adriaen van der Werff, among others. Much of this work is distinguished, but, almost literally, the fire has gone out of it, and in large part, it forms occasions to render the sensual and paint the jazzy ambivalence towards physical, sexual being that Lot and his daughters show—fleshpot Lot. By the time the eighteenth-century painter

Joseph-Marie Vien turned to the subject, this art of incest had been distanced and conventionalized. But the content of Guido Reni's *Lot and His Daughters Leaving Sodom* and the configuration of three pictures, one by Rubens and two complementary paintings by his follower Jacob Jordaens, can illustrate the way Lot did and does shape desires and culture.

Guido Reni's rendering of Lot and his daughters could hardly be more different from Altdorfer's, yet it is every bit as important in representing the history and desire in humanity's Lot complex (Plate V). The three figures appear thoughtful, calm, and dignified. Eroticism is expunged, and images of fire and turbulence are replaced by portraits of three rational, responsible-looking people in a moment of high seriousness—a time of crisis for survivors. In desperate circumstances for which they are not to blame, they are shown conferring. The artist has chosen to uphold the Christian, late New Testament sense of the basic goodness of Lot, the "just Lot" of Jude and Peter, and to figure the three refugees as typological figures of virtue (as Philo and Irenaeus allegorized them). There is much in their expression to show that they are admirable, fully worthy of salvation, as the Bible first reported. If the Leyden and Altdorfer *Lot and His Daughters* expose the fear and menace latent in father-daughter, cross-generational relationships, Reni's portrays the hope.

The burning cities, the fire and brimstone, the sins of the fathers, the shameful nakedness of incest are subsumed—sublimated—in the red robe of Lot and the billowing dress of the elder daughter. Her gown and drapery fall in such a way as to indicate decorously the coming pregnancy, but that fertility shows as the product of her reason. What dominates the scene are the highlighted faces and expressions of the daughters. Look at what's not in the picture: overt, possessive sex, irrational sensual passion, flaming towns, and violence. That's one reason that makes this a subtle, but exciting work. If you realize the full moral implications of Altdorfer's art, it's easy to find moving the hope and possibility of domesticating the story of Lot and his daughters that Reni imagines. Whatever his intention, the painting shows you what the hope for the free operation of women's agency and intellect might sometimes come to mean for many in the last two centuries. The daughters are thoughtful, fully clothed, intellectually engaged with the problem of social survival. The elder is speaking with mindful intensity, directly focused on her attentive sister, looking past her father. The younger, carrying the wine jar, listens with an obliging, concerned countenance of resignation. The father's portrayed as a sage. His expression, meant perhaps to convey the loosening effect of drink, doesn't match the alertness of the women, but there's nothing about it that looks frivolous or improper. Even wearing the symbolic red covering, his venerable goodness comes through in his upright demeanor, his strong sensitive hands, and his serious regard for the speaking figure. It's important to see the father listening, paying attention to the daughters' discourse. He's in on the conversation; he heeds the daughterly plan. Everything is out in the open—no feminine plot to fool the father, no patriarchal projection of lechery. The elder holds pink material in a gesture that will lead to preserving the father's seed, and he seems to be following her with his hand on his robe. One way or another, this image takes hold: the father follows the daughter's lead for the sake of the future.

Stephen Pepper writes of Guido Reni that this painting is part of the painter's whole ideology.[7] It expresses a moral judgment that sees the rational character of the universe and a progress that eventually will lead to "the perfectibility of mankind." I'd add that what it shows primarily is the potential progress of humanity through a fusion of womankind's intelligence and authority with so-called "mankind." Whatever Reni's intentions or the seventeenth-century theological context in which he worked, to my eye there's a forward-looking, almost Victorian aura about the painting: Jane Austen and George Eliot could be conversing about and before a weary old patriarch, whose life they're trying to save and make meaningful.

VI.
Peter Paul Rubens,
Jacob Jordaens, and Ringling:
Pictures from an Institution

One motif in Lot art is that when the crisis comes and the beset, aging patriarch needs young women to regenerate his seed, the matriarch suffers and is effaced. Rubens's fine painting *The Departure of Lot and His Family from Sodom* (1613–1615), though it presents Lot's daughters as fleshy, buxom, and ripe, as you would expect of the artist and his school, in fact features the aged faces of the parents and their anguish (Plate VI). They hold the dramatic emotional focus. Lot's wife, her grim expression etched in the gray confusion of senility, is not looking back, as you might expect, but forward in misery, wiping a tear, as if living only in future loss. Her countenance looks almost like a death mask; life is over for her. It's white-bearded Lot who looks back, but unhappily, heeding one animated angel who gestures towards the laden daughters following the father, while another angel, vigorous in his gauzy red garb, hurries him on his desperate way. Lot's face looks troubled and regretful, as if in distress at what he hears, and it shows not the slightest trace of lust. He appears older and sadder than almost all other painted Lots.

The picture does hold the signs of the future: the wife and mother's countenance is set against a pillar, as is Lot's, but he looks away, back at the girls to whom the angel points as he counsels the father. The older daughter, touching her rounding stomach, already looks pregnant. The younger daughter, her blond hair coming undone, carries golden vessels (presumably for wine), and the older bears the shape of the calabash on her head. The mien of both daughters is modest and solemn. Though one daughter has the famous dimpled, mottled Rubenesque flesh, the scene hardly contains a shred of joy or eroticism.

This work may be the best-known painting in The John and Mable Ringling Museum of Art in Sarasota, Florida, and I see it as the central piece of an allegory whose meaning is as clear as if a giant had scrawled graffiti across the facade of the building: "Lot lives!" It hangs featured on the north wall in Gallery 13, a rather small room. On the adjacent west wall are displayed twin pictures, *Boaz* and *Ruth and Naomi* (1641–1642), by Rubens's one-time assistant, Jacob Jordaens. What the viewer immediately confronts, then, in this confined area, is the narrative, mythic, aesthetic, and historical progeny of Lot and his daughters. The setting and circumstances of this display blend the themes of the pictures and make them reverberate.

In the Bible's Book of Ruth, Ruth, the attractive young Moabite widow, chooses cross-generational unity with her Jewish mother-in-law and mother-figure, Naomi, and goes with her as a refugee back to the Israelite land. There Boaz, a rich, kind old relative of Naomi, befriends Ruth and protects her against the erotic assaults of the young men harvesting his fields. In the King James version, he repeatedly calls Ruth "my daughter." Instructed by Naomi, she wins, with sweet woman's wiles, the love of good old Boaz and gets him to marry her. Their seed generates the House of David. The story of Ruth, the descendant of Lot's elder daughter, can thus be read and seen as the legitimization, even the justification, of the Sodom-Lot story. And

Ruth has lately become a central focus of feminist biblical scholarship and discourse.

The effect of Jordaens's full-length portrait of Boaz (Plate VII), in this museum setting, is uncanny. By itself, you would see the picture as an interesting example of a biblical patriarch, but here, next to Lot, you see that what Jordaens has done is to take Rubens's image of Lot's face as a model and turned it into the face of Boaz. They're exactly alike: Boaz is Lot reborn, but redeemed; the intercourse with a daughterly woman who plots with another woman to seduce him becomes a source of glory rather than shame. And since Jordaens had made an exact copy of Rubens's *Departure of Lot* (it hangs in Tokyo) and very likely worked on the original, this reappearance of Lot's head on Boaz's shoulders is not all that surprising. The fusion implies the equivalency of such figures; these are good, kind old men, but subject naturally to the physical attraction of young women—that's how males are—and the women may seek union with them for their own purposes.

More surprising, in retrospect, is Jordaens's portrayal of Ruth (Plate VIII). In a reversal of tradition, there's nothing refined or sensitive about her. Voluptuous, with bared, bulging breasts proclaiming her fecund, sexual nature and her physical appeal, she sits amid the alien corn being touched and counseled by a wrinkled old Naomi. Ruth looks like a sexpot—a Rubenesque baggage as immodest as if she were Calvin's notion of Lot's daughter being tarted up by an old bawd. She sits perching with knees akimbo over the golden sheaves, with one golden slipper showing on her visible foot. In the companion Boaz frame on the left, the old man holds up ostentatiously another, matching golden slipper (a young woman's missing slipper found by a man of power equals a time-hallowed vaginal symbol of desire). The slipper in the patriarch's hand proclaims that he the aging man means to possess her. If Boaz is Jordaens's reincarnation of Lot, Naomi as craggy-faced crone bears a strong resemblance to Lot's wife in Rubens. Everything here is related. The relationships of older men and younger women are not, in these representations, discrete. In Ruth, the dutiful handmaiden of integration, you can see the traces of the incestuous, plotting daughters and in Rubens's images of the daughters you can see germinating the dutiful handmaid.

The strains of the Lot story in the pictures fuse with the history of the circus magnate who made their public display possible and bring home how enduring and insinuating Lot patterns and complexes can be. Pluto-crat circus boss and compulsive art collector John North Ringling, married but childless, decided in the roaring 1920s to build for Sarasota (where the big circus wintered) and Florida a museum in which he would install his acquisitions and leave them to the public. He set about his plan, but in the late '20s financial troubles began raining down on him. The stock market crashed in 1929 and his loyal wife Mable died. Less than a year later, in 1930, at age 64, Ringling married Emily Hague Buck, a 34-year-old divorcee (he later claimed she was older—maybe even 45). For him getting the attractive Emily made him feel he hadn't lost his own vitality, but the story turned out badly. He made her sign a prenuptial agreement and allegedly bor-rowed money from her for his cash flow problems. She didn't share Mable's philanthropic or aesthetic interests. They squabbled, he lost his money, and broken, the roaring tiger of the Big Top became an invalid—the circus an-imal deserted. They were officially divorced just days before his death in 1936. She, along with other relatives, sued his estate to keep the art from the public. They were finally unsuccessful, but the paintings, artifacts, and the museum were tied up for ten years (1936–1946) in probate.

In Gallery 13, it's tempting to see allegories and read in the paintings the typological experiences of Lot, Boaz, and the founding father of this art house. The museum acquired the Boaz and Ruth paintings by Jordaens later, long after Ringling had bought the Rubens and died, his will had been settled, and the painting had become public property. The new acquisitions look like a stroke of curator genius. They can make you see and understand both Lot and Ringling better and why it's enlightening to conjoin them. Boaz looks old, willful, and confused and Ruth looks like a young woman who can arouse an old man. But he looks also like a figure who can repre-sent the adage *there's no fool like an old fool*, and she, with her smirk and big tits, looks like a malleable poster girl whose questionable image stands out and becomes just that, a cynical question for posterity: "Is this really what patriarchs want and Ruth looks like—cross-generational prostitution sanc-tified by marriage and religion?"

Chapter 5

Embracing the Daughter

THE RIDDLE OF LOT, SHAKESPEARE,
AND THE ENGLISH HERITAGE

A
s the structure of the family develops through time, how should daughters be regarded? What good are they? Can they redeem men's lives? The Lot story raised such questions. In early English literature, two medieval writers—the *Pearl*-poet and John Gower—both used Lot material to show father-daughter interactions, the problem of incest, and the quest for faith in a prophetic light. What each does, though in very different ways (the *Pearl*-poet's work is still drenched in Scripture but not so Gower's *Confessio Amantis*), is to embrace with new urgency the importance of the father-daughter relationship and the implications of the Lot episode for it. And Shakespeare, in all his power, would follow them, dramatizing for posterity the heartbreaking passion, longing, failure, and hope that characterize the history of father-daughter ties.

I.
Making a Pearl out of Incest

The *Pearl*-poet, in *Cleanness*, offers a positive view of Lot and his daughters. There, in his graphic exposition of Genesis 18 and 19, he portrays the whole Sodom story, with one exception—no incest. He shows "noble Lot" to be good and decent, a "meek" and "thoughtful" man, and he refers to the girls as "dear" daughters, "seemly" and "sweet," "beckoning beauties," "graceful, young girls," and, finally, "lily-white ladies."[1] They appear in a wholly positive light. Lot's wife, however, is a "wretched" shrew from the dead sea of misogyny. Out of spite, she pours salt in the angels' dinner sauce; hence, says the poet with cold irony, she ends up as a salt-lick for beasts. But he leaves out the father-daughter intercourse.

It's not that he's squeamish; sex is a big subject in his version of Lot. The poem describes the Sodomites' homosexuality so vividly that it might bring a blush to the cheeks of the young person. More surprisingly, in a religious poem, he celebrates heterosexual copulation as a touch of paradise—something so "hot" ("hote") that all the troubles of the world can't kill its delight; nothing on earth is better. It may be just this sense of the joy of sex that made him flinch from mentioning the incest. Having described the allure of the daughters, he might well have needed to avoid and transcend the erotics of the cave. In *Cleanness*, father and daughters escape God's devastation of "filth among men," only to vanish completely (1051). Where you might expect wine and speluncular sex from a poet so versed in Scripture, he suddenly switches scenes and gives you instead "a pearl" (1068).

That substitution, I maintain, stands as one of the most revealing symbolic moves imaginable for understanding the Lot complex. To draw the lesson of Sodom-Lot and preach Christian purity, the *Pearl*-poet moves abruptly from God's vengeance to the high-flown, symbolic language of courtly love—if you want to be loved by a lady, he says, you must imitate her actions:

> Look to that loved one to learn of her ways;
> If you do this, no doubt, though disdainful at first,
> She will love you at last. So be like her in all.
> And if likewise you long for the love of our God,
> If you fain would befriend Him, then follow His lead.
> In His cleanliness copy Christ's ways on earth—
> *As a pearl* [emphasis mine] He's perfectly polished and clean.
> Bear in mind He emerged from a maiden, was born
> In a marvelous miracle, mighty and pure;
> For no virgin was violently vanquished that time,
> But was better for being the bearer of God. (1062–1072)

That's the gist of the *Pearl*-poet's pearl of wisdom and his jewel of Christian redemption. Instead of Lot the father impregnating his virgin daughters in a cave, you have God the Father siring Christ from the Virgin Mary. But if you know the Scripture, traces of the cave linger.

II.
A Pearl of a Girl:
Sanctifying the Daughter

It's no accident, no mere musty detail of literary history, that this meta-phorical pearl displaces and replaces Lot and his daughters. In *Pearl*, the poet's mysterious poem of Christian salvation which elaborates every possible implication of the "pearl" lines of *Cleanness*, he builds his faith on the transformation of a mourning father's love for his dead 2-year-old daughter into a dream-vision of radiant immortality. It's important to see that the suppressed and missing father-daughter intercourse shows up sub-limated in the concept, image, and fluid hieroglyph of the daughter-pearl. Love of the daughter can be the means by which blessed life is regenerated; here, she bears and ripens the precarious seed of the father's faith. But the love must not be carnal. In this vision, the paternal seed of life and sanctity is preserved not by sexual instinct but by dedication to progeny—to the child. That child—that daughter—can lead you to Jesus, who, famously, suffers little children to come unto him. Wittingly or not, the poet, with the pearl in *Cleanness* and the whole allegorical structure of *Pearl*, literally *cleans up Lot's act.*

Through the power of symbolism, the pearl appears as the poet's lost infant daughter "on the other side," then as a wise expounder of Christian doctrine, a beautiful woman, and a potential bride of Christ whose essence brings into vision the Virgin Mary and Christ the Lamb himself. The pearl-girl also merges into a jewel, the physical substance that in Revelation rep-resents the City of Heaven's shining promise of eternal life. First, you see the deep love of the father for his 2-year-old girl; then you get, in a celestial context, feminine beauty and attraction (with their suggestive possibilities of regeneration) in the manifestation of the "pearl" as a lovely lady. At last you discover that the allegorical and physical properties of the pearl fuse and form a visionary ideal of salvation. The poet imagines a spritualizing process that works like a Christian version of the Platonic ladder of love reaching up to God and the perfect good.

The problem, then, in both Lot's cave and in *Pearl*, is how, in the midst of death, to preserve human existence and any hope for the future. In both, the daughter offers the solution, but the *Pearl*-poet chooses to infantilize the daughter. By doing so he removes the threatening idea and disreputable

history of physical incest, but keeps and celebrates the rejuvenating potential of the daughter. For him, it seems, the benevolent affection that a father
feels for his little girl represents a starting point from which to seek out the
kind of loving emotion on which sustainable faith can be based. Since you
can know that such an affinity really does exist, it proves that spiritual life
is real, that the physical may be transcended, and that "pure" love is possible. And notice that for the male speaker of *Pearl*, the daughter, not his wife
or mother, is the key to opening the way to metaphysical existence—to,
that is, the triumph of continuing life over death. The transcendent daughter in the poem becomes the moral guide and superior of the man. Potentially, this high value set upon the daughter can mean a dazzling future for
women. A pearl of a girl can lead you out of the cave of darkness.

Or can she? From another perspective, a mind that can reduce the wife
and mother to a salt-lick and inflate the daughter into a father's pearl of
great price may still inhabit cultural darkness. The man who gloats over
beasts lapping at the salty remains of a dead wife and imagines salvation in
the form of a daughter whose mother gets no mention at all—this man
who goes to sleep dreaming of ideal regeneration with the daughter but
seems to know nothing of how his spiritual intercourse with her works—
is surely comparable to Lot. That "pearl" in the poet's vision can also hide
away what if not recognized can turn the female into either an object (as a
salt-block or as a beautiful jewel, she's still not a human subject) or the
gassy hot air of men's idealism. I refer, of course, to sex. A pearl's creation,
after all, depends on the slimy oyster's dirty speck of impurity around
which the gem forms, just as the generation of the loveliest child depends
on the mixing together of body fluids and slippery organs. Conceal or suppress sex and you risk devaluing physical being and courting delusionary
fantasies that can and do put people in grave danger.

As I indicated in Chapter 2, two novelists, Nathaniel Hawthorne and
James Joyce, deal with issues the *Pearl*-poet raises by imagining daughters as
pearls. In *The Scarlet Letter*, as in the medieval poem, the existence of its
"Pearl" (the daughter) forms the center of the work, but the child is conceived in sin. The novel, full of matter and imagery that uncannily parallels
Pearl, is revisionary (the poem wasn't published until the 1860s, but it's
possible Hawthorne might have read the manuscript). Little Pearl, the animated scarlet letter, saves her father's soul by bringing him to confess his
sexual sin and his relationship to her. In both *The Pearl* and the novel, the

daughter leads the father to heaven, but in Hawthorne, it's as if a film of human history has been reversed and the child Pearl, in order that the seed of faith in the goodness of the father-daughter bond be preserved, must take the father back to Lot's cave, to his sexual temptation and fall, and open to light the hard fact of life that pearl-children, like Lot's progeny, come out of blurry, messy fornication.

James Joyce, in *Finnegans Wake*, sums up in that one stunning, punning phrase the repressed but ultimately irrepressible connection I'm stressing between Lot's daughters and *Pearl*'s maiden. Wanting to show how incestuous desire keeps breaking out in the human unconscious, Joyce describes the enticing little girl of his model human family at home in her bed: "She is daddad's lottiest daughterpearl" (561.15). He finds what's latent in the *Pearl*-poet: the will to idealize the daughter as a child and a stuttering, hapless effort to purge erotic feeling and tensions out of the relationship of big men and little women.

III.
John Gower and the
Riddle of Incest

Taken together, the pregnancy of Lot's daughters by their father and the pregnancy of the Holy Virgin Mary through God symbolize the psychological contradictions of the Lot complex and represent the conflicted feelings about the nature of incestuous desire that develops and drives history. The following Shakespearean lines describing the shocking life of a princess living in carnal incest with her father, the king, fit both Lot's daughters and the Virgin Mary perfectly:

> I sought a husband, in which labor
> I found that kindness in a father.
> He's father, son, and husband mild;
> I mother, wife, and yet his child.[2]

John Gower helped father that verse. Through him, *Lot* leads to Shakespeare and his world-historic, dramatic embracement of the daughter. In his *Confessio Amantis*, discoursing at length on incest, Gower uses the example of Lot as a lead-in to "The Tale of Apollonius of Tyre," which explores father-daughter relations and incestuous impulses. He wants to tell about "fathers and daughters with an indefinable desire for each other,"[3] and *Lot* makes a good starting place. That desire, as it plays out in different lives, can mean cruel lechery, misery, and death, but it also can be the way to hope, virtue, and self-transcendent love. Georgiana Donavin writes:

During the Middle Ages the meaning of *incest* was paradoxical: when used liter-ally, the word signified the abominable sin of consanguineous sex; when repre-sented allegorically, it signified mystical union with God. Both a sin and a way of remediating sin, *incest* illustrated the workings of Providence in miniature for the medievals. It showed them how God could manipulate an apparent evil toward Eternal Good. (9)

How can the incestuous become the virtuous? "[I]ncestuous longing," says Donavin, could be "a trope for mystical union" (7), but a major secu-larizing theme in the art, literature, and social life to come would actually be a reversal of that trope: to make the mystical union of faith a trope for the healthy and morally regenerative managing of the ambiguous longings and love of fathers and daughters. When faced with the story of Lot and his daughters, the early devotees of the Bible felt they had to uphold its holy authority and rationalize the shame of the cave. The incest on the page had to be dematerialized and made into something spiritual and moral. *And that is just what cultures and individuals have striven to do with the possibil-ity of father-daughter incestuous desire:* turn the dangerous potential for sex and sensuality into responsible affection, civilized affectionate love, sym-pathy, and concern for the future.

Gower is a key transition figure in the grand human project to show how Lot's progeny could be turned to good.[4] His moral aim in the *Confes-sio* may be to subordinate erotics to Christian and political orthodoxies, but the effect is to bring Lot and its religious overtones into narratives of per-sonal, secular life. This conflation matters. It shows that the meaning and aims of sacred texts would be shaped not only by clerical, sermonizing in-terpreters, but also—increasingly—by artists taking up scriptural subjects and rendering them imaginatively for the entertainment and enlightenment of audiences. Lot and his daughters would move out of Scripture and reli-gious commentary directly into the earthy realm of classic father-daughter stories, fantasies, relationship problems, and their consequences in the world. Gower, conjoining Lot's incest with classical narrative and inquiry into the ethics of father-daughter relations, opened a line that runs directly to the Shakespeare of *Pericles* (his version of "Apollonius" in which "Gower" is made to be the play's chorus) and *King Lear* and all the way down through the psychoanalytic inquiries of Freud and Otto Rank, to such contemporary works as Jane Smiley's *A Thousand Acres* (*King Lear* as an incest novel set in the American heartland).

Gower specifically connects Lot's incest to the blatantly erotic incest of King Antiochus and his beautiful daughter and then builds upon the incest theme to explore father-daughter relations in the tale, culminating in the complex but hopeful relationship between Apollonius and his daughter Thais. In Antioch, bad Antiochus, mateless after the death of his wife, rapes his daughter, then seduces her into accepting her role as his sexual mate. Wanting to keep her for his own, he sets a riddle that his daughter's suitors must solve or die. When Apollonius seeks to marry her, he reads the riddle, sees the appalling answer, then flees for his life, knowing the father will try to kill him. Thus begins Apollonius's odyssey of adventures, featuring—amid shipwrecks, violence, calamities, real and false deaths, partings, and reunions —his romantic marriage to the princess daughter of a good and wise father, his own daughter's birth during a storm at sea, her disappearance overboard, his wife's apparent death, the girl's tumultuous life and trials in exile, his alienation, madness and despair, his later redemption by the grown daughter, the resurrection of the mother, and the daughter's eventual marriage.

Two Lot hot spots in all this: (1) In the plot, Apollonius's would-be destroyer Antiochus and his victimized daughter are themselves struck down by fire from heaven, a conscious echo of God's rain of fire down in Genesis 19; (2) Antiochus's riddle in Gower's "Apollonius" and then in Shakespeare's version in *Pericles* is essentially *the riddle of Lot and his daughters—verbal smoke whose haze reveals the smoldering fire of incestuous history*. In the *Confessio* the lines are these:

> With felonie I am upbore,
> I ete and have it noght forbore
> Mi modres fleissh, whos housebonde
> Mi fader for to seche I fonde,
> Which is the sone ek of my wif. (405–409)

(With crime I am upborn,/I eat and am not forborn/When seeking mother's husband, my father,/My mother's flesh I found/In the child of

my wife [trans. Donavin, 71]). The implied speaker is the king-father, Antiochus, and the general meaning, though muddled in its particulars (is
Oedipal desire here a screen for the sexual possession of the daughter?), reveals a blurring of parental, filial, and sexual roles and also the father's incest with his daughter. *Pericles* offers a crucial revision that makes the daughter the implied speaker and the incest even more obvious:

> I am no viper, yet I feed
> On mother's flesh which did me breed.
> I sought a husband, in which labor
> I found that kindness in a father.
> He's father, son, and husband mild;
> I mother, wife, and yet his child.
> How they may be, and yet in two,
> As you will live, resolve it you. (1.1.65–72)

The riddle of incest, then, lies in the genesis of both the tale and the drama,
as it lies embedded in Genesis itself, the biblical beginning of everything.
The larger riddle here is *"what is the place of father-daughter desire and behavior in the story of humanity?"*

IV.
Shakespeare and
Lot's Riddle in 'Pericles'

To the man's world of potentates and priests the *Pearl*-poet and Gower say,
"Fathers, look to and cherish your daughters properly; daughters mind and
save your motley fathers," and Shakespeare builds gloriously on them. In
Gower, through many mishaps, Apollonius's chaste daughter Thais is caught
in a brothel, talks her way out, and near the tale's end, is sent into a dark
cabin to revive a woefully distraught royal visitor. (The biblical analog here
—besides Lot—is the maiden Abishrag sent to warm up failing old King
David.) Unbeknownst to them both, the man is her father, plunged into
near comatose depression, thinking her dead, like her mother. Incest is
somehow in the air: "[I]n the derke forth sche goth, / Til sche him toucheth"
(1691–1692). Apollonius is attracted to her. She talks to him, rouses him, and
when she reaches out to him, he responds with a violent slap that has the

potential of sexual assault. But the daughter protests with the voice of moral authority. She tells him who she is, he tells her who he is, and joyously they reconcile. Gower carefully sets the scene against widower Antiochus's rape of his daughter in the dark and her subsequent silence. These passages "in the dark" are highly charged. Gower seems fascinated by the potential intimacy of fathers and daughters and by the ways that intimacy can shape life.

Pericles tones down the incest.[5] Unlike Gower, Shakespeare doesn't render the sexual intercourse of Antiochus and his daughter, and Pericles's reunion scene includes neither the ambiguous darkness nor the overt assault on the girl. Moreover the play transfers Gower's name for the daughter, Thais, to Pericles's wife, Thaisa, and dubs the girl Marina, meaning the daughter is not simply a stand-in for the mother. Pericles gives her the name when they are literally flailing about in their sea of troubles, and the original name is a sign that the daughter is born out of special circumstances with her own individual history and identity, which are not her mother's.

The sordid opening of *Pericles* with its transparent riddle of incest ("He's father, son, and husband mild; / I mother, wife, and yet his child") finds its answer in the blessing of blooming progeny in the end. Pericles wants and needs a daughter. Marina wants and needs a father. Out of this desire comes Shakespeare's explicit solution to the riddle, Lot's riddle—a second solution ("yet in two") to purge that wrong one in Antioch: in the happiness and renaissance of his spirit at seeing the beautiful, good person his daughter has become, Pericles exclaims to her: "O, come hither, / Thou that beget'st him that did thee beget" (5.1.188–189). Through the daughter the father is born again.

It's a religious concept. The existence of lovely new generation renews life, brings back faith, hope, and charity, makes it possible to move into the future. The father can be the hopeful child of the daughter; so he proclaims. The seed of the father, if it is good, can be preserved, made fruitful by the daughter's being. In the rhythm and the phrasing of what follows after the father calls the daughter the begetter of his true self, you can hear and feel the Christian creed of the supernatural savior flowing into a faith in the daughter as redeemer: "Thou that wast born at sea, buried at Tarsus, / And found at sea again" (5.1.190–191). The daughter resurrects life—spiritually, she is mother to the father.

But the playwright still shows that the blessing for Pericles is strangely close to incest. When Shakespeare wants to convey the full, happy force of the reunion for the father, he has him project the imagery of ecstatic orgasm onto the occasion and onto Marina. Pericles fears, "Lest this great sea of joys rushing upon me / O'erbear the shores of my mortality / And drown me with their sweetness" (5.1.186–187). The father, in the reunion scene, keeps seeing in Marina his beautiful wife as she was when young. He can hardly control himself, scares the girl, interrupts her and hushes her, and seems transported by memories of his conjugal bliss with Thaisa. Shakespeare, then, makes the father's relationship with the daughter central to the generation of faith, but his vision is based on a paternal desire to recapture the buoyancy of earlier love and then—*crucially*—on the diffusion of the desire for physical joy into metaphysical feelings. The end of religious mystery would seem to be self-transcendence, and one way of reaching it in Shakespeare is through the love of a flourishing daughter. Incestuous impulse, sublimated, may transmute into such love, but physical incest itself is narcissistic: anything to please the self—even the whoredom of kin. You could imagine an Antiochus saying to his daughter in erotic rapture, "Come hither / Thou that beget'st him that did thee beget," but you can't imagine him spiritually reborn out of her concubinage.

Pericles rejoices in his daughter, but it's interesting that Marina's joy doesn't seem to match his. He is a loving father, but he has a hard time listening to her speak about her own experience. And hearing the daughter's authentic voice becomes for Shakespeare a major subject and a problem. Both the active and the silent daughter of Lot figure in Marina and—even more to the point—in Shakespeare as a whole, especially the later work. Something made the aging Shakespeare seize on the raw material of Lot complexes—incestuous instincts, devastating family crises, paternal obtuseness, deceased or missing wives, the drama of father-daughter interaction, and the daughter's influence on the father's reconciliation to the world. In *The Winter's Tale* the supposedly dead wife becomes a statue (in the Vulgate, the "pillar of salt," Lot's wife, is translated "statue of salt") that the "lost" daughter, Perdita, helps to revivify for her redeemed father; in *The Tempest*, Miranda, with her lovely nature, helps bring her wise father to find peace of mind in a sometimes brutish world; and in *Cymbeline*, the reformed king learns to appreciate and honor his virtuous daughter Imogen. The answer to the riddle of life, in late Shakespeare, is some form of paternal understanding that the worth and survival of humanity ultimately depends on the daughter, her condition, and her moral fertility: "Thou that beget'st him that did thee beget."

V.

Shakespeare's Renaissance Lot:
'King Lear'

Little in drama is more moving in Shakespeare than the Lear-Cordelia, father-daughter reconciliation scene, and similar wording in the Pericles-Marina reunion shows how emotionally close he sensed the dilemmas were of these disillusioned fathers caught for a time in madness. From *Lear*:

CORDELIA. Sir, do you know me?
    . . .

LEAR. Pray, do not mock me.
I am a very foolish fond old man. . . .
Do not laugh at me;
For, as I am a man, I think this lady
To be my child Cordelia. (4.7.49–72)

From *Pericles*:

MARINA. My name is Marina.
PERICLES. O, I am mocked. . . .
    . . .

This is the rarest dream that e'er dulled sleep
Did mock sad fools withal. (5.1.137–157)

One thing these passages point to is how little confidence fathers might have that they can or deserve to be close to their virtuous daughters. Lear is a major father-figure in Lot history, and in the play you can sense a great reformation of family life starting to take place. Shakespeare, here, moves the Lot complex to the center of the stage where it will often dominate the action right down to the present.

The absence of the mother (the Lot's wife pattern) and of maternal feeling defines the world of *King Lear*, but in it the coming together of Lear and Cordelia after conflict becomes the hope and passion of its art. The play dramatizes both the desperation of aging men who, no matter how high up, still must "crawl toward death" (1.1.41) *and* the mixture of love, rage, envy, hate, and deference of daughters towards fathers and their authority. Shakespeare thus imagines the seedbed in which the conflicts and resolutions of modern Lot complexes have taken form and features the huge potential for evil and good in the Lot myth that gives it such explosive life.

The play teems with Lottish analogs and implications. Like Lot with the offer of his daughters to the Sodomites, Lear begins by pushing Goneril, Regan, and Cordelia into a form of prostitution—verbalized filial whoredom. The two eldest then act like vengeful beings who've been subjected to degrading, patriarchal pressure and conspire to take power, act, and determine history, even as Cordelia attempts to preserve the father's life. Lear is a "child-changed father" (4.7.17) and "bound/Upon a wheel of fire" (4.7.47–48). The old wife is gone and catastrophe threatens. Railing in the storm to the heavens, Lear adopts the familiar fire-and-brimstone imagery of Sodom's apocalypse:

You sulph'rous and thought-executing fires,
Vaunt-couriers to oak-cleaving thunderbolts,
Singe my white head. And thou, all-shaking thunder,
Strike flat the thick rotundity o' th' world. (3.2.4–7)

Shortly after that, Lear decries the "simular of [pretender to] virtue/That art incestuous" (3.2.54–55) and utters the famous phrase, "I am a man/More sinned against than sinning" (59–60). Like Lot in the cave, Lear doesn't seem to know what he's doing. He acts as though his seed must be preserved through the daughters, but he doesn't seem to know them or what his relationship to them should be. The older daughters are plotters, like Lot's girls, and, after coldly acting out their profession of incestuous desire for the father, both succumb to fatal adulterous sex with Edmund, the bastard engendered from taboo sex—as if they were condemned to repeat until they die, their sick sibling rivalry for the love of the same man. On the morally positive side of the Lot complex, Cordelia speaks the very sentiment a sympathetic reader of Genesis 19 might ascribe to Lot's daughters: "We are not the first/Who with best meaning have incurr'd the worst./For thee, oppressed king, I am cast down" (5.3.3–5). *Lear* can show just how much civil hope a father can invest in daughters, and it can also show how dangerous, agonizing, and conflicted that relationship can be.

VI.
Lear's Daughters

Shakespeare begins by dramatizing the fusion of statecraft, psychology, and the inevitable mixing up of the social and the libidinal. After working out the official division of the kingdom, Lear, the father, jeopardizes all his public plans with his narcissistic, semi-incestuous question to his daughters, "Which of you shall we say doth love us most" (1.1.51). It's worth looking at the language of the opening scene to spotlight crucial issues in father-daughter history:

LEAR. Tell me, my daughters
(Since now we will divest us both of rule,
Interest of territory, cares of state),
Which of you shall we say doth love us most. . . .
GONERIL. Sir, I love you more than word can wield the matter;
Dearer than eyesight, space, and liberty;
Beyond what can be valued, rich or rare;
No less than life, with grace, health, beauty, honour;
As much a child e'er loved, or father found;
A love that makes breath poor, and speech unable.
Beyond all manner of so much I love you.
CORDELIA. [*Aside*] What shall Cordelia speak? Love, and be silent.
LEAR. . . . What says our second daughter,
Our dearest Regan . . . ?
REGAN. I am made of that self mettle as my sister,
And prize me at her worth. In my true heart
I find she names my very deed of love;
Only she comes too short, that I profess
Myself an enemy to all other joys
Which the most precious square of sense possesses,
And find I am alone felicitate
In your dear highness' love.
CORDELIA. [*Aside*] Then poor Cordelia;
And yet not so, since I am sure, my love's
More ponderous than my tongue.
LEAR. . . . Now, our joy,
Although our last and least . . .
what can you say to draw
A third more opulent than your sisters? Speak.

CORDELIA. Nothing, my lord.
LEAR. Nothing?
   . . .

Nothing will come of nothing. Speak again.
CORDELIA. . . . I love your majesty
According to my bond, no more nor less.
   . . .

You have begot me, bred me, loved me. I
Return those duties back as are right fit,
Obey you, love you, and most honor you.
Why have my sisters husbands if they say
They love you all? . . .
Sure I shall never marry like my sisters,
To love my father all. (1.1.48–104)

From the start, then, Lot complexes swirl. The old man wants young women to tell him he's still lovable—the most unforgettable man they'll ever meet. The desire behind his question is both the will to control the emotional lives of one's children and the wish for immunity against time: *If my daughters will give me unqualified love, I can go on living through them.* For the daughters, the offer is an old enticement: *power in exchange for love.* Cordelia offers a devastating critique of the incestuous posturing of her sisters and also of the father's demand for a subjugating emotional incest. More generally, her speech points out the danger of Lot-complex desire running wild. Cordelia, like the whole play, insists that the love her sisters profess for their father is not only false, but perverse. Their cynical speech (bargain abasement) comes across as an attempt to intoxicate the father and seduce from him the last seeds of potency. The show of love without the spirit of love can't produce anything but a progeny of envy, lies, and infectious hostility. The elder daughters' speech also parodies, in its crazy hyperbole, the wish-fulfillment of all egotistical parents and authoritarian solipsists of any gender down through the ages.

Shakespeare, in the over-the-top "I am alone felicitate / In your dear highness' love," is dramatizing the plague of *father fixation.* Daughters can become obsessed figures reduced to the essence of bitterness as surely as backward-looking wives. It's hard to make good marriages if you're stuck on your father. Cordelia refuses the seductive paternal masterplot of domination. As Jane Smiley in *A Thousand Acres* (1991) would see it four centuries later, Goneril and Regan's avowals represent both meglomaniacal paternal projection (good girls say and do what *I* want) and a charade of fil-ial worship ("my heart belongs to daddy"—bat-bat-batting of eyelashes) that poison the lives of offspring who, individually and collectively, come to resent such abjection. High tragedy and daily life both tell you that the abject will seek the abjection of others.

It would be hard to overestimate the psychoanalytic significance of King Lear and his relationship to his daughters. In the Lot myth, the father, in a sense, replaces the mother in the lives of the daughters, and that is, no doubt, one unconscious male wish in the complex. The kind of unqualified love Lear is shown seeking is one that seems hardly to exist outside of the loving feeling people have had for the *mother*. In such diverse, telltale signs as Lear's bitter curse of infertility for Goneril, his projection of maternal functions on Cordelia, and the striking absence of almost any reference by the daughters to their mother, you can infer male womb-envy and the desire for a mother's intimacy with her children. Lear is a Lot's wife as well as a Lot. Swearing and disinheriting Cordelia "in hideous rashness," he blurts, "I loved her most, and thought to set my rest / On her kind nursery" (1.1.124–125). The words imply that time at the end of the father's life could run backwards, and to a favorite daughter he could be "father, son, and husband mild." Lear's fury would seem mere senile raving, if it were not that Cordelia speaks precisely and publicly the news an aging man might least wants to hear: the de facto phasing out of the father from the daughter's primary focus of concern, re-placement by other, younger men, and, thus, in effect, the equation of him with a Lot's wife, who for the sake of the future must be left behind.

VII.
Lear and the Curse of Lot

Lot is a above all a myth about the ultimate need to preserve life, fertility, and some form of continuity between generations no matter what, but it's also a myth about the seeds of conflict and family turbulence that lie in that necessity. *Lear* the play and Lear the character express and make literal what I call "the curse of Lot." That curse, growing out of the frustration and tension that the desire for intimacy between fathers and daughters can bring, turns their relationship back to the dead-end of obliterated Sodom and lost generation. As I mean to show, this curse could and would roil in various forms through modern social history, psychology, and art in figuring the lives of fathers and daughters.

Lear in his first scene swears at Cordelia in shocking terms: "[H]e that makes his generation messes/To gorge his appetite, shall to my bosom/Be as well neighbored, pitied, and relieved,/As thou my sometime daughter" (1.1.118–121). Later Lear, out of his own suffering and impotent paternal being, curses the sadistic Goneril, laying on her a destiny of both infertility *and* perverse progeny that destroys her life:

Hear, Nature, hear; dear goddess, hear:
Suspend thy purpose if thou didst intend
To make this creature fruitful.
Into her womb convey sterility,
Dry up in her the organs of increase,
And from her derogate body never spring
A babe to honor her. If she must teem,
Create her child of spleen, that it may live
And be a thwart disnatured torment to her.
Let it stamp wrinkles in her brow of youth,
With cadent tears fret channels in her cheeks,
Turn all her mother's pains and benefits
To laughter and contempt, that she may feel
How sharper than a serpent's tooth it is
To have a thankless child. (1.4.271–285)

Sigmund Freud—himself looking more and more like a battered old king of psychology, naked on the heath of scientific postmodernism—writes passionately about Lear in his illuminating, if wrong-headed, "The Theme of the Three Caskets" (1913). Here he uses folklore's three-choice riddles in Shakespeare (*The Merchant of Venice* and *King Lear*) to ponder myth's revelations of basic mysteries in the human condition. In turning *Lear* into a reductive Oedipal story and the daughter into a disguised mother and a symbol of death, he raises Lot issues in Shakespeare that would keep on haunting male and female imaginations down through the millennium.

Lear is an old man. It is for this reason . . . that the three sisters appear as his daughters. The relationship of a father to his children, which might be a fruitful source of many dramatic situations, is not turned to further account in the play. But Lear is not only an old man: he is a dying man. In this way the extraordinary premise of the division of his inheritance loses all its strangeness. But the doomed man is not willing to renounce the love of women; he insists on hearing how much he is loved. Let us now recall the moving final scene, one of the culminating points of tragedy in modern drama. Lear carries Cordelia's dead body on to the stage. Cordelia is Death. . . . She is the Death-goddess. . . . Eternal wisdom, clothed in primeval myth, bids the old man renounce love, choose death and make friends with the necessity of dying.

The dramatist brings us nearer to the ancient theme by representing the man who makes the choice between the three sisters as aged and dying. The regressive revision which he has thus applied to the myth, distorted as it was by wishful transformation, allows us enough glimpses of its original meaning to enable us perhaps to reach as well a superficial allegorical interpretation of the three female figures in the theme. We might argue that what is represented here are the three inevitable relations that a man has with a woman—the woman who bears him, the woman who is his mate and the woman who destroys him; or that they are the three forms taken by the figure of the mother in the course of a man's life—the mother herself, the beloved who is chosen after her pattern, and lastly the Mother Earth who receives him once more. But it is in vain that an old man yearns for the love of a woman as he had it first from his mother; the third of the Fates alone, the silent Goddess of Death, will take him into her arms.[6]

Wonderfully suggestive on the plight and desire of the father, Freud, as so often, just cannot see and hear the daughter clearly. In fact, it's hard to think of a more "fruitful" dramatic situation than the "relationship" of Lear and Cordelia, when the old father begins *trying* to see and love her (4.7 and 5.3). Goneril and Regan may be forms of death, but Cordelia is *murdered life*, something very different. She is not a Death Goddess, not Mother Earth the undertaker, but a vibrant, tough, smart, young female character terribly sacrificed.

Once, teaching *Lear* in a class of 18-year-olds, I had the students prepare and put on the final scene. The director cast a bright, beautiful young woman as Cordelia, and when the student playing Lear, howling, carried her in, dead in his arms, we were forced to see and imagine this vital girl—this real person—having no more life—"never, never, never, never, never" coming back (5.3.315). The point of the play is not the renunciation of love for death, but the necessity of love and its true reciprocity between father and daughter in a world where physical death is the universal prescription.

One tragedy that *Lear* brings home is the killing of the daughter's potential and the father's ancient blindness to the individuality and living plight of daughters. And one answer to the riddle of Lot that *Lear* offers and that the life and power of the play would help infuse into culture is that "attention must be paid" to daughters as something more than projections and emotional crutches for old men to lean on, if new and kinder modes of life are to develop.

Near the end of Shakespeare's play, Lear has learned to honor the great qualities of Cordelia, and he can imagine nothing finer than basking in her goodness and loving her reverently: "When thou dost ask me blessing, I'll kneel down/And ask of thee forgiveness" (5.3.10–11). I don't want to minimize what a radiant historical moment and image the father-king begging pardon of his daughter makes. From one perspective, the scene and lines have the spiritual calm and magnanimity of the Bible's Ruth and Boaz story amid all the scriptural narratives of violence. Lear fantasizes about living in a private heaven above it all with his beloved daughter, and the sweet musing shows human progress *is* possible:

> So we'll live,
> And pray, and sing, and tell old tales, and laugh
> At gilded butterflies and hear poor rogues
> Talk of court news; and we'll talk with them too—
> Who loses and who wins; who's in, who's out—
> And take upon's the mystery of things
> As if we were God's spies (5.3.11–17)

Through the daughter and his intense spiritual coupling with her, an old man comes to believe that he can find the holy mystery of being and of God.

Looking at those lines from another perspective, however, they show that the father's focus is still on what *he* wants and feels. The vision of life Lear's words imagine suits him perfectly, but what about the beloved Cordelia? Just before her father's fantasizing, she tells him that as prisoners they'd better try to get the sisters to intervene for them. "For thee, oppressed king, I am cast down;/Myself could else outfrown false Fortune's frown./Shall we not see these daughters and these sisters?" (5.3.5–7) "No, no, no, no" says Lear. Shakespeare makes it clear that the old man has had his life of agency and power, and now loving his faithful daughter and feeling her love, he can look down on the world of action, his soul saved. But Shakespeare still doesn't imagine him able to see her as a subjective being other and different from himself. Cordelia doesn't need to save her soul— she needs to save her life. Though figured as Lear's redeemer, she's still a relative creature. Things always revolve around him.

She answers the riddle of his life by giving him new life: "Thou that beget'st him that did thee beget." The riddle of her life gets no such answer. The new life that the character of the daughter Cordelia needs but does not get would seem to lie in the germinating tragedies of the once-powerful father aging in desperation and of the absent mother. One movement of the Lot complex henceforth will be not only towards the discovery of the daughter, but towards the generation and preservation of the seed of her subjectivity—towards the sacrificial lines that the father of the play cannot yet speak: *for you, oppressed girl, I am cast down.*

VIII.
Descendants of Lot,
Descendants of Lear

Just as Lot is an indispensable part of the heritage that made *King Lear*, so the heritage of *King Lear* gets folded inexorably into the subsequent history of fathers and daughters, of aging men and young females growing up, of powerful men under the scrutiny of newly influential women—in short, the modern history of Lot. *Lear* becomes a flexible tool by which imaginations can understand their times. Here are two very different, but telling examples.

1. Three hundred years after *King Lear* appeared, Jane Addams, the great social worker, reformer, and founder of Hull House (in whom a benevolent Cordelia's spirit surely lived), gave a talk called "A Modern Lear" to the Chicago Woman's Club. She spoke of the bloody Pullman railroad strike and labor battle of the 1890s and its protagonist George Pullman, the headstrong industrial tycoon Pullman. "Her idea," as Louis Menand puts it, "was that the conflict between Pullman and his workers was analogous to the conflict between King Lear and his daughter Cordelia in Shakespeare's play: an old set of values, predicated on individualism and paternalism, had run up against a new set of values, predicated on mutuality and self-determination."[7] These new values—mutuality, conciliation and inclusion—which Addams found in Labor, were in fact her own values, now being championed (though she didn't say it) by the civilizing force of public-spirited women like herself—maturing daughters, as it were, of the old patriarchy. The allegory of hope here is the redemption of the system by the

new and successful Cordelia—Jane Addams and all she stands for. *Lear* is tragic, but within it lies the seed for a historical change that can abrogate the tragedy.[8] There's hope in the daughter coming to power potentially redeeming and reforming the authoritarian patriarch. By projecting the faculty of "affectionate interpretation," Addams imagines that the spirit of a new Cordelia can work to show the world the commonality and democracy of existence.

2. *A Thousand Acres* (1991), Jane Smiley's late-twentieth-century version of *King Lear* as a water-polluting, cancer-spreading, incestuous farmer-patriarch who forces his two oldest adolescent daughters to have sex with him and then forget about it until the onset of their middle age (Goneril and Regan as martyr-victims to the so-called repressed-memory syndrome), shows her to be a literary Lot's daughter who uses *Lear* as a mode of understanding the dangers of the Lot myth. Like Jane Addams's piece, the most important thing about Smiley's novel may be that it shows so clearly how *Lot* and *Lear* continually merge and evolve in history and action: a modern woman writer preserves the seed of the great literary patriarch but makes of it her own feminist hybrid amidst the alien corn of contemporary Iowa. Smiley both symbolizes and recapitulates what has happened to Lot and Lear since Shakespeare. The relationship between Shakespeare and herself makes clear and literal the living dynamism of the Lot complex, as the daughter takes control of the cultural forefather's issue.[9]

A half-century after Shakespeare, his recognized successor to greatness in English poetry, John Milton, participated in a strange intellectual Lot charade. Unhappily married, a proponent of divorce, theologically masculinist, and prey to misogyny, the poet of *Paradise Lost* sired girls. According to one biographer, "Milton and his three daughters is a sad story, vague in its chronology, sordid in some of its details, fragmentary and elusive in its essential facts."[10] When he went blind, it seems he forced his daughters Mary and Deborah to read by rote material in languages they did not know and could not understand. They did this hour by hour, day by day, to tedium and exhaustion. The blind father used his girls as handmaidens to help him review, uncover, and preserve the knowledge he needed to generate his creative art, but he didn't deem it worth the effort to teach them what the words, lines, and works meant that, like a superior pair of mynah birds, they enunciated for him. The task and experience seems now, looking back, like some weird, symbolic, intellectual form of incest—daughters servicing the blind paternal mind. What the father wanted was selfless labor and total dedication to his imagination. They had to serve, but were shut out of his life and kept ignorant of the codes that made the diverse human record meaningful to him.

"These things are a parable," wrote George Eliot two hundred years later, in *Middlemarch*, where, with Milton somewhere in the back of her mind, she created the pedantic old scholar Casaubon, who wastes and ignores the intellectual vitality of his young wife, thirty years his junior. Whatever the precise truth of the Milton story, the image of ignorant daughters, whose need for higher education and intellectual endeavor is ignored as they supplicate the blindness of the father, would find its way into cultural memory. And what shaped the modern history of *Lot* and crucial relations between daughters and fathers and between young women and older men, is the great fact that, unlike John Milton's girls, some daughters stopped reading to the blind and started writing for them.

part ii

Generating and Representing
Modern Daughters of Lot

Chapter 6

Reflections from the Cave

JANE AUSTEN'S 'MANSFIELD PARK'
AND MARY SHELLEY'S 'MATHILDA'

E arly in the nineteenth century, two major writers, Jane Austen and Mary Shelley, face the future poised between the chief hopes and dangers of the Lot complex. The first imagines the great opportunity for progress in moralized, legitimized Lot alliances featuring the daughter's growing empowerment and the domestication of the patriarchy; the second imagines the killing blight of incestuous sexual desire.

I.
Creating the Modern World

Before looking at novels by these two, I want to stress the importance of the story I'm using them to tell. It should not be taken for granted. If I say men of the last three centuries used science to create the modern world, it may seem obvious and banal. But what also seems true is this: *women of the last two centuries used imaginative literature—fiction and poetry—to create the modern world.* The way people have come to talk and think and see and feel, in the English-speaking world at least, is unimaginable without the cultural influence of novelists like Austen, Mary Shelley, the Brontës, George Eliot, Harriet Beecher Stowe, Edith Wharton, Virginia Woolf, Toni Morrison, and on and on. They have made reality.

The professional field of literature, with its ability to represent and shape identity, personal relations, conceptions of self and society, and the modes of communication, opened up to women in the last 250 years. It may be the first traditionally male field in which women proved themselves men's equals—*no "separate sphere" in writing*. How did this happen? One answer lies in the complex relationships of literature-loving fathers with their daughters and another in the figuring of older men–younger women relations in the literary record.

II.
Austen and the Politics
of Lot's Daughters

In talent, in the mysterious ability to impose her imagination on succeeding generations, in her feeling for the romance of daily life, and in the suggestiveness and range of symbolic implication in her work, Jane Austen shows herself now as a true heir of Shakespeare. Like him, she was fascinated with the drama of what are, broadly speaking, Lottish dilemmas for both aging men and daughters, and she, too, explicitly looked for and imagined ways to turn the real and potential tragedy of daughters' lives into comedy. She was the first woman in England—arguably in the world—to write great comedy that has lasted, and that in itself makes her a historic figure. The making of that human comedy and her quiet assumption of authority—moral and aesthetic authority—reflect and shape the great movement of modern gender history.

Austen is neither a conservative (that leaves you stuck in old mud) nor a revolutionary (the visual image in that word implies you just swing wildly around and end up in the same place), but a reformer who wants—and gets—her patrimony. In her last novel, *Persuasion*, she shows her wonderfully perceptive, much oppressed heroine, Anne Elliot, getting fed up with the foolish selfishness of the people around her: "Anne longed for the power of representing to them all what they were."[1] That was Austen's own desire, and she matters because she found the power to do it. She assumed agency and asserted the right of daughters to tell their own stories in their own language and be heeded.

Those stories are ones of hope and possibilities, but she was no softheaded idealist. She knew—no one better—that she was born into a world where male-dominated history weighed like a nightmare on the brains of living girls, and she had no illusions about the inescapable fact of female dependency—how could she when she lived nearly all her life in her father's home or in a cottage provided by a rich older brother? She saw women's historical condition as, in effect and symbol, that of daughters patronized by men, but the great thing was that social life could, would, and needed to change for the sake of both women and men. She imagined how: in the final sentence of *Persuasion*, she is summing up the happy love story, and representing, from a powerful woman's point of view, how things might be. She sees the marriage of a put-upon, misprized daughter and a new man of power as a fusion, an incorporation, and a "profession" (*utterance of faith* as well as *vocation*) of what she calls "domestic virtue" and "national importance" (252). It's as if she were saying the personal has become political, the political is personal, the "women's sphere" is now the globe, and the fate of the realm is fused in the mutual evolution of daughters and patriarchs into men and women who can share life wholly. Commonwealth and empire need to be domesticated, and domestic responsibilities and moral values need to become imperial.

If you can see that women's issues constitute a big part of the world's news, Jane Austen is a political novelist of deep insight, as *Mansfield Park*, her longest and most ambitious work, shows.[2] (Among other things, this extraordinary book allegorizes both the French Revolution and the Romantic movement as an amateur theatrical that goes awry when moral authority and the real interests of women get lost or dislocated.) Austen's novels are so experimental and different from one another, so full of various meanings, that she resists reductive reading—or more precisely, like most great artists, she continues to invite fresh readings over time that repay special interests and cast light on a multitude of subjects for different people. I, for instance, now read her as one of the first and most important modern literary Lot's daughters, a novel-writing life-preserver animating the *presentness* of past issues. In *Mansfield Park*, a novel that you can interpret so many ways, I simply want to point out that it tells a tale about the changing relationship and alliance of an older man and a younger woman that opens up new possibilities for the next two centuries.

III.
Discovering a Daughter and the
Meaning of 'Mansfield'

Austen revises and updates the Lear theme, recasts it in upper-middle-class, imperialist, turn-of-the-nineteenth-century Britain, imagines at its very center a new Cordelia as a bourgeois Cinderella, and gives it a happy ending. In the novel a poor little "timid and exceedingly nervous" girl is taken from her own disorderly home of deprivation into her uncle's home, Mansfield Park, as an act of patronizing charity.[3] There she gets lessons in the reality of material advantage, class subservience, and her own deficiencies. Her two older female cousins brag of their cultural education ("[W]e used to repeat the chronological order of the kings of England, with the dates of their accession, and most of the principal events of their reigns. . . . and of Roman emperors as low as Severus; besides a great deal of the Heathen Mythology, and all the Metals, Semi-Metals, Planets, and distinguished philosophers" [18–19]), but quickly the frivolous girls, trained in the superficial, adjourn, says the acidly allegorical Austen, "to whatever might be the favourite holiday-sport of the moment, making artificial flowers or wasting gold paper" (14). Yet neurasthenic Fanny—in faithful love with her kind, mentoring cousin Edmund from the moment in her childhood when he pities her and treats her kindly—learns to read books, nature, and people deeply. In the end, when her two Goneril-and-Regan cousins self-destruct, Fanny becomes the daughter of a great house that loosely but surely stands for England. She ends up as moral savior of the father and a creative mother of the future.

To get at the scope of Austen's intention in her sophisticated art, it helps to see how carefully she chose the name *Mansfield Park* in order to make it carry key allusions to both patriarchal structure and its reformation. Lord Mansfield (1705–1793), born William Murray in Scotland, was a great and powerful chief justice of Great Britain from 1756 to 1788 and a walking epitome of stern patriarchy who helped to shape the law in the modern era.[4] He was famous—and even now remembered—for two reasons that struck Austen: first, his estate was notoriously burned and sacked by the anarchic city mob in the Gordon Riots of 1788, and, second, it was widely thought that Mansfield abolished slavery in England with one judicial decision. He ruled that an escaped slave from Virginia could not be forcibly removed from England for punishment. Moreover, Austen, who said she wanted to write a novel about "ordination," also may have have picked "Mansfield Park" for a title because the German town Mansfield was known and celebrated as a place where Martin Luther, besieged by crisis, had to live and make his stand as a Protestant and a reformer of faith.

When poor little Fanny Price comes to Mansfield Park, she's not only moving in with rich relations, she's occupying the allegorical grounds of history.

With the title word "Mansfield," then, Austen floats the subject of slavery in relation to female life and its deprivations. She, growing up with her beloved sister in a big, supportive family—a literary prodigy mentored proudly by her intellectual father and patronized by the admiring affection of a talented band of brothers (at least two of whom she adored)—doesn't say or believe anything as simplistic as "women are nothing but slaves." She does, however, strongly imply an analogy between the *emancipation* of slaves and rational progress for women. She specifically makes Fanny Price's uncle and the patriarch of the book, Sir Thomas Bertram, proprietor of Mansfield Park, a beset absentee property-owner in slave-holding Antigua, where he must make a dangerous journey during the time of abolition of the slave trade.[5] And she connects his critical recognition of his mistakes of judgment and his lax paternal guidance of his own daughters, together with his shaken hopes for preservation of what's best in his established way of life, to his need for, and reliance on, the growing authority and the love of Fanny, this civilized and civilizing young woman. Fanny, disparaged and ignored when a child, later looked down upon, unappreciated, taken advantage of, and at times bullied even by those who like her best, becomes his true, spiritual daughter and in the end marries his newly ordained son. Austen makes her the far-seeing moral agent who redeems the basically good, but flawed patriarch. If the estate is to thrive and flourish, the father needs Fanny to renew his faith.

Fanny was indeed the daughter that he wanted. His charitable kindness had been rearing a prime comfort for himself. His liberality had a rich repayment, and the general goodness of his intentions by her, deserved it. He might have made her childhood happier; but it had been an error of judgment only which had given him the appearance of harshness, and deprived him of her early love; and now, on really knowing each other, their mutual attachment became very strong. (472)

These things also are a parable. That taming of the patriarchy shows the type of mutual benefit and connection that Austen hoped could and would evolve between men and women.

IV.
An Act of Patriarchal Oppression

True as it is, that last statement of mine sounds flat and sentimental; it tends to sweeten Austen and blunt the challenge her book posed and poses for future daughters and fathers—women and men looking for social progress. There's a terrible scene between Sir Thomas and Fanny, when he urges her to marry rich Henry Crawford, whom she knows to be a philanderer. Besides, she loves Edmund forever, though it appears unrequited. You can see a modern equivalent of Lot's desperate offer of his daughters to the Sodomites in the intense patriarchal pressure that can be brought to bear on a girl to wed a man she doesn't love or like (see Richardson's *Clarissa*). The moral shoddiness of such a business shows through in Sir Thomas's shameful rant at Fanny when she turns Henry down:

For I *had*, Fanny, as I think my behavior must have shewn, formed a very favourable opinion of you from the period of my return to England. I had thought you peculiarly free from willfulness of temper, self-conceit, and every tendency to that independence of spirit, which prevails so much in modern days, even in young women, and which in young women is offensive and disgusting beyond all common offence. But you have shewn me that you can be willful and perverse, that you can and will decide for yourself, without any consideration or deference for those who have surely some right to guide you—without even asking their advice. (318–319)

This nasty tirade and Fanny's reaction to it mark both the end of a line and a new beginning. But the momentous change ordained to come is not, as righteous indignation might expect, the alienation of the hard patriarch and the young woman tormented into independence—him casting her off; her rebelling against cruel treatment. Instead a difficult process drawing them and their interests together gets started. In an overview of the history of men and women, that's what gives *Mansfield Park* a special place. Paternal error and bad behavior make one theme, but another is the necessity for a young woman to assume responsibility for the best interests of all, including her erring guardian, no matter what the pain—and the pain is great: "Her heart was almost broke by such a picture of what she appeared to him; by such accusations" (319). The whole passage is about the improper disposal of women, but it is also about the elder man's inability to control life, see clearly, and make the girl bond to him as a project of his will and desire.

Austen could have been an early star in the English novel's parade of female victims, but that was not her plan. These characters, as she imagine them, are both sympathetic and worthy, which makes her views here both original and provocative. Instead of leaving them ogre and victim, this confrontation begins to make possible an alliance of hope—Sir Thomas doesn't always know what he's about, and he needs Fanny's acute sensibility and faith:

It was over, however, at last; . . . but she trusted, in the first place, that she had done right, that her judgment had not misled her; for the purity of her intentions she could answer; and she was willing to hope, secondly, that her uncle's displeasure was abating, and would abate farther as he considered the matter . . . and felt, as a good man must feel, how wretched, and how unpardonable, how hopeless and how wicked it was, to marry without affection. (324)

The young woman has become the mature moralist.

V.
The Power to Offend and the Necessity of Abjection

Mansfield Park, says Lionel Trilling, is a great novel, "its greatness being commensurate with its power to offend."[6] It offends because it can tell you what you don't want to hear, even as it informs. It tells a story in which "creepmouse" Fanny Price, who condemns the worldly, self-assertive dazzle of good-natured but amoral Mary Crawford—not to mention the usurpations of authority by her Aunt Norris—makes peace with the sometimes unjust and insensitive father figure, Sir Thomas. Race and gender relations are very different matters, of course, but the novel can seem offensive to contemporary feminists in ways that *Uncle Tom's Cabin, Huckleberry Finn*, or a paean to the life and theories of Booker T. Washington can sometimes offend enemies of racism.

In Patricia Rozema's stylish movie of *Mansfield Park* (1999), you can see in the basic changes the film makes in the story just how the book can and does offend modern sensibilities.[7] The movie Fanny Price is a witty, self-assured young woman who writes fiction (as well as actual passages from Jane Austen letters—*sic*!). She looks like a prom queen who has booster-rocket SAT scores too. The clever, gorgeous Mary Crawford, upon whom Edmund, Fanny's love and husband-to-be, has a callow crush, even makes a sweet lesbian pass at Fanny. The film's version of Sir Thomas now becomes the hypercritical, arch-bad-guy "patriarch," an enemy of freedom who exploits his slaves in Antigua (according to his elder son's sketches in the movie, he even got public blow jobs from them). And of course he's a sexual harasser, ogling and poking at Fanny. In Rozema's technicolor *Mansfield*, it's all black and white—gone, in the euphoria of feel-good righteousness, are the moral complexity, suffering, self-doubt, and the need for compromise that Austen's novel makes the awful tax a thinking woman in her time had to pay for progress and opportunities to come.

Still, there's no denying the power to offend in Austen's tough idea that makes repressed Fanny (shown to be emotionally crippled by her early life and given to judgmental priggishness) and authoritarian, class-conscious Sir Thomas into admirable figures—a symbolic duo dependent on one another and indispensable to the good of the commonwealth. What may be most offensive about the book for a modern reader is the fact that Fanny Price, Jane Austen's typological daughter-reformer of *Mansfield Park* and the moral center of a world on the brink of modernity, is the most neurotic, male-identified, and unprepossessing of her heroines—nothing like the bold Elizabeth Bennet–Jane Austen-like Fanny of the film. Underprivileged, wallowing in the fate of her own feckless parents, her only chance to move forward in life is through male *kindness* (the word, with its connotations of benevolence and a familial relationship, appears again and again in the novel) and a patriarchal sense of duty. It is only through the "kind" notice of Sir Thomas, for example, with all his faults, that she can obtain a heated room of her own—with all the potential that the phrase "a room of one's own" signifies.

It's hard to read of Fanny's abjection in first two volumes, yet Austen's rendering of that abjection is one of the most moving things about *Mansfield Park*. Abjection—spasms of mental wincing—flows out of emotional fear and an inculcated sense of inferiority. Fanny's makes her at times horribly shy, depressed, self-effacing, psychosomatically ill, and given to bouts of semi-hysteria. If she, in this novel of symbolism, in some sense may be said to stand for women (as the Park stands somehow for Britain), and if girls get hurt by social oppression of one kind or another, then she will naturally be wounded—and scars are not pretty to look at.

Jane Austen can be tough on women. She hates and mocks whining females (Lucy Steele, Mrs. Bennet, Mrs. Norris, the Bertram sisters, Mary Musgrove) because she imagines a strategy of complaint and perpetual victimhood, besides making you obnoxious, doesn't help people. But, in fact, she shows how very much there is to complain about. Moral progress is not a fuzzy wish, but an imperative in her imagination. A kinder, gentler morality, however, depends on the improvement and reformation of the well-meaning, if doubting, Sir Thomases of the world by the domestic influence and imagination of intelligent women. It depends also on that influence supporting enlightened, reformist sons of the patriarchy. And for that to happen young women must be both knowledgeable and engaged with men's interests.

Fanny depends upon the kindness of patriarchy's men: her uncle, the land-owner with colonial holdings; the Christian son Edmund bound to the Church; and her own sea-going, beloved brother William sailing proudly in the imperial navy. In a key section of the novel, when Fanny is coming into her own, but still fluttering with feelings of inadequacy, Austen brilliantly fuses her domestic realism with radiant symbolism. She creates, in a few particulars, a portrait of one young lady in the seed-time of new life, but also an image of general female life and its historical contingency. Sir Thomas decides to honor and gratify Fanny with a ball. He wants to show her off as her affectionate patron. She, hating display, frets about what to wear. Austen has her obsequiously choosing to wear around her neck the cross that William has brought her from his Mediterranean campaign on a chain that Edmund has given her. In other words, as the nineteenth century begins, the repressed girl finds herself dancing to the elder man-of-property's tune, wearing a cross and chain, and happy to make the best of it, having already come a long way up and wanting to stay close to both the man of faith and the man of war. In this novel, only through abjection to patriarchal males can you gain the affection, power, confidence, and space in which to change the patriarchy.

VI.
A Patronizing Process and the Complexity of Women's Lib

Austen's little England, therefore, like my whole story of Lot, may seem deeply offensive in retrospect, but her point is surely that when you imagine daughters in the world, you need to think of the particular history into which women are born and must live. Self-projecting fantasies that claim the free pass of victimization, and then somehow assume anachronistic power on the part of victims—their spirit is not altered or damaged by injustice—are, for the author of *Mansfield Park*, deceiving fictions that can do great harm. Billie Holliday sings of rich relations: "You can help yourself/ But don't take too much . . . / God bless the child that's got his own;" like most girls in history, Fanny doesn't have her own. She's a dispossessed, hurt child, but then what follows? Disregard and suffering for the sensitive girl will inevitably maim the spirit, but injustice and mental torment don't mean you have to give in to whining bitterness, despair, or rage. By trying to make men better, feeding their moral desires for spiritual well-being, and showing them their best interests, you can get some of your own and more for your sisters and daughters to come. Still, that's a hard story.

One scene, subtle but revealing in its intimations of how much importance Austen invests in the changing relationship of Fanny and Sir Thomas, can serve as a positive pole for the Lot complex in the modern world. (It's on and in the father's son Edmund, in the novel, that this change is registered, so that he becomes a new kind of man in whom paternalism is mediated by rational, feminine moral judgment.) Sir Thomas has returned from the Caribbean to find that Fanny has bloomed. She and Edmund talk of how his father's return after two years has put a damper on the gaiety of the other young people. "I suppose I am graver than other people," said Fanny. . . . I love to hear my uncle talk of the West Indies. I could listen to him for an hour together. It entertains *me* more than many other things have done—but then I am unlike other people I dare say" (197). This character, Austen imagines, is hungering for knowledge, hungering to be serious in the way of responsible men. What follows is not only a capsule, sexist moment that epitomizes how women exist as objects of physical and aesthetic evaluation by men, but also a dialogue in which the whole world can be said to be moving:

"Go to my father if you want to be complimented. . . . Ask your uncle what he thinks, and you will hear compliments enough; and though they may be chiefly on your person, you must put up with it, and trust to his seeing as much beauty of mind in time. . . . Your uncle thinks you very pretty, dear Fanny—and that is the long and the short of the matter. . . . [T]he truth is, that your uncle never did admire you till now—and now he does. Your complexion is so improved! . . . and your figure—Nay, Fanny, do not turn away about it—it is but an uncle. . . . You must really begin to harden yourself to the idea of being worth looking at.—

You must try not to mind growing up into a pretty woman. . . . Your uncle is disposed to be pleased with you in every respect; and I only wish you would talk to him more. . . . "

"But I do talk to him more than I used. I am sure I do. Did not you hear me ask him about the slave trade last night?"

"I did—and was in hopes the question would be followed up by others. It would have pleased your uncle to be inquired of farther."

"And I longed to do it—but there was such a dead silence! And while my cousins were sitting by without speaking a word, or seeming at all interested in the subject, I did not like—I thought it would appear as if I wanted to set myself off at their expense." (197–198)

Look what's going on. Austen figures that a young woman's good looks might dispose a man of power to see the potential of her mind. But she implies also the distress the girl feels that new respect for her by both the father and son may depend on her looks. And yet she presents the disposition for serious conversation with a bright, idealistic girl as real and full of import. She imagines that Fanny's curious mind wants to know about the slave trade, as meaningful a general subject as there could be for the nineteenth century, and that this reserved patriarch, tired of the vacuous "dead silence" of childish girls about the vocational affairs that occupy him, wants to tell her about it. In *Mansfield Park*'s subtle art, Fanny's question and her uncle's approval of her bringing the subject up only make sense if Austen means you to infer that their sentiments coincide. Sir Thomas of Mansfield would seem to be a figure just back from participating in the historical transition out of slavery and repressed Fanny believes in the moral enfranchisement of the soul. This mutual desire of the young woman and the older man to share the knowledge of power, thought, and action is a germ of hope and freedom in Austen's world. Of course, it is *just* a seed in a long gestation of change—a promising, but limited momentary alliance, as its origin in the appraising male gaze and Fanny's dither about separating herself from the other girls go to show.

VII.
Two Daughters: "How Wonderful!"

The bleakest part of Austen's vision in *Mansfield Park* is the separation of the moral heroine from the witty woman of sophisticated charm and worldliness. When most readers think of Austen, they think first of Elizabeth Bennet and Emma Woodhouse, her feisty, funny heroines; but in *Mansfield* she divides the qualities she most values in them—a comic spirit, moral striving to be a better person, and the ability to love wholeheartedly—between Mary Crawford and Fanny.

The novelist expressly gives Mary deft, *Austenian* powers to satirize society's manners and *mores*. But Austen cannot reconcile her entertaining Mary with the need for a serious-minded feminine sensibility that can understand and enter into the vocational and religious interests of men and provide them with a steady role model of virtue and duty. She gives Mary great lines and jokes, even makes her generous, but represents her as morally slack and purges her in the end from the novel's world.

For Austen, it must have felt like suicide. Both Fanny Price and Mary Crawford represent vital qualities and desires within the disposition of Austen, her art, and her sense of the world. Fatalistic, cynical Mary delights in urban amusements, wit, gossip, flashy performance, pleasure, occasional (and much-deserved) male-bashing, worldly power, music, and beautiful people and things; she distrusts romantic love. Passive-aggressive, domestic Fanny longs to improve the world around her and values moral judgment, modesty, order, quiet, security, Christian stoicism, family loyalties, privacy, kindness, intellectual curiosity, and the beauties and harmonies of nature. She believes in true love and assumes the role of moral arbiter for her milieu.

As the two characters saunter together, through a beautiful garden, "in a sort of intimacy" but with little in common, Austen gives them dialogue and thoughts that mark them both as geniuses as well as harbingers of things to come for women. Mary, in her self-centered musing and easy acceptance of the fundamentally male values in her world (wealth, influence, and social success), speaks with the entitlement of triumphant female individualism. She wanders untouched and alienated through the growing green things that Fanny rhapsodizes about. "To say the truth," says Mary, "I am something like the famous Doge at the court of Lewis XIV; and may declare that I see no wonder in this shrubbery equal to seeing myself in it" (209). But Austen gives Fanny, struggling to maturity in Mansfield Park, a broader sense of wonder—wonder that seems the very basis of faith in the future. In language that lets Fanny both predict and celebrate a whole range of intellectual activity and curiosity to follow, Austen imagines an eloquent humanism in a damaged young female's comprehensive consciousness:

How wonderful, how very wonderful the operations of time, and the changes of the human mind! . . . If any one faculty of our nature may be called *more* wonderful than the rest, I do think it is memory. There seems something more speakingly incomprehensible in the powers, the failures, the inequalities of memory, than in any other of our intelligences. The memory is sometimes so retentive, so serviceable, so obedient—at others, so bewildered and so weak—and at others again, so tyrannic, so beyond controul!—We are to be sure a miracle every way—but our powers of recollecting and of forgetting, do seem peculiarly past finding out. (208–209)

In *Mansfield Park*, then, Austen does show you two Lot's daughters: Fanny is ordained to come first as the book's central moral guide and to put first things first (the miracle of life). She become the "true daughter" who sets the domestic tone, preserves the seed of culture and forces the issues that make progress possible. Mary, the female egoist with the talent to amuse and the honesty to strip away hypocrisy and illusion, is a sleeping beauty whom the world will wake when the distance between fathers and daughters has lessened and more equality exists between men and women.

The famous opening of the last chapter, sometimes cited as a profession of Austen's faith, sounds on its surface more like Mary Crawford than Fanny Price: "Let other pens dwell on guilt and misery. I quit such odious subjects as soon as I can, impatient to restore every body, not greatly in fault themselves, to tolerable comfort, and to have done with all the rest" (461). And yet that first sentence—not at all an apt description of "the pen" that wrote *Mansfield Park*, but a perfect segue-way into the spirit of *Emma* and *Persuasion*—does fit nicely Fanny's move out of misery and away from fixation on the guilt of those who oppressed her. The passage bespeaks a broadly political, forward-looking sensibility and a practical strategy. It imagines, like the book, what is so hard to recapture now—and so offensive to many—and yet so necessary for understanding the advances and successes in modern times: the potential of a Lot's daughter story to be a happy one.

VIII.
'Mathilda' and Mary Shelley

One pen that did dwell on guilt and misery was Mary Shelley's. Less than five years after *Mansfield Park* (1814) came out and just after the publication of her sensational *Frankenstein* (1818), she wrote *Mathilda*, a novella fixated on father-daughter incest. This odd little work makes the Lot complex into a deadly erotic nightmare, and it has some of the myth-making potential for modern domestic relations that its predecessor *Frankenstein* has for science and the careerist ambitions of intellectuals. I can begin to make clear *Mathilda*'s disturbing significance (and maybe the reason why it was ignored for so long) by crudely putting the basic questions it raises for almost any thoughtful modern reader: would a loving, civilized, well-meaning father really want to fuck his daughter? Could his adoring, smitten daughter subconsciously want him to tell her that he does and learn the sexual facts of life from him? Could she—stunned when she sees his sexual lust for her— really remain hopelessly in love with such a man? And if a brilliant, creative young woman like Mary Shelley can imagine that he does and she does, what does that say about the whole subject of father-daughter relations and the history incestuous desire? The shocking point of *Mathilda* is that it renders the Lot syndrome without sublimation and brings it close to home— out of the obfuscating cave of ancient history, alibis, and legend. It directly implicates two contemporary, sympathetic souls, a father and a pubescent daughter, in sexual passion and love.[8]

Barely 22 when she wrote this incestuous story, Mary Shelley was already a veteran of sex scandals, dysfunctional families, and the ravages of death. Few writers ever had a better literary pedigree or such a weirdly doom-ridden erotic seedtime. As her consciousness formed and her life developed, love and death inevitably ran together. So did the commitment to writing and the pull of revolutionary lifestyles. She was the daughter of the radical social reformer and writer William Godwin and Mary Wollstonecraft, the daring feminist author and pioneer of women's rights (*Vindication of the Rights of Women*). But when Wollstonecraft died only ten days after her namesake daughter was born, the mother metamorphosed for the girl into an oft-visited gravestone, a portrait in her father's house, the memories of her father, and various maternal writings—in other words, Mary's psychological Lot's wife. Wollstonecraft, a passionate rebel against conventional marriage, had married Godwin only after she found herself pregnant by him, and she already had a bastard daughter, Fanny, fathered by Gilbert Imlay, her American lover. But Imlay abandoned her, leaving the champion of female independence so depressed that she twice tried to kill herself. That was the chance for the austere, 40-year-old bachelor Godwin. These two radical intellectuals went from the meeting of minds to bodies, but then her devastating death from childbirth left the celebrated author of *Caleb Williams* with two little girls to raise on his own.

From her earliest days, Mary focused on her father as her all-in-all.[9] He was a great man, and, not surprisingly, she says that growing up she had an "excessive & romantic attachment" to him.[10] But she could not be *his* all-in-all; when she was four, he married Mary Jane Clairmont, who already had two children. Soon he and his new wife had a son of their own, and Mary found herself with two stepsisters, two stepbrothers, and a stepmother she detested. Not only did *she* resent this woman coming between her father and herself, but the stepmother, it turned out, was jealous of *her*. Mary, after all, was the visible sign that the second wife had a legendary predecessor against whom she could never measure up. And Mary's intellectual abilities, specifically her literary promise, far surpassed the other children and made her father admire her—when he had time. Always busy, writing away, working to stay on top in the literary world, supporting causes, running publishing ventures, scrambling to keep out of debt (he didn't), Godwin gladly turned family responsibilities over to his wife. Feeling both his approval and neglect, Mary grew up wearing the bipolar cap of moody highs and lows.

She was Little Orphan Mary and he was Daddy Morebooks. Fascinated by literature, she benefited from his large library and the freedom he gave her to read what she wanted. He praised and encouraged her own early writing (he published a long comic poem of hers when she was 10); and his prominence meant she had the chance to see, hear, and meet the major figures of the Romantic movement in her own home. Godwin, by fits and starts, gave her informal, but serious mentorship and recognized her talent. He taught her to value the life of imagination. But he could be icy. He often ignored and shut her out emotionally while he pursued his career, and he usually took her stepmother's part against her in quarrels. When friction between Mary and his wife got worse as the girl moved into puberty, he sent her away to live in Scotland with a friend's family.

The night after her return six months later, she met at dinner Godwin's new disciple Percy Bysshe Shelley and his wife Harriet. Mary again spent most of the following year in Scotland, but when she returned in the spring of 1814, the 16-year-old girl began seeing the unhappily married Shelley every day. Two beautiful people churning with erotic desire, they would go together to Mary Wollstonecraft's grave, and there one rare June day by the maternal stone, they vowed their love for each other. In the realm of the dead mother, Mary transferred her romantic father-fixation onto this golden-boy writer, and he passionately embraced the incarnation of the Wollstonecraft-Godwin free-love union.

Godwin found out and forbade Mary to meet Shelley again (within the libidinous male seducer may lurk an aging patriarch waiting to save daughters from a fate worse than death—except his own). In the next three weeks Mary tried half-heartedly to obey her father, Percy threatened suicide, his own wife Harriet swelled with child, and very likely Mary worried about pregnancy too. Then the lovers fled to Europe with Mary's stepsister Jane Clairmont (later known as Claire Clairmont, she became Byron's mistress and, it seems, Shelley's lover too). Godwin condemned Mary's "licentious" love and saw her as a home wrecker.[11] He refused to see her or communicate with her for almost three years, and Mrs. Godwin never forgave Mary for ruining, so she thought, her daughter Jane—something of a Romantic groupie. When they returned in September, Mary, as well as Harriet, was pregnant.

In the eight wild years to follow, Mary lived with Percy Shelley at the heart of Romanticism, helped shape its vision, and bore the word and cost of its experimental erotics. But she never really could get away from the grave of the mother, that symbolic site where she first pledged love. Born in February, Mary's first child died in March 1815. In the next four years, she and Percy had two more children who died. Before he drowned in 1822 she was pregnant two more times: she had a son, Percy Florence, who lived, and then a miscarriage. Altogether: five pregnancies, four deaths. In 1816, Mary's distraught half-sister Fanny, the Wollstonecraft love-child, found, in her depression, the one thing she could do better than her mother and committed suicide. So did Harriet Shelley, found drowned and pregnant, a month later (making it possible for Mary and Percy to wed).

Between the time her *Frankenstein* appeared in 1818 and August 1819, when she began *Mathilda*, Mary fell into heavy bouts of depression, and why not? She lost her two children; her husband, with his polygamous nature, betrayed her with her own stepsister, maybe their maid, and who knows how many others; the shadowy libidinous influence of Byron and his libertine ways and friends hung over the Shelleys in Italy; moreover she remained estranged from her father, the man whose undivided love she had longed for and never had.

If *Mathilda* carries passive-aggressive, displaced rage against Mary's father, as well as a longing for him, Godwin's correspondence to Mary at the time of its writing shows why. Just when she was finishing up *Mathilda*, Godwin wrote her as follows: "I cannot but consider it as lowering your character in a memorable degree, and putting you among the commonality and mob of your sex, when I had thought you to be ranked among those noble spirits that do honor to our nature. Oh! what a falling off is here! . . . you have lost a child; and all the rest of the world, all that is beautiful, and all that has a claim upon your kindness, is nothing, because a child of three years old is dead."[12]

Her Romantic star-bard spouse couldn't make up for the failure of paternal love, and in her suffering mind Percy had fallen into her father's pattern of diffusing among undeserving others the love that rightfully belonged to her. But instead of trying to kill herself, like so many near and/or dear to her, she wrote a piece of fiction probing conflicted incestuous feelings that could make people fall in love with easeful death.

IX.
The Shelleys' Dialogue

In effect, Mary and her husband conducted a literary dialogue and expressed very different views about father-daughter incest and its meaning, and that dialogue still resonates. To see why, *Mathilda* needs to be set in context with Percy's work. In Rome in 1819, the year their son William died from malaria, the Shelleys read an account of a Renaissance incest and murder case in which a Count Cenci raped his own daughter Beatrice, and she in revenge had her father killed. Percy wanted Mary to take up the subject, but she said she felt inadequate and instead urged him to write it. He plunged into *The Cenci*. It was the only work he shared with her during its composition, which indicates how interesting the subject was to both of them (after his death, she claimed it contained his very best work). Percy, disowned by his own father, used the incestuous Cenci, a sadistic aristocrat in league with a venal Church, to embody the evil corruption of authority. In *The Cenci* Percy took the half-century heritage of popular, English gothic-novel sensationalism and tried to make it into neo-Shakespearean tragic art (heavy traces of *King Lear*, that echo-chamber of father-daughter issues and "the curse of Lot" [see Chapter 5] show up everywhere in the play). The real problem in the drama is not so much incest and sexual crime, as the monstrous patriarchal tyranny that rapes the world. The poet imagines the violated, but noble-hearted daughter Beatrice as a justified parricide and a tragic symbol of oppressed humanity, but he's not really interested in personal relations in this play. Paternal incest becomes for him a political trope for the perversity of entrenched power.

For Mary, it was the psychology of father-daughter incest that she found fascinating, and *The Cenci* inspired her at last to write her own, very different "tragic history" of incest in *Mathilda*.[13] Its premise is startling: what if, for the daughter, the incestuous father, instead of being hateful, should be lovable? For the freedom-loving Percy, who despised his own father and could and did take male privilege for granted, it was easy to condemn the patriarchy and make the father a devil. For Mary, who loved her father, admired his work, and wanted to share his intellectual patrimony, the symbolic meaning of incest was much more complex. *The Cenci* uses incest to show the necessity of moral and social revolution, but *Mathilda* concerns itself with incestuous longing in characters you can feel for and even like. And there is something else implicit in Mary's treatment of incest that differs from her husband's: *Mathilda* insists, against implicit attitudes of men like Godwin, Percy Shelley, and other male political reformers and optimists, on the primal sway of parent-child relationships—the ineradicable residue of mutual desires that grow out of them—in determining the shape of life.

Mathilda is a short, sad, and arresting human document. What's daring about it for its time and makes it, in the long run, so much more subversive and unsettling than *The Cenci*, is that it shows how a nice girl can have powerful incestuous feelings for her father and that a father with a conscience—not a villain—might try to replace a wife with a budding girl and focus his life on his own child. Mary Shelley makes obvious both the latent sexual desire in a daughter's love for her father and the driving sexual passion in a father's love for the daughter. She does not "*other*" incestuous feelings. She presents with sympathy a father and daughter who feel "monstrous" erotic desire for one another, and that makes her subject deeply troubling.

She made *Mathilda* out of the emotions and experience of her life, but not simply or directly—which helps also in seeing why it matters. "I was born, and my mother died a few days after my birth" she writes on the first page.[14] But though Mary figures into her tale desires and conflicts she no doubt felt, it is no more straight autobiography than *Mansfield Park*. In the new secular world, the story psychologizes, complicates, and ultimately moves to revise the Lot myth.

X.
Mathilda's Tale

A very young man of promise, talent, and charm, raised by an indulgent, blue-stocking mother, marries Diana, a sweet, accomplished young woman of virtue. After a brief time of happiness in remote Yorkshire, they have a child, Mathilda, but the mother dies in childbirth. The devastated father, losing his beloved, cannot bear to live in Britain and gives the baby over to the care of a dour half-sister in Scotland. He disappears in his agony, wandering the world over, like some Byronic hero (and in fact Mary Shelley conceived the father in the mold of the seductive, incestuous Byron himself). Lonely Mathilda, starved for affection, lives with her aunt until puberty, dreaming and thinking about her father obsessively. When she turns 16, he suddenly returns, and the two come together like ecstatic lovers. For him she's the resurrected image of her mother, and he, youthful in form and spirit, becomes her adored Romantic hero, mentor, and friend, bringing joy and meaning to her life.

Mary Shelley, like the proto-Freudian she is, imagines the adolescent girl's psyche teeming with unconscious sexuality. She eroticizes Mathilda's language describing her paternal reunion and their delightful period of "intercourse" (her word). When she talks of leaping "in his arms," of "happiness" with him that exceeds her "sanguine expectations" ("sanguine" seems to carry here a bloody trace of the pubescent girl), of his exotic wanderings where he "penetrated" the space "of the natives with a freedom permitted to few Europeans," and of his desire to live with her on "a fertile island forever" (187), her language expresses both the innocent awakening of a girl to sex *and* the stain of sexual guilt in her after-the-fact, "polluted" (again, her word) memoir.

When the aunt dies her father takes her to into London society, and it's worth quoting Mary Shelley's exact language here because it epitomizes, at the beginning of the nineteenth century, what the requited desire of a knowledge-hungry, love-hungry, identity-hungry daughter for her father's regard might feel like:

My improvement was his delight; he was with me during all my studies and assisted or joined with me in every lesson. We saw a great deal of society, and no day passed that my father did not endeavour to embellish by some new enjoyment. The tender attachment that he bore me, and the love and veneration with which I returned it cast a charm over every moment. . . . [W]e lived more in one week than many do in the course of several months, and the variety and novelty of our pleasures gave zest to each. (190)

When a young man begins to pay court to Mathilda, the father suddenly turns cold, spurns her, and soon takes her back to Yorkshire. There his continued alienation from her and his obvious unhappiness crush the girl. He won't have anything to do with her. That leads to the climactic scene of the novel, a classic fantasy of father-daughter incest and desire. In the remarkable Chapter 5, Shelley, if you read her florid language carefully, not only makes incestuous desire literal, she also encodes incestuous orgasm symbolically. Mathilda leads her father to "a mossy hillock" in the woods (198), confronts him, and begs him to tell her what's wrong. Passionately she longs to probe his mind, possess his feelings, open him up—know him. "Alas! You have a secret grief that destroys us both. . . . Tell me, can I do nothing? You well know that on the whole earth there is no sacrifice that I would not make" (199).

"Do not urge me to your destruction," he begs her (200).

She cannot stop: "Dearest, dearest father . . . I must not be repulsed; there is one thing that although it may torture me to know, yet that you must tell me. I demand, and most solemnly I demand if in any way I am the cause of your unhappiness. . . . Ah, dearest friend! . . . Speak that word; it will bring peace, not death. If there is a chasm our mutual love will give us wings to pass it, and we shall find flowers, and verdure, and delight on the other side."

She then throws herself at this feet, grabs his hand, embraces his knees. "[I]n violent disorder," he moves away: "[Y]our words . . . will make me mad, quite mad, and then I shall utter strange words, and you will believe them, and we shall be both lost for ever."

Shelley, through Mathilda, explicitly imagines the driving power of the unconscious: "When I repeat his words I wonder at my pertinaceous folly;

I hardly know what feelings resistlessly impelled me. . . . I was led by passion and drew him with frantic heedlessness into the abyss that he so fearfully avoided." What you have is a fantasy of the daughter seducing the father, but without the guilt of conscious intent.

She emotes, swears all love for him, wails that he must hate her, and drives him over the edge:

"Yes, yes, I hate you! You are my bane, my poison, my disgust! Oh! No!" And then his manner changed, and fixing his eyes on me with an expression *that convulsed every nerve and member of my frame*—"you are not of all these; you are my light, my only one, my life.—My daughter, I love you!" The last words died away in a hoarse whisper, but I heard them and sunk on the ground, covering my face and almost dead with excess of sickness and fear: a cold perspiration covered my forehead and I shivered in every limb. (201; emphasis mine)

The father confesses in a paroxysm of grief that he wants to live entwined in his daughter's arms. What the text renders, then, is that, even against his will, he, the man who adores this girl and is responsible for her good, cannot help wanting her sexually. That idea in Mary Shelley would have huge implications and consequences for gender history down to the present.

The main sin here would seem to lie not in the father's forbidden feelings, which are beyond control, but in the irresponsibility of telling Mathilda about them. Some truths are too hard to bear/bare. His confession makes the girl whose passionate love he has aroused have to know, face the fact, and remember that her beloved father wants to conquer time and death by mating with her. He puts her on the hottest Lot spot imaginable. She can resist his tabooed desire, but since his erotic life has shaped her own, she cannot help but live in the prison of his desire. Mathilda reacts with "speechless agony" (202). Her father faints away in passionate despair, and she runs off, vowing never to see him again. What stands out in the chapter is the absolute moral code upholding the taboo on father-daughter incest together with the mutual impulse of the two characters to go against what they consciously know to be right.

That night Mathilda has a dream of her father in which she follows him to the sea and sees him plunge off a cliff. When she wakes she finds him gone, and, fearing he'll kill himself, she chases after him. Heading for the coast, she arrives to find that her father has indeed plunged into the sea and, dragged out dead, now lies on a bed in a cottage, like some giant, defunct phallus: "[T]he bed within instantly caught my eye; something stiff and straight lay on it, covered by a sheet; the cottagers looked aghast" (214).

Mathilda never recovers; as she says, "[T]he real interest of my narration is now ended," though almost half the novella remains (234). She stays fixated on her father: "I believed myself to be polluted by the unnatural love I had inspired" (238). She flees to Scotland and lonely penance. There, Woodville, an idealistic young poet whose fiancée has died, visits her. Mary Shelley doesn't bother disguising the origin of this figure: from her description, he could be named Percy. He befriends her, but in her despair, Mathilda decides they both should die in mutual suicide. Woodville then gives an impassioned Shelleyan speech inspiring her for the moment to live.

But the Lot complex holds her. She walks out into nature and thinks of her namesake in Dante's *Purgatorio*: "I pictured to myself a lovely river such as that on whose banks Dante describes Mathilda gathering flowers. . . . and thought it would be sweet when I wandered on those lovely banks to see the car of light descend with my long lost parent to be restored to me" (241).[15] Paradise, for the maiden daughter Mary Shelley imagines, means the resurrected and purified father. Mathilda's pitiful life is over. She loses her way, gets caught in a drenching rain, and catches a fatal disease. Her text, in the form of a short memoir to Woodville, ends with her imminent death.

Mary Shelley imagines a story whose concerns will reverberate again and again in the life and art of the next century: the heart that belongs to daddy can petrify like the heart of Lot's wife; the daughter's obsession with the father can be the killing backward glance that binds her to the bitter fate of Sodom and Gomorrah. The father-daughter (and older male–younger female) relationship is subject to deadly corruption. About *Mathilda* critic Anne Mellor says that at "a psychobiographical level, the novella is pure wish-fulfillment," but most of these wishes are contradictory (194). Shelley gets at logically irreconcilable, but nevertheless psychologically real, strains and veins in modern culture and society:

The "male gaze" of my father brings me to life, but the father's gaze can transfix me into an object hateful to myself.

I love my father and I want him dead.

If I loved my father enough, he would not die.

Whatever people say, you are stuck forever with your desire for a parent's love and what they can give you, and stuck too with their desire for what they wanted from you.

We must not talk about it, but I, the daughter, not only behave seductively to the father, but long to see him under my sexual power.

The father's sexual desire is dangerous, irrational, barely controllable and often horrible; it pollutes the lives of women and brings the whole world to life.

XI.
A Daughter's Curse

Girls shouldn't swear: until recently, that was a social rule. Before *Mathilda* it was a rare, almost unheard of thing in literature for a daughter to curse a father, but of course daughters often heard their fathers swear. Cursing, in fact, was (and usually still is) a sign, for good or bad, of male assertiveness training and combative will. It could imply a man's power to speak to the deity (orthodox, monotheistic faiths gendered God male), assume his voice, identify with him, and usurp his authority against your antagonists. It was the rude privilege of male ego. Mary Shelley knew what it felt like to want to curse your father, and when she imagined "a daughter's curse" in *Mathilda* it was a signal that things were changing: the daughter could appropriate the right to curse.

That "daughter's curse" still resounds. It exposes the terrible conflicts that would permeate modern family psychology. It condemns the father for his "savage" sexual urges and it pleads for age to desex him so that he can no longer menace his "child." At the same time, it pledges devotion to him. After her father shatters Mathilda's faith in him and herself by exposing his profane desire, the daughter composes her curse:

To this life, miserable father, I devote thee!—Go!—Be thy days passed with savages, and thy nights under the cope of heaven! Be thy limbs worn and thy heart chilled, and all youth be dead within thee! Let thy hairs be as snow; thy walk trembling and thy voice have lost its mellow tones! Let the liquid lustre of thine eyes be quenched; and then return to me, return to thy Mathilda, thy child, who may then be clasped in thy loved arms, while thy heart beats with sinless emotion. Go, Devoted One, and return thus!—This is my curse, and a daughter's curse: go, and return pure to thy child, who will never love aught but thee." (204)

The daughter consigns the dangerous, virile father to the wilderness of old age. As she prays for time to bring him to hoary impotence, the words express a deep fear of patriarchal sexuality, but then a huge ambivalence about the daughter's desire.

Symbolically, the curse seeks to make the patriarch senile ("all youth be dead") and the daughter infantile ("child"). It desperately beseeches a physical reality for each of them that would remove both potent male sexuality and female sexiness, with their sometimes painful, hideously improper impulses, from the father-daughter relationship. It is a pleading, feminine avowal that the daughter's natural intercourse with her father must be devoid of sex. It doesn't seem too much to ask.

But maybe it is. The wish for pre- or post-sexual being means that even among devoted family members the sex drive—repressed, sublimated, displaced, or rearing its ugly head—exists. And the very form of language shows the daughter affirming the lasting bond and identity with the father. "Devoted" describes and fits them both in the passage, and this father and this daughter, in their morbid devotion to one another, are each other's curse. The daughter's curse finds and condemns physical incest even though the erotic life of the father forms inevitably her own erotic bent and becomes for her the only model of true love. Psychologically, that is her "curse." The father is irreplaceable and the permanent focus of desire. The problem this curse reveals is not assault and harassment by an evil, detestable man, like Cenci, but the overwhelming of a good man's moral will by the anarchic force of eros. The simultaneous banishment of the father and wished-for union with him points up inherent sexual discontents in nature, civilization, and families. Erotic tension, whatever form it takes, is liable to exist or develop between fathers with libidos and sexually maturing daughters. *Mathilda*'s "curse" stands for, bemoans, and tries to deal with, and heal, the awful power of sex to destroy rational life. Ironically it conveys exactly the same skeptical female attitude towards the physical imperatives of sexuality that the telling old slang term for menstruation, "the curse," does: in effect, you can't keep the blood from flowing and rising, but what a pity! And yet this daughter's curse also seeks both the father's salvation and his selfless love.

With "a daughter's curse," Mary was responding directly to the father's horrible curse in *The Cenci*. There her husband had taken King Lear's curse of the vicious Goneril and reshaped it into the depraved utterance of the incestuous count. Percy makes Cenci rant as if the spirit of a Marquis de Sade had taken over the role of Lear—and it has. The father's curse here bespeaks sadism, misogyny, and an insanely jealous hatred of fecundity. It makes incestuous rape the sign of absolute power corrupting absolutely, and it reads like a perverse cities-of-the-plain anthem. Shelley's Cenci lets loose a verbal avalanche of resentment against anything that subordinates the desperate libido of an aging man to the interest of future generations, or sexual acts and desires to the purpose of procreation. Look how the imagery of his speech moves to recreate the biblical catastrophe, turn the daughter into Lot's wife, and the daughter's progeny into the very essence of human accursedness:

> If this most specious mass of flesh,
> Which thou hast made my daughter; this my blood,
> This particle of my divided being;
>
> . . .
>
> Which sprung from me as from a hell, was meant
> To aught good use; if her bright loveliness
> Was kindled to illumine this dark world;
> If nursed by the selectest dew of love
> Such virtues blossom in her as should make
> The peace of life, I pray thee for my sake,
>
> . . .
>
> That if she have a child . . .
> . . . May it be
> A hideous likeness of herself, that as
> From a distorting mirror, she may see
> Her image mixed with what she most abhors,
> Smiling upon her from her nursing breast. (4.1.133–172)

In the *Cenci* version of the Lot complex, then, patriarchy—in the form of this wicked father—is an incestuous curse to be cursed. The ideological appeal of this judgment would become powerful and useful for many reformers—especially in the later half of the twentieth century. Paternal rape and incest as the ultimate example of sexual victimization could and would be seen as both evidence and a trope of the oppression of women. Bringing to light incest would move people to support the cause of liberation.

But for Mary Shelley, the paternal curse that *The Cenci* dramatizes, though real and terrible, was not the curse that most daughters had to face and live with. In Mathilda's "curse" and case, the daughter still cannot help wanting to swear allegiance to the father because it's through the mirror of his regard that she first sees that she's lovable and gets her own special identity and worth; it's through him also that she first imagines the intellectual possibilities and fullness of a life beyond the conventional woman's lot. She hopes that time will emasculate his gaze, take away his power, but reunite them.

The daughter's curse hangs over the age to come. It stresses the place and power of sex—it may even be said to privilege the importance of sexual thoughts and desire in the manner of Freud and much twentieth-century psychology. It makes the control of male sexuality crucial to women, to the family, and to the survival of intergenerational harmony. Though the physical act of sex does not literally occur here, the curse nevertheless focuses on the reality and force of incestuous erotic attraction. Mary Shelley finds incestuous sex, with the emotions and thoughts it arouses, the human experience that epitomizes the vulnerability of women, the potential for moral degeneration in family structure, and the need to control raw male lust. In *Mathilda*, however, the issue is not simply power and its perversions, as in *The Cenci*, but being in love with the father and facing up to the fact that the father's genuine love—even against his own wishes—might sometimes involve sexual feeling. Mathilda's curse shows how you need strategies that will divert and police this love, but what's fascinating is that it still leaves the daughter's relationship with the beloved father the most important thing in her life. It expresses both hope for life-with-the-father and a crippling psychological form of infantile paralysis.

To sum up: you can read in this Lot-complex curse ways of altering, displacing, and surviving the erotics of incestuous desire that social history has by now made familiar. It makes the daughter morally superior to the father, but it appeals to his moral responsibility and sympathy. It makes her his teacher, and it stresses his guilt. It identifies and warns of some primitive, animal quality in the father, but makes the domestic world a desirable haven of peace and civilization: rationally the man should want to protect and join it. Rhetorically the curse conjures up for the father the image and identity of the daughter as a child, an innocent being who doesn't naturally arouse sexual desire in a mature man—that is, it previews the coming popular ideology of the purifying girlchild ("return pure to thy child"). It vents hostility against the father's body and, as both a personal and historical metaphor fulfilling the daughter's wish, it imagines the decrepitude of the patriarch. It also seems to threaten him with death for his misbehavior, and it features, with the stress on the age difference and the father's physical deterioration, the grotesquerie of old-young erotics. But what it offers the father is the daughter's care, moral absolution, and undying devotion—his preservation through her love and agency. Finally and prophetically, the curse, whose imagery recalls the dramatic vision of old Oedipus at Colonus succored by his daughters, rewrites Oedipus into Lot: for Mary Shelley, the unfolding story of Oedipal sexual guilt and gender relations lies in the problematic history of father-daughter love and bonding.

XII.
'Mathilda' Suppressed

The fate of *Mathilda*, the material book itself, can stand for much of the story's real significance in the following two centuries. It had a hard time coming to light. Mary sent it back to England for her father to read and publish through Godwin's firm. He didn't publish it. He thought highly of parts of it, but he found the subject "disgusting and detestable."[16] She asked him to revise it and publish it or return it to her. He refused and kept it. After Percy Shelley's death she returned to England and reunited with her father. She lived near him and they met almost every day. She wrote and worked to pay his debts as well as her own, and they were very close in his old age. The benevolent part of her "curse" came true, and she no longer thought it prudent to publish *Mathilda*. The manuscript stayed buried in Godwin's papers. Years later, it was deposited by the Shelley heirs in the Bodleian Library, where it remained unpublished until Elizabeth Nitchie dug it out for publication in an obscure academic edition in 1959 (a year after the American publication of *Lolita*). It was soon went out of print until 1990, and only lately is it getting much scholarly attention.

In truth, like Jane Austen and her character Fanny Price, and unlike poor Mathilda, Mary Shelley, through her imagination and life, made out of the evolving Lot complex an opportunity for the change and development her expanding feminine soul craved. I want, therefore, to give the last word on *Mathilda* and all that little book might mean for modernity to Jane Austen (who of course never read it). In *Northanger Abbey*, her hero

Henry Tilney is inventing and parodying gothic fiction for the impression-able, novel-loving heroine Catherine Morland. Henry is mocking some silly scene in which a girl rummaging in drawers comes upon "a roll of pa-per": "[Y]ou seize it—it contains many sheets of manuscript . . . 'Oh! thou —whomsoever thou mayst be, into whose hands these memoirs of the wretched Matilda may fall.'"[17] Even a decade or so before Mary Shelley, the name Matilda has become a cliché for put-upon female figures in popular gothic thrillers, and Henry finds the whole business of reshaping old plots of terrorized women for the delectation of a modern young woman a comic business. Catherine longs for him to go on, but he then is "obliged to entreat her to use her own fancy in the perusal of Matilda's woes." The con-junction of Austen's wry hopefulness, "Matilda's woes," and the need to use the fancy you can bring to the texts of the past, makes a good framework for investigating the working of the Lot complex and images of Lot's daugh-ters in the modern age.

Chapter 7

The Cave and the Mask

THE BRONTËS

Charlotte and Emily Brontë preserved the seed of their father Patrick in writing, most notably in their famous novels *Jane Eyre* and *Wuthering Heights*. In literary history there is no more pregnant, courageous, or painful example of the Lot complex at work, no clearer instance of its cultural force and influence in modern times than in the life and novels of the great Brontë sisters. They were daughters—and mothers—of genius. But their importance transcends literary history. What they uttered from behind the mask of Victorian patriarchy shaped the imagination of the future.

I.
The Father

I told them all to stand and speak boldly
from under the cover of the mask.

—Patrick Brontë

Patrick Brontë (1777–1861) had the seeds of greatness in him, and his daughters made them live. He came to England out of Ireland and lower-class life. His people were story-telling peasants, tenant farmers, traders, day-laborers, and their women—flowers born to blush unseen. There's little hard information about his early years. What is known comes from a few recorded facts, Brontë family lore, and the speculations of various Brontë biographers.[1] The chances that Patrick Brunty (or "Prunty"—the spelling is uncertain) would become an educated gentleman were one in a thousand; that he would be remembered in the twenty-first century, close to nil. What he did was at least as hard to bring off as the comparable achievement of a poor, black Mississippi sharecropper boy last century who made it to Harvard, joined the professional class, and became a leader. Born poor in a thatched, mud-floor cottage in County Down, raised up in hungry Ireland on "fadge" potatoes and oatmeal, he was the eldest child of barely literate parents: a tale-spinning Protestant father and a mother who may have come from Catholic stock. Through brains, imagination, ambition, and luck he learned to read, got some education, got religion (Wesleyan Protestantism), developed a lifelong passion for letters, taught and ran a school, miraculously won sponsorship and entrance to Cambridge, changed his name and land, and became an Evangelical minister of the Church of England, a published, if undistinguished, author, and the enabling father of as amazingly creative a set of daughters as the world has seen.

1.

EARLY LIFE

For a laboring Irish boy to become a successful clergyman and jump class in nineteenth-century England took talent, discipline, and a will to compromise and repress natural impulses. First-generation success requires the emotional sacrifice and exile from the personal past. It means being a slayer of old loyalties and desires within yourself. A dramatic rise in the world doesn't prove you've sold out, but it does mean you've paid an awful toll.

Patrick was a precocious reader, and when he was only 16, he decided he could run a school. A gifted teacher, he did so successfully for five years.[2] But pedagogy, as life and books teach (Charlotte Brontë's, for instance), can lead to erotics. The story goes that when he was 21, one of his students, a nubile 15-year-old named Helen, fell in love with him. They were caught kissing, and some amorous poems of his were found in her pockets. Her father put a quick end to the affair. But by then Patrick had won the regard of the most important man in the district, Thomas Tighe, an influential vicar who had been a disciple of John Wesley. Tighe chose him to tutor his sons and then offered him an extraordinary chance: if Patrick would follow the righteous Christian path and agree to work for the revitalized faith as an ordained minister, Tighe would smooth the way for him at the advanced age of 25 to become an undergraduate at Cambridge and find a vocation and preferment in the Church. That happened.

What enabled Patrick to better himself so remarkably was the Evangelical religion he embraced. It was the way out and up for him, but he was no hypocrite; he believed it to be the foundation for moral life and salvation. Nevertheless, that religion and his vocation worked to condemn and divert his real passion for the world, the flesh, and the tempting devil of his romantic imagination. The key to understanding the soul that generated his daughters' genius is to see that he loved the world of secular education, politics, and military power; loved the flesh of erotic life; and loved the dazzling, dangerous words of profane literature.

At Cambridge, where he changed his name to Brontë, he was caught up in England's struggle with France. He came to identify strongly with the two great warriors who beat Napoleon: Admiral Nelson—after Trafalgar, made Duke of Brontë—and, most significantly, the great Irish soldier and savior of the English, Arthur Wellesley, the Duke of Wellington. Martial matters fascinated him. Later, as a clergyman in the North, he was involved in pacifying the Luddite rebellion. Charlotte Brontë's novel *Shirley* features the workers' uprisings and the political and military maneuverings in 1812 Yorkshire where her father had found himself in the midst of raging public conflict. It takes much of its complex social vision from Patrick's experience and imagination, and it clearly shows the tension in him between an allegiance to the world and an allegiance to piety.

That tension shows in another vein. When he was a newly ordained curate and courting pretty Mary Burder, who loved him, he wrote her a poem for her 18th birthday. He begins by celebrating the day and her beauty. Soon, though, the verse lapses into religious scare tactics that might give a girl pause:

> Full soon, your eyes of sparkling blue,
> And velvet lips, of scarlet hue,
> Discoloured, may decay.
> As bloody drops, on virgin snows,
> So vies the lily with the rose,
> Full on your dimpled cheek;
> But, ah! the worm in lazy coil,
> May soon prey on this putrid spoil.[3]

Happy birthday, sweetheart! They didn't marry.

Patrick had a passion—even a vocation—for literature, but it was a guilty passion; he had to censor and make safe what he wrote. In 1811 he published his *Cottage Poems*, a small collection of didactic verse. His writing is spoiled by the verbal smog of piety, but he can't keep his pride and joy in writing from showing through: "When released from his clerical avocations, he was occupied in writing the Cottage Poems; from morning till noon, and from noon till night, his employment was full of real, indescribable pleasures, such as he could wish to taste as long as life lasts" (Lock and Dixon, 98).

In 1815 he wrote a preachy little narrative, *The Cottage in the Wood*, about a cottager who discovers a rich, drunken young man in trouble. The youth falls in love with Mary, the rustic's daughter, whom he tries to seduce. She rejects him in disgust. Later, she inherits a thousand pounds and devotes herself to good Christian works. The man continues drinking away his life. One night lightning strikes an oak tree under which he and two friends are carousing. The other two are killed, but he's spared; and with the help of Mary, he accepts Jesus Christ and reforms. After passing all the tests of Evangelical orthodoxy, he at last wins Mary, and they spend a blessed married life together.

Brief as it is, this banal parable is virtually unreadable—even my dreary summary makes it sound better than it is. Nevertheless, its plot and pattern mark it as a key source for *Jane Eyre*. Later, Patrick would make sure that his children knew his literary work, and, though generally ignored, its influence on them was considerable. Since they didn't have to uphold clerical orthodoxy, they could use the hollowness in his writings as breeding space for their imagination.

In particular, his writing stimulated Charlotte's literary bent. In the poem "Winter-Night Meditations," for instance, he writes in detail of a faithless whore:

> Through her, the marriage vows are broke,
> And Hymen proves a galling yoke.
> Diseases come, destructions dealt,
> Where'er her poisonous breath is felt,
> Whilst she, poor wretch, *dies in the flame.*
> [emphasis mine][4]

Patrick Brontë calls this strumpet "Maria" (by chance, that would be the name of both his wife and first-born daughter). Imagine the reaction of Charlotte reading this poem, showing as it does a prurient fascination with sexuality joined with a fierce moralistic bent. Compare this verse to Charlotte's description of the debauched Bertha Mason and her fiery death in *Jane Eyre* and you can see how the father's writing could work on the daughter.

2.

A NEW LOT

It's easy to see Patrick Brontë as a new Lot. He separates from his kin and heritage. He leaves Ireland and moves to an England comparatively prosperous and, at first, flowing with opportunity. In 1812 he woos and marries Maria Branwell, an Englishwoman. It's a love match. Patrick, approaching middle age, proceeds to father six children in six years: Maria (1814), Elizabeth (1815), Charlotte (1816), Patrick Branwell (called Branwell, 1817), Emily (1818), and Anne (1820).

Money for a parson is always tight, but, in the Evangelical North of his new land, he finds a living in the Church, gains respect, makes friends, publishes newspaper articles and letters as well as his moral poems and stories. In 1818, he published his longest fiction, *The Maid of Kilarney; or, Albion and Flora*, expressing his political and religious ideas. What gives the book its shape, however, is a love story set in a dreamy, mystical Irish realm, and that romantic bent would touch his children. Brontë, as perpetual curate, took over the parsonage at Haworth in 1820 and in the next year, came disaster. His wife died miserably from cancer, leaving six motherless children. The family desolation was terrible. Charlotte, barely 5, and Emily, only 3, found bitter salt indeed, and the ache and rage of orphanhood drive all their novels. Having no mother can mean hell on earth—the reign of death and the rain of brimstone. Brontë psychology in part turned into Dead Sea territory, where for evermore you had to fear and wait for the aftershocks of God's devastation.

Patrick's biographers call him "a man of sorrow," and that describes him pretty well in the long, definitive period beginning with the death of his wife. This passionate man was left alone and celibate. He sought a wife and a mother for his children, but three women turned him down. He was too poor and had too big a family. As far as he had come, he was still a marginal figure, Irish, living up in Yorkshire in shabby gentility, fixed in a vocation that makes heavy demands and offers little pay. He continued to carry out his duties and obligations responsibly, but sometimes he lapsed into deep depression and hypochondria. His melancholy was tempered by his affection for his children, but his own ambitious dreams of flourishing success in a land of promise were over. The Haworth parsonage at intervals sparkled with his fitful inspiration and the life of his brilliant children, but often it resembled a gloomy cave. Like Oedipus, Lear, and Milton, among others, Patrick Brontë would move into old age menaced by blindness and dependent in dark times on daughters.

That household offers a particularly striking instance of a Lot complex in full swing. Had Mrs. Brontë lived, it's unlikely *Jane Eyre* or *Wuthering Heights* could or would have been written. No wife or mother mediated between the father and children or served as a role model for the girls.[5] There was no maternal lightning rod to defuse the inner emotional fires and fantasies he set burning in the siblings. For them, he was a magnetic, if sometimes distant personality, and like most parents he had his rages and oddities.

Mercurial, Patrick could be very aloof, but then suddenly he would zoom in and focus on his children and their souls. He would preach dread, but give them libertine Byron to read; spout Tory doctrine, but push liberal causes and expose them to radical writings; condemn the world, but instill in them his passion for politics, books, and the glories of nature. A conservative with a deep sense of original sin, he embraced radical, Rousseau-like ideas of education. He would treat his daughters with warmth and coldness, neglect and concern, love and indifference; he would make probing raids into their lives and minds, then retreat into seclusion.

By fits and starts, he rallied to believe that he would live on not only through God, but through his offspring. He would try to form and guide these intelligent beings—educate them as he had wanted to be educated, find their special talents, feed their imaginations, tell them stories (many from his own past), get them to read widely and freely, train them to articulate what was deep and true in themselves. He failed with his wastrel son, but not with his daughters.

3.
THE FATHER'S MASK

Many years later, after all his children had died, the father reported an episode that became famous. Whether or not it happened as he said, Patrick's family catechism comes across now with historic force and meaning.

When my children were very young, when, as far as I can remember, the oldest was about ten years of age, and the youngest about four, thinking that they knew more than I had yet discovered, in order to make them speak with less timidity, I deemed that if they were put under a sort of cover I might gain my end; and happening to have a mask in the house, I told them all to stand and speak boldly from under the cover of the mask.

I began with the youngest (Anne, afterwards Acton Bell), and asked what a child like her most wanted; she answered, "Age and experience." I asked the next (Emily, afterwards Ellis Bell), what I had best do with her brother Branwell, who was sometimes a naughty boy; she answered, "Reason with him, and when he won't listen to reason, whip him." I asked Branwell what was the best way of knowing the difference between the intellects of men and women; he answered, "By considering the difference between them as to their bodies." I then asked Charlotte what was the best book in the world; she answered, "The Bible." And what was the next best; she answered, "The Book of Nature." I then asked the next what was the best mode of education for a woman; she [Elizabeth] answered, "That which would make her rule her house well." Lastly, I asked the oldest [Maria] what was the best mode of spending time; she answered, "By laying it out in preparation for a happy eternity." I may not have given precisely their words, but I have nearly done so, as they made a deep and lasting impression on my memory. The substance, however, was exactly what I have stated.[6]

Patriarchy can be a helpful term and concept, but it loses explanatory power, loses its potential to expand knowledge and understanding, if it's only used to mean *bad, bad, bad*—just an evil system by which men, for their own selfish ends, have run the world and oppressed women and children. Patriarchs have made and shaped history because life and motherhood were precarious, and the power and the laws of fathers did sometimes seem to work to develop the existence, maintenance, spread, and development of humanity and its capabilities. First comes the crude structures of enduring life; then the refinement of morality and justice becomes possible. Patriarchy, however, is not one unchanging thing, but a historical process. If you look closely at the father's interrogation and the Brontë children's responses from behind the mask, you get a defining, symbolic image of the nature of patriarchy in the nineteenth century and a social structure ripe for change and reform. It's a family affair, but family affairs are mutable and resonant.

Patrick's strategy follows the Lot pattern. It's like a juvenile, domestic version of the start of *King Lear* featuring the father's questioning of the daughters from which all the action plays out: "What shall Cordelia say?" What shall Charlotte and Emily say? The darkness of Lot's cave finds an analogue in the Brontë mask. Small and vulnerable people in the world require cover. They need safety devices and strategies that will let them hide in order to get at, face, and tell the truth—as, for instance, confession booths, psychiatrists' inner offices, "truth" serums, hypnosis, and, most definitely, the institutions of the art of fiction (literature, drama, cinema, videos, hypertexts) all prove.

Imagine the mask scene, and you can see how prophetic it is. It seethes with inventive talent, sibling rivalry, and subtle mind-games that potentially could boomerang on the father. The widower senses depths and essences in his children that they either keep from him or can't express. His grief has put him out of touch. He's lonely and wants to know them better. The father wants to lay bare the core of their being—make them see, hear, and define themselves to him and each other. And—more—he wants to project what he will discover.

In his clerical garb, he herds his charges into the parlor, lines them up by age: *Stand up, put the mask before your face, and answer when I question you.* Imagine them shuffling, bouncing around nervously, getting scared waiting their turn. Branwell pokes a sister and pinches another (see the father's question to Emily). Some fun. But maybe it *was* fun. Maybe the charade of play, the bizarre mask, the unpredictable behavior of the father make them feel *we're something special; no family's like us; father's playing with us, paying attention, putting us—putting me—at the center of things; he cares about me. I count. I have my place and role.* One lesson for the siblings, of course, is *disguise can lead to truth; a structure of fiction and play can get at basic realities.* Another is *I'm playing my father's game. I'm speaking through his mask.* When people question children, whether they know it or not, they generally like to play the ventriloquist before anatomically and neurologically correct, intuitively obedient dummies.

He begins with Anne. To her being identified as "a child like her" must mean the littlest, *the youngest girl.* Sibling position in the family can determine identity and destiny. The question fixes on the girl a sense of her life as desire—*what do you want?*—and incompleteness—*a being like you must certainly lack and need something.* She doesn't think or dare to answer what she misses in her life: *a mother.* She has no choice, no incentive of memory to look back. Her life, her future, lies with the father. Her answer, "Age and experience," is ironic; they are what Anne, dead at 29, would never have. But what would be enough age? What would be the right experience? How can a little girl get attention? It was a daughter's dilemma. One meaning of the response is, of course, *I want to be like you.* In this setting, only her father has "age and experience."

Next comes Emily. Her reply to the father could stand as an epithet for one strain in modern feminism: *reason with him, and if he will not listen to reason, whip him.* The question of what to do with a naughty boy challenges her, a 6-year-old girl, to assume the paternal role and responsibility. In context, it reveals a conjunction that exists in the father's mind between his only son and Emily. It's also the father's most personal, least abstract question. It's both flattering and demeaning. It suggests an implicit closeness, a conspiracy, conscious or not, between the father and Emily, but it also centers on the boy, rather than on her, and makes her a mediator—her brother's keeper—in life's business. He doesn't ask her, *when* you *are naughty, what should I do?* His words define her specifically by her relationship to himself and Branwell. The question presupposes, however, that Emily could easily put herself in her father's shoes and both comprehend a boy's misbehavior and imagine using male authority to discipline and punish for the sake of long-term good. It implies, *I trust you; you could be like me.* Her answer, which comes like a lash, epitomizes the spirit of *Wuthering Heights* (where Catherine Earnshaw, asked by her father what she'd like for a present, answers, "a whip"). It gets at Emily's hardness and freedom from sentimentality. It also gets at that cruel streak in her that rages to hurt the hurt of existence. Her words would be unthinkable for her sisters, who suppress and/or displace their cruelty and anger. The reply shows a manifest desire to *whip* boys in every sense of the word. In front of her older brother, she dares to say he must be good or be beaten. Emily's answer from behind the mask lacks the tact of conventional Victorian femininity. It sounds virile.

The father, however, speaking in front of all his daughters, asserts the difference between the minds of men and women and asks Branwell how we can know about these differences. The father's question assumes it's up to males to speak authoritatively on gender matters. Historically, sex was what both fathers and "naughty" boys like Branwell got to talk about and define. That's one practical lesson for the girls here. Branwell's answer, in effect, "look at bodies," implies *anatomy is destiny.* But how would the 7-year-old naughty boy know anything about bodies? From living, sleeping, and playing with so many sisters in close quarters, of course. Siblings are curious about bodies, and in this question and reply, you can begin to imagine the real nineteenth-century domestic seedbed out of which twentieth-century psychoanalytic theories of "infantile sexuality" (its formative importance on personality) and the so-called "phallocentric" nature of "the symbolic order" (i.e., *language*) would develop. In this scene, the son wears the father's mask as a sex and gender expert. *Wuthering Heights* and *Jane Eyre* would offer evidence of how provocative that pose and subject could be—how much resentment, sibling envy, and creative interest the alleged differences in mind and body might stir in the sisters' minds.[7]

The question to Charlotte, *what's the best book?*, singles her out as the family literary agent. It suggests her vocation for literature. The right book is the proper response to the father—the right answer. Value lies in literary achievement, and, in her answer, religion and being are transformed into texts. She sees God as an author. Her words transmute faith, nature, and God (the subject and author of the Bible) into writing, and later, in her novels, she'll seek to do the same. Her familial role, her father, ambition, religion, nature, and desire are all bound up for Charlotte with letters and writing. To be a knowing reader of God's work and then a writer who can make existence vivid is a way of assuming almost divine powers and of transcending the sex and gender problems implicit in the previous question and Branwell's answer. Life can be made into books and literary competition, and a girl can be a bookish star.

The next question, for Elizabeth, about female education, opens up what would be called *the Woman Question*. Her answer that a girl should prepare to rule her home well previews the Victorian ideology of the separate, domestic sphere for women, and woman as queen of the house. But in this family context, Elizabeth's home rule looks very much like a poor consolation prize.

The question to the eldest, Maria, the father's pride and joy and his right-hand girl, whom the whole family adored as a good and kind—almost holy—little mother-substitute and a prodigy (Charlotte would base the martyr Helen Burns in *Jane Eyre* on her), elicits a saint's response and the ultimate Christian solace. For a churchman wracked by death, hers is the winning answer. The reply, however, also marks a retreat from the world. As a climax of Papa's anecdote, Maria's response may leave him on the road to heaven, but it comes close to fixing the post-maternal life of the Brontës in the realm of a death-wish. Life behind the paternal mask was anything but a carnival.

This family was looking for other worlds, and Brontë, remember, was a great teacher. You have here in the father's mask experiment a remarkable meta-fiction governing the fate of the family and the daughters' imaginative output. You have also significant historical patterns for female lives: a girl may be small and quiet, and look up to her father; a girl may be smart as a whip, tough-minded, firm, rational, passionate, and vengeful, and she may serve as a potent alter-ego to her father; a girl may become the master of arts and letters her father dreamed of being; a girl may preside over the home for her father's comfort; a girl may be an angel in the house (or under a gravestone) who takes away the sins of the father. Each question masks a paternal desire, and each answer offers a means to fulfill it. Every teacher, pollster, and lawyer knows the questions you ask determine the answers you get; the father sires the different responses, scattering seeds in his children's short lives. He himself wanted a mask to speak through, and in his progeny he got it.

The relationship between imagination and reality, however, is always two-way. Patrick Brontë remembered and wrote down the mask scene long after his daughters were dead and their novels published. Their books, in turn, helped to form what *he* recalled. His recreated overview of them speaking from behind the mask was, no doubt, partly determined by their later work. The child may be father of the man, but the father may be the child of the girl who grows articulate and influential. There is no living past, no enduring consciousness, no memory that does not somehow depend on the pre-existing, artful language of creative imagination—on stories.

4.
IN THE SHADOW OF DEATH,
THE FATHER'S GIFT

Shortly after the mask scene, the Brontë death march continued. Patrick, wanting formal education for his children, sent the four eldest girls to Cowan Bridge, a new school for clergymen's daughters founded by Carus Wilson, an Evangelical with a fanatical disdain for the flesh (condemned for the ages in *Jane Eyre* as "Brocklehurst"). There, according to Charlotte, saintly Maria was horribly mistreated, and her sisters had to watch her suffer. Both Maria and Elizabeth fell badly ill. Taken back to Haworth, Maria died, and, within weeks, Elizabeth followed. Fetched home by Patrick, Charlotte and Emily avoided sickness, but again death had ravaged the family. To be a Brontë after this was to live life as if it were always under deadly siege. Charlotte, with survivor's guilt, now became the eldest daughter. She, explicitly, and Emily, implicitly, would imagine their sisters' deaths as barbarous sacrifices condoned by religious authority; and they would both put cruelty to children at the heart of their fiction.

Patrick Brontë's two great gifts to the children—gifts they needed to bear their excruciating losses—were to make them know, first, that they mattered—that to be a Brontë was something important—and, second, that a lively mind could expand life and make it fascinating. Directly or indirectly, by encouraging free mental play and honoring letters and arts, he let them know that it was good to fantasize—to make, play with, and take seriously imaginary figures. Whatever his faults as a father and man, whatever just and unjust resentments he provoked, he enabled and empowered his children to make up stories and to create alternative lives and worlds. Against the dogma of his own religious sect, he sanctioned their fantasy lives.

What children do and are is often what the parents wished to do and be but had to suppress. The father longed to express himself though the mask of fiction, and he wanted to command troops, follow adventures, and govern affairs of state. He put his faith in the Duke of Wellington. The making of the Brontë children's Angria and Gondal (the invented realms of their collective, ongoing juvenile writings that, for more than a decade, shaped the core of their inner lives) and then the making of their poetry and romantic tales both developed quite literally out of the soldiers, dolls, figures, and toys that Patrick would bring home to them from time to time. You can see how his seed germinates in the account Charlotte Brontë gives of how she and her brother and sisters began their authorial lives:

Our plays were established: *Young Men*, June 1826; *Our Fellows*, July 1827; *Islanders*, December 1827. Those are our three great plays that are not kept secret. Emily's and my bed plays were established the 1st December 1827, the others March 1828. Bed plays mean secret plays; they are very nice ones. All our plays are very strange ones. Their nature I need not write on paper for I think I shall always remember them. I will sketch out the origin of our plays more explicitly if I can.

. . . Papa bought Branwell some soldiers from Leeds. When Papa came home it was night and we were in bed, so next morning Branwell came to our door with a box of soldiers. Emily and I jumped out of bed, and I snatched up one and exclaimed, "This is the Duke of Wellington! It shall be mine!" When I said this, Emily likewise took one and said it should be hers. When Anne came down she took one also. Mine was the prettiest of the whole and perfect in every part. Emily's was a grave-looking fellow. We called him "Gravey." Anne's was a queer little thing, very much like herself. He was called "Waiting Boy." Branwell chose "Bonaparte."[8]

Charlotte and Emily, and for a while Branwell, turned the father's presents—not just his toy soldiers, but also his interests, opinions, lore, memories, pain, passion, and conflicted, personality—into the source of their texts. The man fathered six children and had to bury every one of them. He didn't have a single grandchild. But his progeny lives in the radiant fiction of his daughters.

II.
The Older Daughter

"Do you think because I am poor, obscure, plain and little,
I am heartless and soulless? You think wrong!"

—Charlotte Brontë

Charlotte Brontë (1816–1856) had a loving, murderous, and incestuous genius. She wanted to embrace her father's life—to make it her own—and she wanted to transform it too. By her own account, her creative life began with the toy-soldier fetishizing of her father ("the Duke of Wellington") and then her projection of him into her first writings. Her mother was a gaping blank in her mind. To be a female in this family was to risk disappearing. All Charlotte consciously remembered about her mother was an image of the ill woman being carried downstairs to play with Branwell—*not* with the daughter, that is, but with the son, the male. After Mother Maria died in 1821, daughter Maria, the father's favorite, got even closer to him. Charlotte's life and writings indicate a needy child longing to be Daddy's girl, the chosen one; it's likely that she never got over her resentment that Maria was Patrick's first daughter.

1.

RAGING AMBITION AND
GIVING GOOD DAUGHTER

Something in the traumatic history of Charlotte's early life made her realize that you could die for—even want to kill for—your father's undivided attention and approval. She wanted Maria's privileged place, and the ghastly family tragedy at Cowan Bridge School left her the eldest child. It also left her with survivor guilt that needed to be assuaged. Homicidal impulses might come true, and such impulses, the dark side of highly competitive people, need to be sublimated and justified in righteousness. From her early school days she remembered and took to heart two things that shaped her vision: the evil reality of child abuse (on which she could blame the death of Maria) *and* a chain of events that eliminated rivals.

The loss of the sisters on top of the mother's also left her with stored-up infantile anger. *Jane Eyre*, *Shirley*, and *Villette* indicate how Charlotte's mind could rage at her sense of abandonment, at her father's inability to protect and save his daughters. Such anger could only be diffused in fantasy and art. She was susceptible to hero-worship, and her father was her first hero; but she wished him younger, closer to her, and better than he was. Loving the father, but resenting him could and would cause great conflicts in her life and work. She wanted both his sanction and her own autonomy. She longed to do what he admired, did, and wanted to do—write and preach morality—but deep down she also wanted also to punish, reform, and surpass him. Words and stories might be the means to honor the father, gain the authority she craved, and assert her independence.

Her childhood, then, left her split: in both fact and fiction, she had a tendency to fawn over older men (the way to power and love lay in pleasing them), but, as Matthew Arnold saw, she was also full of "hunger, rebellion, and rage."[9] The vacuum of the absent mother and the intimidating authority of the father would never stop troubling her, but in fiction she could identify with a father-figure, make her young heroine fall in love with him and gain his total devotion (and, along the way, also make him suffer for his sins). Charlotte would follow that pattern again and again. "The loves of her life," says Irene Tayler, "had been her father and her dreams,"[10] and in novels she found a way to bring them together as she liked.

Some years ago, a comparatively young and inexperienced female lawyer was nominated Attorney General on the advice of an aging Secretary of State because, a cynic said, *she gave good daughter*. Charlotte Brontë would have understood. Giving "good daughter" for an ambitious young woman means using and winning the father over in order to preserve and then possess the seed of power. When 20-year-old Charlotte was still deep in Angria, she wrote the Poet Laureate Robert Southey, pouring her heart out about her literary hopes and sending him some verses. The great man, replied—but with a wet blanket:

The day dreams in which you habitually indulge are likely to induce a distempered state of mind. . . . Literature cannot be the business of a woman's life, and it ought not to be. The more she is engaged in her proper duties, the less leisure will she have for it. . . .

Write poetry for its own sake; not in a spirit of emulation, and not with a view to celebrity. . . .

Farewell, madam. It is not because I have forgotten that I was once young myself, that I write to you in this strain; but because I remember it.[11]

Charlotte replied by return mail, not with "Thanks for nothing, Mr. Pompous Piggy Poet—I hope you go blind," but with obsequious verbal curtseys of gratitude for getting attention and a straight answer from such a celebrity. She moves to bind with the powerful older man, play the good girl, invoke the father, and yet still go on doing what she wants to do— write with the approbation of authority:

You do not forbid me to write; you do not say that what I write is utterly destitute of merit. . . . I know the first letter I wrote to you was all senseless trash from beginning to end; but I am not altogether the idle dreaming being it would seem to denote. My father is a clergyman of limited, though competent, income, and I am the eldest of his children. . . . Following my father's advice—who from my childhood had counseled me just in the wise and friendly tone of your letter— I have endeavoured not only attentively to observe all duties a woman ought to fulfill, but to feel deeply interested in them. I don't always succeed, for sometimes when I'm teaching or sewing I would rather be reading or writing; but I try to deny myself; and my father's approbation amply rewarded me for the privation. Once more allow me to thank you with sincere gratitude. I trust I shall never more feel ambitious to see my name in print; if the wish should rise I'll look at Southey's letter, and suppress it. It is honour enough for me that I have written to him, and received an answer.[12]

That might seem to be laying it on a bit thick, but not at all: he wrote back inviting her to visit him in the Lake Country. Later, at the height of her fame, she told Elizabeth Gaskell about Southey, but she said that at the time of his letter she didn't have the money to go to the Lakes. With sweet irony —an irony that flashes on the fictional fates Charlotte often imagines for those who cross her heroines—Gaskell writes, "At the time we conversed together on the subject we were at the Lakes. But Southey was dead" (176).

2.

BECOMING THE ELDEST,
BECOMING CHARLOTTE BRONTË

Not until the death of her sisters in 1825, nine years after Charlotte was born, did she become the eldest daughter. She spent the rest of her life making up for lost time, taking the lead, helping her father organize the family and household, striving to better herself, mediating, inventing worlds in stories, coordinating the children's fantasies, planning their careers, prodding them to publish, pushing herself to the fore, representing them, contacting powerful literary men, nursing her father and her own reputation, winning the approval of the world, and preserving the Brontë name. She and Branwell got the siblings writing; she kept them going; and she made herself judge of their work and their reputations.

The story of Charlotte—the end of her desire—is the making of books. She seemed to abstract every reverie, every throb of hope and despair, every slight, every pain and pleasure that touched her and then write them down, She lived to make fiction out of her sense impressions, and her vivid imagination was erotic and even transgressive. She colonized everyone and everything in her life to make her stories.

Little is more suggestive in the Brontë saga than that report of Charlotte's (quoted by Gaskell) of her conspiracy with Emily to create "bed plays." "Bed plays mean secret plays; they are very nice ones." That comes across as a classic moment of daughterly Lot-complex conception. This "bed" is surely the seed-bed of *Jane Eyre* and *Wuthering Heights*. It may seem tediously post-Freudian to read these early Victorian words as somehow erotic and sensual: the sublimation of infantile sexuality into textuality—*play* to *plays*. And yet: *bed play means secret play and is very nice, very strange; it's nature is indelible*—that's not a bad epigram for the two most famous Brontë novels. Imagine the context: two motherless, budding geniuses, 11 and 9, share a bed. In their small world, beloved inhabitants keep dying, and the survivors live in the parsonage like disaster refugees. The girls cling to one another and live—and will always live—precarious lives. Charlotte thinks, takes charge, plots with her taciturn, singular younger sister: *Let's repopulate life with characters and create new realms.* But out of what? Out of their fertile minds. Still, the seed of their creativity comes from the father. He's preoccupied; he's getting old; he's distant; he's eccentric. But what they know, they know from him; what they desire, he either had, or wants. They'll use him, use his writings, use what he provides, to make new life, but they'll keep their creative intercourse with him secret, lest the parson in him disapprove. When the first-born lies in bed, gestating fictions, the creative incubus of the father—though he might not know it—has already come into her.

After the death of her older sisters, Charlotte quickly joined with her brother in developing narratives that would sprawl on year after year.[13] She and Branwell became close, and they dominated the Angria collaboration. After a while, strong-willed Emily and quiet Anne exiled themselves from Angria to join and create their own (lost) world of Gondal. Living geographically and emotionally far from the madding crowd, these Brontës grew up bound together in the shared production of imaginary worlds. Charlotte, though she sometimes needed Branwell or Emily to spark and guide her creativity, was the real leader in this literary apprenticeship, and Angria, mythical kingdom of imperial and sexual intrigue, obsessed her into her 24th year, at least. Working with Branwell, she had imagined as the central hero, a romantic, promiscuous, noble figure, and then over the years she fashioned one heroine after another to encounter him, interact, and vie for his love and favor. She tried out in Angria most of the situations and character-types she later developed in her novels. What's more, she rendered female figures that combine many of the same qualities of strength and abjection that she would later herself show when she fell in love with Constantin Heger, with whom she studied in 1842–1843.

Between the start of the juvenilia and the writing of *Jane Eyre* (1829–1846), the major events of Charlotte's life beyond Haworth and outside the family circle were:

• her schooling as a teenager at Roe Head, where she made the intense friendships with Ellen Nussey and Mary and Martha Taylor that taught her about both female bonding and privileged bourgeois life;

- her sad experience as a teacher at Roe Head School where she came to realize that she lacked her father's pedagogical talent;
- her two short stints as a governess in big houses where she learned to despise both unmerited class privilege and the exploitation of child-care workers, but to fantasize about the governess as a potential Cinderella;
- her education in Brussels, at the Pensionnat Heger, when, in 1842–1843, at first accompanied by Emily, then alone, she sought—futile plan—to prepare herself to open with her sisters a school of their own (her father being hard up for money);
- and, finally, the crushing, doomed passion she developed there for Constantin Heger, the married head of the Belgian girls' school.

All of this she fused with family psychology and the heritage of Angria and then channeled into her fiction. She tried to follow primly in her father's path, projecting a career in education and hoping to be a writer, but instead she ended up absolutely obliterating his tracks in the swath of her amazing success.

3.

FALLING HOPELESSLY
IN LOVE

Before going to Brussels, she rejected two offers of marriage from clergy-men she hardly knew,[14] but she'd never loved or been close to any men except her father and brother. At the Belgian school, where her father deposited her with Emily, she fell madly and hopelessly in love with Heger, the headmaster and a happily married father. Her lacerating passion, a classic case of transference, determined her art. She had to move her love out of childhood to adulthood (and to the edge of adultery) in order to write a great love story.

"Falling in love with love is falling for make-believe" is a perfect lyric for Charlotte Brontë. Falling in love is often falling into the vulnerability of the past, but with the giddy hope and joy of satisfying the frustrated desires of early life. It can be a way of trying to change the past through intimacy with another, but lots of people seem formatted to keep getting it wrong. It figures that Charlotte, attached to her father, would fall in love with some unattainable man. Later writing that very man, she told him he was "*mon*

maitre de literature," the only master she ever had.[15] That, however, was un-
true. Before "Maitre" Heger, her father taught her.

A fine, charismatic teacher like the young Patrick, Heger, 33 and in his
prime when he knew Charlotte, poured out energy—some of it erotic. He
was oddly seductive, what the French call *beau laid*—the ugly frog who's
really a prince (like Rochester in *Jane Eyre*). About his students, this big
little-man cared. He wanted them to learn, and he was driven to find out
what they knew and didn't know, what they thought, what they could do,
what their secrets were. He spied on them (he went through Charlotte's
things, opened her desk, read her notes). He saw that girls were ignorant
but that some, like Charlotte and Emily Brontë, were hungry to know and
intellectually fertile—virgin intellectual territory.

Educational history of the last two centuries features an academic Lot
complex. A whole gender that, relatively speaking, had had few educational
opportunities and wanted to learn, became a project for reform. Men of
good will, power, lust, missionary zeal, idealism, need, and what-have-you
could now sow the seeds of intellectual curiosity and achievement among
young women. Heger was dedicated to opening his students up to the life
of the mind. Gruff and intimidating one minute, he could be solicitous and
helpful the next. (Brontë would portray him with little disguise as Paul
Emanuel, the nominal hero of her great novel *Villette*). A benevolent des-
pot in his little realm, he could be a kindly, bossy egoist full of hyperbole,
bluster, and sexist rant. Basically, he was wise and good-natured. He loved
to challenge his pupils, and he didn't mind bullying them into tears and
anger, if he could provoke them to think. He also provoked crushes and
adoration. Like Charlotte, he was both a doer and a voyeur, a moralist and
a plotter, a strict Christian and a devotee of passion and romance. To him
the brilliant Brontë sisters must have looked like a pedagogical bonanza.

Charlotte Brontë, at 26, was Heger's oldest pupil (as well as his tutor in
English) and she found herself happy under his gaze. When he stared hard
at her, talked to her about religion, morality, and literature, praised her
writing, gave her books, and, in his bantering, hectoring way, communi-
cated his high regard for her, it thrilled her soul.

But she had an unbeatable competitor: Heger's wife, Zoe, who would
bear him six children (the same number as Patrick's wife). Madame Heger,
a politic, charming, hard-headed woman kept the place running smoothly
by making it her business to know everything that went on. In this little spy

state, she was chief of surveillance. At first Madame welcomed the Brontë girls and took Charlotte into the family. Even in the second year of her stay, when homesick, anti-social Emily had gone, the wife, pregnant with her fifth child, still tried to make lonely Charlotte feel at home. But by then Brontë was in despair, obsessed with the husband—far gone in love—and Zoe acted. Quietly, she waged a cold war over the months, freezing Charlotte out, getting her husband to end his English lessons, and making sure that he and the English girl rarely laid eyes on each other.

Charlotte stewed and sank further into depression. Her identity was righteousness, but how can a woman who loves a married man be righteous? Her dilemma was terrible. What to do? She gave in to brooding paranoia, and out of guilt and desire, she demonized her rival. Her beloved master had disappeared with the hateful woman into a forbidden part of the living quarters. Madame Heger therefore became the mother of the detestable women in her fiction—Zoraide Reuter in *The Professor*, Madame Beck in *Villette*, Bertha Mason in *Jane Eyre*—women who try to trap the heroes through the lure of sex, money, false religion, deceit, and corrupt family ties. In this painful love story, passive-aggressive Charlotte's Brontë found another inspiration for articulating resentment—the fierce *resentimentality* that marks her fiction and, not coincidentally, modern life.

4.
DYING TO BE AN AUTHOR

At the start of 1844, Charlotte finally had to go back to Haworth where her father was beginning to lose his sight. From there for the next two years, she wrote pathetic letters to Monsieur Heger in this vein: "To forbid me to write to you, to refuse to answer me would be to tear from me my only joy on earth. . . . I pine away."[16] No answer came, but living out erotic agony somehow quickened her creative will.

Imitation, the sincerest form of flattery, is also surely the sincerest form of memory. In late 1845 Charlotte famously went through her sister's private things. She found and read without permission Emily's verses, and then pressured the reluctant genius as hard as she could to publish them together with her own and Anne's poems. The whole business looks suspiciously like the plotting first-born using subtle, coercive Heger tactics to further her ambitions. The project also seems like an adult replay of the "bed play" cooperation with Emily to create Brontë literature.

The years 1845–1847, when all of the siblings were home together in the aging father's house, were crucial for literary history. By the end of 1845, all three sisters were hard at work on novels. In that same year, Anne had left her governess post at the Robinsons and Branwell, dismissed by an outraged Mr. Robinson, had returned home to dissipate the rest of his life away in drink, drugs, and mania ("Here's to you, Mrs. Robinson!"), apparently crushed by his sordid affair with the older woman; he died in 1848. The sisters all, in one way or another, figured his sottish degeneration into their work. By the middle of 1846, *Poems by Currer, Ellis, and Acton Bell* appeared, and Charlotte, Emily, and Anne had, respectively, finished versions of *The Professor*, *Wuthering Heights*, and *Agnes Grey*, which the ambitious older daughter sent off together trying to find a publisher.

Charlotte started work on *Jane Eyre* under circumstances that read as if I'm making them up to fit my Lot theories: She found herself with her father in dark exile. When Patrick's eyesight deteriorated, Charlotte with Emily took him to an eminent Manchester eye specialist. The doctor advised a cataract operation, but said Patrick would have to stay in Manchester for some weeks after the procedure. In August, therefore, Charlotte, alone with her father, went back to the city to stay with him during the surgery and recuperation. On the day of the operation, she got word that her first novel, *The Professor*, had been rejected, though her sisters' had been taken. Now, residing in gloomy Manchester lodgings, where she lived trying to preserve her father's vision in his seventieth year, she began the romantic story of Jane and Rochester. Patrick rested in the dark, wounded, and totally dependent on her. Old and near blind, he couldn't write. But she could. Out of their dimmed and joined prospects, she began to bring forth the issue that would justify and transfigure for posterity both their lives.

5.

'JANE EYRE'

AND THE LOT COMPLEX

There are a thousand good ways to read a novel as rich in meaning as *Jane Eyre: An Autobiography*.[17] I stress *Lot* and the historic figuring of desires that Charlotte Brontë felt and imagined in her own life. This daughter's fantasy, transmuted to visionary art, is a young woman's marriage to a father-figure who will love her, talk intimately to her, give her a say (in every sense) over both their lives, and make her the center of his being and

his destiny. And the wishful fantasy she so shrewdly projects onto this father Rochester is that the younger woman will bind up his wounds, understand him, love him in spite of his moral failures and his hurt, imperfect,
deteriorating body and mind.

In the novel, the stern Christian soul-saver St. John Rivers tells Jane not
"to yield to the vacillating fears of Lot's wife. . . . I counsel you to resist,
firmly, every temptation which would incline you to look back: pursue
your present career steadily" (318). Through the autobiographer "Jane Eyre,"
Brontë tries to do exactly that demanding and needful thing. St. John is, in
fact, ironically repeating the warning to Jane of the apparition of her resurrected mother—a form of Lot's wife: "My daughter, flee temptation."
"Mother, I will" (281). A woman's life may now be salvaged and regenerated
by following a *career*. Charlotte Brontë's is writing. The solution that she
seeks is to find and create in her imagination a metaphorical father and
reconcile incestuous longing to law, civility, and morality. As a writer and a
new woman, she would mediate between generations. She would create the
text that would be her patrimony and give her access to her father—to
what he *meant* to her.

In the end, Jane writes famously of Rochester, "Reader, I married him,"
and continues in the next chapter:

Mr. Rochester continued blind the first two years of our union: . . . I was then
his vision, as I am still his right hand. Literally, I was (what he often called me)
the apple of his eye. He saw nature—he saw books through me; and never did
I weary of gazing for his behalf. (397)

"Literally" means *in letters, in written language*, and "putting into words"
was the right way for the daughter to keep her father's seed alive.

Jane Eyre is so bound up in Lot fantasy and Lot drives that just telling
what happens proves the point. A badly oppressed girl grows up in a cruel,
religiously debased society in which those who can't break free seem
doomed to burn up (e.g., Helen *Burns* and St. John Rivers in fevers, Bertha
Rochester in a fire). This girl redeems her patriarchal world and bears new
life into the new age. When young, she passionately longs for a sympathetic
father-figure to save her. Later, three men of authority (Brocklehurst, Rochester, and St. John Rivers) are willing to sacrifice her well-being—and that
of other daughters—in the name of their God and/or their male egos. Two
irresponsible older women (Mrs. Reed and Bertha), of an age to protect

and mother her but trapped by their past sins, persecute her until they die miserably. More than once, what looks like divine intervention leads the girl away from sexual danger to safety.

At 18, she finds herself living in lonely refuge with a man old enough to be her father, tutoring his bastard daughter. He's charismatic, unconventional, sexually experienced, but world-weary—apparently past his prime. She falls in love with this morally questionable survivor and wants to share his life and renew his faith. As for him, he relishes her obscurity and her candor; he delights in calling her "child" and other diminutives. He's more than willing, however, to deceive her and take her virginity. He himself is a refugee from a slave land of lust and greed (the racially exotic, financially exploitable West Indies). The girl intoxicates him with her fresh, probing mind, and moral strength, and he too falls in love. A housekeeper sums it up: "She was a little small thing, they say, almost like a child. . . . Mr. Rochester was about forty, and this governess not twenty; and you see, when gentlemen of his age fall in love with girls, they are often like as if they were bewitched" (375–376). To him she represents innocence and hope—another chance—and she points the way forward out of the despair of the past.

She even saves him from being burned up in his bed by a big, bad woman. He's hiding a crazy wife who's unchaste, diseased, and dangerous— she can't understand him and she does shocking things upstairs. Against the law, he decides to mate with the girl, even though his spouse lives, not-so-secretly, wallowing in her own fleshy pollution. The husband talks fantastically of taking Jane to live in a lunar landscape, like Lot's refuge above the scorched cities of the plain: "I shall seek a cave . . . among the volcano-tops, and mademoiselle shall live with me there, and only me" (234). Even near the end, with his wife dead, he says to Jane, "I suppose I should now entertain none but fatherly feelings for you: do you think so? Come—tell me" (383).

After the exposure of his bigamist plot, Rochester gives a creepy little speech that bears serious scrutiny. In retrospect, it epitomizes the Lottish specter of incest that haunts this narrative (not to mention Christian myth and anthropological history): "Your pity, my darling, is the suffering *mother* of love: its anguish is the very natal pang of the *divine* passion. I accept it, Jane; let the *daughter* have free *advent*—my arms wait to receive her" (270; emphasis mine). In that extraordinary, incestuous trope of desire, anyone can see both the lasting significance and the fluid potential of the Lot theme and complex from Old and New Testament times to the present.

When, at a climactic moment after finding out Rochester is married, motherless Jane is trying to leave him, Brontë imagines a version of the "Remember Lot's wife" warning coming to her in the form of a maternal vision shining forth out of the night sky:

She broke forth as . . . not a moon, but a white human form shone in the azure, inclining a glorious brow earthward. It gazed and gazed and gazed on me. It spoke to my spirit: immeasurably distant was the tone, yet so near, it whispered in my heart—"My daughter, flee temptation!"
"Mother, I will." (281)

Jane heeds that call to flee "temptation" and presumably the same fate as Rochester's wife, who dies in an inferno from which the husband barely escapes, maimed and sightless.

What Charlotte Brontë did in *Jane Eyre* was to marry the Lot complex to modern social history, love, the marriage plot and the novel—an act of imagination that still reverberates, even for people who don't know the book.

The abstract logic of the novel says something like this: *The long-existing fascination of the girl with the older man's power and experience and the older man's fascination with the young woman's fresh, erotic appeal and hopeful mind must be recognized and dealt with as part of history's ongoing flow. This mutual attraction—this passion for communication and love across gender and generation lines—has been, and is, so ripe for exploitation that it needs to be socialized, controlled, and made legitimate through new female agency. Before Lot's wife can be properly remembered, the daughter must gain respect and authority.*

6.

O BRAVE NEW GIRL

Jane Eyre is a key feminist text. The character Jane Eyre faces a changing world in which a girl, in order to be saved, must leave the past, act on her own, and seize the present day. That's why the parable of Lot's wife is so powerful (and disturbing) now. Look at the story Brontë imagines for Jane: she must prepare herself to make her own way, get learning, get ahead, and somehow earn a living, much in the same way that an ambitious male (like Patrick Brunty) had to do. She must take new responsibility in making changes in the world of the fathers, a world she, like her creator, wants to inherit and reshape. She must assert a woman's right of free thought and speech, sexual passion, and equality. She must try to overcome traditions of male privilege and authoritarianism (John Reed, Brocklehurst, Rochester, and St. John Rivers), and—almost as important here—female irrationality, and jealous irresponsibility (Mrs. Reed, Miss Scatcherd, Blanche Ingram, and Bertha).

Crucially, she must learn to stand up and speak out against child abuse, those customs of early mistreatment of body and mind that stain the Brontë imagination (vicious confinement and humiliation in the death-haunted, symbolic "red-room" at the Gateshead foster home; beating, mental torture, bad hygiene, and starvation at the Lowood school administered by Brocklehurst, minister of a perverse Christianity). She must deal with a new age that, for many of the most thoughtful, brought the loss of a sustaining faith in Christian resignation, with its pie-in-the-sky pay-off. Jane needs to get the attention and win the love of those who, like Miss Temple, Rochester, and the Rivers family, can help her find dignity and identity in a community of moral worth. And she must try to reconcile her moral sense with an intense erotic desire that's bound up with the seductiveness of male power.

She has to create a new family out of the wreckage of the old and become, in effect, her own mother. She must face the emotional upheavals and conflicts that grow out of the intensifying relationships of the nuclear family and the developing cultural expectations for marriages based on, and maintained by, personal love, sexual attraction, intimacy, intellectual equality, and friendship as well as economic interests and religious dogma. She has to join in the scramble for money in the emerging nineteenth-century economy where good fortune means wealth and wealth offers new possibilities for freedom and influence. Moreover, she must filter her perceptions of the world through a self-conscious psyche and a personal history that make her unique. She moves in a new era of psychological individualism, a world where "nerves," introspection, enigmatic dreams, the private truth of memory's stories, and fluid, violent images flood the single mind, and unconscious desires as well as social motivations mirror and shape the course of life.

In a famous passage, Charlotte Brontë imagines Jane speaking up for generations of her younger sisters:

Millions . . . are in silent revolt against their lot. Nobody knows how many rebellions besides political rebellions ferment in the masses of life which people earth: but women feel just as men feel; they need exercise for their faculties and a field for their efforts as much as their brothers do; they suffer from too rigid a restraint, too absolute a stagnation, precisely as men would suffer. . . . [T]hey seek to do more or learn more than custom has pronounced necessary for their sex (96).

That's her real answer to Southey. Those words claim a right to the so-called *man's world*. Though many may now criticize Charlotte Brontë on particular issues of race, class, and gender, feminism in all its guises has spoken Jane's language in pushing for the great modern, revolutionary cause, *the career open to talent*.

Virginia Woolf, in a haughty moment, writes, "The drawbacks of being Jane Eyre are not far to seek. Always to be a governess and always to be in love is a serious limitation in a world which is full, after all, of people who are neither one nor the other."[18] But what "to be a governess" in the nineteenth century actually meant was to be a female aspiring to middle-class status who labored in a difficult vocation where the possibilities for women of professional life and, not incidentally, the professionalization of childcare and education generally were being pioneered. And if you also think of all that loving and being loved by a thoughtful older man who could see her intellectual force meant to Charlotte Brontë and Jane Eyre, you see that Woolf's words actually do point to historical *needs* of ambitious women and show why Jane Eyre has seemed such a prophetic figure.

A generation of feminists, in the decades after World War II, rediscovered the "nourishing" force of this novel. Adrienne Rich, for example, wrote that Jane's marriage "is not patriarchal marriage . . . but a continuation of this woman's creation of herself."[19] And Sandra Gilbert called Jane's story "a pattern for countless others . . . in which the problems . . . are symptomatic of difficulties Everywoman in a patriarchal society must meet and overcome."[20] But such testimony to the novel's inspirational force tells only part of the story. It tends to tame and dilute the novel's *outrageousness*—its original force—by making proper and formally coherent what is, after all, one of the most shocking and problematic of Victorian narratives. *Jane Eyre* is not Mary Wollstonecraft's *A Vindication of the Rights of Women*, but a violent story full of raging desire for *both* justice and transgression.[21] The novel *is a scandal*—a destabilizing work that churns together taboos, idealistic behavior, criminal wishes, virtuous hopes, and suppressed drives in the turbulent mind of Jane. That's what makes her such a large figure. In this book, *the wife* is the sex-mad home-wrecker, and *the other woman*—a "young girl" (258)—is the domestic savior, the mother-to-be and the sympathetic, first-person self.

What does it mean for the most famous teenager in Victorian fiction to love, empathize with, forgive, and cleave to a powerful older man who, living in the same house, betrays her by plotting to sham a marriage, take her to bed, and make a concubine of her? Nothing morally simple, trivial, or comfortable. There's no getting away from the fact that the plot features a girl who falls in love with a father-figure, displaces his wife, triumphs in her death, saves and marries the older man, and then has his baby. And this wish-fulfillment, rooted though it may be in male power and libido (and—figuratively speaking—in the evolving anthropology that will make divorce common), is here a woman's fantasy, not a man's.

Important literature, such as *Jane Eyre*, breaks out of cloying red-rooms of repressive self-censorship; it sets fire to houses of ideological purity and smug colleges of orthodoxy, be they Christian, patriarchal, collectivist, Freudian, Marxist, feminist, economic, ethnic, professional, or whatever, because it will not suppress—in fact, it insists on and renders—the fluid insatiability of desire and the limitless contradictions within self and society.

Charlotte Brontë says something more challenging than *women should be free*. *Jane Eyre* shows that a woman should and wants to be free, but may continue to have erotic needs and cravings for masters to adore, talk with, hurt, suffer for, abase, nurture, and reproduce. As a harbinger for major themes of late twentieth-century life and literature, it says that one way to freedom, progress, and true love for women is to embrace and use a conspiracy-theory model of patriarchy: belief in, and exposure of, a male father-lover's master-plot to keep the wife shut in and to seduce the daughter. It says that before you can really move to freedom and equality, you must feel and dramatize your own victimization. It says that the way to reach and appreciate the mother and establish a healthy tie to the past is first to escape the mother and turn your back on the past. (Before Jean Rhys could write *Wide Sargasso Sea* paying homage to Bertha Mason and all such Lot's wives, Charlotte Brontë had to imagine victory in the destruction of the backward-looking wife.) It says that a man may try to avoid the despair of aging and lack of fulfillment by finding a younger woman, and a younger woman may try to conquer her inequality with men and other women by finding a sympathetic older man whom she can both love and outlast (thus escaping the threat to older women of being cast aside, one way or another, by men.) It says that people wish to flee temptation and then return to it with a clear conscience; that those who suffer unjustly long not so much for the triumph of virtue as for the chance to punish the wickedness of others.

What often shapes personality and political movements even more than positive goals is the drive to *get even* (in every sense), and Charlotte Brontë is the novelist-laureate of the scorned daughter's *get even*. Look what happens to characters who cross Jane: Mrs. Reed dies unmourned; John Reed ends up a bankrupt suicide; the Reverend Mr. Brocklehurst suffers the "mortifying" public exposure; Bertha kills herself burning down the house; St. John Rivers burns up trying to convert the "heathens;" Eliza Reed's shut up in a cloister; and, of course, Rochester is blinded and disabled until he becomes a good papa. Brontë makes Jane an author you shouldn't refuse.

7.

THE MADWOMAN IN THE ATTIC

A Victorian Lot's wife, Rochester's spouse Bertha represents both the mania that comes from sexual corruption and the doom that threatens women (and men) who wallow in bitter unreason and can't move out of the past. Lately, however, the plight of Rochester's first wife has sparked much sympathy. She's even taken on a feminist crown of victimhood, most notably in Jean Rhys's *Wide Sargasso Sea*. Sandra Gilbert and others have seen Bertha as Jane's symbolic alter ego acting out the repressed rage of women. But such revisionism, enlightening as it is, distorts Brontë's original project if it leads to the sentimentalization of Bertha. The narrative features the deadly rivalry between brainy, moral Jane, the girl making the future, and the old wife of the bad past. Jane Eyre is meant to represent a progressive, emancipating woman; Bertha is meant to represent a revolting, reactionary woman —deranged, trapped in compulsive sexuality, and out of her mind—a modern maenad inimical to procreation and the future.[22]

To read Bertha primarily as a rebel sister instead of a menace to good daughters is to screen or purge the fact, force, and meaning of Jane Eyre's ideological and psychological matricide. Helene Moglen calls the "madwoman" "the jealous, vengeful mother who prohibits marriage to the be-loved father."[23] Brontë's rhetorical and ethical problem is how to make it seem right to get rid of a woman twenty-five years older than the teenage Jane so that the girl can have the woman's husband—that is, *how to legitimate incestuous desire.* She solves it by distancing and demonizing Bertha, the wife, as a sexual outlaw, and by transforming Jane from a daughter of Lot to a new Ruth. Jane is fit for motherhood; Bertha is not. The "mad-woman" is in part *the Mother as Other,* an older woman from an embit-tered, flamboyant generation whose lechery and mindless alienation threaten the emergence of a "new woman." And she is an image of the wild, uncontrollable power of sexuality that looms over the girlchild.

Recent critics may ignore or downplay Bertha's syphilitic mania and promiscuity, but Jane Eyre and Charlotte Brontë, in setting down Roch-ester's words, stress them: "[T]he doctors now discovered that *my wife* was mad—her excesses had prematurely developed the germs of insanity" (270); "no professed harlot ever had a fouler vocabulary than she" (271); "de-bauchery: . . . That was my Indian Messalina's attribute: . . . Any enjoyment that bordered on riot seemed to approach . . . her vices" (274). Brontë's por-trayal of Bertha attacks the monster of indiscriminate sex and lust that much modern feminist theory, like traditional religion, condemns. Roch-ester's sexuality needs to be and can be controlled—men are like that—but only by Jane, not Bertha, and only if Jane gets equality.

The making of modern feminism and social history has meant finding female role models from the past and celebrating women's buried achieve-ments, but it has also involved venting, through art and criticism, hostility to women whose bondage to the past held back the advancement of daugh-ters. Brontë gets at the flaming, contradictory desire, repressed and cen-sored, that wants to honor the mother, wants the mother's blessing even as it wants to get rid of the woman defined chiefly by sexuality, passion, the re-generative potential of her body, and the degree of her physical beauty. Jane Eyre's language and imagery split the mother, but Brontë's diction and vi-sion link the two figures—Bertha is a "lunatic," and the "Mother" appari-tion that leads Jane from temptation literally comes out of the moon. What Jane describes in the visionary woman-in-the-moon scene is a wise mother you could love and remember, but who disappears and leaves you free. These two fantastic figures together tell of contrary impulses to obliterate mothers—women of the past—but also to idealize and aestheticize them.[24]

8.

"LITTLE NERVOUS SUBJECT"

Jane Eyre is a prophetic book, and nowhere more so than in Jane's recounting of her dreams to Rochester. These show conflicts and danger in one young woman's life, but they also symbolize brilliantly general fears, ambiguities, and dilemmas in the history of modern gender relationships. It's easy enough now to give Freudian readings to these dreams, but what's more interesting is the way Brontë's Lottean dreamwork and the issues it raises help in reading "Freud" and the post-Freudian aftermath. There would have been no psychoanalysis without the testament and history of daughters. Consider the case of "Janet E." (whose narrator is the father-fixated, love-starved "Currer B."): a highly emotional young woman confesses her complex dreams to an experienced older man who has employed her to mind his child:

"During all my first sleep I was following the windings of an unknown road; . . .
I was burdened with the charge of a little child: a very small creature, too young
and feeble to walk, and which shivered in my cold arms and wailed piteously
in my ear. I thought, sir, that you were on the road a long way before me; and I
strained every nerve to overtake you, and made effort on effort to utter your
name and entreat you to stop—but my movements were fettered; and my
voice still died away inarticulate; while you, I felt, withdrew farther and farther
every moment."
  Rochester responds, "Little nervous subject!
  " . . . I dreamt another dream, sir: that Thornfield Hall was a dreary ruin. . . .
I wandered, on a moonlight night, through the grass-grown enclosure within;
here I stumbled over a marble hearth, and there over a fallen fragment of cornice.
Wrapped up in a shawl, I still carried the unknown little child: I might not lay it
down anywhere, however tired were my arms—however much its weight impeded my progress, I must retain it. I heard the gallop of a horse at a distance on
the road: I was sure it was you; and you were departing for many years, and for a
distant country. I climbed the thin wall with frantic, perilous haste, eager to catch
one glimpse of you from the top: the stones rolled from under my feet, the ivy
branches I grasped gave way, the child clung round my neck in terror, and almost
strangled me: at last I gained the summit. I saw you like a speck on a white track,
lessening every moment. The blast blew so strong I could not stand. I sat down on
the narrow ledge; I hushed the scared infant in my lap: you turned an angle of the
road; I bent forward to take a last look; the wall crumbled; I was shaken; the child
rolled from my knee, I lost my balance, fell, and woke." (247–249)

What she describes, it seems, betrays a deep conflict coming out of her perceived female duty to bear and nurture children, her fear of pregnancy, and her desire not to be left behind by a powerful male figure whom she loves. She's afraid of both dropping the child and being strangled by it. To keep up with the father and take the road of progress might mean leaving the baby behind and it might mean disastrous falls. (You can see the drama and tension of Jane's dream acted out every morning in every day-care center in the world.) But the point of the setting is that the older man of power is present and part of the revelation of the young woman's dreams. He's neither detached nor objective, but deeply involved in her fantasies and her transfer of early fears and memories to the symbolic ordering of her present experience. The girl opens up her dreams and her "unconscious" to a figure who desires her well-being, but wants to use her, wield power, and project his own designs onto her. This pattern will recur.

9.
INTENTIONS, IMPLICATIONS, AND INFERENCES

Charlotte Brontë fused with the character and composer of Jane's "autobiography"—not for nothing did the Victorians, behind her back, call her "Jane Eyre." That authorial, textual, first-person entity is large, contains multitudes, contradicts herself, and is untroubled by that hobgoblin, foolish consistency. Here are some resounding intentions and implications you could infer from this elder daughter's most famous book:

- If I think I was abused, I was abused.
- I want to hate, adore, hurt, get free of, and make love to the patriarch.
- I want a different father who will be enthralled with me.
- Christianity provides a model of faith and hope for immortality, but pastors and Church fathers are liable to think and behave like sadistic misogynists.
- The call of love and writing is stronger for me than the call of Christianity.
- I champion the cause of females, even though I may despise, disparage, and patronize the lives of women [Bertha, Mrs. Reed, Celine Varens] and girls [Georgiana Reed, Adele].

- I must and can make a good story out of my life.
- The way to fulfillment is through the love and power of an older man.
- The way to fulfillment is through the virtue, love, and intelligence of a young woman.
- Men—even the men you love and who love you—lie to you, use you, plot against you, turn you into jewels, trinkets, and labor-saving devices; they are not monogamous, they have other women, they exploit you if they can.
- The double standard can be used by bright, enterprising young women to narrow the field of competing females and obtain power.
- If the man you love has another woman, she's hideous and should die.
- The spirit of my mother—of all women—will save me.
- If some powerful man knew how badly they treated me, he'd make it right.
- Marriage drives women crazy, and wives and mothers—good or bad—for the most part live like lunatics.
- If I want to find the "good" mother and wife, *I* must create her in myself.
- Promiscuity in a man is not a sin.
- Promiscuity in a man requires punishment by all means.
- Sisterhood is powerful and ennobling.
- Sisterhood is a destructive deathtrap full of spite and hate without the mediation of a virtuous father's power and love.
- The sexual nature of men must be controlled by law and the threat of violence.
- Help, they're starving us girls!

When, as a reader, you feel righteous and vicariously liberated by Jane's memories exposing child abuse at Gateshead and Lowood; when you're transported to Thornfield to register the drives of a rich, middle-age man and a young woman to merge bodily and spiritually with one another and possess the qualities of the other; when you try to puzzle out the strange dreams that Jane Eyre narrates to the beloved male authority figure in her life; when you see a female mind—trying both to transcend the past and bond with it too—split the mother-figure into vampire and angel; when you read about a fundamentalist religious faith that offers little but self-righteousness and glorified death; when you read the story of a determined, brilliant, pious and impious woman using the full powers of imagination and fantasy to make a good and resonant story—when you take in such things, you are smack into allegories of modernity and the regenerating life of the daughter from out of the cave and behind the mask: "Millions are in rebellion against their lot."

III.
The Younger Daughter

Emily Brontë (1818–1848) had a short, remarkable life of stunning achievement, but unlike Charlotte she left almost no record of it—no diary outpourings of the heart, next to nothing in the way of letters and documents. The older sister liked to write friends, loved her first-person voice, wanted to be known, wanted to impress people. Emily was different—enigmatic, antisocial, living in her private realm. She didn't care to relate to people outside her family. A mysterious, daunting creature, she diffused the articulations of her complex self into her characters. Like Lot's silent younger daughter, she expresses herself directly only through her act of generation—her literary issue. But what an issue! Her novel, *Wuthering Heights*, transgresses decorum to render life as an angry, collective hive of desire, and love as a necessary multiple personality disorder. It conveys the force of erotic passion and death as intensely as anything in fiction, and it transcends the orthodoxies and soothing moral painkillers that sap the truth of even great books. What's more, it transcends gender.

The Lot plot of the older daughter's *Jane Eyre* expressed an ambition to supplant the mother and to reform and share power with a chastened, loving patriarch whose redeemed life she can wed to her own, to a better future, and to a higher morality. That is the "seed" of Charlotte Brontë's issue. The plot of her sister Emily, however, is not to replace the mother, not to win the love or the power of the father, not to save him and civilize humankind, not to celebrate the good daughter, mother, wife or feminist moonangel, but to break through the historical limits of gender, selfhood, creed, and physical being and claim for her imagination boundless freedom. And that includes the freedom of casting off "female" identity altogether and *being male*: "I *am* Heathcliff." When Emily Brontë has Catherine Earnshaw speak those self-defining words, you have the crucial utterance of *Wuthering Heights*.[25] The forms of gender, love, and identity become subjects of imaginative construction.

1.

WHY CAN'T A WOMAN
BE LIKE A MAN?

By the time of *Wuthering Heights* and Branwell's ruin, Emily, according to Lock and Dixon, "had indeed, become, for Patrick, the son he had so longed for" (369). That may seem an odd thing to say about a daughter who did not—and could not—leave her family circle, earn her living, travel alone, make friends, marry, preserve her writing, or see to its publication. Nevertheless, the remark *is* a key in opening up both the genesis and meaning of her novel. This daughter is not a Daddy's girl, but a Daddy's boy. Emily was by far the tallest of the children, and her siblings, sometimes afraid of her, called her "Major." The anecdotes, legends, and most critical commentaries about her stress her so-called "masculine" traits: independence of mind and will, physical bravery, disregard of pain, love of the outdoors, stubbornness, taciturn stoicism, brutal honesty, rudeness, a pronounced streak of sadomasochism, disdain for sentimentality, and both a tough rationality and a private, consciously worked-out metaphysical faith. No one ever calls her girlish, womanly, ladylike, refined, proper, dainty, tearful, self-sacrificing, nice, or nurturing.

After the sisters were dead, Charlotte's beloved mentor Monsieur Heger would say of Emily that she had "a head for logic, and a capability of argument, unusual in a man, and rare indeed in a woman": "She should have been a man—a great navigator. Her powerful reason would have deduced new spheres of discovery from the knowledge of the old; and her strong, imperious will would never have been daunted by opposition or difficulty."[26] That's shrewd: she certainly does explore fantasy life, and she discovers how to create novel spheres in *Wuthering Heights*. But somehow I can imagine her saying of Heger in turn, "He should have been a woman —a great midwife," and that sort of free-minded refusal to be patronized may indicate what matters most about her art: its potential for opening up the imagination.

Emily Brontë gets beyond essentialism—the idea that a woman or a man is, by nature, essentially *this* or *that*. She could see, feel, and render a woman's imagination, embodying a nervous, nurturing Nellie, a bleeding, intrusive ghost-girl trapped in childhood (Cathy I as dream-waif), a spoilt, petulant wife and wonderfully eloquent lover (Cathy I), a conventional female redeemer of the uncouth male (Cathy II), and—just as powerfully— a cruel, charismatic male devotee of erotic faith (Heathcliff) and a banal, voyeuristic, gentleman narrator (Lockwood). She didn't worry much about oppressive patriarchy, suffering womanhood, or moral uplift. Her book rages with both the anarchy and fight that, I'm arguing, opened up possibilities of life for women. It avoids the "virtue" trap of self-justification and defensive gender pride that can censor honest expression. She does what "group identity" backers of political and religious movements can almost never do—get quit of mind-numbing piety. She renders, as no novelist before her quite had, the androgynous *savagery* that lies at the core of human love, human being, and historical change. And because she could express that fierce reality, in its complexity, her work, like her contemporary Darwin's, explodes the sentimentality of Victorian life and fiction.

Her whole means of narration from different points of view and the brilliant use of dialogue show an imagination impatient with the limitations of individual identity. By imagining the anarchic, amoral Heathcliff and Cathy, their consuming love, their transfiguring deaths, and their impact on a second generation, Brontë expresses the desire to obliterate distinctions between male and female, to be free of prescribed gender roles altogether, to be and love anything you please—to be a bad boy and a bad girl as well as a good girl, to realize the fusion of the living and the dead, of good and evil, of parents and children, of old and young, of illicit desire and lawful procreation. Like Charlotte, Emily wages war on so-called "female disabilities," but by sometimes identifying with Heathcliff and using him as a mask to speak through, she also crosses—even crosses out—the gender line.

To the Old Testament orthodox, the issue of Lot's daughters had meant outlaw progeny descended from the depraved cities of the plain. One thing the daughter Emily offers is a story integrating the erotic outlaw into the on-going, earthy flow of the world's life. Readers have always felt her book's transgressive mood. The phrase "I *am* Heathcliff" signals the primacy of erotic identity to the self and a great change coming. It's time to recognize that the emotional thrust of her wild novel points the way to the modern redemption and reformation of the cities of the plain—especially that second city of the plain, Gomorrah.[27]

2.

EMILY VS. CHARLOTTE:
GENDER VISIONS, GENDER TROUBLE

Of the creation of Heathcliff, disapproving Charlotte writes, "Whether it is right or advisable to create beings like Heathcliff, I do not know: I scarcely think it is. But this I know; the writer who possesses the creative gift owns something of which he is not always master—something that at times strangely wills and works for itself."[28] If the older daughter is right, one possible implication of Emily's unconscious art is surely: *I am Heathcliff. He's in me: and since that's the truth of my imagination, I do not have to accept the conventional life of a heterosexual woman as an immutable human condition.*

The point is not that *Wuthering Heights* is somehow a homosexual book, but that it makes gender a matter of imagination and puts erotic desire, self-definition, and fate before everything else. The key point of the fire-and-brimstone destruction of the Lot story as it evolved is the wickedness of sexual activity in and for itself without regard to the future: the Sodomites would not subordinate erotic life to lawful procreation and the nurture of progeny (that is, to God's will, self-transcendence, moral culture, and the good of civilization). The great sin of Sodom and Gomorrah is to choose erotic desire over species procreation (and survival). Love pursued as an end means irresponsibility in the eyes of God; it has no future and thus can lead to annihilation. The second Brontë daughter revisits this conflict and revises the past to make it part of the future. She imagines that libido, erotic faith, and the generation of the world to come are integrally bound together in dynamic tension.

Any account of Emily Brontë is bound to be impressionistic. If you want to understand how her mind grows and works, you're forced to speculate on a few second-and-third-hand scraps from witnesses of varying credibility. You have to pick your way through the theories and guesswork of Brontë scholars, and, of course, draw inferences from her surviving texts. What little is known of her life proper comes mainly through Charlotte's mediating words—her succinct "Biographical Notice" of 1850; her letters; the accounts, correspondence, and practical discretion of her friends and devotees (including her authorized biographer, Elizabeth Gaskell, who didn't have "a pleasant impression" of Emily, and Charlotte's strait-laced husband, Arthur Bell Nicholls, who didn't even want *Charlotte's* life made public); her patronizing preface to *Wuthering Heights*; her fictionalized portrait of Emily in *Shirley*; and the selected materials she preserved (including Emily's four brief diary entries from 1834, 1837, 1841, and 1845 totaling less than 2,000 words). "An interpreter," said Charlotte, "ought always to have stood between her and the world,"[29] and she took on the role. She regarded her sister with wary, protective awe: Emily was a genius, but she and her writing sometimes got out of control. (Charlotte may even have gone so far as to destroy "Ellis Bell's" second novel.[30]) Something about Emily evidently *did* need to be toned down if not covered up, most likely episodes of spaced-out, manic-depressive behavior—varied bouts of autistic withdrawal and ecstasy, emotional tyranny, anorexia, and temper tantrums by the semi-madwoman in the parsonage.

But there was more to the censoriousness. The little big sister was jealous because at times Emily had what Charlotte longed for, both as a daughter and as a writer. I quoted earlier from the end of *Jane Eyre*, when Jane says of her erotic father-figure Rochester, "I was then his vision, as I am still his right hand. . . . I was (what he often called me) the apple of his eye." And yet, according to John Greenwood, the Haworth stationer who knew the Brontës, those are the exact terms that Patrick had already used to describe *Emily*—not Charlotte—when she delighted him by learning how to shoot a gun: "She is my right-hand, nay the very apple of my eye!"[31] Self-contained Emily had a freedom from the usual constraints on female consciousness (and conscience) that Charlotte couldn't help but envy, even though she considered it dangerous. After she "found" Emily's poems and launched the publishing scheme—to become authors and thus wield authority—she remarks that her sister's poetry is "vigorous and genuine," "wild," "elevating," "*nor at all like the poetry women generally write*" (emphasis mine).[32] But *Wuthering Heights* is much too wild for Charlotte; it scares her.

With all they had in common, with their faith in love and imagination and their shared creative life, the sisters were rivals. In their fiction, they saw deep into the future, but they didn't see eye to eye, and the conflict comes out in the issue of the father and the relation to authority symbolized by the father. The essential difference between them—of far-reaching importance—becomes clear if you set next to one another what may be the most famous lines, respectively, from *Wuthering Heights* and *Jane Eyre*: "I *am* Heathcliff" and "Reader, I married him." Charlotte could never have written the former, nor Emily the latter. Cathy and Heathcliff choose erotic

anarchy; Jane Eyre chooses stable marriage. The younger daughter suppresses her traditional gender identity; the older stresses it. Here are their
respective words in fuller context:

If all else perished, and *he* remained, I should still continue to be; and, if all
else remained, and he were annihilated, the Universe would turn to a mighty
stranger. I should not seem a part of it. . . . Nelly, I *am* Heathcliff—he's always,
always in my mind—not as a pleasure, any more than I am always a pleasure to
myself—but as my own being—so, don't talk of our separation again— . . . (64).

Then he stretched his hand out to be led. I took that dear hand, held it a moment
to my lips, then let it pass round my shoulder: being so much lower of stature
than he, I served both for his prop and guide. We entered the wood, and wended
homeward.
  Reader, I married him. (395)

In Emily's imagination, a woman doesn't need to be separate from a
man. In this passage, she's not interested in *relationship* between Cathy and
Heathcliff, but in *identity*—human identity as an imaginative continuum
and mystery in the face of death. I'm not arguing that Emily Brontë *is*
Heathcliff. I'm saying that she can identify fully in her art, when she wants,
with a morally suspect, anarchic male figure of great consequence, and in
doing so, she claims a dynamic authority beyond gender. In *Wuthering
Heights* she does not identify either as a woman or as a man, but as an
imaginative force that can incarnate either and join both.

To Charlotte, the man is still the *other*. She clearly identifies with the
little bride and makes her relationship to the man and the evolving partnership of marriage the point of her story. And by addressing the reader,
she makes it all a public business, in effect: *You are a gendered and socially
conditioned being. If you're female and you don't see a woman and her plight
in historical perspective, if you don't see the need to control men and check
their force by resistance and education, by the sanction of law and/or by seducing them into some sort of practical, moral or erotic dependency, you cannot alter the continuing pattern of victimization. You delude yourself if you
think you can be free of the problem of women's oppression.* The image of the
diminutive female figure as prop to the sinning, chastened, widowed older
man carries weighty allusions to gender history and shows *Jane Eyre* as part
of women's long struggle for patrimony and empowering love. For Charlotte marriage and motherhood are still the proper womanly ends for her

heroine (and for herself, as her final year tragically showed—wed, pregnant, and dead all in nine months' time before she turned 40).

For Emily, however, the point is to find transcendent love in the brutality of existence and imaginative power in the teeth of impending death. The fact of death is the basic human condition, and the need to overcome it diminishes all other concerns: you delude yourself if you don't give it the highest priority. Worrying about gender inequality and sexism for her is like us worrying about fair play and etiquette in Auschwitz or the Twin Towers. What's needed is what the Bible's Song of Songs calls the "love that is fiercer than death."

The old question about Emily Brontë—in essence, *how could a provincial Victorian virgin and parson's daughter who lived such a brief, uneventful life have written such that passionate, ferocious novel?*—still holds. One answer is that it came out of her special relationship with her father. Patrick, according to a man who talked to him in 1850, "considered Emily the genius of the family."[33] "Nature had made Emily . . . his most beloved, his favourite" (368), say Lock and Dixon, and her biographers all agree they were temperamentally alike. The last short interchange between Mr. Earnshaw and his daughter Catherine in *Wuthering Heights* reveals a confident creative mind, relaxed and close in spirit to the father, claiming a bond, and it can also stand for a whole slew of gender histories to follow:

> "Why canst thou not always be a good lass, Cathy?"
> And she turned her face up to his, and laughed, and answered—
> "Why cannot you always be a good man, father?" (34)

Emily's way of preserving the paternal seed is to *be* that seed. She doesn't seem to envy the father's status, resent him, adore him, hold him in awe, or vie with her siblings for his regard and approval. Though she rejects the orthodox, sermonizing parson in him, she moves to subsume his creative spark into her imaginative self. She dwells in her father's house nearly all the days of her life, finding it unbearable to live elsewhere. At home she can inhabit a world of her own, but she creates that world out of what she first inherits and absorbs from Patrick Brontë. She takes in his Irish lore, his repressed Irish dreaminess and violent-mindedness, his mercurial spirit, his loneliness, his life history, his passion for God, immortality, books, art, ideas, and discipline, his inwardness, his courage, and his quirky idealism, but she transforms it all into her unique, virile imagination—hard, fierce, earthy, and visionary. The legacy of Lot churns through Emily Brontë and *Wuthering Heights* into modern life.

3.

NO MOTHER, GHOST SISTER,
SPOOKED AND SPOOKY SELF

As a child, Emily lives in a post-maternal world. Mother love is missing, literally a thing of the past. Mother Maria died when she was barely 3, and there's nothing to show that Emily remembered any real involvement with her at all. Any vague or reconstituted memory she has likely carries with it the concept of death. To Charlotte (and the two older sisters), the mother is a lost figure who can be imagined and idealized, even replaced in fantasy projections, but for Emily motherhood means a Lot's-cave sense of aftermath and suggests a climate of the irrecoverable or never-possessed. In *Wuthering Heights* mothers don't survive. They simply aren't there, or they disappear and their children don't think about them—something rare in a family chronicle. Emily can identify with fathers and children, with servants —even with dogs—but not with a living mother. But because she doesn't know a mother, she doesn't have to dwell on motherhood or feel she should *be* a mother. She's free to think through other figures.

The domineering human presence for Emily as she comes to consciousness is the image of her father, and what she sees him doing is mourning and missing his beloved mate. Where had she observed anything like Heathcliff's love for the dead Cathy and his longing for reunion in eternity? Where had she seen first the rage against death and the need to transcend it? The answer of course is in her childhood and in her father. As in her novel, what's central in her childhood is a love story that's already happened. The real memory of her mother comes in the form of her father's lonely grieving for his wife and his frustrated erotic need. Patrick told others of the unhappy outbursts of his dying wife, and he surely let his children know of her anguish, his tormented memories, and their mutual love.

Some famous dying words of Cathy express sentiments perfectly apt for Maria Brontë—and Lot's wife:

"I wish I could hold you," she continued bitterly, "till we were both dead! I shouldn't care what you suffered. I care nothing for your sufferings. Why shouldn't you suffer? I do! Will you forget me—will you be happy when I am in the earth? Will you say twenty years hence, 'That's the grave of Catherine Earnshaw. I loved her long ago, and was wretched to lose her; but it is past. I've loved many others since—my children are dearer to me than she was. . . . ' Will you say so, Heathcliff?" (123)

If her father had heard, felt, and remembered such torturing language from her mother, his children certainly knew it. When Emily is coming to consciousness and "taking in" her father, the absence of the mother first presents itself to the child as an erotic absence in *his* life. The father's thwarted desire and love romanticize and eroticize in a particular way her childhood and her sense of life: *I'm missing something and it must be like what my father's missing; my absent mother means tragic love.*

Her own knowledge of the agony and loss mortality can make you suffer comes to Emily directly with the ghastly end of her two oldest sisters. Her mother is mostly an abstraction, but the mother's namesake, Maria, along with Elizabeth, her aunt's namesake, nurture the little girl and build her sense of confidence and identity in this vibrant society of siblings. (The doubling and similarity of names of *Wuthering Heights* parallels the repetition of names in the successive generations of the Brontës: i.e., the mother and daughter Maria, aunt and daughter Elizabeth, father Patrick and son Patrick Branwell.) In retrospect childhood becomes for her a time when intimacy is possible, but that time is doomed. Emily—said to be the "darling child" and "pet nursling" of Cowan Bridge School, where the beloved Maria and the dutiful Elizabeth find miserable death—feels for her oldest sister what little children feel for a loving mother. But also she senses that she feels for absent Maria II what her father feels for the absent Maria I. The sisters' demise scorches her with the knowledge that earthly life means an inevitable alienation from all you love. It makes transcendence a matter of life and death, but it also reinforces her desire to recapture the past and feature childhood as the time when life is most intense, most worthwhile, and least lonely. Imagination becomes her means of hope. In "To Imagination," she writes, "So hopeless is the world without/The world within I doubly prize."[34]

Like an early saint, she figures the mortifying of the flesh can express both her contempt for the world and the faith necessary to overcome the treachery and pain of physical existence. In her novel, Lockwood, the conventional gentleman narrator, falls into a troubled sleep at Wuthering Heights and dreams of reaching out a window and feeling the grip of the ghost-child Cathy's dead ice-cold hand:

"Let me in—let me in! . . . I'm come home. . . . "

As it spoke, I discerned, obscurely, a child's face looking though the window. Terror made me cruel; and, finding it useless to attempt shaking the creature off, I pulled its wrist on to the broken pane, and rubbed it to and fro till blood ran down and soaked the bed-clothes: still it wailed, "Let me in! . . . I've been a waif for twenty years!" (20)

In the time-scheme of the book, this chronology makes little sense: Cathy doesn't die twenty years before this incident, nor does she perish in childhood. But the daughter Maria Brontë did—when Emily Brontë writes this passage, Maria and Elizabeth *have* been dead for just twenty years.

The seed that produces this ghost-girl comes from the father and his habit of telling ghoulish, supernatural Irish stories to the children even when they had nearly grown up; Emily, in particular, is held rapt by them. But now, here, I want to argue that the specter of the child Cathy and that sadistic piece of torture can conjure up for us both Maria and Emily, the one insufficiently protected by the father and martyred by an institution for "clergymen's daughters," the other emotionally damaged by the capricious reign of mortality and in deep conflict between a longing to have the dead back and the need to break free from death's grip. The text at this point identifies with the wounded, victimized child as importuning lover, with the "ordinary" man who fears the terrible intrusion of the uncanny and morbid into life, and with the living, monomaniacal male love-seeker (Heathcliff) begging for union with the child-form of his beloved ("'Come in! come in!' he sobbed. 'Cathy, do come. Oh, do—*once* more'" [23]). The whole scene can be read as an eruption of the excluded, mistreated, disillusioned daughter into male consciousness. The time in the book is 1801. The next two centuries will feature the struggle of the daughter to get from the outside to the inside of things and penetrate the "man's world."

The wrist-rubbing episode must surely be one of the most striking metaphorical images of repression that fiction offers. Lockwood's dream and Cathy Earnshaw's ghost enact the agonizing internal war between the unmet desires of the past and the threat of the past to make anarchy of the self and society in the present. They render the spooky hunger for love and care in the enduring child without and within—battered and rubbed a thousand wrong ways—who is both the self hurt and cut off from love in the past and the victim of the present self enraged at the abuses of the past. The suffering little ghost represents the erotic and tortured history of childhood—the wounds, needs, and urges formed back then and inefficiently suppressed and expressed later—that so terribly and inexorably assaults consciousness: Cathy's, Heathcliff's, and Lockwood's fictional consciousness; Emily and Patrick Brontë's real consciousness; all consciousness. And you have here an image and memory of the haunting desperation of girlhood that man cannot shut out.

4.

TOYLAND, GIRL-AND-BOYLAND, AND
THE FATHER'S ISSUE

Mr. Brontë brings home toy soldiers which the children play with, fantasize about, and use to make up stories. Charlotte explicitly and Emily implicitly come to understand that this paternal gift triggers their creative vocations. They project their imaginative life onto his presents, and for Emily the fetish from the father over the years turns into the most important thing in her existence: the fantasy world that becomes her reality. When the 7-year-old takes up that "grave-looking fellow," she starts a process through which "Gravey" metamorphoses into Heathcliff and her novel. At first, she and Charlotte make up secret plays, then she and Anne are junior partners to Charlotte and Branwell in the sagas of Glasstown, Verdopolis, and Angria. But Emily, impatient with the abjection of Charlotte's women and Branwell's political intrigues, needs the liberty to control her own world. When Charlotte goes away to school at Roe Head, Emily breaks off from the collective saga, takes Anne with her, and creates the imaginary realm of Gondal. Her diary papers show how completely she integrates her Gondal life with her so-called "real" life. This entry from June 26, 1837, is typical: "Papa gone out. Tabby in the kitchen—the Emperors and Emperesses of Gondal and Gaaldine preparing to depart from Gaaldine to Gondal to prepare for the coronation which will be on the 12th July. Queen Victoria ascended the throne this month."[35] Gondal, England, Haworth—in her mind it's all the same.

It's clear—though no one seems to have noticed—that when she comes to write *Wuthering Heights*, she makes Heathcliff up out of the impetus and memory of her father's fiction-generating gift. As Patrick brought play figures home to his children, the father in the book, after the children have asked him for gifts, brings home the swarthy little foundling Heathcliff who becomes the focus of the narrative and a figure through which the author projects desire and savage fantasy. This analog is surely no coincidence. Heathcliff and *Wuthering Heights* are what she eventually makes of Patrick's toys. She gives the world Heathcliff as her father gave the children figures to play with, but she inhabits Heathcliff too. She thus imagines herself not only as the receiver of her father's gift, but also as that very gift itself, and she both shapes and becomes her father's issue and bounty.

5.
PSYCHOLOGY DISPLACED ONTO CANINES— LOVE ME, LOVE MY DOG

Patrick, who remembers pets and watchdogs fondly from his own childhood, insists on keeping big dogs in his house, and Emily—unlike Charlotte—makes his enthusiasm for animals her own. She fetishizes dogs, and her intense relationship with them stands out (see Chitham, 114). As a child and later as a woman, she can pet, discipline, tussle, and romp even with fierce ones. They serve as a source of, and an outlet for, love. Nancy Gars, a servant in the Brontë household when the Brontës were small, said Emily had "the eyes of a half-tamed creature and cared for nobody's opinion, only being happy with her animal pets."[36] That feral streak in her shows up again and again in her fiction (*Wuthering Heights* teems with vicious dogs), and so does the intimidating independence and the feeling for primal nature that Gars's words imply.

To keep and master animals for a nineteenth-century young woman was to exercise an authority that could look and feel very much like traditional male power, and creatures for Emily would seem to be rather like what the metaphorical flock is to the Old Testament Lord: a vital connection with the world, a responsibility, and a catalyst for exploring the pent-up violence and sacrifice inherent in creation. Like that of many others, her passion for dogs shows a need for affectionate contact with living beings, but it can also mask psychological projections onto them, aggressive misanthropy, and a drive for control and obedience born out of the frustrating behavior of people. When Emily was miserably failing in her attempt to teach at the Law Hill girls' school, she snapped to her pupils that the dog of the place is "dearer to her than they." She meant it. She needed to reconcile her impulses for loving attachment with what she saw as the cruel ferocity of life, and one instinctive way to do that was through dogs.

One afternoon the menacing Brontë mastiff Keeper, which Emily had made *her* dog, is discovered lolling on the father's bed. Elizabeth Gaskell, writing Charlotte's life, sets the scene: "Keeper was lying on the best bed, in drowsy voluptuousness. Charlotte saw Emily's whitening face, and set mouth, but dared not speak to interfere; no one dared when Emily's eyes glowed in that manner out of the paleness of her face" (269). She drags the growling dog downstairs, but it becomes more and more enraged and, slavering viciously, sets to spring at her throat. Suddenly Emily uses her bare fists to hit him again and again in the face, beating him furiously until his gleaming eyes are swollen and running with blood, and he's half-blind. She then guides him to his lair, takes his poor puffy head in her lap and soothes him with her love.

Obviously she's courageous—physically brave in the way that only males were expected to be—but psychologically such a dog-day afternoon reveals a sensibility roiling with self-lacerating, sadistic impulses. It points to an imagination capable of creating Heathcliff, the "half-savage" Cathy, and the whole *Wuthering Heights* world. Emily identifies strongly with both the humane and the bestial. She finds in her female self both a disciplinarian and a beast, and that leads her to feel and project an odd continuum of identity—daughter, dad, and dog.

No wonder she could imagine in her novel a famous scene of fleshly mortification, cruelty, and stoicism (the boy Heathcliff is describing the attack of the Linton bulldog set loose on Cathy):

The devil had seized her ankle . . . I heard his abominable snorting. She did not yell out—no! She would have scorned to do it, if she had been spitted on the horns of a mad cow. . . . A beast of a servant came up . . . shouting—

"Keep fast, Skulker, keep fast!"

. . . The dog was throttled off, his huge, purple tongue hanging half a foot out of his mouth, and his pendant lips streaming with bloody slaver. (38)

That's Emily Brontë's vision of some virulent "mad cow disease" infecting and defining life in the world.

That extraordinary scene occurs only a few pages after Lockwood's bloody dream of mutilating the ghost-child Cathy at the point of entry. Together with the earlier passage, the words suggests both outrage at the brutal suffering inflicted on girls and a terrible masochistic reaction to the fate of *being* a girl. The imagery shows a displacement of human sexuality into

animal ferocity, and it conveys, in the obvious phallic symbolism, an appalled fascination with the bestial amorality of fecund, violent nature. Her
mind and art include both the stoic girl and the vicious dog as integral,
connected parts of the unfolding, mysterious processes of life. The "civilized" Lintons loose their dog on Cathy, and that starts a chain of events
that issues in the birth and flourishing of the daughter Cathy II. Sadism
and masochism, like dog-eat-dog, are inescapable facts of life to Emily
Brontë, and what you need is some rational way of seeing and accepting
cruelty as an ineluctable part of existence and nature.

In Brussells, she wrote an essay for Monsieur Heger: "Nature is an inexplicable problem; it exists on a principle of destruction; everything must
be a tireless instrument of death to others or else cease to live itself, and in
the meantime we celebrate the day of our birth and praise God for having
entered into such a world."[37] She also writes an excercise on "the cat." She
liked cats, but not as much as dogs. Why not? *Cats are the animals most
like humans. Watch them and, just as in people, you see hypocrisy and ingratitude, as well as cruelty.*[38] This comparison may sound cynical, but, as
in her novel to come, she is really working to comprehend the mystery of
things and to find a vision of inclusiveness. It's not a matter, in E. M.
Forster's famous words, of "only connect." We *are* connected. It's not *nature* on the one hand and *culture* on the other, or humanity versus bestial-
ity, but all in all.

Brontë imagines the grown-up Heathcliff carrying the memory of the
"refined" Lintons setting their dogs on children, and she shows him re-
venging himself viciously. After marrying Isabella Linton, he tells Nelly,
"The first thing she saw me do, on coming out of the Grange, was to hang
up her little dog." Nelly replies, "Mr. Heathcliff . . . this is the talk of a
madman." (117). But the savage pain of life can drive you mad, can pervert
your humanity, can make you question naive ideas about the goodness of
being. Just before the bulldog had mauled the child Cathy, she and Heathcliff had been peering into the beautifully adorned, plush Linton drawing-
room, watching their cultured little counterparts Edgar and Isabella fighting over which one would get to fondle and pet their little white poodle.
The scene then renders supposedly civilized children torturing the dog by
pulling it apart.

Victorians like Emily Brontë and Darwin turn to the animal world and
render its savagery partly to combat the distortions and deceptions of reli-

gion that, in the expectations it sets up, can break hearts and leave hurt people without plausible faith. The point is that savagery is actually bound up with the whole process of survival, a process in which individual death is absorbed into collective immortality. Brontë's representation of humanity would seem to evolve out of her attitude towards animals, and that parallel helps you understand one of her distinctive qualities: by normal standards, the main characters of *Wuthering Heights* can hardly be called sympathetic, and yet the novel still manages somehow to convey great sympathy for life and its passion—including most definitely the love-life of the moral outlaws Heathcliff and Cathy.

Though Emily renders deeply flawed characters, conventional moral blame figures hardly at all in her work. If you love your dog and your dog behaves badly, you don't make a huge moral case out of it, because you don't idealize the ethical life of dogs or expect them to be angels. It's the same with humans: Emily isn't shocked by human misbehavior, because she sees savage humanity as part of immortal nature.

6.
"A MORAL TEETHING":
THIS IS NOT MY FATHER'S CREED

Emily learns from her father and her life that you must seek salvation. But she can't do it his way. She is writing *Wuthering Heights* and, clenching her teeth, she composes in a passion this wild speech for a Heathcliff furious at all that keeps him from the dying Cathy and wholeness of being: "I have no pity! I have no pity! The more the worms writhe, the more I yearn to crush out their entrails! It's a moral teething, and I grind with greater energy, in proportion to the increase of pain" (118). No other Brontë—no English novelist, nobody else at all—is writing like that. It's an amazing outburst—vicious, crazy, manic in its anger, but somehow daring, even exhilarating, in its honesty about the mind's savagery. It puts "I *am* Heathcliff" in a grotesque new light. It suggests both a Nietzschean "moral teething" from an ethical tradition gone dead and a Freudian regression back to the time of such libidinous infantile pleasures as biting: it's *beyond* good and evil and *before* good and evil. And "moral teething" (an astounding phrase splicing body and soul) reveals in two words the tremendous intensity, both physical and metaphysical, of Emily Brontë's sensibility.

Philosophically, she needs to accommodate the existence of cruelty into a viable faith, and that's one reason why this passage and Heathcliff matter so much.

How can you face and justify a world and a species in which such monstrous sentiments and urges exist, and, what's worse, exist in yourself (*I* am *Heathcliff*)? For her father, as well as Anne and even Charlotte, the answer lies in Christianity and its doctrines, but not for Emily. Orthodoxy—organized and institutionalized creed—casts out; it damns, rains down fire and brimstone on wicked others, turns the disobedient to salt, separates sheep from goats, tells accursed ones to depart, and lets loose the poison gas of self-righteousness. It proclaims "I am *not* Heathcliff." It's always judging and, for her, that means it condemns much of life. It can and does lead to cant, rant, hypocrisy and lies. What's needed is an *indiscriminate*, inclusive imagination that can find integrity in the fact of enduring life and in the divided self.

Emily Brontë's most famous poem "No Coward Soul Is Mine" asserts an intellectual courage that matches her physical courage.

> No Coward soul is mine,
>
> . . .
>
> Vain are the thousand creeds
> That move men's hearts, unutterably vain,
> Worthless as withered weeds
> Or idlest froth amid the boundless main
> To waken doubt in one
> Holding so fast by thy infinity
> So surely anchored on
> The steadfast rock of Immortality.

The words "No coward soul is mine" have come to define her spirit. The poem enunciates her faith in immortality, but obviously a belief in eternal life would require no courage at all, if it were simply a matter of acquiescing to Christian ideas or even to a benevolent deism or an idealistic romantic pantheism. Emily's bravery lies in implicating the self in whatever *is*, in embracing pain, identifying with the perpetrator as well as the victim, rejecting the exclusions of moral superiority, and taking it all in. What's daring is that she can and does imagine, for example, Heathcliff, ecstatic suffering, blood-slavering dogs, immanent death, Cathy's drunken brother

Hindley, and the impotence of moral sentimentalism all as ineradicable parts of immortality, which for her is the eternal process of being.

Her problem is the same one her father has made his vocation, the problem of faith, but she rejects his—even as it brings to life her own. Two famous lines defiantly proclaim: "Vain are the thousand creeds/That move men's hearts, unutterably vain." Those are fighting, radical words. The point is that the "creeds of men" work to create doubt in immortality because they condemn much of *what is*, ignore the mysterious integrity of existial processes, and can't accept the totalizing interdependence of all things and all streams of life. Without Heathcliff there would be no passion in *Wuthering Heights*, no redemptive love between Cathy II and Hareton, no story, and no Emily Brontë in our consciousness. But Christian doctrine—Patrick's and Charlotte's too—would burn up a "Heathcliff."

Emily Brontë's intellectual blasphemy rests in her claim to have no limits—that there are no limits to her imagination, that she recognizes no boundaries between God, herself, nature, history, thought and all that is and may be. When she comes to refashion much of "No Coward Soul is Mine" in Cathy's famous speech, and make Heathcliff the focus of her faith, she substitutes—outright basphemy—Heathcliff for the abstract God of the poem:

I cannot express it; but surely you and everybody have a notion that there is, or should be, an existence of yours beyond you. What were the use of my creation if I were entirely contained here? . . . If all else perished, and *he* remained, I should still continue to be; and, if all else remained, and he were annihilated, the Universe would turn to a mighty stranger. I should not seem a part of it. My love for Linton is like the foliage in the woods. Time will change it, I'm well aware, as winter changes the trees. My love for Heathcliff resembles the eternal rocks beneath—a source of little visible delight, but necessary. Nelly, I *am* Heathcliff—he's always, always in my mind—not as a pleasure, any more than I am always a pleasure to myself—but as my own being—so, don't talk of our separation again— . . . (63–64)

Emily is making more vivid, less wooly, and even more provocative the mystery and implied heresy in the poem: that immortality, God, and life are inseparable from the desires of a self that is both particular and boundless. In *Wuthering Heights*, she is really imagining what a wide-embracing love might mean, and it means a moral teething.

7.

PRESERVING PAPA'S SEED:
HEATHCLIFF SIRES EMILY'S GRANDFATHER

Emily listens all agog. Her father tells her how his Irish great-grandfather Hugh went to Liverpool to trade cattle, and there found a dark, hungry Welsh street urchin, took him home, called him "Welsh," and raised him as his own son. Welsh, he said, dazzled the old man, turned into a shrewd trader, became Hugh's favorite, and drove the Brunty brothers wild with jealousy. After the father's death, said Patrick, they drove Welsh out, but, with money-shrewdness and vengeful will, he came back to take over the place from the impoverished brothers and marry their sister, the youngest daughter of the family. It's a cuckoo's tale that Patrick tells. Welsh in turn adopted a son (young Hugh) of one of these poor, drunken Brunty brothers. But Welsh lost his money, turned mean, and badly abused Hugh. The boy's only joy and companionship in misery was his dog Keeper, and that's how Emily's dog got its name. Emily's racing mind imagines what it's like to take over a family, how it feels to be an outsider and then a usurper, what it's like to be victimized and become an abuser, what it's like to love a dog more than anything, what it's like to *be* a dog. Patrick finishes his story. When Hugh got old enough, he ran away from the farm, got a job in a limekiln, met and married the golden-haired Ellis McClory, and Patrick was their first-born.

Later Emily thinks *those are my people, they made my father and me.* In her private world she feels that a Brontë is the heir of impulse, of early incestuous feeling, of passion from beyond the pale. She is the descendant and scribe of the love-struck, the dispossessed, the self-fashioned, the canny, the obsessed. She comes from freedom-seeking, noncowardly souls. She muses on the childhood of Welsh and his foster sister and what Welsh suffered and how he lived his life. As Welsh was welsh in a strange land, so, she thinks, we are still Irish here. She comes to imagine and know the torrent of love and ferocious family feeling that roils in banal circumstances and forms human life—her life in particular—even though English gentility and manners work to suppress such knowledge and its expression. When she fantasizes the emotional life of Gondal and then composes *Wuthering Heights*, she transmutes her father's ancestral history into her art.

The only trouble with this view of Emily bonding with her father's heritage is that it's almost certainly false. In 1995, after Juliet Barker's massive biography *The Brontës* appeared, Lydia Brontë, a writer and a direct descendant of Patrick's brother William, wrote to the *New York Times* asserting that Barker had "missed a crucial fact," namely the story of Welsh and Emily's indebtedness to it.[39] Barker, who had dismissed such material as a late nineteenth-century fabrication, replied that the Welsh-and-Emily legend was hogwash circulated by a man named William Wright a half century after *Wuthering Heights* because he wanted to bolster his intuitions about the Irish connection. The late Victorian Brontës, says Barker, knew little about their family history.[40]

The fact is that Heathcliff, in effect, was Welsh's ancestor, not the other way around. Other scholars, however, still maintain that Patrick's Irish history and his tale-telling at least planted the seeds of Heathcliff, the two Cathys, and the novel in Emily's imagination. What's most telling in the Lydia Brontë version and its variants is posterity's need to make Emily her father's vessel. People thought that the erotic and violent nature of *Wuthering Heights* must necessarily come from male experience and the father. The idea seems to be that such a strong and *original* novel necessarily depends on and is dictated by masculinity.

Two points need stressing. One is that in order for Emily to write such a story in such a form, she *would* need to be a new kind of woman—really, by Victorian standards, a sort of man. The second point is that this daughter has not only preserved the seed of the father, she has literally *invented* it. The daughter's art has recreated the father's heritage and significance for later generations, and that power is what makes modern Lottish history. To preserve the seed, you must regenerate it through the imagination. The Brontë myth reverses the myth of Athena springing from Zeus's head: here the Father springs from the head of the daughter: Heathcliff—*mon semblable, mon frère, mon père, mon grand-père—c'est moi*. Posterity reads the father's life through the daughter's imagination.

8.
PISTOL-PACKIN' DAUGHTER:
"LOAD AGAIN, PAPA"

Emily sprawls on the floor next to her dog, oblivious to the world, reading Scott, reading Byron, sucking in vicarious life. Devouring *Rob Roy* one day, she is struck by the rebel figures of the heroic Di Vernon, who can fight like the bravest man and of Rob's de-gendered, mannish wife Helen MacGregor, who leads an armed band of guerillas. Another time, taking in Byron and his description of what it's like to have a gun pointed at you, she can almost hear the click of pistols being cocked. What she actually has heard ever since she can remember is the big bang of her father shooting off his revolver.

Patrick's eyesight is failing, he's growing old, and in 1843 Emily is the only child living at home with him. He decides, for their safety, to teach her to shoot, and she becomes, according to the stationer Greenwood, a star pupil. When her father wishes, she comes out of the kitchen, sets up a target, takes the gun from him, and blazes away with skill: "She knew she had gratified him, and she would return to him the pistol, saying 'load again papa,' . . . 'I'm ready again, papa.' And so they would go on until he thought she had had enough practice for that day. 'Oh!' he would exclaim, 'She is a brave and noble girl.'"[41]

If, as Mao said, "power flows from the barrel of a gun," then it could mean a lot for a daughter to take up arms and shoot like her father. She might feel a dramatic new forcefulness, and her sense of gender and the possibilities in her particular imagination might well change and expand. In *Wuthering Heights*, Isabella Linton Heathcliff tells how her drunken brother Hindley lets her see his weapon:

[A] hideous notion struck me. How powerful I should be possessing such an instrument! I took it from his hand, and touched [it]. He looked astonished at the expression my face assumed during a brief second. It was not horror, it was covetousness. He snatched the pistol back, jealously . . . and returned it to its concealment. (108–109)

The transgressive, gender-bending spirit of this little scene between secondary characters does, in fact, permeate the book. And it's well to remember that, as a cigar is sometimes just a cigar, sometimes a gun is just a gun. It may be that the supposed phallic symbolism in much modern discourse is misnamed, and, as in *Wuthering Heights*, what's operating is not penis envy but pistol envy. What does a woman want, Herr Doktor? How about an equalizer? If a young woman has a means to power—can wield the gun, and/or wield the pen—she might construct gender as she wishes and according to her own nature. Preserving seed might come to mean taking over from the father and delivering your best shot.

9.

SQUEEZING OUT A THE NEW CATHY
AND THE INTEGRITY OF EROTIC LIFE

Daughter Emily, sister Emily, imagines a Lot story vital to modern experience. Look what happens at the heart of *Wuthering Heights*: the pattern and dilemma of Lot's wife, the destruction of Sodom, and generation out of the cave take shape, but in a new form. Midway through the book, Heathcliff and a pregnant, mortally ill Cathy, both married to others, renew their love for one another in a frenzy of illicit desire. Their emotional language soars, and they rage against their physical separation and her imminent death. Their fierce embrace stuns her into unconsciousness and then into mindless labor. She gives birth to Cathy II and immediately dies. A terrible conflict between unsanctioned love and the necessity of childbearing kills her, but leaves new life, a daughter, to replace the mother, and an erotic history that becomes part of the future.

In this central Chapter 15, the dramatic agony of Cathy and Heathcliff features a desperate looking back to a doomed world of childhood intimacy, a looking back to a time when libidinal feeling and closeness didn't mean the restrictive demands of a sexuality channeled within marriage to produce progeny, but to an age of polymorphous love—what Freud would call "polymorphous perversity." Since the book first appeared, many readers have tried unsuccessfully to prove that Heathcliff, rather than Cathy's husband Edgar, must be the biological father of her daughter, but Brontë's story actually suggests something different and less banal: there's more to the generation of life than an act of genital sex. Whatever follows from and out of this encounter is touched and somehow possessed by the bearing and inflicting of pain in this scene, the violent feeling of sacrifice, and the spiritual and verbal intimacy of these wild ones in this time of mortal crisis. Cathy II is the issue of a lawful marriage, but this girlchild and her subsequent destiny are also born out of the fatal passion of the mother, the savage force of Heathcliff's desire, and the intoxications of life in the past as well as the present. The personal experience and the erotic bent of early life determine procreation, identity, and the changes and developments that mark human nature. And erotic life has an integrity that runs through generations. Just as it's vital to see (though, for various reasons, it's easy to miss or deny) that the Lot family history floods into the history of Ruth, David, and Jesus and becomes an integral part of the whole scriptural tradition, it's important to see how from out of the passion of Heathcliff and the first Cathy flow both the love story of the daughter Cathy and, beyond that, a radical vision of erotic experience that is *inclusive*. Like *Lot*, "the text offers the diversity and power of erotic appetite and even suggests that amoral, sexual besotment" are sometimes necessary for survival and progress (see Chapter 1 of this book).

To think of Heathcliff is to remember his dedication to love and his cruelty. He is like one of those men of Sodom who defies God to pursue the object of desire, caring nothing for future life beyond his erotic need. The book's plot does end with regenerative images replacing tragic obsession and the appeals of civilization overcoming the force of selfish eroticism. Brontë presents the conflict between desire and sanctioned love, ultimately choosing, in the end, to bring love into harmony with law, through the coming together of Cathy II and Hareton Earnshaw, whom she redeems from brute ignorance by teaching him to read. In these last pages, it might seem that Brontë negates Heathcliff and his fanatical love. But she doesn't. In the spirit of her book and her faith, he is a necessary presence. He literally squeezes new life—a new Cathy—out of the woman he loves. Without their erotic transgression, the text indicates Cathy I would have died without giving birth. Brontë is recuperating the wholeness of things, including the dark side of eros, and she insists that the backward look and visionary memory animate being in love. The seed of amoral passion creates life and meaning, creates the imagination and voice of love. It makes possible regeneration and the revision that leads to progress. Generation and regeneration come from the power of language and narrative and what inspires it—not just copulation. For example, it is really the bent of Emily's novel, rather than Charlotte's *Jane Eyre*, that kindles the possibilities for the sympathetic resurrection of the demonized older woman Bertha Mason: *Remember Rochester's wife; remember Linton's wife and Heathcliff's love. Wuthering Heights*, analogically remembering Lot's wife and cities-of-the-plain erotics, insists on the interconnection and integrity of erotic history. The point is that the creation of Heathcliff with all his force and rhetorical complexity shows exactly the kind of imagination that would bring the rehabilitation of Sodom and Gomorrah, and of Lot's wife and daughters too, into the central plot line of twentieth-century humanity.

There is, of course, great ambivalence in the text about Heathcliff, as well as Cathy I. The novel not only kills off mothers, it kills off fathers too.

Significantly, in its second half, in Edgar Linton and Heathcliff, it splits and doubles the father figure for Cathy II, but winds up eliminating each. They both act as fathers, the one loving but tame and conventional, the other strong, but harshly controlling and even, at times, maniacally vicious. Lot gives us two daughters, and Emily Brontë, after the death of the mother Cathy, gives us two fathers. Psychoanalysis has told us that myth and literature often present two mother figures, one "good" and one "bad," who represent an important mode of dealing with the disturbing ambiguity that people feel about their childhood experience and about their mothers. Emily Brontë, stressing daughterhood's growing agency, makes a similar move regarding fathers—"the patriarchy" (split feelings respecting fathers —they're kindly allies of empowerment and monsters of treachery—would come to drive texts by and about daughters down to the present moment). From Edgar, who loves his daughter and whom she loves without reserve, Cathy II gains self-confidence, civility, and a sense of her own value. Nevertheless he is weak, his power is illusionary, and he dies. In the latter part of the novel, Heathcliff, who makes himself into the patriarch of the Wuthering Heights property, takes her under his roof. By an act of will, to secure both the Linton and Earnshaw estates to himself, he forces her into a marriage with his snivelling, dying son Linton. His coercion might well be called legalized, paternal rape—except that the expiring boy is obviously incapable of sex. Though the age difference between Heathcliff and Cathy II is no greater than that between Jane Eyre and Rochester, Emily Brontë imagines no erotic flow, no older man-younger woman attraction, between them. His desire is fixed on achieving immortal identity with Cathy II's mother. Hers is to live and survive the older generation. Heathcliff, in the aftermath of his own frustrated passion, is shown tormenting her into the sullen knowedge that she as a woman has little control over her life, and that if she is to preserve the Linton and Earnshaw seed, she must resist and outlast the father-in-law who loves her dead mother, and she must not look back sentimentally to her mother's life. She must move on.

The logic of the plot structure, however, is not the same as the tone, mood, and feeling of the book and its effects on readers. *Wuthering Heights* is a fire and brimstone novel. The rendering, for instance, of the unspeakable dangers of childbirth for a woman and of the erotic glory to which even baseborn sinners can aspire, tinge the text with a pro-Sodom quality. Moreover, the power of its visionary imagination, the verbal force of its erotic dialogue, and Emily Brontë's ability to create and identify with Heathcliff and generally to let her focus and sympathy flow back and forth across gender boundaries, mark it as pro-Gomorrah. Grand erotic passion—romantic love in the *liebestod* key—need not be exclusively the province of the male troubadors, the courtly love poets, the seventeenth-century tragedians, the Stendhals, the Wagners, or the Tolstoys; it need not have a phallic point.

IV.
Inferences to be Inferred from the Younger Daughter's Issue

- Sodom and Gomorrah are immortal sites in the psychological landscape, the body politic, and the historical memory.
- Without passion and desire, there is nothing.
- People lie and lie about the cruelty of existence.
- Society is a sham and discrete individualism is a sham.
- I am Heathcliff and you are Heathcliff, and I am not Heathcliff and you are not Heathcliff.
- The death of the mother provokes a hardness that diminishes life, but makes it endurable.
- Cruelty and sacrifice lie at the heart of faith and erotic renewal.
- Bearing pain is prayer.
- Passion is greater than virtue.
- Question piety, question authority.
- Truth is relative, perspective multiple.
- The creative soul can transcend gender.
- The pain and joy of childhood are indelible.
- Desire defies death and is immortal.
- Love is a colossal, glorious whip.
- The virgin is born out of bestial savagery.
- Life is a burnt-out wasteland traversed by love-struck refugees and their chroniclers.
- Hush, hush, sweet Charlotte: I am my Father's Keeper.

Chapter 8

The Maiden Tribute

Jane Austen, Mary Shelley, George Eliot, and the Brontës especially make
it clear that the daughter would loom larger and larger in the modern
imagination. Daughters needed to find ways to share the father's life,
but men needed to honor and identify with girls and save them from the
commonplace fate of abuse—physical and mental—that plagued their sex.
Vivid reflections on nineteenth-century girls and their place in the world by
two eminent Victorians, William Stead (1849–1912), the influential journal-
ist and editor of the *Pall Mall Gazette,* and Lewis Carroll (1832–1898), author
of the *Alice* books, pay tribute to the daughter-figure as the being who
brings the quality and moral potential of civilization into focus and gives
purpose to life.

Like Dickens, both men were seduced by the ideal and ideology of innocent girls as redeemers.[1] In very different ways, they were deeply involved with young females, moved by girls' sexual vulnerability, and passionately concerned with their well-being. For thoughtful Victorians, like
Carroll and Stead, bettering female life seemed to depend on controlling
customary forms of violence towards women and girls and increasing their
freedom and self-esteem. Each imagined himself as a Victorian knight serving little damsels (Stead championed the cockney girl Eliza and thousands
more in his "The Maiden Tribute of Modern Babylon" report; Carroll portrayed himself literally as Alice Liddell's bumbling, comic White Knight in
Through the Looking-Glass).

They came into conflict, however, about how best to deal with the threat
and violence of male sexual desire in their society, and that disagreement
has profound implications in the modern quest for female empowerment.

Stead, believing in the righteous power of the press to bring about a political solution, set out to publicize rich older men's victimization of young girls. For Carroll, trumpeting the details of men's sexual wickedness would just make things worse. He imagined that men's temptation to glorify and eroticize power was itself the biggest problem for girls (and everyone else), and he used the girlchild in his *Alice* books to undermine, mock, and belittle traditional male authority and patriarchal pretentiousness. I want to focus on Stead and his famous 1885 "Maiden Tribute" articles,[2] which he wrote in order to get the age of consent for females raised from 13 to 16, on Lewis Carroll's horrified reaction to the series, and on the issues for gender history and the theme of Lot's daughters that Stead and Carroll raise.

I.
A Dubious Act of Heroism

Consider the following events: A man of means and power in London, wanting a virgin girl for his purposes and acting through a former prostitute and brothel-keeper, arranges for Lily, a 13-year-old cockney child, to be procured from her mother and father for five pounds. The girl is deceived. She thinks she is going as a servant to a new "situation," but instead the man has her taken to a shady midwife and abortionist who holds her down, strips her, and examines her genitalia in order to certify her virginity. The girl is so small that the examiner fears that she'll suffer terribly from her deflowering, urges that she be drugged, and agrees to try to patch her up later, if need be. The child is then taken to "a house of ill-fame" where the procuress undresses her, puts her to bed and tries to chloroform her to make her sleep. The woman leaves and the man who bought her—he orders whiskey for himself and lemonade for the girl—comes in the room, locks the door and turns around to find the girl suddenly awake, scared to death, and wailing to go home. Then she falls silent, her body and being wholly at his mercy.

After a while he takes her to a Harley Street doctor to certify her virginity again, and once more she's bared, prodded, and poked—this time unconscious under chloroform—and then put in a hotel with the bawd. The next morning, the man and his agents ship the girl across the Channel to Paris. There she's kept incommunicado for eleven weeks. In London, her distraught mother goes to the police about the missing child. Eventually, the father searches with the authorities in France, and they find the girl. Finally the man who bought her is exposed and put on trial with his accomplices. Within half a year, he's convicted and sent to jail for two months.

He is, however, regarded not as a villain, but a public hero, and the whole affair becomes a huge moral triumph for him. Reform-minded people see him as a Christian soldier doing God's work, and even his sentencing judge, while deploring his methods, credits him with being a man of the highest moral principles. Meanwhile the reformed whore whom he lured back to help him goes to jail for six months. As for the midwife who pitied the girl, she gets thrown in prison and dies miserably.

Does anything really justify the outrageous treatment of this particular girl, her parents, and the two pathetic veterans of the Victorian "gay life"? Was that strip necessary? The man is, of course, William Stead; the victim of the violent scheme is a girl named Eliza Armstrong (Stead called her "Lily"); the reformed whore is Rebecca Jarrett (protégé of female rights advocate Josephine Butler); the midwife is Louise Mournez; and the purpose of the whole charade is to prove sensationally that poor little English girls can and are being sacrificed on a massive scale to rich men's lust and then sold into international prostitution rings—"white slavery," as the reformers called the practice. Social activists like Josephine Butler (vehement opponent of the Contagious Diseases Act that mandated the coercive inspection of prostitutes' bodies) and Bramwell Booth of the Salvation Army had lobbied the flamboyant Stead to help them get Parliament to pass the Criminal Law Amendment Bill. That bill, besides raising the age of consent, would allow young minors to give testimony against men accused of sex crimes. The new law would also more closely regulate sexual behavior deemed immoral, including prostitution generally, sex with children, and—notoriously—homosexual relations. It would mean more rigorous and widespread policing of erotic practices right down through the twentieth century. Its main aim was to prevent supposedly widespread sexual violence against girls that, it was said, raped "the daughters of the poor" and wrecked their lives. Legally and ideologically, it was meant to extend girlhood, setting aside three more years as a protected age of innocence.

Stead's campaign succeeded. He inflamed the nation with his series, got the public excited about the assault on working-class girls, and, in less than a month, the Criminal Law Amendment Bill sailed through Parliament.

II.
"The Maiden Tribute"

London, according to Stead, had become in 1885 "a resurrected and magnified City of the Plain, with all the vices of Gomorrah, daring the vengeance of long-suffering Heaven" (Stead, "Maiden," pt. 1). In "The Maiden Tribute of Modern Babylon" he was consciously offering a new version of Genesis 19 and portraying the Lot complex as a collective social nightmare of male lust and patriarchal conspiracy. Stead regenerated the old fire-and-brimstone story, but he now centered it on the victimology of Lot's daughters and the need to protect them.

"The Maiden Tribute" ran in four parts from July 6 to July 10, 1885. Since Stead's purpose was to prevent young girls from having sex with older men and being lured into prostitution, he decided the best way to do that was to focus on poor virgins procured for privileged old lechers. That would make people actually have to face up to the violation of children and make them do something about it. Stead had informed the Archbishop of Canterbury and other religious leaders about what he was doing in order to gain their support. In the prologue to the series, he set out to get a huge audience for the sex and scandal to come:

We have . . . determined . . . to publish the report of a Special and Secret Commission of Inquiry which we appointed to examine . . . sexual criminality. . . . Nothing but the most imperious sense of public duty would justify its publication. . . . [W]e have no desire to inflict upon unwilling eyes the ghastly story of the criminal developments of modern vice. Therefore we say quite frankly to-day that all those who are squeamish, and all those who are prudish, and all those who prefer to live in a fool's paradise of imaginary innocence and purity, selfishly oblivious to the horrible realities which torment those whose lives are passed in the London Inferno, will do well not to read the *Pall Mall Gazette* of Monday and the three following days.[3]

In other words, *Victorians, start salivating.*

They did. Crowds stormed the office and rioted to get papers throughout the week. The huge news agent chain W. H. Smith banned the sale of the *Pall Mall Gazette*, but newsboys, volunteers (one was George Bernard Shaw, who would mine the whole affair for *Pygmalion* and *Mrs. Warren's Profession*), and the Salvation Army distributed copies. People and Parliament read, raged, and reacted. The tone and style of Stead's project come through in his list of the crimes that the series would expose:

I. The sale and purchase and violation of children.
II. The procuration of virgins.
III. The entrapping and ruin of women.
IV. The international slave trade in girls.
V. Atrocities, brutalities, and unnatural crimes.[4]

All these categories of sexual evil and violence appear in the purchase and possession of "Lily," which concluded the first article. That case immediately made Stead's point and at first seemed to offer proof of his veracity and responsibility. "Lily" turned out to be Eliza, though Stead, in league with the unreliable ex-bawd Jarrett, would sometimes deny it later. But by the time his botch-up in trusting Jarrett's word that she had actually purchased "Lily" from her parents (she had not) was exposed in court and he was convicted of abducting the girl, his goal had been accomplished.

When the child cried in terror in the room that night after Stead had verified that her "maiden tribute" was intact, he thought of lines to end his bombshell opening article: "For the child's sob in the darkness curseth deeper/Than the strong man in his wrath." The important thing was to be on the girl's side and speak in the girl's name—even if you weren't actually sure of her name.

Claiming personal knowledge, "a knowledge purchased at a cost of which I prefer not to speak," Stead described the girl he ostensibly bought:

Lily was a little cockney child, one of those who by the thousands annually develop into the servants of the poorer middle-class. . . . Her education was slight. She spelled write "right," for instance, and her grammar was very shaky. But she was a loving, affectionate child, whose kindly feeling for the drunken mother who sold her into nameless infamy was very touching to behold. In a little letter of hers which I once saw, plentifully garlanded with kisses, there was the following ill-spelled childish verse:—

> As I was in bed
> Some little forth (thoughts) gave (came) in my head.
> I forth (thought) of one, I forth (thought) of two;
> But first of all I forth (thought) of you.[5]

Lily-Eliza sent that verse (it reads like early Lewis Carroll) to her mother, though her Salvation Army "rescuers" would not deliver it. Because Stead addressed a collective problem, he describes the girl in generalized terms, and he, a good progressive man, still could not help seeing her as another class of being—real but lacking individuality and interchangeable with thousands. To save such girls from violence, he felt he had to use violence against her.

The excitement of getting the "Maiden Tribute" story out put Stead in a fever. Overwrought and needing rest, he paced up and down with an icepack on his head dictating his prose. He got carried away in his melo-dramatic role-playing. Impersonating a debauchee, he, a teetotaller, drank champagne, smoked cigars, and rouged his cheeks (like Proust's Baron de Charlus). Picture him when he shut and locked that door and found him-self alone in a bawdy-house with the drugged 13-year-old girl. What went through his mind? Was there, as usual in a brothel room, a looking-glass? Did he see a monstrous reflection of himself that he could sublimate into print? In retrospect, he rationalized and dramatized the scene as one of holy sacrifice: "There was a brief silence. And then there rose a wild and piteous cry—not a loud shriek, but a helpless, startled scream like the bleat of a frightened lamb." It seems the girl is the new lamb of God whose sac-rifice is holy and redemptive—according to Stead, she was even born on Christmas. Erotic violence against a young girl had become the unforgiv-able sin and the ultimate "blasphemy."[6]

The metaphorical power of the scenario in Lot's cave, when drunken-ness drowns civilized repression and frees the patriarch's natural lust for his daughters, reverberates down through the ages. That scene, a version of which Stead enacted, is what he knew could no longer be tolerated or ig-nored, and his determination to end it may have depended on susceptibil-ities within himself. His project to root out sexual sin can, in retrospect, look like a self-purging.

III.
A Man of Contradictions

One day in 1860 a girl, playing with boys in a dirty little English town, stopped to fix her garter. A 13-year-old bully tried to look up her skirt, but suddenly an 11-year-old boy flew to the rescue. And though the younger boy got his head punched, he saved the girl from the bad lad's gaze. The hero was little Willie Stead, who later said, "I often think that little scrimmage was prophetic."[7] And he remembered telling to his father, "I wish God would give me a big whip that I could go round the world and whip the wicked out of it." In 1877, when he had already proved himself a *wunderkind* of journalism, he wrote in his diary about a compulsion to author an "'Uncle Tom's Cabin' on the slavery of England [i.e., prostitution]" (Terrot, 140).

Stead was a fabulous character, bigger than life and a man of huge contradictions. He crusaded against sexual misconduct, but it fascinated him. The home-schooled son of a nonconformist minister, he was an outsider whose "personality became one of the controlling forces in English public life."[8] A believer in democracy and socialism, he championed Tsarist Russia because of his infatuation with a young Russian Countess. A decrier of Mammon, he still figured out how to get pornographic material into his journal and boost circulation. He idealized prostitutes and felt "respect and admiration for the extraordinarily good behaviour of the English girls who pursue this dreadful calling" (Stead, "Maiden," pt. 4). Happily married, he bragged that all over London women were dying for him. Loving, as he put it, to worship "my wife with my body, as the Prayer Book has it," he nevertheless admitted that he limited intercourse to twice a week because, "if thrice or four times in the week I got deaf with apparent wax formation in the right ear."[9] According to Havelock Ellis, the pioneer taxonomist of sexual behavior, Stead loved to talk to him:

The main subject was always sex. He told me that his friends considered him "mad on sex." He did not dispute that opinion. In his life and actions he was undoubtedly a rigid moral Puritan and his strong self-control kept him in the narrow path. But in his interests and emotions he was anything but a Puritan, and in the absence of that stern self-control he would have been quite a debauched person. The mastery of sexuality was a great problem with him. His repressed sexuality was, I consider, the motive force of many of his activities.[10]

A worldly manager of political and commercial affairs, Stead believed in the occult, and published *Letters from Julia*, a book of messages purportedly sent through his hand from a deceased American woman, Julia Ames. He said he'd become her amanuensis, and Julia's wisdom and feminism flowed through him "from the other side." The history of his discarnate, out-of-body dealings was written for the most part by two devoted younger women—his daughter Estelle and Edith K. Harper, whom Stead befriended when she was a girl. Sixteen years later, when Stead was 58, Edith became the adoring secretary of psychic affairs for this man who, she said, loved so much the "Woman Soul of the World." He died heroically on the maiden voyage (fittingly) of the Titanic in 1912 helping to save women and children as the great ship went down. Reportedly, he contacted psychic mediums on both sides of the Atlantic before the keel hit bottom, and his friends and spiritualist allies (one was his fellow admirer of the beautiful Maud Gonne, W. B. Yeats) said he kept coming back to them like a boomerang from the great beyond.

IV.
Making a Sensational Impression

Judith Walkowitz has shown how "The Maiden Tribute" combines victimization, popular melodrama, and pornography in one narrative.[11] It could appeal, therefore, to a complex desire to identify with a righteous cause, participate in a story of menaced virtue that might have a happy ending (moral progress), but also savor vicariously the thrill of erotic *transgression*. The series *is* obscene—titillating, gossipy, irresistibly readable, and full of lascivious innuendo, as you can see from the subheadings of the July 6 inaugural piece: "Virgins Willing and Unwilling," "How Girls Are Bought and Ruined," "The London Slave Market," "Why the Cries of the Victims Are Not Heard," and "Strapping Girls Down." Stead knew the secret joy of the prurient, which is that you don't have to give up guilty pleasures; you just have to say you're against them.

Though the historical significance of "The Maiden Tribute" has been recognized, most notably by Walkowitz, it's still underestimated. It helped spell the doom of the English-speaking public's reticence about sex as a social issue. It encouraged official surveillance of sexual activity, eroticized the popular media, and popularized the theme of sexual exploitation. It politicized the concept of the innocent maiden and identified patterns of female victimization that still haunt modern consciousness. In its metaphorical structure and even its title, Stead fused together and made relevant for contemporary urban culture the dark heritage of both Hebraic Scripture and classical Greek mythology regarding sex and gender history (both Freud and Joyce would do the same). Stead opens his brilliantly sustained rhetorical enterprise with stately but inflammatory prose meant to burn up with moral fervor the resurrected cities of the plain:

In ancient times, if we may believe the myths of Hellas, Athens, after a disastrous campaign, was compelled by her conqueror to send once every nine years a tribute to Crete of seven youths and seven maidens. . . . The vessel that bore them to Crete unfurled black sails as the symbol of despair, and on arrival her passengers were flung into the famous Labyrinth of Daedalus, there to wander about blindly until such time as they were devoured by the Minotaur, a frightful monster, half man, half bull, the foul product of an unnatural lust. . . . Then it was that the hero Theseus volunteered to be offered up among those who drew the black balls from the brazen urn of destiny, and the story of his self-sacrifice, his victory, and his triumphant return, is among the most familiar of the tales which since the childhood of the world have kindled the imagination and fired the heart of the human race. . . .

   This very night in London, and every night, year in and year out, not seven maidens only, but many times seven . . . will be offered up as the Maiden Tribute of Modern Babylon. Maidens they were when this morning dawned, but to-night their ruin will be accomplished, and to-morrow they will find themselves within the portals of London brotheldom. . . . The maw of the London Minotaur is insatiable, and none that go into the secret recesses of his lair return again. . . . Yet, so far from this great city being convulsed with woe, London cares for none of these things, and the cultured man of the world, the heir of all the ages, the ultimate product of a long series of civilizations and religions, will shrug his shoulders in scorn at the folly of any one who ventures in public print to raise even the mildest protest against a horror a thousand times more horrible than that which, in the youth of the world, haunted like a nightmare the imagination of mankind. Nevertheless, . . . I am not without hope that there may be some check placed upon this vast tribute of maidens, unwitting or unwilling, which is nightly levied in London by the vices of the rich upon the necessities of the poor. . . . If the daughters of the people must be served up as dainty morsels to minister to the passions of the rich, let them at least attain an age when they can understand the nature of the sacrifice which they are asked to make. . . . That is surely not too much to ask from the dissolute rich. Even considerations of self-interest might lead our rulers to assent to so modest a demand. For the hour of Democracy has struck, and there is no wrong which *a man* resents like this. [emphasis mine][12]

That's rousing stuff, especially when followed by all sorts of flamy particulars on how the Victorian sex trade worked. Stead, a new Jeremiah, transposes the Minotaur into privileged men who desecrate modern secular faith by violating the girlchild. He moves quickly to feminize the tribute sacrifice—maiden daughters become the sex victims and boys drop right out of the picture. Notice also the implied need for a new male hero (and who do you suppose *that* will turn out to be?) and the shift in focus to the just grievance of the democratic man. Stead fuses and absorbs the cause of sexually exploited girls into that of socially exploited *men*. He's dealing in demonology, as symbolized by the monster, and he turns demonic evil into the sexual plunder of daughters by the rich—by, that is, unjust economic power and an unfair class system. But in this attack, there's still a nagging little hint that girls are the disposable property of men—democratic men. Walkowitz, pointing out a contradiction not only in the supposed feminism of "The Maiden Tribute" but in the history of feminism generally, shows how a stress on victimology can actually weaken the drive for female agency and once again leave female destiny as the ultimate responsibility of men.

Stead, however, finds the Minotaur in actual Establishment figures and assails the hyprocrisy of patriarchal respectability. For rhetorical purposes, he links police and paternal authority to incest and prints an unproved allegation:

A. B., an officer of high standing in the force, fifteen years ago violently seduced his daughter who was then sixteen years old. After this intercourse had continued some time she left home. . . .

Now if this story be true—and we publish it merely in order to challenge the most searching inquiry, and if possible to secure its immediate contradiction—what a piece of wickedness is here exposed to light! (Stead, "Maiden," pt. 4)

At the huge rallies in the weeks following publication, supporters of Stead and the Criminal Amendment Bill would repeat as gospel an "urban legend" about the wealthy gentleman who arranged to buy a virgin, and when he came to ravish her, found his own little daughter. Stead saw that, to make his case, he could play on the new cultural value placed on the purity of daughterhood and on the fears and revulsion against incest.

V.
Charles Dodgson
and His Reaction to the Exposé

People of all opinions knew immediately how important "The Maiden Tribute" was. Something had changed. It signaled, as one social worker for children said, a social revolution. Nothing was off limits to the press, provided it could wrap itself in motives of moral purity. Sex would get more public attention and increasingly become a matter of social concern, policy, and political demagoguery. Those who ignored or seemed to tolerate a society's supposed sexual abuse of its children—especially daughters—could and would be pilloried and condemned.

Politics, sex, daughters, abuse, and the power of prurience, however, made a volatile mix. Nobody wanted to defend men violating girls, but Stead's many detractors thought graphically describing forms of erotic sin might lead to more, not less, sex and violence. Their point was that blatant texts featuring sex would fuel uncontrollable, libidinous desire.

Charles Lutwidge Dodgson, the shy, eccentric bachelor, mathematician, Oxford don, and cleric who, taking the pen name "Lewis Carroll," made up famous tales for little maidens, wanted "The Maiden Tribute" suppressed. This loving friend of Alice Liddell and other girls was appalled by its obscene contents. After he read Stead's opening screed, he wrote Lord Salisbury and asked him to decide whether "the publication, in a daily paper sure to be seen by thousands of boys and young men, of the most loathsome details of prostitution, is or is not conducive to public morality," and, if not, to take "legal steps."[13] His logic was that the image of wanton sex was so powerful that some would succumb to its perverse appeal: the articles would actually foster the spread of erotic violence. It's not a stupid view. No doubt, however, personal revulsion and unconscious impulse caused him to react.

As a child, Dodgson was the eldest son of a large family with eleven children. He identified emotionally not with his authoritarian, clerical father, but with his kind, child-burdened mother who died when he was 19. As a boy he loved to amuse and entertain his siblings—his seven sisters especially—with stories, games, and nonsense. Derek Hudson claims that the great psychological lesson Dodgson learned in his childhood was that he

could not, so long as he lived, be without the companionship of children—
and by children he meant little girls.[14] They were a necessity to him; "they
are three-fourths of my life," he once said. Conventional, adult, genital sexuality and marriage were not for him, and there's no evidence that he ever
engaged in physical sex with anyone else. His sublimated libido, it seems,
flowed compulsively, but with kindness and propriety, towards the figure of
the girlchild. Thus you can see how and why Stead's "Maiden Tribute"
would spook him. If men genitally desire and pay for prepubescent and pubescent virgins, and if *you* love prepubescent girls and the beauty of their
bodies and like photographing them naked, how can you be sure that your
relationship with them is pure and innocent?

Two weeks after the Salisbury letter, in all the furor Stead had wrought,
Lewis Carroll (he used his pen name because it had become synonymous
with empathy for the girlchild) wrote an extraordinary letter in the *St.
James's Gazette*, "Whoso Shall Offend One of These Little Ones—,"[15] setting forth his case. It begins with a complaint about the mushrooming
power of the print media to stir mass emotions and overwhelm thoughtful
civic responsibility:

I know that any writer who ventures to protest against what happens to be a
popular cry has little chance even of respectful attention. The rapid inter-
communication of our age has brought us one evil from which our forefathers
were free: the mass is moved too suddenly and too violently: Each tide of popular
feeling runs headlong in one direction, sweeping all before it, and back again
with an equally dangerous reflux, leaving ravage and ruin behind it. . . . [A]
horrible fashion seems to be setting in, of making all things public, and of
forcing the most contaminating subjects on the attention even of those who
can get nothing from them but the deadliest injury. . . . The question at issue is
not whether great evils exist—not again whether the rousing of public opinion
is a remedy for those evils. . . . The real question is, whether this mode of
rousing public opinion is, or is not, doing more harm than good.

In Carroll's mind, Stead, "in the sacred name of Religion," was ramming
pornography down the throats of a public that would become addicted to
it. The letter goes on to "plead for our young men and boys, whose imaginations are being excited by highly-coloured pictures of vice." According to
his biographer Morton N. Cohen, this child-lover went through struggles of
conscience about his "bad Habits," had shameful dreams and fantasies, and
felt remorse at being tempted by erotic images and thoughts that could heat

up desire and put you in peril of sin.[16] Taking up Stead's title word "maiden" and his rhetoric sacralizing the child, Carroll writes, "I plead for our pure maidens, whose souls are being saddened, if not defiled, by the nauseous literature that is thus thrust upon them—I plead for them in the name of Him who said 'Whose shall offend one of these little ones which believe in me, it were better for him that a millstone were hanged about his neck, and that he were drowned in the depth of the sea.'" He abhorred anything he thought might threaten girls and his faith in them.

The rest of Carroll's critical reflection on "The Maiden Tribute," in its personal context, is candid and moving. He drags out a long quote from an obscure sermon by E. Monro published in 1850 (he must have read it and taken it to heart long before Stead portrayed the Minotaur). Its gist is that you should avoid images and thoughts of sex and sexual desire. Now Carroll, whose friendship with girls gave meaning to his life, sometimes photographed girls in poses that, as many have said, look unmistakably sensual and, in our era at least, convey sexuality.[17]

The facts are these: Dodgson, one of the most distinguished photographers of the nineteenth century, gave up photography for mysterious reasons, and there was some gossip about his desire to be in the company of girls and take nude pictures of them. His attention to their daughters annoyed a few mothers, including Alice's, and he castigated himself more than once for his impure thoughts and his sinfulness. His heirs cut a page out of his diary, and entries from the time of his closest involvement with Alice Liddell are missing. It's with this background that I see Carroll, in his letter, quoting Munro against Stead and on behalf of his own soul: "By all means, and on all occasions, avoid dwelling on the object of impure sensation. . . . The mere dwelling on its forbidden pollutions, even to combat them, forms evil habits, and withers holiness." Munro's words that follow, steeped as they are in the idiom of photography, would seem to have deep meaning for Dodgson (and likely explain why he gave up photography). And they can make you feel something of the erotic longing, shame, and conflicts that shaped Carroll's avocations and his particular focus:

But on all these occasions as far as possible shun the image; do not let the coloured lights fall into a shape or outline, nor suffer, if you can help it, your vision to centre them in a focus; if they are dimmed, leave them so, and do not restore the view; repress even the slightest image, lest it should strengthen and invigorate evil desire; you are too weak to bear it. If you have to pray against it, to examine yourselves on it, let the object be an imperfect memory, a recollection of something past, rather than of the object itself; mean it without expressing it, intend without defining it. Let no excuse avail to dwell on it.

Carroll adds:

This contrast between these wise words and the conduct of those who are doing their best to "centre in a focus" the soul-destroying picture, and to add yet more "coloured lights" than the devil has already supplied, needs no words of mine to emphasize it.

"The Maiden Tribute" presents his worst nightmare. The world is out of control. Girls can be violently possessed, dirtied, ruined, and the horror is that self might actually be implicated; imagining such a thing might trigger some hellish impulse that makes you or others want to do it. What's needed is to focus on the girl in a new way and to create an irresistible, kindly, comic diversion that becomes reality. That was Carroll's way in the *Alice* books and in his life generally.

VI.
The Force of
Sexual Hubris vs. Lewis Carroll

The issue between Carroll and Stead is about the wielding of power. For Carroll, it's male power and the fetishizing of it that really harms girls, so for him the way to protect them is to neutralize people's insidious love affair with power—whatever their erotic bent.

When I read that Dodgson condemned Stead's series, my first response was a smugly superior knowingness: *It hits too close to home for him; he has a sneaking sympathy with Minotaur men; little girls excite him, etc., etc.* In retrospect, how typically patronizing—and revealing—my reaction was. Never mind that Dodgson, like Stead, supported the Criminal Law Amendment provisions. Most people know sexual deviance when they see it, and the way to see it is to look down on the suspected deviate. Vladimir Nabokov, for instance, who owed a huge debt to Carroll's art and translated him into Russian, said, "I always call him Lewis Carroll Carroll because he was the first Humbert Humbert." In an interview, he proclaimed in his own high style, "He has a pathetic affinity with H.H. but some odd scruple prevented me from alluding in *Lolita* to his wretched perversion and to those ambiguous photographs he took in dim rooms. He got away with it, as so many other Victorians got away with pederasty and nympholepsy. His were sad scrawny little nymphets, bedraggled and half-undressed, or rather semi-undraped, as if participating in some dusty and dreadful charade."[18]

There's a marvelous irony in *Lolita's* creator taking the Savonarola line towards the Victorians and Carroll, and it just shows how the topsy-turvy zaniness of the *Alice* books is actually realism. Nabokov's outlook, steeped in the spirit of Stead, meant that somebody might come along to write, as Paul Taylor said, "a piece with a mock-Wonderland trial scene in which an adult Alice—claiming to have retrieved the memory of repressed child abuse—puts Dodgson in the dock."[19] Louise Doughty, reviewing Christopher Hampton's 1994 play "Alice's Adventures Under Ground," was that somebody. She seized on what she called, "the sadistic undercurrents implicit in Carroll's manipulation of his most famous 'child-friend'" and asserted, "Carroll was clearly a potential abuser in thought if not in deed and what this production does not consider is whether the innocent Alice is at all aware of or damaged by his attentions. . . . [I]t made me feel sick."[20]

People like Doughty and Nabokov feel free to assault Lewis Carroll and make such accusations because they, in their time, have been caught up in an ongoing, very complex "maiden tribute" saga.[21] Jackie Wullschlager, for instance, writes, "In our post-Freudian age, the sexual undercurrents seem blatant and these friendships unhealthy. The truth was more ambiguous."[22] It's important to note that not one shred of evidence has come to light that any child Dodgson ever knew suffered, as a result of his behavior, trauma, damage, or physical, emotional, or verbal abuse of any kind, and—as all honest parents know—very few adults could make a similar claim. On the contrary, Lewis Carroll brought joy and kindness to children and comic genius to the world. Keeping in mind the hostile disdain of Doughty and Nabokov and Stead's strange time in that dark room with Lily-Eliza, consider this cheerful, unconsciously erotic memory of the grown-up Alice (Mrs. Reginald Hargreaves) about making pictures with Dodgson:

Much more exciting than being photographed was being allowed to go into the dark room, and watch him develop the large glass plates. What could be more thrilling than to see the negative gradually take shape, as he gently rocked it to and fro in the acid bath? Besides, the dark room was so mysterious, and we felt that any adventures might happen then! There were all the joys of preparation, anticipation, and realization, besides the feeling that we were assisting at some secret rite usually reserved for grown-ups! Then there was the additional excitement, after the plates were developed, of seeing what we looked like in a photograph. (Cohen, *Selected Letters*, 164–165)

No poor, bedraggled little victim here.

What hubris, what aggressive bent in people, then, makes them feel that their own erotic lives are morally superior to Carroll's? It's a momentous question whose answer has to do not only with recent history, but with Lot's cave and daughters, with the nature and linkage of libido and power, with entrenched reverence for manliness, with deep-seated fear of feminine agency, with the danger of sexual exploitation (see *Lolita*), with a religious heritage that sanctions sex only for reproduction, and with the love of exercising control over the sexual behavior of others. Sexual acts, emotions, and thoughts can easily come close to violence; strong social, group, and parental pressures squeeze individuals to want to be and feel sexually "normal"; and the nurture and culture that promote and very early on impose obedience to sexual authority leave men and women with the will to project that obedience onto others. People could and would look down on Carroll's penchant to spend time with, on, and for little girls because authoritarian impulses, moral surety, and good conscience—or the need for it—about sex, and residual fears about sexual misconduct encourage scapegoating and rampant hostility against erotic nonconformists.

Sex, violence, and power are intertwined, and how that explosive amalgam can be managed and civilized drives both Stead's blast and Carroll's response. The dispute between them is about how best to stop the mistreatment of children and young women. It seems simple for a man like Stead, at ease with his own masculinity and "normal" sexuality, to understand life as a violent sexual melodrama of good and evil with himself as a potential hero. If he has power, he knows that's a good thing. Gain power and suppress, forcefully if necessary, wicked oppressors. He understands instinctively how using a young girl as an object for good can empower himself and his interests (in fact "Lily" owes much to Carroll—she is in part the abstract idea of Alice democratized and popularized). He makes her a sexual object and ignores her individuality in order to turn her into a symbol that will move people. She becomes first of all a cause and an appendage to his will, and she herself is of real interest only as she can affect others through the stirring words of his moral crusade.

Now think of Dodgson. I suspect he knew the pornographic potential of Stead's articles was real because he felt them. For him, the problem is not to empower, but to *disempower* himself and others. His texts and life show that he is interested in ceding power to Alice and other girlchildren. Lewis Carroll wants to undercut the dignity of authority and minimize the sway of violence—even righteous violence. Cohen's carefully researched biography convinces me that Dodgson behaved impeccably with Alice and the rest of his little girl friends and models, but that he knew that some of his erotic desires were unacceptable—even shameful and potentially dangerous. It's quite likely that he struggled to control and repress urges he may have felt, but knew were contemptible. He cannot be a hero, cannot imagine starring in a melodrama of virtue, because in his mind, he partakes in sinful eroticism. He had feelings that, if dwelt or acted upon, might implicate him in sin. Lewis Carroll, then, works, through the art and fantasy of the Alice stories, to belittle violence, authority, and himself. He understands his otherness, his marginal erotic being and his problematic relationship to power. Therefore he throws the subjective stress in his work onto Alice. He uses the real name of Alice Liddell. He's interested in imagining her agency, her individuality, and the possibilities of identifying with this child. Modern Babylon sucks up Eliza Armstrong, but Alice sucks up the environment through her looking-glass into her Wonderland. You might call the *Alice* books Babylon's long overdue tribute to the maiden.

VII.
Mocking Male Authority
and Empowering the Daughter

The normal sense of power was reversed in Dodgson's erotic life. Children had affective, emotional power over him; he depended on their good will, but they were not dependent on him. Therefore he doesn't eroticize or idealize power, and that's what makes him so interesting on the subject of power and on the advancement of daughters. Between would-be male heroes and little girls, he chooses the little girl every time. Carroll, looking at Alice Liddell, sees that the girlchild is real; he understands her uniqueness and the fact that she is different from himself with different needs. He senses that the girlchild must be protected from his own love, and the way to do that is to diffuse and exorcise the sexual violence in himself and, beyond that, to diminish the charisma of violence and male entitlement in the imagination.

Lewis Carroll's great move in his mock war on authority is to place the beloved girl Alice Liddell in the midst of weirdos, autocratic fakes, and ridiculous, infantilized, would-be heroes, and then project himself into that world of folly in self-caricatures, such as Humpty-Dumpty, the Gnat, the White Rabbit, and the White Knight.

The revolutionary, subversive attitude in Carroll towards male authority and its threat of force needs to be emphasized. You find it everywhere in the *Alice* books—in "off-with-his head" royal pronouncements, "sentence first–verdict after" judgments, in the violent nursery rhymes, in "Speak-gruffly-to-your-little-boy-and-beat-him-when-he-sneezes" child-care maxims, in the send-up of the very idea of heroism. The figure of the White Knight becomes in Carroll a foolish, fond autobiographical entertainer for Alice, and then he ends up as a photograph in her memory. In his own photography, Dodgson may eroticize children and he may even aestheticize infantile sexuality, but he does not eroticize violence or power. He simply—or complexly—wishes to make the childishness (in the pejorative sense of the word) of force obvious, and to reduce violence to a prepubescent stage—that is, to a stage in which it cannot breed.

To recapitulate: the mode of Stead is to magnify sexual violence as a way of mobilizing political power to crush the trade in girls. The mode of Carroll is to defuse, minimize, and trivialize the forces of violence, including patriarchal power, because to dwell on images of heroism and strength in the service of righteousness is to risk fetishizing power. Before Stead invented the modern Minotaur, Carroll imagined the Jabberwock (Tenniel's drawing of the Jabberwock—see Figure 8.1—could serve as well for the Minotaur), and "Jabberwocky" and its context take us back to basic questions about violence, male power, sexual desire, and their linkage.

> The Jabberwock, with eyes of flame,
> Came whiffling through the tulgey wood,
> And burbled as it came!
> One, two! One, two! And through and through
> The vorpal blade went snicker snack!
> He left it dead, and with its head
> He went galumphing back.

FIGURE 8.1 The Jabberwock. Illustration by John Tenniel from Lewis Carroll, *Alice's Adventures in Wonderland*, London, 1866. Rare Books Division, The New York Public Library, Astor, Lenox and Tilden Foundations.

"And, hast thou slain the Jabberwock?
Come to my arms, my beamish boy!
O frabjous day! Callooh! Callay!"
He chortled in his joy.

"It seems very pretty," [Alice] said when she had finished it, "but it's *rather* hard to understand! . . . Somehow it seems to fill my head with ideas—only I don't exactly know what they are! However, *somebody* killed *something*: that's clear, at any rate—."[23]

Carroll's girlchild can see that heroics and demonizing seem usually to mean that somebody has killed something. She does not show respect for the world of male violence. Stead longs to be the beamish boy, to give "one, two, one, two" to the wicked, to be embraced by women, and to chortle in victory. Carroll's project is to reduce such phenomena as the Minotaur to child's play and, as a way of combating evil, to divert attention to the girl-child rather than to the righteous hero—to the new power of the daughter rather than the old power of the man.

Stead and Carroll bring you two symbolic daughters of Lot: Lily, the victim who points up the need of political and social reform to develop female opportunities, but whose own identity disappears into the abstraction of a powerful man's cause and desire; and Alice, the figure of projected female agency who diminishes and shrinks the man's world—that violent, power-mad world of the fathers.

Chapter 9

The Lot of Freud and Dora

H ere, from the very eve of the twentieth century—the century of the Holocaust and women's liberation, of the nuclear family and the nuclear bomb—is the famous dream of a disturbed Jewish girl of 18:

A house was on fire. My father was standing beside my bed and woke me up. I dressed myself quickly. Mother wanted to stop and save her jewel-case, but Father said: "I refuse to let myself and my two children be burnt for the sake of your jewel-case." We hurried downstairs, and as soon as I was outside I woke up.[1]

Reading closely, anyone familiar with the Bible can find in this dream a version of the Lot story and see that its content and form relate to the scriptural fire and brimstone. This "First Dream" of "Dora" appears in Sigmund Freud's best-known and most controversial case history, *Fragment of an Analysis of a Case of Hysteria*. It offers one key to understanding Freudian complexes and, more broadly, twentieth-century gender psychology and history. Freud's case can be read as a secular new testament of Lot-Scripture, and its importance for many through the twentieth century and beyond—feminists, psychologists, historians, literary scholars, and cultural critics, among others—is intimately bound up with the implications of collective Lot history. For Freud and Dora (Ida Bauer), both Viennese Jews, the cultural language, myth, and imagery driving the case lay closer to home than Oedipal Greece.[2] The whole psychoanalytic project from the start can look like a return to Sodom and Gomorrah. A curse of psychological perversity and sexually driven hysteria plagues Freud's land, and he must try to find an intellectual refuge where humanity can escape and renew itself.

The heritage of the Lot family and its flight from Sodom flows into and out of Dora's dreamwork. The neat biblical parallels—unconscious or not—make prophetically clear for the following century the developing prominence and complex significance of father-daughter, older men–younger women relationships and the "paralyzed mother" theme. The Freudian meta morphosis of "Remember Lot's wife" into "Remember Mother's jewel-case" (jewel-case in German, *Schmuckkastchen*, is slang for the female genitals) goes to show how the critical, cultural significance of Genesis 19—its relevance to the history of gender, sex, family, race, morality, and social faith —keeps on evolving. Dora needs to get out of a bad situation, and her case shows how modern culture needs to understand, transform, and sublimate for good the powerful desire of older men and younger women, including fathers and daughters, to merge with one another.

The Dora case goes on living and generating controversy because it offers the best and the worst of Freud. Here you have the daring seer who explodes Victorian family pieties and hypocrisies, strips away smug cultural cover stories, exposes the subtleties of motive and inner life, and shows clearly the sins of the fathers against daughters. But here also is the "expert" who comes on as the Svengali Papa you love to hate—an arrogant, sexist, reductive mesmerizer projecting his obsessive sex ideas onto a very young woman, turning her into a textual fetish, and treating her feelings like so many twigs in the storm of his psychoanalytic passion.

Freud, it seems, really did want to empower young women and liberate them from oppressive restrictions, *and* he really did want to use them for his own intellectual purposes and benefit. You need only read Carroll's *Alice* books, Stead's "The Maiden Tribute," or Henry James's *What Maisie Knew* to sense what the social realities surrounding bright young females might be in Freud's age. Freud wanted to save these girls and women from destructive repression, oppression, sickness, and harm, *but* he also he wanted their maiden tribute in the form of his own lasting greatness and immortality.

I.
Reviewing the Case

1.
BACKGROUND OF AN ANALYSIS

A rich,   late 40s (Philipp
Bauer)   ings his attractive
daught   anded her over to
me for   c," depressed, irri-
table, a   igraines, sleepless-
ness, s   ss of voice, a mys-
teriou   y she left a note
threat

Tl   ooks," "in the first
bloom   attached" to her father (da Bauer the same
name   *Copperfield,* one of
his fa   uffered from many
ailme   iarlotte Brontë's father, had eye trouble and   ment in a darkened
room on account of a detached retina" (12). The clever but illness-prone father and daughter had a deep bond of sympathy with each other, and both
were alienated from the mother (Katharina Bauer). This woman, according
to her husband and daughter, concentrates all her attention on "domestic
affairs," displaying what Freud calls the "housewife's psychosis" (13)—mind-
paralyzing obsession with cleanliness and order and a lack of intellectual curiosity. "Dora," says Freud, was "on very bad terms with her mother" and
"looked down on her" (16, 14). The daughter wants to be an intellectual. She
doesn't want to be like her mother, defined by the scope of home drudgery.

As a child, Dora had taken her bright older brother as an intimate and
a model, but as they grow up and tend to side in family conflicts with different parents—the girl with her father, the boy with his mother—they become more distant. Lately the unhappy girl has avoided people, but, when
her health allows, she attends "lectures for women" (16) and attempts serious studies. Dora has come to resent and ridicule doctors, who, it seems,
can never cure her. Her father first brought her to Freud two years before

to treat her nervous cough, but when it cleared up by itself, they turned down his offer of analytic therapy.

Now the father tells Freud why he thinks she's sunk into melancholia. When Dora was 12 and he got badly sick, "he and his family . . . formed an intimate friendship with a married couple" (18), Herr K. (Hans Zellenka, who first brought the father to Freud), "still quite young and of prepossessing appearance" (22n15), and Frau K., "young and beautiful" (25). Dora's mother would have nothing to do with his sickroom; instead Frau K. nursed the father through his illness, gaining "his undying gratitude" (18). He told his wife that he was so depressed he even went into the woods to commit suicide, but Frau K. found him and talked him out of it (Dora later claims this was a lie to cover a tryst). Frau K. befriended Dora, becoming the adolescent girl's role model—like some wonderful big sister. Herr K. also had been very kind to the girl, walking with her, giving her flowers, presents, and lots of attention. Dora, her father said, had often taken care of the K.'s two children, becoming, at times, like a little mother to them. Shortly after Dora and her father first saw Freud, they visited the K.s at their summer-house on a lake. The father stayed for a few days and arranged for Dora, then 16, to stay longer. But just as he was going away, Dora made a scene and left with him. Two weeks later she told her mother that Herr K. on a walk by the lake had propositioned her, saying, in so many words, he got "nothing out of [his] wife" (90). After her father wrote the man for an explanation, Herr K. wrote back, professing esteem for Dora, but when later the father confronted him, he denied Dora's charge outright. He said that, according to Frau K., the girl was hipped on eroticism and sex books. Her tale of the scene by the lake, he said, was a teenager's fantasy.

Ever since, Dora has been "pressing" (19) her father to break off with Frau K. He tells Freud, however, that he cannot. He thinks Dora's story *is* a fantasy. Besides, he's bound to Frau K. by "honourable friendship" (19) and gratitude. Frau K., also unhappily married, has herself suffered from nervous disorders, and now he's her only support. Dora's father assures Freud that his own relationship with Frau K., because of his crippling venereal condition, remains proper. They are both, he says, "poor wretches," and he tells Freud (in a repeated theme and verbal formula of the case), "I get nothing out of my own wife" (20). But Dora, feeling betrayed by the K.s, keeps harping on the subject, and her latest crisis follows another try to make her father give up Frau K. He asks the doctor to make Dora see reason and drop her allegations.

Freud, however, decides that Dora is *not* fantasizing. Skeptical of the father's story, he begins treating Dora, eager to test his hypothesis that psychological trauma rooted in sex triggers pathology. The case comes to him in his early 40s, when he's on fire creating psychoanalysis, but still relatively unknown and isolated in a milieu hostile to his ideas. After his father's death in 1896, he analyzes his own psyche, writes *The Interpretation of Dreams*, and keeps on refining his theories on the psychology of sex, including infantile sexuality. He's hungry, though, for clinical material to support his theories. He wants to prove that unconscious motivation drives behavior and that repressed sexual desire and knowledge erupt in, through, and on the body. To know and help people, you must read the signs of their unconscious and lead them to understand the mind's power over the flesh. They do not know the contents of their own minds, nor the meaning of great chunks of their lives, but through analysis they can learn.

A person, he is discovering, is a psychological text to be interpreted, and if you are to know the real meaning of self and experience, you must learn to read and decode a hidden language inscribed beneath the surface of daily life. For Freud, this young woman is like a Torah passage for a rabbi, the writing on the wall for Daniel, or the riddle of the Sphinx for Oedipus—she embodies the message of fate.

2.

HOW THE CASE DEVELOPED

Dora now sees her father's relationship with Frau K. as a common love affair, and she's filled with resentment. But the case is complicated. Her last governess, a free-thinking, sharp-witted woman, had been in love with her father. Dora had been close to her (Freud thinks the woman mentored her in "the facts of life"), but when she decided that the governess only paid attention to her to get close to her father, Dora got the woman fired. And she tells Freud that two years before the lakeside proposal, when she was only 14, Herr K., on a pretext of watching a church festival parade, got her to come alone to his office, where he suddenly embraced and kissed her. That disgusted her, but she told no one and remained deeply involved with the K.s until the lake incident. And far from condemning her father's friendship with the wife, Dora had appeared to welcome it and revel in her own close-ness to Frau K. In fact, when she visited the K.s, she would share a bedroom with Frau K. and hear secrets about her unhappy marriage. It was almost as if an elder and younger sister were in a kind of incestuous conspiracy. Freud sees Dora's repressed, bisexual desire hovering about the affair and infers her vicarious, if unconscious, participation in it—noting, for instance, that when Dora talked about Frau K., she used to praise her "adorable white body" (54). Annotating the case twenty years later, he comes to see the girl's homosexual feeling for Frau K. as key.

The sessions, several days a week, last for three months, ending on De-cember 31, 1900, the last day of the old century, when Dora suddenly breaks off the therapy. By the end, Dora doesn't bother to deny Freud's assertions that she was in love with Herr K., who, it appears, acted towards her as both a thoughtful suitor *and* a cad. In her final session, she tells Freud that an-other "young girl" who was the K. children's governess confided to her just before Herr K.'s proposition that this same K. had seduced *her*, telling *her* he got nothing from his wife (97). Dora said K. made "violent love" to this governess, had sex with her, got her pregnant, and then dropped her. When, by the lake, Dora saw Herr K. making the same moves on *her*, she got mad, slapped his face, and left. And when later she decides that Frau K. has be-trayed her by telling Herr K. things the girl has shared with her, Dora, in a slough of despond, tries desperately to make her father once and for all choose her over Frau K. This *other woman* now makes her miserable be-cause Dora sees that her special early affinity with her father is broken and that people just try to exploit her. Either they play up to her to get near her father, or else, as in Herr K.'s case, they think of her as an interchangeable sex object.

Freud maintains, over the short course of the therapy, that she's pas-sionately in love, without knowing it, with her father, with Herr K., and with Frau K. (and later he realizes, he says, that she has transferred complex erotic feelings onto *him*). He cleverly shows the fluidity of the sexual iden-tity and desire of a young woman, but he seems uneasy about delving into the ways general culture and social experience form Dora's various pas-sions. Her real problem, which he perceives but doesn't much explore, seems to be that the people she cares most about and depends on are willing to sacrifice her for some interest of their own. That means she cannot learn from them how to sustain love and trust—or maintain health.

Dora tells Freud that she can't stop thinking about her father's love for Frau K. or forgive him for it. Freud theorizes that she acts like a jealous wife because she's long been in love with her father and, in her unconscious mind, replaces her mother in the role of his mate. Dora resists this idea at first, but, Freud notes (almost gloating in triumph), she immediately talks about a 7-year-old cousin who told her, "'You can't think how I hate that person!' (pointing to her mother), 'and when she's dead I shall marry papa'" (50). Freud claims Dora also identifies with the woman her father now loves, the mistress. And later he thinks that she, unconsciously a devotee of Gomorrah, resents her father for loving the woman *she* loves, Frau K. At their final session, Freud insists that she waited to tell her parents about the lakeside incident because she really wanted Herr K. to renew his proposals and never leave off until she married him. Dora then tells him good-bye "very warmly, with the heartiest wishes for the New Year, and—came no more" (100).

3.

SEXUAL HARASSMENT

Any way you look at it, it's a sordid little story. Like Maisie in James's *What Maisie Knew*, Dora is an "ironic centre" that "has the wonderful importance of shedding a light far beyond any reach of her comprehension" (James, 29). But unlike Maisie, Dora gets sucked right into the sickness of her world and has to deal with such shocking, tabooed subjects (for their time) as venereal disease, female masturbation, and fellatio. And unlike James's novel (and more like the Bible) this case is replete with the symptoms of a veritable plague—diseased flesh, leaky bodies, and raddled nerves. Its milieu, like William Stead's in another context, is a new city of the plain in both spiritual and pathological crisis—nearly all the principal figures in the case suffer, directly or indirectly, from the effects of syphilis.

Dora characterizes her father, whom she loves, as a devious man who thinks mainly of his own advantage. Like Lot, he seems willing to sacrifice his daughter, and what most embitters her is her sense that she has been "handed over to Herr K." (27) by him, her ultimate guardian, as a sop for his liaison with K.'s wife. It's striking that Freud uses the same expression, "handed over," to describe the father's action in bringing Dora to *him*. The analyst has much to gain from her. To his own confidante, Wilhelm Fliess, he writes, "It has been a lively time, and I have a new patient, a girl of eighteen; the case has opened smoothly to my collection of picklocks."[3] She's a valuable object of knowledge to be examined and employed for *his* advantage. He does realize he's sacrificing the girl's trust to his scientific ambitions, but Father Freud knows best:

[T]he patients would never have spoken if it had occurred to them that their admissions might possibly be put to scientific uses. . . . But in my opinion the physician has taken upon himself duties not only towards the individual patient but towards science as well. . . . Thus it becomes the physician's duty to publish. (2)

Nevertheless, he means in his vocation to play the good, responsible patriarch. His masterplot is that psychoanalytic interpretation can reveal unconscious subtexts and incestuous urges that determine the course of a life, and that by making people aware of truths they repress, it can free them—individually and collectively—from their mind-forged manacles.

Freud is eager to give to—and through—Dora "French lessons" (to use the sexual code of Henry James in *Maisie*), and he falls into it himself when he has to justify indoctrinating young females with his theories of sex and its influence: "No one," he says, "can undertake the treatment of a case of hysteria until he is convinced of the impossibility of avoiding the mention of sexual subjects. . . . The right attitude is: '*pour faire une omelette il faut casser des oeufs.*'" (42). "It is possible," says Freud, "for a man to talk to girls and women upon sexual matters . . . without doing them harm and without bringing suspicion upon himself" (41), and he continues: "I call bodily organs and processes by their technical names, and I tell these to the patient if they—the names, I mean—happen to be unknown to her. *J'appelle un chat un chat.*" He equates French with technical language that he uses to give himself objective authority and to feminize the patient, but he's also using it metaphorically and symbolically—and maybe defensively. That "*chat*" in an alien tongue reads like a bit of deflection and unconscious guilt about letting the pussy out of his ideological bag in Dora's presence.

Freud displays dazzling intelligence in the case, but he also presents bizarre speculations about Dora as matters of assured fact. He writes, for instance, of her shock and flight when Herr K., with a palpable hard-on, suddenly grabbed and kissed her: "[T]he behavior of this child of fourteen was already entirely . . . hysterical. I should without question consider a person hysterical in whom an occasion for sexual excitement elicited feelings that were preponderantly or exclusively unpleasurable" (22). And later, in analyzing her dream, he offers this: "I came to the conclusion that the idea had probably occurred to her one day . . . that she would like to have a kiss from me" (66). Satirizing male egotism eighty years later, Carly Simon has the perfect lyric for this Freudian moment: "You're so vain, you probably think this song is about you."

4.
THE REST OF THE STORY

Dora rejects Freud. After eleven weeks, she abruptly leaves—as suddenly as she left Herr K. Freud has been so intent on teaching her the root causes of her symptoms and what her experience and dreams mean, so wrapped up in getting her to face unpleasant truths (and see his own uncanny intelligence), that he missed some of her resistance to him and—crucially, he says—the transference onto him of complex feelings she has for other older figures in her life. He believes, though, that he has helped her and that leaving him with an unfinished analysis is an act of displaced spite.

He adds a postscript. Fifteen months later, using facial neuralgia as an excuse to see him, she returns to tell him that, while paying a visit to the K.s ostensibly to console them for the death of a child, she confronted Frau K. with her knowledge of the affair. She says also that she got Herr K. to admit the truth of the scene by the lake and took the news of her vindication back to her father. Since then, she says, she's been in reasonably good health—except for a bout of aphonia caused, it turns out, by a meeting in the street with a bewildered Herr K. who, in bumbling abstraction, got hit by a cart. She tells Freud that when people mention her father's affair with Frau K., it causes only a ripple of emotion. She's now absorbed in work. On the last page he writes condescendingly: "I promised to forgive her for having deprived me of the satisfaction of affording her a far more radical cure for her troubles" (112). He reports that eventually she married, and he sees that as a move towards health.

But Dora, it seems, never found much health or happiness. In the somber, real-life postscript to Freud's case, she married a man who did not please or satisfy her—an unsuccessful music composer. The husband depended on her father as his employer and patron (Herr Bauer even hired an orchestra to perform his son-in-law's music). Her spouse suffered severe ear and head injuries during World War I. The couple had one son, but when in 1922 Ida briefly consulted the psychiatrist Felix Deutsch for what were diagnosed as psychosomatic ailments (ringing in the ear, dizziness, loss of balance, and headaches—the symptoms of her wounded husband), she told him of her "frigidity," her disillusion with men and love, her abhorrence of pregnancy, and her resentment of her maturing but apparently feckless son's womanizing and neglect of her.[4] She also, with flirtatious pride, told him that she was the famous "Dora." Her parents, it seems, both died of tuberculosis, but she retained her bitterness towards them. Her father lied, was promiscuous, suffered from mental confusion, and didn't take care of her properly. Her mother didn't love her. She shared her mother's compulsions about the unclean and the clean, but transferred them to the body. She was terribly bothered by constipation, vaginal discharges, and the dirty, impure nature of physical being in general.

In his unsympathetic article, Deutsch quotes a source who called her "one of the most repulsive hysterics" he ever knew (43), and characterizes her as an emotional sadist. He sees her husband as a masochistic milquetoast—the only sort who could live with her—and comments on her lasting resentment for her father and her contempt for spouse and son. The husband died of heart failure in 1932, brought on, Deutsch insinuates, by Dora's disdain and scorn. Only her brother, Otto, who became a Socialist leader in Austria, retained her respect. But Otto Bauer was chased out by the Nazis and died in France in 1938. She and her son also got to France, and eventually her son got her to America.

According to Deutsch, Dora the aging émigré always remained a difficult person in bad health, full of complaints. Her life in the United States was a hard scramble, although she, who always had something of her father's entrepreneurial cleverness, is said to have made money in her last years as a professional bridge player and teacher. Amazingly, one of her partners was her onetime idol, Frau Zellenka. In 1945, she died in New York of colon cancer—uncleanness of the bowels. As for her errant, maligned son, Kurt Herbert Adler, he became a musician, conductor, and impresario of great distinction who, in the 1950s and '60s, built the San Francisco Opera into a world-renowned company. Ironically, then, anxious, miserably dissatisfied Dora did bear a distinguished son for a new world.

5.

THE MEANING OF THE CASE

What stands out about *Dora* is the mystery of psychological reality and difficulty of knowing what's true about others. This strange case is part medical history, part social history, part hearsay, part fact, part fiction, part self-serving testimony of a sullen teenage girl who feels victimized, part projections of a system-making, authoritarian genius out to prove what he wants, and part a lasting work of imagination. And that imagination may be any reader's own, for the work is of, by, and for interpretation, with definitive certainty for none and fruitful speculation for all. It's a text for each reader to process into sense. The Dora case logically assumes that a dream, an illness, a form of speech, a choice of words, a symptom, a gesture—indeed the whole motley plenitude of human experience and behavior—have underlying, unconscious meanings, messages, and motivations that can and must be read and interpreted subjectively. You're the doctor here as well as Freud, and you see that doctors have hidden agendas—hidden sometimes from themselves.

The case I read features a pregnant encounter between a leading patriarch of modernity and a representative daughter of the new century, dissatisfied with the past. Freud bases his comprehension of Dora on her dreams because, he says, he has learned "to translate the language of dreams": "The dream, in short, is one of the *détours by which repression can be evaded*; it is one of the principal means employed by what is known as the indirect representation in the mind" (9). What he asserts as true for the dream, you can claim also for the images and fantasies of myth, story, narrative scripture, and literature in general—including case histories. Ostensibly, Dora is the author of her dream: it belongs to her, and Freud poses only as the recorder and translator of its meaning as her unconscious mind devises it. But, like Lot's daughters' plan to sleep with their father, the dream and its significance are actually full of male projections. Dora's first dream, which Freud, of course, narrates in words of his own choosing, is a product of their strange intercourse, and it opens up one way to see *Lot* as the living, subjective contents of people's lives. *Dora* changes and personalizes that often repressed old story of fear and desire.

"Which Dreamed It?" is the title of Lewis Carroll's last chapter in *Through the Looking-Glass*, and there, in words that fit Dora and Freud perfectly, Alice muses, "He was part of my dream, of course—but then I was part of his dream" (208). Carroll ends by leaving the question of who has the dream up to his readers, "Which do *you* think it was?" In Freud, that final question is implicit but unavoidable. He has nothing to work with but what Dora tells him, and often she may be, if not exactly lying, then unconsciously making things up, distorting memories, mixing up visual images, getting things wrong, or pushing for her own views and interests. And as any thoughtful person can see, it's much the same with him. How much of the printed text of Dora's dream embodies her words and imagery and how much has been shaped by Freud cannot be known.

Almost against his will, Freud later recognizes the problem. In *An Autobiographical Study*, he describes how common sense and personal knowledge finally made him realize that most of the stories emerging at the beginning of his career from his female patients about their fathers having sexual intercourse with them couldn't possibly be true. Of many, he says, "they were only phantasies which my patients had made up *or which I myself had perhaps forced on them*."[5] That's a key. He admits he has the power to coax patients to give him what he wants. People, whether they know it or not, tell those in authority, those they want to impress, those they depend on, those they love or fear, what they think will please them. Freud wanted to hear that early traumatic sex causes physical and mental illness, and by his own theory about how the wording of denials can actually express confirmation, his lame follow-up to his point about forcing people to say things reads like a veritable confession: "I do not believe even now that I forced the seduction-phantasies on my patients, that I 'suggested' them" (21).

Dora's dream, then, is a collaborative process between a young woman and an older man. It is also a collaborative process of reading and readers. The last line of *Through the Looking-Glass* is "Life, what is it but a dream?" In the Dora case, that question is not rhetorical, but one to be patiently analyzed and explored.

II.
Freud's Lot Complex

1.

BACK WHERE HE CAME FROM

In *Dora* Freud writes, "A daughter usually takes her mother's love-story as her model" (99). Whatever the truth of that statement, it's full of projection. It shows he's interested in generalizing about young women's love-lives, but implicitly—since according to his idea that to express troubling thoughts about yourself you often reverse the terms, it also means "a son usually takes his father's love story as his model." Freud did, but he sublimated it. He was born from the cross-generational union of an older man and a younger woman. Amalia, his mother, at 20 became the third wife of Jacob Freud, who was 40. Jacob, in fact, had a son older than Amalia; Sigmund was a year younger than his eldest nephew and first playmate. Thus the model love story that Freud took from his father and that shaped his imagination had both serial partners and a very clever and assertive younger woman as its fertile object.

Freud, growing up as the eldest of his mother's seven children, couldn't help but see his aging father's potency renewed again and again by a woman young enough to be his daughter. Moreover, his father, a slippery character from a family of dubious respectability (Jacob's brother was jailed for fraud), was a reputed womanizer with a racy history. It follows that a curious, precocious boy like Sigmund, finding his own identity, would think and fantasize about this older man's past and present sex life. Exposed to Jacob's sexual attitudes, he would likely take them in and feel the urge to match the father in sexual experience and sophistication.

But Freud, I suggest, would also be in conflict—conflict from which gratification would come in the form of a grand sexual sublimation. As first child of one parent, but not the other, his familial role and loyalties would be split. Feelings and empathy for both father and mother would move him. He would somehow be imbued with his young mother's jealous disapproval of Jacob's erotic past, and he would be disposed to shy away from the taint of personal sexual scandal. And because he was in a sense a generation closer to Amalia than his father, he might unconsciously identify with a young woman in her relationship to an older man. If he ever projected himself into his mother's life story—and he surely did—he would find a classic Lot pattern in which the daughter-figure (in age) becomes mate to the father and then mother to the future.

2.
SUBLIMATING LOT

For a boy of his time, however, conscious identification with a woman would carry shame and demand repression. Inevitably the father's desire and knowledge, his proven way with younger women—his "love story"— would work to form part of the son's core of being. Freud would move to seek erotic intimacy with younger women, but in a way that would escape moral censure and avoid the guilt of promiscuity. He would possess the sex in their heads, as he sought ways of being like his father, while being able to repress and plausibly deny doing so. In *Dora*, Freud writes on sublimation of people's odd sexual bents: "They are a development of germs all of which are contained in the . . . sexual pre-disposition of the child, and which, by being suppressed or by being diverted to higher, asexual aims— by being *sublimated*—are destined to provide the energy for a great number of our cultural achievements" (43).

Freud would prove his superior moral goodness and be a loyal son to his mother by trying to cure what ailed young women. One way of "having sex" is to talk about it. Remember his words in *Dora*: "It is possible for a man to talk to girls and women upon sexual matters . . . without doing them harm and without bringing suspicion upon himself." Developing his own "talk" version of his father's sexual prowess with young women, he too became an erotic explorer.

The working of the Lot complex in the Dora case also depends on its presence in Freud's earlier professional development. Elder teachers and colleagues who exerted therapeutic sway over girls excited his interest. He learned much from Charcot, who hypnotized susceptible, hysterical young women and made much of "the sexual thing" in explaining nervous disorders. And, as I said before (see Chapter 2), one of the key episodes in the founding of psychoanalytic thinking and the modern history of the unconscious, "The Case of Anna O.," features a patient's frustrated love for her dying father, her transfer of those feelings to Dr. Breuer, her desire for the older man, and her relief from grief and frustrated sexuality through "the talking cure."

In 1895, Freud's newborn daughter was given the same name as psychoanalysis's first case-history protagonist, Anna. She would become a perfect embodiment and sign of Freud's particular Lot complex. Their interests and careers would merge, and she would further his work and gratify her own intellectual curiosity and ambitions. Her father had impregnated her, that is, with his passion for psychoanalysis, and it became her (re)productive life. Though at the end of his own life he called her "Anna Antigone," his youngest child's role was more precisely that of a scientific, sublimating Lot's daughter dedicated to the preservation and development of Freud's discoveries. In Freudian terms, what drives her impressive accomplishment and this whole remarkable father-daughter relationship of achievement looks very much like intellectual incest.

The daughter figure, I repeat, is a mother of that which we call and mean by "Freud." In Dora's first dream, the analyst sees Oedipus, but not Lot with his wife and daughters, nor the fire-and-brimstone heritage of wicked, sexual Sodom and Gomorrah. Why not? One reason is that he, who is always showing you how you try to avoid admitting to yourself what's hard and humiliating, is like other people. It's important to see that Freud, by choosing (in middle age, after all) the terminology of the Oedipus myth for his universal complex, himself disguises and in part suppresses what is so evident and vital in his own early perceptions of life and his developing psychological theory: namely, an older man's passion to opt for a younger woman, the active role of the female daughter figure in opening up new worlds, and the replacement and disappearance of old wives.

Oedipus may be shocking, but it can be distanced into impersonal abstraction or relegated to childhood, like the memory of an infant disgrace. Men do not often mate with their mothers, nor, proportionally in history, have many men actually married women from the older generation. As adults they have not usually seen the older woman as a forbidden prize. On the other hand, as Freud knew well, aging men do feel tempted to renew their creative vigor with younger women, do project desires and sexual urges on them, and do use them to fight off time's wingèd steamroller. He knew too that young women are often drawn to the power and expertise of older men and sometimes feel an urge to seduce them or to respond to the erotic drives of authority figures.

For Freud too, the Oedipus complex, with its classical reference, follows and fulfills one motif in the history of Lot—namely, the universalization of

Jewish experience for the rest of the world. Three points here apply particularly to Freud and the Dora case: (1) The story of Sodom and Gomorrah and of Lot and his daughters insists that sexual history *does* determine history; psychoanalysis, with its stress on the psychosexual origins of fate—an eternal return to the ancient cities of the plain, as it were—points to the vast general importance and symbolic meaning of the flight of the Lot family. (2) The whole edifice of Christianity, strictly speaking, is founded on the incestuous experience of a poor Jewish girl. (3) When the Bible moves from Hebrew to forms of Greek (and, later, Latin), it can be said to become international and all-embracing; the belief of a Jewish sect becomes a catholic faith. By appropriating the language of Greek myth for his theories, Freud was looking to move beyond sectarianism and any taint of the ghetto in a world rife with anti-Semitism. But still, he was using Dora to preserve his seed.

III.
Lots of Dreamwork

1.
DORA'S DREAM OF AUTHORITY

Look again at Dora's dream: "A house was on fire. My father was standing beside my bed and woke me up. I dressed myself quickly. Mother wanted to stop and save her jewel-case; but Father said: 'I refuse to let myself and my two children be burnt for the sake of your jewel-case.' We hurried downstairs, and as soon as I was outside I woke up."

Fire means danger, passion, and crisis. Traditionally, it also stands for the ultimate form of punishment. For Dora the burning house can mean fever in her body, violent inner rage towards others, big changes that menace her, and/or the desperate longing to escape from the hell she's in. And fire proverbially signifies the heat of sex (as, for example, the flames over Sodom and Gomorrah, or—relevant for Freud's later report of Dora's love for Frau K.—Byron's hot line in *Don Juan* celebrating the torrid isle of Lesbos, "Where burning Sappho loved and sung"). Her father's will and being wake Dora to the peril she's in, and he appears as a savior. She must flee with him, but she needs first to put on her clothes and cover her naked self. As in Lot, the mother appears as an obstacle from the past who delays and hinders the flight to the future. Dora's dream father, though, won't let his wife's obsession with the "jewel-case" destroy the girl. The father leads Dora with her brother out of the deadly domestic space, and then—it's an odd and telling detail—*she wakes up for the second time.*

The girl learns in analysis that she, like everyone, expresses desires through her dreams. A quick study, she sees that dreams are daughters' milk to Freud, and in the dreams she expresses her need for his understanding and support. One day he's looking for something dark in her childhood, when she suddenly tells him that a few nights before, she had the burning-house dream and that she's had the exact same dream many times before. Maybe she did and maybe she didn't. "A periodically recurrent dream," Freud writes, "was by its very nature particularly well calculated to arouse my curiosity" (56). Dora often seems to be telling Freud, for her own purposes, what he wants to hear. When she tells him she first had the dream three nights running at the lakeside with the K.s, it pleases him. It's doubtful whether people *do* have the same exact dream over and over, but in retrospect, to make sense of themselves and their waking life, they may say they do. She wants an ally, and a good, "recurrent" dream served up to the great unweaver of dreams might help to get him on her side. Indeed, he decides this "first dream" deserves an "especially careful investigation" (56) and bases much of his analysis on it.

Freud, analyzing Dora, keeps insisting that people's sex lives and libidos, like dreams, emerge out of floating mental conflations of times, people, experiences, talk, and memories. He manages to convince her what a big part sexuality plays in her milieu and psyche, but the case shows how confusing sex can be for a budding girl. It's full of contradictions. It grabs hold of you, but you have to learn about it from others. It's very bad, but it's a jewel of great price. It gives you power, but it takes away your power. You get lessons that it should be repressed and kept secret, but when you talk to a doctor, you're told to get it out in the open. It makes you want to touch your "private" parts (which others seem to want to make into a public affair), but then when you do and get pleasure, you learn to hide and regret it. It's improper, but if you're healthy you should want it. It's dangerous and "dirty" because, as the pathology of her parents' show, it can make you ill and burn you up. But it must somehow be good too because without it your family falls apart. Since it can draw the people you love, like Father and Frau K. together and away from you, it's bad; but, then again, it can make people like Herr K. and Frau K. be nice to you. On the other hand, the sex appeal that makes a man sweet to you can also turn him into a scary and ridiculous groper.

There's a notorious, much-discussed passage in which Freud notices that Dora is wearing a stylish reticule at her waist and that, as she lolls back on his couch, she keeps fingering it. He tells her that she's acting out a wish to masturbate, which she did as a child. When he tells her that the reticule of her dream, the "jewel-case," is a bawdy German term for *vagina*, Dora replies, "I knew you would say that" (61). Recent commentators see here Dora kvetching with good reason, tired of Freud pushing sex at her, but it's possible that she's simply acknowledging that she's right about what will interest him. The whole business of opening, shutting, and fondling the little purse looks rather like a sly, manipulative put-on bringing the symbolic object from her dream into real life and drawing attention to her predicament. Maybe he'll see that she's in danger of being used as a sex object to be admired, poked, owned, devalued, and passed on, and that if it all doesn't stop, she'll go crazy.

It's obvious that Dora longs for union with a responsible, powerful paternal authority who will protect her. Her wish is that the father should recognize her feelings, empathize with them, rouse her to a better life, and wake *himself* up to the peril she's in. He should put her first, choose *her*, leave other bedrooms and come to hers. Beyond that, however, in speaking in the name of her father in the dream, she moves to identify with him, assume his nature, and act decisively. It seems she wants, in the dream of rescue, to find her power and very being in the father. And she projects her desires from him onto Freud as well.

2.

THE COMPLEX DREAM FATHER

Freud wants her to see that her dream is a fantasy collage and the man in it has a plural identity. The different figures in Dora's life conflate in her dream, but they play different roles and mean various things at different times. Her "father" is her papa, but he can also stand for Herr K. and Freud too. One bit of the analysis epitomizes the muddle in Dora's psychoanalytic situation: in recalling her dream, "[s]he had forgotten to relate . . . that each time after waking up she had smelt smoke" (65). Freud, who more than once said to her, "There can be no smoke without fire," tells her the smoke relates the dream to himself. She replies that she smelt the smoke in her dreams before she saw Freud, and that both her father and Herr K. are "passionate smokers." "I am too," says Freud. He then muses that Herr K. smelt of smoke when he kissed Dora and concludes—in that classic moment of counter-transference—"that she would like to have a kiss from me" (66). Sometimes, as he later said, a cigar is just a cigar, but sometimes it's a symbol that might fit in a jewel-case, and how can a girl (or her doctor) know which?

The three "smokers," Papa, Herr K., and Freud—father-figures all—play various Lot-complex parts in Dora's burning dreamhouse. Her real father bonds with the new generation and chooses their mutual salvation. Dora obviously wants him to revert to his protector role in her childhood. His concern for her brings him back to her bedside. In dream logic, he finally acts to keep her safe from pawing and premature sex, and he validates her resentful rivalry with her mother. He opens up new possibilities and provides an escape route. That's one basic meaning of her father's command to go with him. Another, less savory one, shows up in the heat (pressure) she feels in her life from his desire to preserve his own life by coming to the bed of a younger woman. He may also be acting out a tabooed, incestuous wish of hers. If the flight-from-Sodom story is part of Dora's imagination, and if, in her life story, she has seen Frau K. as an older sister intimately related to her beloved father and herself, then the father's "two children" in the dream could stand for Dora and Frau K. (the brother transposed). Dora, then, would unconsciously be binding herself sexually to both Frau K. and her father in a plot that gets rid of the disobedient mother (disobedient to her daughter's and husband's desires).

Overall, Dora's dream reflects both the daughter's historic dependence on the father for safety and her complex role in putting in focus the historic patriarchal responsibility for preserving life into the future. But what jumps out is Dora's second awakening. What does it mean? One answer would be that once paternal action has helped her out of immediate danger Dora realizes she must wake up again, take charge herself, and, with a new perspective from outside the burning wreck of family life, recognize that faith in paternalism is a dream of the past. She knows her father lies to himself and others. She's like him, but she wants to be better than he is. She needs to get the father on her side, then be free of him.

Freud insists and shows that the dream father also serves as a screen for

Herr K. That means that K., who according to Dora, did walk into her bedroom at the lake house, then becomes the older lover saying, in effect, *let me take you away from all this; I'll be your father now and give you romantic love besides.* The worldly man offers flattering attention and the possibility of sweet refuge from a disintegrating home. Projected onto Herr K., "I refuse to let myself and my two children be burnt for the sake of your jewelcase" would also express Dora's enmity towards her father's mistress, condemn Frau K. as a bad mother, and betray a wish to replace her.

In Freud's reading of Dora's dream and libido, a touchy but important subject and sociological pattern in the last century emerges: the drive— conscious or not—of an ambitious, dissatisfied younger woman to prove herself by taking a married man away from his wife. Everyone knows of married (or divorced) men who hit on young women to boost their egos, but everyone also knows of women who seem to delight in seducing men attached to other women. Why? One motive is mimetic, triangular desire: you're programmed to seek and love what someone you admire and look up to does. For example, *if Frau K., whom I idolize, married handsome Herr K., then I want him.* More cynically, you could say of both the larger pattern and this case specifically that the damsel needing to be led out of the fire offers a battered male another chance for innocence and hope in a sour world, and the older man's love and concern wake the bright young thing to her own worth and to the joy of beating out an older rival. Freud, at one point, suggests not only that Herr K. was serious about marrying Dora, but, more surprisingly, that it might have worked. If you see, behind the dream father, Herr K., you see how the older lover can make a young woman feel attractive and worthwhile—one wish that drives Dora's Lot complex.

But Dora's second wake-up with regard to Herr K. would seem to reveal her basic skepticism. The older K. turns out to be flawed goods. It appears he wants to use her crudely for physical sex, and he just tells her what he tells all the girls. He's weak and won't stand up for her against his wife; he doesn't protect her like a man should. And, of course—it's one of the basic points of the dream—the literal protector in it, her father, disdains him. More broadly, the final wake-up ending looks like a rejection of wishful, but often dangerous erotic nonsense about good, masterful, mature romantic saviors.

James Joyce's parody in *Ulysses* of girlish desires and male projections mocks Lottish erotics with an irony that's perfect for Herr K. and Dora:

No prince charming is her beau ideal to lay a rare and wondrous love at her feet but rather a manly man with a strong quiet face who had not found his ideal, perhaps his hair slightly flecked with grey, and who would understand, take her in his sheltering arms, strain her to him in all the strength of his deep passionate nature and comfort her with a long long kiss.[6]

That's the dream world of Jane Eyre and Rochester. In the real world, according to Freud, the "still preposessing" Herr K.'s efforts at a "long long kiss" revolted the 14-year-old girl, and his proposition two years later to take her—like a governess—into his "sheltering arms" drove her away. She got the message: *wake up, little Dora.*

That is, if you believe Dora on Herr K. What she says about him might be contaminated by her relationship to Freud and (to use his terms) the process of *transference* onto him during analysis. Transferences and counter-transferences between Dora and Freud color the text and suggest that, except for the certainty that he did treat her in some intense psychoanalytic sessions and wrote up the account, it's wise to take almost nothing about the case and its particulars at face value. If, for example, Dora wants Freud to act like a guardian, then she might want him to believe some very bad things about Herr K. And if she gets it in her head that Freud, for his own purposes, is trying to foist sex on her, as she says Herr K. did, she might abruptly decide to quit him, just as she ran from the K.s house. That means that he goes wrong when he so blithely says, "It is possible for a man to talk to girls and women upon sexual matters of every kind. . . . There is no necessity for feeling any compunction at discussing the facts of normal or abnormal sexual life with them" (41–42). Such easy male presumption belies the force of sexual transference and sexual history.

3.

TRANSFERENCE AND AUTHORITY

The fact that Dora comes up with her "recurrent" dream during treatment and that Freud is evidently merged in it with both her father and Herr K. gives her case and complex its enduring significance. Strictly speaking, *transference* means that in the psyche of the patient during treatment, the therapist comes to stand in for or replace a previous figure (often a parent) in the patient's life. *Countertransference* is the reverse: the patient evokes and represents for the analyst a figure (or figures) of the past. Feelings, desires, thoughts, memories, fantasies that were aroused by the earlier person get redirected—*transferred*—onto the doctor (or patient) and then, often, out into the world. The implications and effects of what I'll call the *Vienna transfer* extend far beyond the psychoanalyst's office and run right down through the twentieth century. The process becomes both evidence and model for the oscillating movement between the personal and the socio-logical, between the individual and history. People, whether they know it or not, make transfers in order to continue a journey, move on, and get to somewhere new.

Freud says "mastering the transference in good time" (108) is necessary if an analysis is to be successful, and though he failed to do so in Dora's case, the logic of his phrase assumes that the physician controls—can mas-ter—the transference. That assumption of authority matters. The psycho-analytic transference and countertransference between a younger woman and a prominent older man of course have roots in the ancient past—Lot's cave, for example.[7] Not only do people ascribe to authority figures the characteristics and functions of others from their past, they often learn to do so from those authorities. Under Freud's prodding, Dora may show, understand, or at least grudgingly acknowledge that she does look for power, love, knowledge, respect, freedom, and even vengeance in her rela-tions with her father and Herr K., and when Freud's influence takes over her mind, she may also seek these things—or ways to get them—through him. Freud might not directly dictate to Dora how the transference be-tween her father, Herr K., and himself works, but in a hundred ways, he pushes her to see what he sees. "Mastering the transference" can mean pro-jecting it onto Dora and others. Not only does the psychological mentor fuse with father and paternal lover in her dream, he interacts with her to recreate and define the very identities of father, lover, mother (and other figures) that make up her present reality. He can thus help to get her be-yond the past by reshaping it and bringing it into manageable focus. But he may also reinforce an old sense of daughterly dependence on patriarchal authority that becomes intolerable.

If Freud is a surrogate father in Dora's dream, she can say things to him—and maybe through him—which she could never say to her real fa-ther. She might get her story heard. The case shows how Freud reversed two major paternal negatives that often faced turn-of-the-twentieth-century girls: he didn't tell them they talked too much and he didn't think that what they said was insignificant or trivial. In the so-called "talking cure," analysts don't try to make daughters (or any patients) shut up, and they do find deep truths, buried or not, in what they say. That may be one reason why— no matter how justified the backlash against Freud in recent decades may seem—the psychoanalytic movement from the beginning has attracted the articulate interest of so many, ambitious, mold-breaking, forward-looking women (Bertha Pappenheim, Sabina Spielrein, Lou Salome, H.D., Anna Freud, Melanie Klein, and many others).[8] Another reason is that the transference process lets you see how your familial experience connects with cultural structures of authority, and it can show you how to move between private life and the larger world.

4.
THE END OF THE DREAM:
ANALYTICAL TENSION AND CONFLICT

In the dream itself, the transfer of the father's role onto Freud offers Dora a model of the ideal psychoanalytic project and cure. The "doctor" appears at her bedside, dedicated to her well-being. As the analysis shows, the dream returns Dora to helpless infancy and then revisits traumas of her childhood and pubescent life. Her devoted "father" gives her a chance to repair the damage by making her aware of the meanings and the menace that may lurk in the symbolic residue of memory (e.g., the "jewel-case"). She can then move to wide-awake, independent maturity.

But the dream in the end also represents the daughter's rebellion and the rejection of the father figure. Freud recognizes in writing up the case that the dream previews Dora's decision to abandon his therapy and his plans for her. The tension and conflict that the dream's end symbolizes in the Freud-Dora relationship break out all through the analysis—as they have in modern gender history. Here are a few pregnant instances (and ones that have— and will—call up highly subjective responses from different readers).

First, Freud finds Dora good-looking. She pointedly fingers her reticule ("jewel-case") for him. He thinks she'd like to have a little kiss from him. It's easy to mock his ego here, but it's likely that the older man glimpses at least a partial truth. Her behavior (as Deutsch also attested) could be seductive. Freud tells her he knows how she operates; he's persuasive, the most impressive doctor she's ever seen. She does want to learn things from him. At times she wants to win Freud over, to charm him, to make a confidante of him in order to help her keep her father's allegiance and separate him from the K.s. And certainly this doctor, like other men she knows, is interested in sex. It may have seemed to her that you have to use sex appeal to get away from sex (the K. milieu). She tells him what he wants to know. In the physician's office, sex and a seductive pose might be safe.

But maybe not; they might also be demeaning and dangerous. Dora has seen how fortyish men (Freud was 44—young enough to be "still prepossessing") do seek sex from young women. In the end, Freud writes of Dora, "I do not know what kind of help she wanted from me" (112). But in their dialectical encounter, that question can be—and surely was—reversed: *I do not know what kind of help* he *wanted from me*. Maybe she got scared. It was obvious Freud wanted her to talk forever about sex. Or she may have been confused; Herr K. wanted sex, but this doctor was different. Like some awful inquisitor, he seemed to want to suck everything private and secret out of her. She feels she must leave the man to keep from being swallowed up and digested like a dainty intellectual morsel (he *did*, after all, turn her into a *Fragment of an Analysis*). He believes her and helps reinforce her sense of victimization, but still she can't afford to give in to him completely and lose herself in his system-making and in her old (transferred) need for father's approval. Freud's text makes clear that Dora intuits countertransference and understands that he will take her rejection of therapy personally. By asserting her will against him, she manages to wield some power over him.

The Freud-Dora relationship grows out of an old story, but the twentieth century would revitalize it. It seems she uses sex and hates that she does. Dora counts on her sex appeal with Freud, resents its existence, worries that it doesn't exist, and needs to get away from the erotic attraction of male authority. He tries to help her to define herself, but then she has to resist letting *his* definition possess her. She plays with her jewel-case, talks about masturbation, opens herself to this mental locksmith, but then gives him up. Freud, remember, calls her disgust at K.'s sudden clasp and kiss of her when she was 14 and "hysterical." Such dogmatic twaddle alerts you to the dangers of sticking too close to male mentors, even would-be saviors.

Second, two pieces of information Dora offers about Herr K. seem designed to seduce Freud's sympathy and look, in context, problematic—possibly true, possibly skewed. Only later, after she tells of the lakeside proposition and slap, does she mention K.'s office embrace two years before. The timing seems wrong. That gross, earlier incident would appear much more offensive, but after it, Dora still seems to have remained on good terms with Herr K. (*in love*, even, according to Freud), making little or nothing of what was on its face outrageous. It's suspect, then, because it doesn't quite jibe with the Dora-K.'s history, and also because, at a critical time, it transparently (pun intended) feeds Dora's hope and purpose in enlisting Freud's influence with her father against the K.s. In effect, she says, "You're fascinated by sex and you convince me how important it is in illness. Look at poor little me, open to sexual plots, and what this man did to me." The neglected, mistreated young woman, looking for help, sees that sexual harassment, brought into the open, might actually be the means to appeal to—and gain—authority.

Freud does want to believe the incident for his own reasons, which aren't quite Dora's. Looking everywhere for libido, he's invested in a real love story between K. and Dora. And he seizes upon the physical details in her account as his chance to climb on his hobby-horse, ride sex, and project on Dora such dubious ideas as the memory of K.'s phallus, coughing as a symptom of fantasized oral sex, and a rigid hypothesis about sexual trauma as the originator of pathology. What he doesn't believe—and surely it's one reason why she turns against him—is that she's completely honest about her revulsion for Herr K.'s kiss and embrace.

At her last session, she abruptly produces that story about Herr K. seducing the young governess. It seems a perfect justification for Dora's behavior—maybe too perfect. Again the timing and circumstances don't seem quite right. Why didn't she tell Freud about it before, since it would make everything clear and prove she has nothing to feel guilty about? And would the girl, no friend of Dora, suddenly confide in her "rival" and admit her shame and disgrace? Perhaps so, but it's also possible that Dora, at the end of the analysis and puzzled by Freud's questioning of her sincerity in rejecting Herr K., feels the need to provide him with a pat explanation. It would prove to Freud, the father-figure she's trying both to impress and escape from, her "persecution" (80) by K., the married older man. But whether I'm right or wrong to doubt what Dora sometimes reports, Freud's grudging admission later that he may somehow have forced seduction fantasies on suggestible patients expands the potential meaning of Dora's elaborations. People long to be justified in the eyes of authority, even when trying to leave it behind—or take it on.

Third, though he understates it, Freud points up what was obviously the low point in their analytic relationship: Dora at one point regresses like an angry infant. He has been prying guilty secrets about childhood bedwetting and masturbation out of her, when she, musing on why she fell ill, tells him that she knows her father is to blame. She knows he suffered from venereal disease, knows he infected her mother, knows how her mother's whole being has been poisoned by disgusting genital disorders, and knows how she herself hates her own recurrent vaginal catarrh:

> Her father, then, had fallen ill through leading a loose life, and she assumed that he had handed on his bad health to her by heredity. . . . For several days on end she identified herself with her mother by means of slight symptoms and peculiarities of manner, which gave her an opportunity for some really remarkable achievements in the direction of intolerable behaviour. (67)

Most likely, in the transference, she's behaving towards Freud as she would like to act towards her father: be a bad girl and yet still be accepted, forgiven, and loved. But "remarkable achievements" of "intolerable behavior"? You'd like to know more. What did she do? Scrub his couch? call him a sex maniac? kick and scream? slander people? bash herself and try to set Freud's office on fire?

Whatever the form, she was acting out in therapy rage against her father for his accursed sex life, rage against her mother for the childishness that kept her from ever having a proper female role model, rage against nosy Freud for making her relive the traumatic pains of childhood, and rage against her whole treacherous, sexually sick culture, whose main feature, according to Freud, was that it was infected with the most widespread, virulent venereal disease of all: pandemic, life-blighting neuroses. The earthmoving desire that shows through in this offhand passage in Freud is an impulse in modern civilization for a woman (Dora and her mother are united here) to engage in self-destructive "behavior" in order to shame and pressure authority to pay attention and to change.

A fourth point is that, in tone and spirit, Freud's text when Dora quits his care reads like that of a spurned lover or father trying his best to maintain dignity, but falling into that familiar parental petulance of moral superiority: "Her breaking off so unexpectedly, just when my hopes of a successful . . . treatment were at their highest, and her thus bringing those hopes to nothing—this was an unmistakable act of vengeance on her part" (100). Somehow, he seems more human and appealing here, as he continues, puffing himself up as an intellectual knight to a maiden in distress. "No one who, like me, conjures up the most evil of those half-tamed demons that inhabit the human breast, and seeks to wrestle with them, can expect to come through the struggle unscathed." Dora wounded him, as her dream foreshadowed and she intended.

What follows puts the complexity of the mutual Lot complex of these two in a very broad light—Freud, for once uncertain, seeing Dora's need and looking beyond psychoanalysis to the blurry borders between personal and professional life:

Might I perhaps have kept the girl under my treatment if I myself had acted a part, if I had exaggerated the importance to me of her staying on, and had shown a warm personal interest in her—a course which, even after allowing for my position as her physician, would have been tantamount to providing her with a substitute for the affection she longed for? I do not know. (100–101)

He doesn't have all the answers, but the questions he touches on here go to the heart of many "late patriarchy" issues. Dora does long for "a warm personal interest" and "a substitute" for "affection." Freud might seem too cold, and yet he may be onto something when he indicates that professional competence—vocation—may hold more promise for her then a charade of devotion. His particular school and system, however, may not be able to teach her the right skills and toughness to ease her future, and she may be right in walking out. But the dream's literal fire-and-father imagery makes graphic how desperately she was depending on that "warm personal interest" and how she would turn herself once more into a child to get it. What she did get from Freud was his faith that her account of rampant, adulterous, exploitive, and dishonest sexual relations in her family and set was true. She was *not* crazy.

In the end, though, if you study this "doubting Freud" passage, it seems the older man on whom she is to rely, well-meaning though he may be, can't give her enough. She can't be sure that he makes the right professional decisions about her or that he knows enough about what matters most to her. Freud's phrasing of the problem thus emerges as the problem itself for the girl and one big reason why she wakes that second time in the dream: "Might I perhaps have kept the girl under my treatment?" patronizes Dora and does not even make her grammatically the subject or first person of her case, as she needs to be.

5.

WANTING TO BE

OUT FROM UNDER

"The girl under my treatment . . . ": Almost twenty years later another young woman, Anna Freud, training to become a psychoanalyst, underwent analysis by her father. During that time, she was driven to write poetry about a woman's need for creative independence that bears on the end of Dora's dream:

> Only when my mind was churned more deeply,
> When I was struggling with wild, dark forces,
> Did I, alone in my need, feel with fear
> That each poet sings but his own sorrow.

Her biographer notes that in this poem, "Dichter," her illustrative metaphor comes from the Old Testament.[9] Not surprisingly, it calls up the descendants of Lot and his older daughter:

> I would like to play the harp myself,
> To try the power of my own verse,
> Snatch up my soul from its despair,
> Do what cannot be done by others' words.
> My song should conquer night and pain,
> Reaching in triumph the realm of joy.
> In my own service, I would sing my soul—
> David would I be, and King Saul as well.

So, it seems, would the awakening Dora, uncanny big sister of Freud's daughter.

IV.

Dreaming Becomes Reality:
Two Types of Modern Lots

The Dora case has become a modern myth, and, like mythic figures, its characters have seeped into contemporary consciousness. Besides Freud himself, *Dora* offers both the father and Herr K. as types that Lot's modern daughters must deal with. I see in both of them patterns of behavior and personality that have helped shape the last hundred years of domestic, erotic, and gender relations, especially for the middle and privileged classes. To bring home their importance and the continuing force of the case in general, I want to look at them as representative men who reveal the inevitable fusions of life, literature, reader consciousness, and narrative patterns. That is, I mean my reading of these "characters" to imply and make clear their paradigmatic significance (much as the old scriptural commentators read the figures in Genesis 19 as types who reflected truths of their contemporary life).

1.

THE FATHER

Declining health and aging are the fire and brimstone of existence. They burn up time and power. He used to manage life well when he wasn't sick. He made money. He'd use a little guile, a little authority, a little charm, a little humor, and make people feel that they wanted to please him. He showed them, smiling, who's boss. Relatives, women, men who could help him, managers, workers, his bright son and daughter—they'd all pretty much do as he wished. The firm made plenty. He could do what he liked now—except that his lungs threatened to give out, and the VD he caught in the old days might just finally drive him black-out bats.

He realized he married the wrong woman. Pretty once, she had some money and common sense, and, fool that he was, he judged he could smarten her up. But she turned out to have the mentality of a whisk broom. She can't grow or change and doesn't know how hard he works or even what he does. She's rigid and frigid and doesn't sympathize when he's ill or feel sorry for him in his crazy downswings. He: "I wanted to shoot myself today!" She: "Wipe your feet!" And she's no mother to Dora—nothing but a glorified charwoman. He feels she wants to make him a piece of furniture, dead as her heart, celibate as the old Pope. But he won't let her. He's found another woman.

The daughter from the start was quick and smart—everything her mother wasn't. He and the girl were always close; he'd toss her about, she'd stand on his shoes when he danced. They'd laugh at the same things—puns, picture-books, his son's seriousness, the literal-mindedness of the mother, the goofy flattery of his underlings. She knew what he meant even when she was little, looking at him with those great searching eyes. He taught her she was important and what she did mattered; she admired the way others looked at him. He could feel her pride. She would visit him in his sickroom, chat, and act the little nurse. Later, when his wife muttered, clucked, and stormed away from him, the daughter looked over, rolled her eyes, and winked. When he thinks of himself as the girl's father, he knows he's not such a bad person.

But it bothers him now that his daughter's depressed and angry at him. If only she could see that his relationship with the other woman is a good thing for all. She was such a good influence on the girl. It delighted him to see them with each other, animated and happy, gossiping and laughing together like two beautiful, intelligent sisters—and both devoted to him.

He loves Frau K. for renewing his life. He knows she finds him more attractive than her handsome, silly husband, and she has a body he adores. He feared that part of his life was dead, but it's not. He will not give her up. They might divorce and marry each other, but he worries about finances and complications—especially the girl. Why is she so miserable? Why can't he reconcile her to her former friend, this wonderful woman. After all, the girl's really a protégé of them both. He spoils the girl and always tries to give her what she wants, but now she's so hostile. He may have let her spend too much time with the husband, because it made things easier. Dora exaggerates about him: K. is no marauder; he's too weak. It would be a bad idea for that man to marry the girl. The father worries that this brilliant but nosy doctor of the psyche will get them all nervous, work the girl up and ruin things. He decides to wait things out and—patient as a trained seal— try to balance all the balls in his domestic circus. But he worries that he could soon lose both the erotic spark of the younger woman, his own daughter's faith, and the flow of energy in his life.

2.

THE OLDER MAN

Molester, cradle-robber, libertine, seducer of servants, cast-off husband unable to satisfy an ambitious wife, pathetic, complaisant cuckold, public enemy of innocence, virtue, and feminine well-being, desecrator of church festivals, sick symbol of manhood's general failure: the type of degenerate that fed Austrian Jew-baiting and made Hitler's road easier; that led to Leopold

Bloom masturbating in front of the girl in *Ulysses*; to Woody Allen in child-custody court; to promiscuous politicians preying on pudgy pages—what scorn, what hateful thoughts have not fallen on Herr K., one of literature's all-time losers. That aging has-been's sometime good looks, as they turn to wattles and wrinkles, surely didn't remain "prepossessing." Yet the maids, the child-minders, the office assistants always liked him. He would ask these young women about themselves, and he would truly try to care about how they were doing. They thought he was nice, not stuck-up. Would anyone care, would anyone believe him if he said that he didn't paw the girl, that she led him on, that he meant well, that he fell in love with Dora?

What choice did he have in that whole affair? He depended financially on the girl's father, and when the big man got sick and needed advice, Herr K. took him to a good doctor he knew—Freud. The boss always ogled K.'s wife, and he sent Dora into the K. household. Herr K. had to be good to the daughter. Besides, she was nice to the children, even when they bored and exasperated his wife. He saw that this pretty, precocious girl liked him. And he loved that pubescent shyness, the naïve flirtiness—the firm flesh. And Frau K. would share anatomy books with her young friend—big sister lessons in dangerous liaisons.

It's a cliché, but his wife really doesn't understand him. He used to be happy, but then she always wanted more. She says he's not effective enough, that he lacks drive. She says that Dora's father needs her, and they all will benefit. She refuses to let K. touch her any more.

Tough, arrogant Freud, he knows, thinks little of him. Freud tells him that with his boyish insecurity, K. needs a girl who can look up to him. With an adulterous wife and Dora in the wings, the best thing might be a divorce. Freud teaches him that frauleins' father-transference give him his big hope for self-confidence. He might marry Dora, who would be rich. K. felt sorry for her, but he lusted too. He wanted her. He thought she was pure, a virgin for him. K. enjoyed playing the suitor to this bourgeois princess: candy and flowers; cards and letters. "*Liebchen: Covering the territory for the firm, I think of you in my loneliness. Sweets to the sweet.*"

He thought they were intimate, that she wanted romance. But she slapped him hard before he could finish *I-love-you.* And in his own house, she told him to stay out of her room, which he had made sure was the one he had to go through to get to his own. This when, so *come-hither*, she'd been positively asking for it. The father, that hypocrite, wrote him an irate letter. K. felt guilty. He really did esteem the girl. But his wife convinced him the girl was totally neurotic—a troublemaker; Frau K. said deny everything. He did, and the big man believed him.

Later on he was walking down the street, when he saw Dora on the other side. She looked startled, wide-eyed—so loveable; she hailed him. He was eager to explain everything, so he ran across to her, but he didn't see the stupid cart, and it hit him. Stunned, he went down, spinning, sitting in the middle of the road, the driver cursing him for a fool. K. was mortified. Then when they saw he wasn't dead, he heard them all laughing, even Dora. When they got him up, he looked for her, but she was gone. They took him to an infirmary. He was reeling, but he managed to laugh at himself when this very, very cute young nurse patched him up. Self-deprecation works like a charm—he wanted to see a lot more of the nurse, and he did.

3.
MISSING MOTHER

In the dream, Dora's mother is backward-looking, nothing but trouble, and, in fact, no one in the whole case says anything good about her. She's just the madwoman in the foyer, stuck in the past, polishing furniture and jewels. As many have noted, Freud's account, like Dora's fire dream, denigrates, then effaces Frau Bauer. For father, daughter, and Freud, her mode of life is contemptible, one to avoid. "Remember Lot's wife," at the start of the new century, becomes for many young women in essence "Remember Dora's mother"—that is, *Fight housewives' psychosis: you don't have to live like that.*

But the rejection of the mother by the father-identified daughter leaves her with unmet needs, unconscious longing, and residual guilt. Freud says that the girl, in her psychosomatic symptoms and in that bout of "intolerable behavior," acts out, in her childish irrationality, a latent identification with her mother, who, after all, as Dora knew, was not only scorned, but also infected by her diseased husband. The final wake-up in the dream leaves the mother behind, but it also breaks the spell of the father. And Freud, in his dismissal of the mother, is surely identified in Dora's mind with the father.

Dora's "second dream," which Freud only begins to analyze just before she breaks off therapy, fantasizes the death of the father, but, in elaborating upon it, she recalls a key scene of herself standing for two hours "in front of the Sistine Madonna, rapt in silent admiration" (88). "The 'Madonna' was obviously Dora herself" (96, n20), says a cocksure Freud, projecting onto her a "maternal longing for a child" because, he says, lately she'd had "a phantasy of childbirth" manifested by hysterical stomach pains (94), and "because she had won K.'s love by the motherliness she had shown towards his children." But the dream image represents an even more basic wish fulfillment: *Dora wants to see a good mother.* The Madonna is surely the mother she's missing: a devoted, inspiring, loving and loveable woman, untainted by the sexual pollution and the bad nature of men. Dora's dream history thus recapitulates biblical, incestuous Lot's-daughter history in figuring a situation in which father and daughters, abandoning the superceded wife-mother in the sterile, shameful past, bond in desperation, and start a process that eventually results in spiritual regeneration—the divine miracle of immaculate conception, virgin motherhood, and woman transformed into a sacred figure of redemption. In the return of the repressed, the disparaged, absent mother reappears to Dora as a being to be honored and cherished. Again, these things are a parable for an age to come.

Freud's speculations about the Madonna and Dora here fit in with good old-fashioned male thinking: the girl must be in love with some man; she must want to have a baby; she must idealize the role of motherhood for herself. But these assumptions don't match Dora's psychological makeup or her life. "[T]he notion of the 'Madonna,'" says Freud, "is a favourite counter-idea in the mind of girls who feel themselves oppressed by imputations of sexual guilt,—which was the case with Dora" (96, note 20). Change the word "girls" to "men" here and you might come closer to the truth.

Dora seems much more distressed by male sexual behavior than by her own supposed sexual guilt. Her gaze here at the Madonna makes a fitting image for the end of the case, because where to find and how to resurrect the mother who had to be left behind is one of the greatest problems shaping modern Lot complexes. One challenge in the intellectual life of our time is for women (and men too) to "remember Lot's wife" by discovering a rehabilitating faith in the mothers of the past that, in essence, would sublimate and exculpate Dora's rejection of her mother.

4.

THE REVENGE OF DORA

Dora has had her revenge, which is to turn the tables on Freud, the putative agent of sexism.[10] She shows the necessity for reform in gender relations. Like Mathilda with her daughter's curse in Mary Shelley's work, Dora stands as an avenging diagnostician of patriarchy's illness. This ostensibly hysterical neurotic thus undergoes a miraculous transformation in the consulting room of history and turns into Doctor Dora, psychological expert on what ails society and what it's hiding. It's as if in the arena of interpretation she has practiced a kind of Freudian jujitsu in which she turns the psychoanalytic force and insight used on *her* against the social pathologies of male domination all around her. Dora's revenge on Freud is conceived from the intellectual seed of her world-shaking, bearded therapist, and it goes something like this:

You insist on the power of unconscious motives and drives, on the force of covert sexual urges, on the universality of incestuous impulses, on the inevitablity of repression, transference, and projection in shaping perceptions and ideas. You teach the necessity of being skeptical about people's self-knowledge and their self-representations. You keep on probing childhood history for sex and dredging up repressed memories about it—the more disgusting the better. You find truth in outright fantasies and dreams. You organize your vocation and make your living as a secular confessor and authority for women who often lie supine in your office as they speak. You denigrate their interests to the interests of men and the world of the fathers. But I'll use your own knowledge and methods to sap your authority and burn down the walls of "the man of the house." I'll make the great power of your skepticism mine and turn it onto your own motives, your own words, your own self-presentation, your own behavior, your own libido, your own childhood, and your own subterranean self.

You want me to scrounge up sexual memories from infancy and childhood? I'll show you childhood as a nightmare of sexual abuse. I won't let you or your avatars think of yourselves as benevolent patriarchs. I'll get up off the couch, walk out the door, move into the public space of your published "case study" and beyond, and I'll claim victim status. I'll be a reproach to you for joining in the conspiracy of male privilege, for your fatalistic attitude towards incest and abuse, for your complicity in the outrageous, filthy world of seduction, sexually transmitted disease, and assaults against women, for your implicit prurience, and for your cold, ignorant hauteur about the plight of aging women.

But, ironically, such new determination and independence, such projected sentiments and effects—in other words, such an outcome—had, consciously or not, been instrumental in motivating Freud's own hopes and intentions for Dora's case.

V.
Postscript: "The "Prepossessing Drauma"

More than a quarter of a century after Dora quit Freud and he published his account, James Joyce put his own gifted but unhinged daughter, Lucia, into psychotherapy with Carl Jung and others.[11] As Joyce suffered through father-fixated Lucia's mental agonies and her doctors' incompetence, he turned in *Finnegans Wake* to eroticized father-daughter, man-girl relationships and a whole range of scandalous, textual Lot complexes. Specifically, in a devastating satirical passage, he imagined—in composite, punning overlays of Stead with Lily, Lewis Carroll with Alice in the darkroom, prurient father-confessors with girls in confessionals, and sex-driven therapists, like Freud, Jung, and Ferenczi, with sexy nymphets on the couches of their secular confessionals—the libidinous implications of psychoanalysis. In particular, he focused on both Lucia's clinical history and the Dora case, which he obviously knew well ("prepossessing," Freud's very word for Herr K., as well as the specific details and masturbatory imagery of the last three lines, give proof of how familiar Joyce was with "Dora"):

we grisly old Sykos who have done our unsmiling bits on 'alices, when they were yung and easily freudened, in the penumbra of the procuring room and what oracular comepression we have had apply to them! . . . *father* in such virgated contexts is not always that undemonstrative relative (often held up to our contumacy) who settles our hashbill for us and what an innocent . . . looks like can be suggestive of under the pudendascope and, finally, what a neurasthene nympholept . . . with a prepossessing drauma present in her past and a priapic urge for congress with agnates [any male relatives by the father's side, i.e., the father] . . . fundamentally is feeling for under her lubricitous meiosis when she refers with liking to some feeler she fancie's face.[12]

These lines mock the kinship of psychoanalytic discourse to pornographic sniggering, and they also bring to light the repressed, unsavory history of Lot's cave down through the years—all those shady sites of sleazy sexual probing. They show intellectual authority ready to make use of a seductive girl hot to merge with a father figure. The passage gets at much of modern feminism's quarrel with Freud. But what matters most may be that in the obscurity of Wakean prose as in the tangles of the Freudian unconscious—and in Lucia and Dora both—you find that modernism's daughters are Lot's daughters burning up in, with, and at the prepossession of the fathers.

Chapter 10

Shirley Temple

THE DAUGHTER AS CHILDSTAR

The Temple thing is this: . . .

—F. Scott Fitzgerald[1]

They worshiped her in the 1930s. They loved her. What's in a name? The modern impetus to put faith in the girlchild can be summed up in that serendipitous surname of this most famous and popular of all child stars. Shirley Temple was a sight for millions of sore eyes in the Great Depression. For a few years, she was a curly-topped icon. In the hard twentieth-century secular world, the radiant image of the little Hollywood star, like the star over Bethlehem in a religious age, showed the longing of many for renewal and redemption through the innocence of an adorable child.

Adoring Shirley became a ritual. Just like ordinary star-struck fans, celebrities of every description—presidents, princes, potentates, prelates, governors, bishops, mayors, financiers, agents of dictators and commissars—sought Shirley out, wrote her, begged to see her. President Roosevelt rejoiced in her: "When the spirit of the people is lower than at any other time during this Depression, it is a splendid thing that for just 15 cents, an American can go to a movie and look at the smiling face of a baby and forget his troubles."[2] His wife Eleanor confided in Shirley; dictator Benito Mussolini sent his own son for an audience; Leopold Stokowski, symphony maestro, told her she was "a divine instrument" (134); Amelia Earhart lectured her about feminist principles and assured her Hamlet would have made a bad pilot; Einstein talked to her about his poor arithmetic; J. Edgar Hoover, the chief of the new FBI, wore a Shirley Temple police force badge and invited her to his Washington headquarters; urbane Noel Coward sat on the little star's toilet seat pleading for her autograph. Shirley became a much put upon connoisseur of famous laps, expert at gauging degrees of boniness, softness, and discomfort, both physical and psychological, in lap-land (74, 206). Everybody, it seemed, who was anybody wanted to meet her, touch her, and get a picture taken with her.

It could be argued that Shirley Temple was the first untitled mortal child to achieve worldwide fame and veneration (unlike the most famous children before her, she was neither deity, royalty, nor—strictly speaking—a fictional creation). More people saw her—millions more—than had ever seen any other little girl. By the end of 1937, after only four years in the movies, the 9-year-old star had drawn more than more than 240 million paying customers to see her—nearly double the population of the United States. She was the box office leader for four straight years, a feat never equaled in film history. What *Time* magazine called this "cinemoppet" embodied for the public the promise of childhood and the possibilities of recreation, in the fullest sense of the word, both on screen and off.[3]

Why? The answer is that she was seen to preserve the seed of civilization and joyful energy though bad times—and "seen" is the operative word. Shirley's image epitomized the visual appeal of children—the power of a cute child's image to evoke positive, self-flattering, and highly emotional feelings of sympathy from projecting adults (a main reason for the success of the camera, film, and photo developing industries and a lucrative staple of the advertising business). No child had been so universally gazed upon before, and she came to represent the goodness of children and to focus in her photogenic being people's hope, love, and desire for progeny. And she also embodied and mirrored the complex seductiveness of possessing innocence.

She was the child of an ambitious movie-mother and a banker-father spoiling to handle money. But she was also the offspring of Charles Dickens and Little Nell, of Hawthorne and Pearl, of Lewis Carroll and Alice, of Louisa May Alcott and *Little Women*, of John Millais, Eastman Kodak, and countless portraits and photos of little girls, as well as a sister to Little Orphan Annie. Her full image—with its paradoxes and contradictions—

shows her to be a true modern daughter of *Lot*, strangely fulfilling vital cultural needs and desires.

The record of Shirley, the child, in Shirley Temple Black's fascinating book *Child Star* and the image of Shirley in her films fuse together, all of a piece. I want to compare them to show how popular entertainment and her sense of her own life merge together. I'm making the large claim that Shirley Temple, far from being a cultural footnote from the 1930s, offers a key to understanding what has happened since in gender relations and social history. The desires that were projected upon her and from her show up in both her movies and the account of her early life, and they helped to determine the way we live now.

Her sweetie-pie films show up regularly in the "family favorites" section at video rental stores, in college media collections, and on old movie channels, and her remarkable autobiography can be found in almost any good library or book outlet. As a performer, she is remarkably good, but her movies mostly are not. They're laced with sentimentality and sometimes with dated, naïve sexism, racial attitudes, and American provincialism. Nevertheless they're extremely revealing about what people wanted in the first half of the twentieth century. Deceptively simple, like all wish fulfillments, they can look, from one perspective, like magically answered social prayers: a kinder, gentler nation; rough, willful men tamed; racial harmony; peace between nations and generations; colonial and religious disputes settled; songs and dances of innocence—Little Nell and little Pearl rejuvenated, given celluloid life, tap shoes, dimples, close-ups, and Hollywood endings. On reflection, however, neither the movies nor the life give us pretty pictures only. She's delightful to look at and read about, of course, but sometimes there's something disturbing about what surrounds her image. What, in fact, the typical Shirley Temple film is mainly about and what her recollections in *Child Star* often seem to be about is the crucial relationship—under particular, varying circumstances—between an innocent, winning girl and older men of authority.

If you look at images from four typical movies from her glory years, *Bright Eyes* (1934), *The Little Colonel* (1935), *Captain January* (1936), and *Wee Willie Winkie* (1937), you can see in retrospect how the films feature the girl's civilizing power over men, and how they relate to that transcendent phenomenon, "Shirley Temple," the girlchild as star.

I.
Seeing the Girlchild Star:
The Films

I.
'BRIGHT EYES'

Even in this early box-office smash, contradictions appear around the child figure. Here, reflecting the self-impersonation that characterizes her type-cast movies, Shirley plays a cute curly-locks named "Shirley." In one of her best known cinemoments, she sings her famous *de facto* theme-song, "On the Good Ship Lollipop," that sugar-in-the-sky anthem for down-and-out Depression dreamers and sweet-toothed children of all ages:

> On the good ship Lollipop,
> It's a sweet trip to a candy shop,
> Where bon-bons play,
> On the sunny beach of Peppermint Bay.

What may not be so widely known is that Shirley performs this song in odd circumstances, to say the least. The "good ship" is an airplane taxiing about on the ground in which a group of beefy, unemployed aviators (reportedly the USC Trojan football team) are having a party for Shirley—the little trouper appearing alone with this hunky bunch who sit in the passenger seats, ready to be amused. Soon she's moving up and down the aisle, singing and entertaining them. Throughout the whole picture, these men, to pass the time while they keep waiting for jobs to turn up, befriend her, amuse her, and hand her about like a big rubber doll (or a soft football)—especially the hero, "Loop" (James Dunn), her dead pilot-father's best friend. He cares for her and tries to look after her. On the way to pick her up from the airship party, her mother is suddenly, shockingly struck dead. Loop (who looks a bit like FDR) for the rest of the film seeks custody of Shirley and in the end joins with her in building a new family.

It's easy now to see the Lollipop scene as a Depression allegory with Shirley Temple in her prescribed historical role: while the airship of state spins its wheels around the field, revving up and waiting to get off the ground, a hungry crew of out-of-work veterans is diverted and soothed by the charms and wholesome energy of a lovable girl. The men go to her show and focus on her instead of their troubles. Shirley functions as the germ of hope for the future, a figure who absorbs, but diffuses dangerous male passions that might otherwise go into trouble-making and destructive rebellion. But she's more than an allegory; she's really a cute kid.

In the first scene you see "Bright Eyes" Shirley alone on a country road hitchhiking. It's a scene that at first sight plays off despair and could evoke images of dust-bowl waifs thumbing their way around a failing nation. But Shirley's jaunty and trusting. The road's part of Shirley's big neighborhood. It turns out she's looking for a quick ride out to the airport to see her pal Loop, who's promised to take her up in an airplane. The scene is sunny: the girl thumbs now so she can fly later, and even though this orphan obviously lives in a world of past disasters, she's on the move with purpose—hopeful and perky. That could sum up the popular image and meaning of Shirley for her time. (Imagine how different the effect would be now if you saw a picture of a lone 5-year-old girl hitchhiking on the highway to the nearest airport.) The opening shots of Shirley are juxtaposed with a plane looping-the-loop: *things may be tough now, but look at this happy kid—the sky's the limit.*

When Loop lands his plane, he's glad to see her and soon she's browsing through his scrapbook. She sees a high society picture of a glittery woman, and a sad Loop rails against this rock-hearted beauty who betrayed him. The image of the showy, sexy woman set off against the unspoiled little girl helps compose one message of the film: beware of the lure of sex and social-climbing—*think of the children.*

Shirley's sweet widowed mom is forced to work as a live-in maid for a nasty, nouveau riche couple named Smythe, who have a daughter Joy, just Shirley's age. The Smythe money comes from their rich old uncle, Ned Smith, a curmudgeon confined to a wheelchair. (Uncle Ned looks suspiciously like those two old 1930s plutocrats John D. Rockefeller and Henry Ford.) The cheerful servants, in their below-stairs life, dote on Shirley and take their mean-spirited employers with a grain of salt.

It is Christmas Eve. Shirley's mother has great troubles. Death has come unexpectedly to her husband; life is unfair; bad people like the Smythes bully good people like her; malefactors of wealth inhabit the world; the poor are oppressed. Prosperity might be around the corner, but it and virtue don't seem to go together. Still, as she puts Shirley to bed and has the child pray for everyone—even the rich—the music swells. The strains of "Silent Night" take over the soundtrack ringing with a message of blessed serenity.

In honor of the Nativity, the holy time of sacred love's regeneration, the movie camera moves to climax in the scene by giving us a close-up of the reborn savior, the little child that, by implication, is suffered to come unto God: Shirley asleep in an aural glow.

Later she makes friends with sour Uncle Ned and thaws his icy heart. When her mother is struck dead and the Smythes refuse to help the child, the old skinflint even offers to make her his ward. Meanwhile Loop, wanting to save Shirley and adopt her, volunteers for a thousand dollars to fly an impossible mission through a killer storm. The rich old Republican who turns out to have a heart of gold contests with the Roosevelt-like Loop for the privilege of caring best for Shirley, vessel of hope. Eventually they settle their custody battle (Ned disapproves of Loop because he has no wife) when Loop agrees to marry that repentant, ultimately faithful scrap-book socialite. Thus, with Ned's support, they reconstitute a functioning set of parents and a family for Shirley.

But I neglect one of the most striking figures in *Bright Eyes*: the marvelously hellish Joy, a comic bad seed played for laughs by Shirley's child-star rival, Jane Withers. Bad girl Joy set off against good girl Shirley doubles the image of the girlchild—Lot's daughters in an infantilized, funny, pop-culture version, pregnant (if that's a proper word for little girls) with meaning for times to come. Joy, the mirror opposite of Shirley in every way, is a little monster out of patriarchy's worst nightmares: when poor Shirley goes through a garbage can and salvages one of Joy's castaway dolls, Joy grabs it back, telling her she can't have it because she—Joy—decides she wants to rip it up and "kill" it. In a later scene, Joy and Shirley are pushing their dolls in two toy prams, like two little mothers out for a stroll, when Joy announces she's going to play at taking her "baby" to the hospital where she hopes it will die; then she can do what she most wants with dolly—bury it. Whereas Shirley is always kind and sparkle-friendly to cranky old Ned, Joy torments him, makes faces at him, and hates him. Joy yells, grabs what she wants, sasses her elders, disobeys, detests dolls and pretty clothes, despises the Christmas spirit, refuses to share. Like a boy, she races her trike, plays fire engine, screams like a police siren. Shirley may pray to God the Father dutifully, but Joy, like a little Americanized Dora, goes regularly to a psychiatrist, who says she mustn't be thwarted. Jane Withers is on screen eight minutes at most and always—except for a few seconds—with Shirley, but somehow her image fused with her adorable rival captures, on a small scale, the paternalistic fears for civility that produced a Shirley Temple—as well as some buried resentments and strivings for authority that would spark a later feminism. This split-image of daughters makes a picture with a future and previews two dominant strategies in facing and changing the world of the fathers: (1) attract and win over power to get power; (2) defy convention and rebel.

2.
'THE LITTLE COLONEL'

Here the appeal of Shirley heals the lingering animosities of the American Civil War. As usual her cute charm and energetic sparkle seduce a disillusioned patriarch into civil behavior. In this case crotchety, bitter old Colonel Lloyd (Lionel Barrymore), a veteran of the fallen Confederacy, disowns and refuses to see his daughter for eloping with a Yankee named Sherman. Things go bad for Sherman, and when his wife and their pert daughter Lloyd (Shirley), nicknamed "the little colonel," have to move back to the South near the Colonel's plantation, the little girl wins and warms the heart of the old man—and symbolically puts an end to the past hostility between North and South for the future good of the nation, which she naturally embodies.

But something even more important is going on. Shirley Temple Black, writing in her autobiography about her film appearances in the 1930s with the legendary black dancer Bill "Bojangles" Robinson, quotes director D. W. Griffith's words before this movie: "There is nothing, absolutely nothing, calculated to raise the goose-flesh on the back of an audience more than that of a white girl in relation to Negroes" (90). The best-known shots from *The Little Colonel* show Shirley hand-in-hand with Walker (Bill Robinson), the formally dressed house servant in the Colonel's Southern mansion, dancing up, down, and up the staircase. This sequence is probably the most famous scene in all Shirley Temple movies. She, the magic girl, evidently could smooth bigotry's goose bumps and get American audiences to tolerate and smile at a vision of black flesh and white flesh joined. This child inspired such good will that she could hold out the promise of reconciliation between races, as well gender and generational harmony.[4]

The film and Black's account of its making say a lot about the history of American race relations and white attitudes in the 1930s. Though *The*

Little Colonel has plenty of offensive racialism, that connection between the precocious girl and the graceful black man becomes its dominant image—and literally a "touching" one. Shirley and Bojangles touching and tap-dancing together gives you a picture of bonding, fleeting and unstable though it be. Child, female, black man, menial status—these marginal categories begin to merge in the movie's vision as they do in the Genesis Lot chapter and, later, in influential twentieth-century ideologies. The tie between the little colonel and black folks in the film is strong, though presented with the usual white liberal condescension of the time. Shirley trusts and confides in her mother's cook and mammy figure, Mom Beck (Hattie McDaniel); she plays with, and orders about, her little regiment of scraggly black children; she goes to an outdoor black baptism with Mom Beck, Walker, and her playmates where one (Nyanza) gets a ritual dunking; and she even enacts the role of dying Little Eva in a play-within-the-film version of *Uncle Tom's Cabin* (cut from the distributed video print). Not that *The Little Colonel* doesn't offer plenty of racist pap to segregated America. One paternalistic, negative message in the film would seem to be that Negroes are still very much like children. Though the movie asserts their basic dignity and obvious virtue, Walker and Mom Beck, in one scene, are talking about things they don't want the children to know, and so they spell out the words. But, lovable simples that they are, they spell them wrong—yuk, yuk! Walker, like a good boy, takes all sorts of demeaning abuse without a murmur from the rude old Colonel (like Jackie Robinson, a decade later in the 1940s, forbidden to reply to insults when breaking the color ban in major league baseball).

In writing about the filming of this movie, Shirley Temple Black makes a proud thing of holding Negro hands. When pitiful Nyanza gets scared out of his wits acting with superstar Shirley and blows his lines, she, "taking his small hand in mine," befriends and calms him. When she and Bill Robinson are first introduced and walk across the studio lot together, she keeps reaching to take his hand, "instantly attracted" by "his silky, muscular grace" and "his great round eyes showing whites all around" with "rows of brilliant teeth [how many rows?] showing in a wide smile" (91); Bojangles doesn't notice until his wife tells him. "When he took my hand, it felt large and cool." She asks him if she can call him "Uncle Billy." Yes, he says, if he can call her "darlin'." "From then on, whenever we walked together it was always hand in hand, and I was always his darlin'" (91). Shirley's account here, like the movie, reflects racial stereotyping, but much more significantly, the movie and her life reflect the will of a white girl to reach out, touch, and grow. Despite any gaffes, Black's esteem and friendship for Robinson come across convincingly throughout her book, and it will become apparent just how deeply he touched her.

Behind that "Uncle Billy" and the figure he plays in the film looms American culture's Uncle Tom. In Stowe's *Uncle Tom's Cabin*, Little Eva and Tom, white girl and black man, redeem her father in particular and the evils of the national past in general, and they become centers of faith. In the world of entertainment—in the luminous staircase dance—that's what the image of Shirley and Bojangles looks to do. You can see how Shirley Temple focused and developed in motion pictures for the mass audience of her times wishes, drives, and obsessions that come right out of nineteenth-century history and literature.

There's a sad and revealing moment in her autobiography when Shirley, grown, is reunited in 1944 with Robinson at a benefit and asks to come and visit him and his wife in their home, since in the old days, they often came to buffets at her house. "Leaving the . . . platform, we held hands as we always had" (371). He tells her with regret, "'No way, darlin'.' He gave my hand one reassuring squeeze. 'Just no way.'"

3.
'CAPTAIN JANUARY'

Shirley, here appropriately called "Star Bright," again gives meaning and hope to the lives of old men. The movie is based very loosely on the book *Captain January*, a little seaside *Silas Marner* by Laura E. Richards about an old seadog who finds a baby girl washed up on a Maine shore and raises her happily. In the movie, Star is taken in, named, cared for, and doted upon by a much sourer Captain January (Guy Kibbee), a battered but good-hearted lighthouse keeper who unofficially adopts and makes himself a father to the girl. January squabbles constantly with another grizzled old codger, Captain Nazro (Slim Summerville), who, like him—and like the whole little fishing town—is captivated by Star. Star loves January and sparkles for him, dancing and singing around the snug lighthouse and around the whole village, a winning bundle of joy for all the townsmen—most of whom, in the trough of the Depression, have no work. January and Nazro are seedierlooking than the men you see in most Shirley Temple films; unshaven, they look like geezers. The little girl keeps them responsible and well-behaved, but their down-and-out looks are not prepossessing. The film is a beauty-and-the-beast tale binding generations.

Six-year-old Star provides her Captain with his reason for living. He homeschools her in the Bible and navigation, and she dresses up in her mother's opera clothes to entertain him (a trunk filled with her mother's costumes washed ashore with her). The plot features the false accusations of unfit, improper parenting against January by a spiteful truant officer (she looks like Eleanor Roosevelt) who tries to take Star away. Though harsh, unjust governmental power in the form of this mean woman manages to drag the sobbing child off, Star is united with her Captain in the end—and with her unknown rich relatives to boot. It turns out she has a wealthy aunt and uncle who commission a cruise ship for Star. Captain January ends up skippering it, and the spruced-up townsfolk, given work and dressed in nice uniforms, serve as the crew.

There are, however, distinctly odd features about *Captain January* that make it, at moments, puzzling. Some images can even show why the spirit of its truant officer took hold and why the idea of a cute little girl living alone with an unrelated, grizzled old man who looks like a drinker now makes people shudder. Two scenes seem bizarre. In one sequence, Star's grown-up sailor friend Paul (Buddy Ebsen), dressed in bell-bottoms and a dashing sailor shirt, takes his ukulele and Star alone down to the beach. Inexplicably, supposedly on the cold Maine coast, Shirley Temple wears a little grass skirt, a scanty necklace of seaweed and nothing else. While Paul strums the uke, topless Shirley does the hula.[5] The novelist Graham Greene, reviewing the film, said that Shirley, the redeemer and cleanser of the souls of grown men, appears nevertheless to behave coquettishly at times. Despite Shirley's earlier hula in *Curly Top*, I was dumbfounded to imagine how this wildly incongruous scene could exist—until I read Laura Richards's *Captain January*. In it there's an illustration, surprising in a children's book of any period, of a grass-skirted black woman with big, bare breasts. The movie and Shirley were making innocent the book's odd sexuality—an indecent picture of a naked woman is defused in child's play. But sometimes the very stress on the child as a desexualizing, purifying agent in Shirley Temple movies can work in strange ways. In one of the goofiest sequences in her films, Shirley dreams that old, round-faced Captain January has turned into a great big baby in a bonnet and high chair. Star, in this vision, has succeeded in turning men into big babies and taking away their manhood—for many, no doubt, a consummation devoutly to be wished. At the end of this section, you get Shirley dreaming of diapering the ridiculous figure of Guy Kibbee, and the picture cuts to an image of a huge diaper ready for application. Whose dream is this? The *idea* of little Shirley Temple diapering a gross, naked Kibbee is surely one of the weirdest in motion picture history. And yet there's half-baked symbolic logic here: the child is becoming mother of the man, and the regenerated, purified daughter of Lot expresses the dream of a diaper service to clean up the act of dirty old men.

4.
'WEE WILLIE WINKIE'

This was Shirley's favorite movie—maybe because it meant she could act like a boy. Taking over a boy's role, she could get closer to male power and freedom of action. Shirley had become such a big star that Hollywood would rewrite gender for her. The film was adapted for her from Rudyard Kipling's story "Wee Willie Winkie" about the little son of a British regimental commander in India. With Wee Willie as a girl, Shirley could be the tomboy, get away from cloying sugar-and-spice, and play with guns (which she loved). She could step right into the picture of conventional masculine pursuits—like soldiering, empire-building, and power politics. Images that stand out in this film are Shirley, as usual the darling of many grown men, drilling in her spiffy military uniform featuring kilts; Shirley handling and learning to shoot a rifle; and Shirley, the international negotiator, helping to pacify the subcontinent by winning over the hostile, dark Afghan rebel leader (Cesar Romero) near the Khyber Pass (everything old is new again). One reason she thought *Wee Willie Winkie* her best picture, she says, is "because I finally seemed to earn the professional respect of someone so blood-and-thunder macho as [director John] Ford" (181)—a man of power.

Two notable, vastly different public comments appeared about Shirley in *Wee Willie Winkie*. Eleanor Roosevelt wrote in her column: "I wonder how many people seeing *Wee Willie Winkie* will get the main lesson from it. It took a little child's faith and logic to bring a dangerous tribal chief in India to an understanding with his ancient enemy" (182). For the president's wife, Shirley was the Princess of Peace.

For naughty, iconoclastic Graham Greene, however, she was just a piece. Writing in *Night and Day* (October 28, 1937), he got himself and the journal in big trouble (studio lawyers brought a successful libel suit against the journal and put it out of business):

Infancy with her is a disguise, her appeal is more secret and more adult. Already two years ago she was a fancy little piece. . . . Now in *Wee Willie Winkie*, wearing short kilts, she is a complete totsy. Watch . . . the way she measures a man with agile studio eyes, with dimpled depravity. Adult emotions of love and grief glissade across the mask of childhood, a childhood skin deep. It is clever, but it cannot last. Her admirers, middle-aged men and clergymen, respond to her dubious coquetry, to the sight of her well-shaped and desirable little body, packed with enormous vitality, only because the safety curtain of story and dialogue drops between their intelligence and their desire. (quoted in Black, 184–85)

Whether or not men saw Shirley as a sexual object, the most interesting thing here is what's motivating Greene. "Clergymen" is the tip-off word. Religious faith, not sex, is his main concern. Why, really, would he write such a passage? Greene, a pessimistic Catholic cynical about a wicked world sentimentally fetishizing a little girl into an object of faith, wants to shock people into an awareness of fallen humanity's penchant for perverse fantasies and false idols—even dimpled ones. He's out to pull down the Temple of what he perceives as a false God—or goddess. He risks blasphemy of faith in the child to expose the hypocrisy behind the whole enterprise of *the innocent girlchild* and the corruption of those who promote such idolatries. *He* is the one projecting seductive behavior onto the child to expose men who eroticize the illusion of human innocence and use it for their own ends. And if an aesthetically cute and pleasing Shirley seems to dance vampishly, smile, and show off, or if she appears to act with touching joy, natural spontaneity, hope, and good-heartedness, who taught her these different moves and steps? She was an adult project, mostly of men, and, as her sense of life in *Child Star* reveals, that project was full of contradictions. The movies are just vehicles for the complex phenomenon of "Shirley Temple"—a cinematic, wholesome, moralized version of the Lot complex.

II.
Seeing the Girlchild Star:
Early Life and Older Men

Black dedicates the autobiography to her mother, whom she calls "the dominant pillar of my young life."[6] But a pillar rigidly supports the space of others. It also suggests Lot's wife imagery. Gertrude Temple was responsible for the fact and success of the daughter's movie career, but not for the form, image, social effects, and symbolic impact of Shirley. Mrs. Temple knew what was wanted, and over and over coached her would-be infant prodigy to flash and "sparkle." But the value and consequences of "sparkle" were that they furthered the various plans, dreams, and projects of men.

Powerful men often wanted to associate themselves with Shirley's perceived qualities of goodness and use her for their own ends. And Shirley learned to relate to powerful men. Anecdote after anecdote in Black's indispensable book about the way a girl could figure in the twentieth-century historical imagination recount the interaction between herself and older men. In it she conveys a sense of herself as a human mirror in which their particular, essential selves would be reflected, and in turn shows them as mirrors in which she could see the self she wanted to be. Said one director, "Shirley was the product of her mother, the instrument on which she played" (205). But looking back it would be more accurate to say that it was the individuality and personality of the mother that was effaced. A daughter may absorb, fulfill, and repress the mother all at once.

Shirley's career was born in just that spirit of modern Sodom-and-Gomorrah cynicism that Graham Greene frets over. Unwittingly, Mrs. Temple directed sunny Shirley's little feet to a shady side of the street. Her first pictures, "sexist" one-reelers called *Baby Burlesks*, cast children in adult roles parodying famous films and stars, and they featured, in Shirley's words, "cynical exploitation of our childish innocence" (14). In *War Babies*, a spoof on *What Price Glory?*, 4-year-old Shirley, dressed in a low-cut blouse and diaper, played a tough French bar-girl who did "kootchy dances" for troops off to the front. In another *Burlesk* parody, *Polly Tix in Washington* (get it?), she acted the part of a call-girl paid to seduce Washington politicians: "Aw, c'mon, Senator, you can be had" (24). In another she played a girl named "Morelegs Sweettrick" (Marlene Dietrich) as a little seductress. Evidently, there was a market for children performing such roles. Within two years, however, would come the reverse cynicism of "purity." Hollywood, under severe pressure from censor Joseph Breen and religious pressure-groups, worried about its moral image. It now discovered the girlchild as a marvelous figure on whom to project moral purity as well as hope in a time of economic troubles.

What would now be called child abuse, physical and mental, was frequent on and around the set in Shirley's early, pre-stardom days. She breezily tells how her mother turned her over to Charles Lamont, the director of the *Burlesks*. He punished Shirley for wasting time and got her to do what he wanted quickly by putting her, hot and sweating from the Kleig lights, into a 6' x 6', sound-proof, freezing black-box-on-wheels with nothing to sit on but a block of melting ice. Lamont threatened the kids that they wouldn't work if they tattled on him, and even when Shirley did tell her mother, Gertrude wouldn't believe her. The lesson, said Shirley, was profound and unforgettable.

I've said that a modern form of Lot's cave is the darkroom, where pictures are developed and seeds of the future are preserved in recovered images from the past. Memory—how you preserve the past—depends on the dominant media, and nowadays snapshot photos often trigger the recollections and shape life stories. *Child Star* features lots of photos of Shirley from her early life, usually with celebrated men. The power of photographic images to shape memory and set off nostalgic feelings for the past and for childhood—one meaning of the "Shirley Temple" phenomenon—shows itself here. Often it seems that her written text comments on, and gives a narrative context and form to the photographs in the book. Let me offer prose snapshots on a few of the diverse, important older men who figure significantly in the Shirley Temple picture of things.

1.
GEORGE TEMPLE

A stocky man with a receding hairline, forcing a smile, he sits behind a desk, guiding Shirley's fingers as she, plopped sweetly on the desk alongside an official-looking paper, holds a big pen over a contract. He's beneath her, not on her level in the picture, not at the center, but they're touching, hands joined in this happy moment of generating income. It's Shirley's lucrative signing with Twentieth Century Fox.

FIGURE 10.1 George and Shirley Temple at Fox in 1934. Courtesy of Shirley Temple Black and Shirley's World, L.P.

I choose this picture (Figure 10.1) because it symbolizes something re-markable for its time, though easy now to take for granted: a daughter can appear to equal or surpass her father in importance. In Black's book, fo-cusing on her movie career, George comes across as a nice, normal dad with whom Shirley had a good, easy relationship, but somehow, in her child star days, he doesn't seem a dominant presence. She loves him, but she's not in awe of him. The photo shows, however, that the daughter did become a central presence for him. Pondering her early life, she writes, "I needed Mother's crucially important maternal and professional influence.

She needed Father for business administration. He, in turn, relied on me to produce the income stream" (487). A self-made banker with little formal education, he'd had the drive, pride, ability, and high spirits to make something of himself. His daughter's seed-money now gave him the chance to move his family and himself to a level he could never have dreamed of in his youth.

Shirley's first graphic memory of him comes when she smashes her lip badly and has to have stitches. In the emergency room where George carries her, he—a strong, athletic man—faints at the sight of her blood, and the doctor has to stop, leaving the suture hanging out of her bloody mouth, while he gives smelling salts to the father. Somehow, in that opening vision of the two, they seem equals. Between the first chapter and the next fifty pages describing how this star was born, Black hardly refers to George. When she became famous, she says, he put a life-sized photograph of her handing him her first paycheck at the door of the branch bank he managed. That, he tells the family, led a lady at the bank to proposition him with a stud fee to sire on her another Shirley. Then comes a paragraph first revealing emotional intimacy between father and daughter. Black says, out of the blue, "We had long been 'secret best friends,'" and tells about how they "sneaked thick, chocolate milk shakes" and visited a jail and fire houses (52). This sounds almost like an ongoing conspiracy of siblings to have fun whatever authority figures said. Shirley remembers how in "private moments he would hold me astraddle his lap and croon his only song: ' . . . you are the ideal of my dreams . . . I've known you forever it seems . . . I love you, love you, love you.'" Obviously, these were sweet times for her. When George looked at her on his lap, he could see and *love, love, love* the ideal of his dreams: a wonderful child who was both the essence of all that was good and at the same time a little twentieth-century cash-flow fox. If Shirley comes across as something of a Daddy's girl in her movies and book, one reason may be that, having no fear of her own Daddy and seeing him as a "best friend," she felt at ease with men. About George's singing to her, she says, "Although his voice was thin, tight, and flat, it is recalled now as music from an angel" (52).

But in managing her money, her father was no angel. He took and trusted as a partner an officious Stanford man who professed confidently to have the detailed financial expertise George lacked. It turned out that Shirley's earnings were mismanaged and hundreds of thousands of dollars she made over the years were misappropriated. "Malfeasance," "illegality," and "delinquency" are some of the words she chooses in describing the handling of her money. She discovered this bad news in 1950 when she married Charles Black, the scion of a well-to-do family and a successful financier in his own right. She had to decide what to do, but since she loved her father very much, the decision to preserve good relations came easily. She kept the information quiet while he was alive, protecting him out of respect, deep affection, and her passion to maintain family unity and honor (487). Near the end of *Child Star*, however, she breaks her silence and prints these words from a codicil George wrote nearly a half century earlier in 1940: "There will be those, upon my death, who will without knowledge of sacrifices my family and I have willingly made, accuse me of the wrong course as the parent of Shirley to take her earnings" (484). Shirley Temple was not a destroyer, but a preserver of her father's seed and core of virtue. There may have been better, shrewder fathers, but as a provider and a protector, there was no better daughter. You could say she repaid the amiable, exuberant man who *love, love, loved* her by becoming, as only a faithful daughter could, her father's keeper—an increasingly important role for women.

2.
BILL "BOJANGLES" ROBINSON

There's an abrupt, startling transition in Black's first chapter. Her father, in Shirley's little "stitches" crisis, lets her down by swooning at her bloody lip. In the very next paragraph, with no preparation, she pictures "a veteran black performer" who dances on Broadway, but faces terrible odds against getting a shot at the big money in movies (10). "Nobody, least of all Bill 'Bojangles' Robinson" would imagine that "his professional salvation lay in the babble and confusion created by a bunch of babies at Mrs. Meglin's Dance Studio" 3,000 miles away (11). Straight from her father, she moves on to the memory of talented "Uncle Billy." It's easy now to think of "Uncle Billy" as a demeaning term, but what's more important historically and psychologically is that it claims, however crudely, kinship across America's color line. She feels linked to him, and of no other man in *Child Star* does she write more positively.

A star, but a novelty star (the cute kid), Shirley mysteriously identified with Robinson, another novelty star (the Negro tap-dancer) in 1930s Hollywood. She revered his skill in the art she most loved, dancing. Odd and pretentious though it may sound, Shirley seems intuitively to have felt they shared a communion as outsiders, and she admired him tremendously. At the studio commissary, she says, he ate at "a single table against the back wall . . . alone . . . one remarkable man, proud, self-contained and totally at ease with himself" (224).

With all the racism in the country and its history, it sometimes gets lost how deep, in twentieth-century America, was the longing to overcome racial divisions, how strong was the desire in people, however conflicted, to respect, understand, and sympathize with others who at first appeared unlike themselves. The sentimental but very real bond between Robinson and Shirley gives proof of this. A Harlem reporter wrote that in Robinson's home the walls of his den were covered with autographed pictures from scores of notables, starting with FDR, but "for each one of those others there are two of Shirley Temple" (202). Like so many others, for his own reasons, he saw her as a figure he was more than proud to be associated with. As for Shirley, who in 1974, decades after her stardom, became a successful Ambassador to Ghana, she portrays her friendship with Robinson as one of the most memorable of her life.

Two similar, yet startlingly different pictures make the point. In one (Figure 10.2), Bojangles and Shirley—two hoofers at work—are poised on the lower step of the staircase in *The Little Colonel*, holding hands in a still shot from the movie and looking totally absorbed in their performance and in one another. Their eyes meet and their faces are lit up, especially his, shining with his big smile. Her expression is more tentative—pleased and relieved that she's remembering her steps, doing well, but looking to him thankfully for support and guidance. He's beaming with that (in)famous, once-traditional Uncle Tom "darkie" grin of deferential joy ("See everybody," it seems to say, "I'm devoted to this little white girl—ecstatic to be in this movie, darlin'."). Robinson's look is the visual equivalent of his widely quoted remark about Shirley, "God made her just all by herself—no series, just one" (Windeler, 13). He's costumed in a top butler's black trousers and mourning coat, white shirt, grey vest, shiny buttons—the formal attire that marked the servant's respect for those whom he served. She wears a light dress and black stockings. The white and black hands entwine, bonded, and the whites and blacks of the picture compose happily. The picture seems to imply that art and the inherent goodness of the girlchild can bridge huge

FIGURE 10.2 Staircase dance in *The Little Colonel* with Shirley Temple and Bill Robinson. Courtesy of Shirley Temple Black and Shirley's World, L.P.

chasms between people. And, though it's easy and surely proper, seventy years after the fact, to critique aspects of this image of Shirley and Robinson, you'd have to be pretty cynical not to see in it a sign of hope—a pure Lot's daughter symbolizing with naive good will a promise of integration.

In a different spontaneous shot that gets at what looks like a child's special, unguarded hero-worship (Figure 10.3), Shirley walks hand in hand again with Robinson on a studio street. She looks up at him, away from the camera, with a smile of delight—radiance: he's the coolest guy she's ever seen. She's fixed on him, happy in his company. He's wearing light, sharply creased khakis, a beautifully fitted sport coat, a crisp white shirt, no tie, oxfords—perfect ivy-league casual attire. He doesn't look at her. He looks edgy, preoccupied, serious, in a hurry, in charge. With her, it looks like, he could be himself sometimes, drop the smile, get out of his deferential role. He's like a father holding on to his child naturally, but moving along and

FIGURE 10.3 Shirley Temple holding hands with Bill Robinson in 1935. Courtesy of Shirley Temple Black and Shirley's World, L.P.

thinking of other things. Grasping Shirley Temple, he looks like he can really go anywhere. What's obvious here is what means most: the most famous white girl in the world looks up to a black man with joy and esteem, and he takes it for granted. The photo makes the idea of white supremacy look ridiculous.

Black, in her book, is not a racist, and she shows immense good will, but in her prose she can't get entirely free of the baggage of racial stereotyping. As a child, however, in her gaze at Robinson she did. Amazingly, in fact, Shirley not only saw him as her "Uncle Billy," she also unconsciously projected her friend into the role of a father. Robinson, she reports proudly, warned her first husband, third-rate actor Jack Agar, never to hurt her. And in one of the most extraordinary passages in the book, Black tells the following tale: When a doctor botches surgery during the birth of her son, Shirley comes right to the edge of death. Sensing she's going to die, she feels the presence of Robinson, dead years before, and sees his "round, shiny face. . . . His eyes were filled with the clear and childlike friendliness I recalled so well, and I heard his voice calling . . . : 'Come on up, darlin', it's fine up here'" (511). That may read like something out of a Dickens novel or *Cabin in the Sky*, Hollywood's 1936 try at a movie about "Negroes" and afterlife, but notice she's hallucinating Bill Robinson—not George, not her husband—as the reassuring father who art in heaven. She sees in him a paternal figure mirroring that which she projected on the screen and that which made her beloved: "childlike friendliness." Heaven is integrated, and Shirley Temple, delirious, transcends race and its heartbreaking problems.

3.
J. EDGAR HOOVER

In the 1930s era of the Lindberg baby's kidnapping and death, Shirley, a valuable property, receives extortion threats. She and her mother regularly listen to a radio program, *Gangbusters*, featuring the heroic exploits of the new Federal Bureau of Investigation. Shirley develops a love for weapons. She likes them better than dolls. And she forms her own Shirley Temple police force (89), giving out Junior G-man badges. She's the chief. She, who's always being told what to do, loves to tell others what to do. Darryl F. Zanuck, the studio boss, hires his overweight boyhood crony, John Griffiths (Griff) as Shirley's chauffeur and bodyguard (and, not incidentally, as a spy for Zanuck on Temple doings). On a vacation auto trip up the Pacific Coast, Shirley and her parents get word of two kidnap plots. George Temple buys a gun and they speed home, worried sick. Griff, from whom Shirley sometimes tries to run away just to see him huff and puff, doesn't seem the ideal protector. He takes to driving with an unholstered revolver on the seat beside him, and Shirley rides in back, under a lap robe. Back home her father spooks at bumps in the night and stalks around the house protectively. Her mother stews. They need help. The FBI manages to find and arrest a couple of pathetic would-be teenage extortionists in Nebraska and Georgia. It's then arranged for Shirley to meet J. Edgar Hoover, dashing young leader of the FBI, a genius at public relations and bureaucratic empire-building, and the self-proclaimed captor of gangsters like Pretty Boy Floyd. People tend to think of Hoover now, if they remember him at all, as a portly, balding, quasi-Fascist old closet queen and anti-Soviet fanatic, but in 1937–1938, he's square-jawed like Dick Tracy, handsome, with eyes "like a falcon's" (206). This is the man, they tell her, who protects her from criminals and keeps her safe. Small wonder she's prone to idolize him.

Hoover woos Shirley. He looks at this little girl and sees opportunity. He wants people to see and know the FBI exists to protect everything Shirley represents and that it must have support and a free hand to defend the American innocence and goodness she embodies. He seems genuinely to care for her; and she's a means, he senses, of preserving the seed of all he believes in. He knows she has a "police force." He gives her real police tools (a secret mini-camera, a finger-print set)—and he arranges for her to shoot a real gun at FBI headquarters. He cultivates her, pays careful attention to what she likes, gets through to her, and elicits from her something like hero-worship. He delights her and then, as the photo shows, playfully entraps her.

At their first meeting, "the start of a long, close friendship" (206), Shirley asks him if he's married, and he tells her no; like her, he lives with his mother. Hoover, as if he were Loop in *Bright Eyes*, sits Shirley on his lap. "Hoover's lap was outstanding as laps go. Thighs just fleshy enough, knees held calmly together, and no bouncing or wiggling. One arm circled me protectively, and mine curled around his neck as I rested my cheek against his. For me the whole FBI was romantically encapsulated in his strong, quiet presence" (206). Black here shows a girlish, innocent Lot complex at work and shows also how that complex can fuse personal, political, and historical circumstances. She goes on to describe how Hoover and her family soon meet again, at the famed Ahwahnee Hotel in "legendary" Yosemite.

There, in Yosemite Valley, J. Edgar literally does put Shirley in a trap: she follows him around the Ahwahnee golf course where long tubes of wire fencing protect new trees. Hoover orders an agent to put Shirley in one of these wirework "cages," just her height (Figure 10.4).[7] In it she stands, cheerfully "caught" in jovial bondage, her head sticking up just above the top with Hoover behind her, his elbows leaning on the top wire, hers protruding out, his smiling face above hers—J. Edgar Lollipop, the joshing jailer. He's got her landed like a prize fish or, as he tells her, like a skunk. The FBI, he says, always imprisons skunks. From then on he sends her all kinds of skunk figurines. Hoover's "sub-rosa bureaucratic policy" of friendliness to her and her family puts her for a time into a kind of ideological cage (458). She feels indebted to him. When she grows up, he gives her brother a job in

FIGURE 10.4 Shirley Temple with J. Edgar Hoover in Yosemite Valley, 1938. Courtesy of Shirley Temple Black and Shirley's World, L.P.

the agency, and when she starts thinking seriously about Charles Black as a prospective husband, she calls up the FBI up to get a full rundown on him.

Fifteen years after her caging, with the Cold War going full blast, Hoover has her helping the FBI identify suspected communists. Getting her portrait painted by the artist Sig Arno, she accidentally opens his bedroom closet door and comes across a life-size picture of Stalin. She calls the FBI. Later she finds that Reds are living in her neighborhood in Washington, D.C., and she phones Hoover personally asking him to send out agents to use her house as a stakeout. Black later would come to realize that to some extent she had been used by Hoover. Nevertheless the child star put in the cage by the top cop makes a fine image showing how the Lot complex fuses with very particular social history and how a girl's fears, needs, and longing for strength can bring her to identify with and seek authority and its promise of safety. That's why the iconography of authoritarianism—communist, fascist, nationalist, military, religious, royal, corporate, ethnic, or what have you—has so often featured the image and ideal of the fetching, pure little girl set next to the strong man. Power needs to associate itself and harness the moral force of the girlchild and what her image represents.

4.
PRIME MINISTER
W. L. MACKENZIE KING

Shirley, now a postpubescent star teenager, visits Canada in 1944 to launch some ships on a morale-building tour to support the Allied war effort. The long-time Prime Minister Mackenzie King, a 70-year-old bachelor, takes a shine to her and invites her home to tea. He looks and talks like a superannuated James Mason playing a benevolent version of Humbert Humbert. Like Captain January, his life is as lonely "as a lighthouse keeper's" (371). His beloved mother, light of his life, is dead. Sizing up Shirley, and not one for chitchat, he tells her that he wants her to know that women have the power to communicate to the living "from beyond the grave" (372). He shows her a hand-drawn document of the Allies' D-Day assault on Normandy marked with the places and battles of the historic invasion just as it happened, he says, months before it took place. The spirit of his dead mother, in perfect, telepathic communication, guided his hand.

The adolescent girl animates and intoxicates this leader. He thinks he can say anything to her, be open and honest in a way he could never be with men, and no dire consequences will follow. And it turns out he's right. She's touched by his sincerity. Black writes years later, "What a refreshing perspective, a world leader unafraid to call up spiritual resources to predict events of international importance and unashamed to recount such events to a stranger!" (372–373). Shirley Temple for a moment replaces the dead mother as the confidante of power.

5.
FRANKLIN D. ROOSEVELT

Eleanor Roosevelt visits Shirley at Fox Studios. Testing the waters, since it seemed likely Mr. and Mrs. Temple were Republicans (they were), she asks her if the star likes the President. When the girl answers yes because on the radio he calls people "my friends," Mrs. Roosevelt invites her to Washington. Shirley thinks the president's wife is nice but a bit frumpy; after thinking hard, she decides to give Mrs. Roosevelt two of her police force badges. J. Edgar Hoover makes most of the Temples' arrangements for the trip and the presidential audience on June 24, 1938.

It doesn't go particularly well. In the Oval Office, her parents are stiff and silent. A big, jowly man, Roosevelt sits behind his desk. Shirley walks around and shakes his hand. He stares at her, keeps holding her hand, not talking, awkward. Two of the most accomplished performers in the world seem to have a touch of stage fright. He asks her if she likes boats. She says she likes to catch fish. What kind of a hook does she use? She doesn't know. Ha, ha, ha, he says, sometimes the ends are more important than the means. Nobody laughs but FDR, and it rankles the great man because he's not charming America's most popular female person. "Why aren't you smiling? . . . I thought you were famous for your smile" (233). He's projecting and could be speaking to a mirror. Power loves smiling daughters. The girl is something to turn into political capital. Her mother speaks: Smile, she says. Shirley tells FDR she doesn't smile because she's lost a tooth, and tells how it came out eating a sandwich. He does prime newsreel Roosevelt and throws back his head laughing. It's not funny for Shirley. She doesn't laugh. "It seems as if I have been losing teeth all my life." FDR says something lugubrious like *I guess we all could say that.* But that's enough: he signs her autograph book and it's over.

A revealing follow-up soon occurs. Shirley, chronicled by Fox Movietone News, visits Mrs. Roosevelt at her private house Val Kill in Hyde Park. Shirley gives her pointers on the best way to move and act when the cameras are rolling. And unlike her husband, Eleanor really talks seriously to the child star. These two celebrities, with almost nothing in common, living such extraordinary lives, move in an atmosphere of complex, pervasive paternalism. When Shirley expresses disappointment at not seeing the New York slums, Mrs. Roosevelt agrees: "'But my father always said I had no right to visit slums for fear of bringing home diseases to my own children.' Her voice was inflexibly gentle. 'A wonderful man, so kind. He still seems alive, like someone in *The Blue Bird*'s Land of the Unborn Children'" (236). Of course her father was a drunk, but he seems to have had the virtue that FDR didn't possess of paying attention to Eleanor, of making her feel central and centered. She praises her inebriate father rather than her outstanding husband. Lot is everywhere. Black ponders on her puzzling outburst: "The reference was wholly unfamiliar, but the concept of such a land sounded spooky enough to remember a long while." The concept of future fathers as unborn children, as implicitly preferable to the mighty men of now, would haunt the century as it wore on.

Shirley had visited a president once before—President Lincoln. In *The Littlest Rebel* (1936) she plays the daughter of a captured Confederate officer in the Civil War. She goes North to Washington to plead for her father's life from the one man who can save him: the Great Father in Washington, Lincoln, the savior of the nation to whom Roosevelt was being compared. The adorable little girl saves the father—preserves his life—by touching the strain of mercy and core of humanity in the president. The filmmakers and President Roosevelt's public relations men are one in wanting to show patriarchal power in union with innocent childhood so that, however menacing the present, the future can become a seedtime. Shirley Temple brings together movies and presidents, fathers and daughters.

In one of her very last movies, *That Hagen Girl* (1947), made when she was 19 and unhappily married to Agar, Shirley is cast as an adopted, illegitimate teenager. She's a nice, sensitive girl, but gossip and meanness make her a social outcast. The male lead is a man twice her age whom people suspect of being her father. In real life Shirley has just found out she's pregnant; in the script she is driven to attempt suicide by drowning herself in a river. But the kindly older man saves her. He then passionately kisses her and quickly marries her, "father" suddenly turning "lover" (413). *Time's* reviewer thought moviegoers might find "an appearance of rebated incest as a romantic situation" stomach-turning (November 10, 1947). But things turn out relatively happily. Shirley has a healthy baby, and America's favorite girl again meets and interacts with another president—a president-to-be, that is: her co-star and movie savior is Ronald Reagan.

6.

ARTHUR FREED,
THE HOLLYWOOD MOGUL

The most amazing story Black tells in *Child Star* is one that shows why fears about child abuse and sexual harassment and the rage against men and their sexual desire in much late-twentieth-century feminism became so prevalent and had such a huge social impact. What's so surprising is not just the content of the anecdote, but the casual, semi-comic tone of near resignation in which Black presents it.

In 1940, her childhood days numbered and great days of stardom done, 12-year-old Shirley leaves Fox and signs with Metro-Goldwyn-Mayer. A few months later a studio bigwig appraises her flesh as commodity: "First we get rid of the baby fat" (319). It's Arthur Freed, Hollywood's star producer of *The Wizard of Oz, Singin' in the Rain,* and many other classic hits. Shirley and her mother are visiting the MGM executive suites and they split up. Mrs. Temple goes off with studio head Louis B. Mayer; Shirley's left alone with Freed. Shirley's tickled to death to be given a private audience with "an executive of such stature" (319). But it turns out that Freed is one of MGM's notorious "lecherous older men" (320). Black, the lap expert, writes that the distinguished overseer of Dorothy, Toto, and wholesome family entertainment, "fumbling in his lap," announces, "I have something made for just you. . . . You'll be my new star!"

Obviously, Freed did not believe in preliminaries. With his face gaped in a smile, he stood up abruptly and executed a bizarre flourish of clothing. Having thought of him as a producer rather than exhibitor, I sat bolt upright. Guarded personal exposure by both brothers and Father had maintained me in relatively pristine innocence. . . . I still had little appreciation for masculine versatility and so dramatic was the leap between schoolgirl speculation and Freed's bedazzling exposure that I reacted with nervous laughter.

Disdain or terror he might have expected, but not the insult of humor.

"Get out!" he shouted, unmindful of his disarray, imperiously pointing to the closed door. "Go on, *get out!*" (319–320)

Meanwhile, according to Black, while Freed is offering Shirley his sick preview of coming attractions, Louis B. Mayer has got her mother alone on a soft couch. He's making moves, beginning to paw until the distraught Mrs. Temple escapes by jumping up, warding him off, and backing out the office door.

This now seems fantastic. It's the sort of thing that gives man-hating a good name. And it all happened. Why would Mayer, who could have his pick of beautiful women, come on to a 50-year-old mother? And why did Freed expose himself to Shirley? Why would this man out of the pages of *Who's Who,* with a stable of accommodating starlets, try to embarrass or debauch a 12-year-old? The alleged perpetrator here isn't some furtive pervert wearing a soiled overcoat—though Shirley, at the movies with a high-school girlfriend, later *did* encounter such a man—but a pillar of the film industry. On the other hand, his accuser isn't some whiny recovered-memory victim, but a happily married, eminently sane, fulfilled, Republican ex-Ambassador and matron with absolutely nothing to gain by making false charges—as credible a witness here as you could hope for. These Temple desecrations would almost seem to be a matter of policy: *We do this because we can; we have the power to get away with it. I can flash Shirley Temple if I feel like it. That's the real world. Whatever we say about women, however influential and sacred the myth of the innocent girlchild is, however we market stories and images of of nice, heartwarming little girls, in this business we own and possess you.*

Driving home, comparing notes, the Temples seem for the moment more like confiding sisters than mother and daughter. Black, who wouldn't publicize this incident for almost a half century, shows how they see no means of redress, never think of going public, lashing back, or fighting. In fact, they feel lucky that the contract with MGM is already signed.

That such a thing could happen to Shirley Temple and that she could really do nothing about it shows why the relationship between men and women, men and girls, would have to change. The contradictions—contradictions that are focused in and around Shirley—had become too blatant. You cannot create a faith, spread a faith, incorporate the faith in a child and its image, and then, with impunity, besmirch the object of faith. If Shirley Temple could be harassed and molested, anybody could. You couldn't really trust the fathers to preserve faith. You needed to conspire against them. And that would happen.

Chapter 11

Woody Allen and Mia Farrow

LOT IN THE ERA OF DECONSTRUCTION

L et me begin and focus this chapter with an absurd Lot fantasy. Imagine the offspring of Sigmund Freud and Shirley Temple: it's Woody Allen. Imagine the dreamchild of Lewis Carroll and Henry James's Maisie Farange: it's Mia Farrow. And the two, both with serious Lot complexes, were made for each other.

I see Allen's "visible life" (his films and the public record of his life—what you can look at) bred from a symbolic merging of the Jewish father of psychoanalysis (the interpreter of jokes, sex, and the death instinct, as well as dream fantasies) with the dimpled Depression-darling daughter of popular faith in the redeeming power of girls and movies. But how this visible life unfolds and why it matters is joined intimately with the life of Mia Farrow, who on and off the screen has played the role of both Lot's daughter and Lot's wife. I see *her* visible life generated out of Lewis Carroll's passion for children, for beautiful photographic images, and for the radiant girl passing through the trials and incivilities of wonderland. And a grown-up Maisie Farange, who might come to know about love for attractive older men and the need to preserve a moral identity in a milieu of erotic betrayal, makes the perfect fantasy mother for Mia. In the living history of Lot complexes, Woody Allen and Mia Farrow have made a spectacle of themselves.

In the big picture, they remain fascinating figures of great accomplishment, though they nearly destroyed each other, hurt others, and (like most people) at times behaved appallingly. These two collaborated wonderfully to make each other's art better, but here I want to concentrate on particular issues and images that emerge from the intertwining of their visible lives. These have broad social significance. In their interaction off screen and on, they laid bare the tensions, attractions, and power struggles that figure now at the turn of the millennium in older men–younger women relationships and history. They can make you see both the continuing, ambivalent consequences of that old male habit (and prerogative) of taking up with younger women and a historic explosion of female resentment at men's sexual irresponsibility.

I.
Woody

Making good films is as demanding an art as any. You need creative vision and the will to see it through. Cinema of integrity and excellence requires and shows off the imaginative genius of an artist who can somehow coordinate the skills of all kinds of people working in different media and then fuse them in an evolving electronic technology that's only a hundred years old. It's a bit like playing the croquet game in *Alice in Wonderland* where you use flamingos as mallets and rolled-up hedgehogs as balls, and bogus royalty keeps threatening to cut off your head. You have to be a sly, obsessed organizer of fantasy life to get other talented egomaniacs to do what you want. Woody Allen, né Allan Konigsberg, was such a one.

Allen has made thirty or so films over more than three decades, including, arguably, as many good ones as any other director ever. Yet because of his bitter legal and public relations war with Mia Farrow and his liaison and marriage to her adopted daughter, Soon-Yi Previn, his reputation has sunk even among many who value his work. "Irretrievably creepy," prissed columnist Maureen Dowd, a onetime admirer, "I think I'll do without Woody Allen."[1] He's tainted with the scandal of Lot's cave: incest, sneaky exploitation of young women, betrayal of older women, and bad faith.

1.
BECOMING WOODY

If Lot did not exist, it seems it would have been necessary for Allen to invent him. The self-interested urban Jew somehow alienated from both the righteousness of Abraham and mindless heathen hedonism, estranged from the culture of male dominance and male-bonded louts, caught up in the tyranny of the senses, trying to make deals, fearful of the mob, getting laughs but disrespected, wanting to do good—a sly charmer, a man of half-assed schemes and women troubles—much harder and cannier than his public persona, running one step ahead of disaster, aghast at life outside the city, easily intoxicated by nubile girls, sliding disgracefully into oblivion, scared to death, preserving his seed through art—that's the Lot Woody Allen was born and raised to play.

How did Allan Konigsberg become Woody and his movies? One simple (and complex) answer is that he chose *the daughter* over *the mother.* He was born in Jewish Brooklyn and the Depression and came into full consciousness during World War II. His parents' Yiddish-speaking families came to New York from Europe around 1900. This was the famous population influx whose descendants burst out of shtetl life to imagine, reshape, liberalize, entertain, and reconceive twentieth-century America and, not least, to cast the reflections by which it came to understand and laugh at itself.

Allan's grandfather Isaac Konigsberg made a fortune—he even owned movie-houses—but lost it in the 1929 crash. By the time Isaac's son Martin and Nettie Cherrie, a bookkeeper, met and married in 1931, he was scrambling to eke out a living, and after Allan was born (December 1, 1935), he found he wasn't making it. Nettie, a sharp woman, had to go back to work when the boy was barely a toddler, and Allan's day care passed to a series of hired girls. Some were incompetent; some were scary; some were pretty and nice. None stayed with him long. What did stay were feelings of rejection and abandonment by his mother and the unconscious lesson that you need to placate young women, wheedle their good will, find in them nurturing substitutes—and be ready to replace them.

Of love, money, and support in the family, there wasn't enough (there never is). Criticism was rampant. "[A] compliment," he later wrote in *Side Effects,* "had not passed through the lips of any [family] member during my lifetime."[2] His mother and father needled each other constantly. Clever children of battling parents often adopt two strategies: they learn to distance and withdraw from the commotion, often into fantasy, and they learn to be diverting. Years later, speaking about being funny for a living, Woody said, "When you do comedy, you're not sitting at the grown-ups' table, you're sitting at the children's table."[3] But if the grown-ups are screaming at each other, maybe you don't really want to be at their table; maybe you're actually dying to upset the so-called adult table by mastering that art of psychological table-turning that is comedy.

Allan was a quick, active child with a morose streak, and Nettie was no mother of the year. Decades later, when he reminded her how often she hit him, she admitted, "You were very bright and you ran and jumped. I didn't know how to handle that type of child. . . . I wasn't that good to you."[4] He had that incomparable guide to the ways of the hard world, the critical mother who, in a flash, turns the milk of human kindness to salt. When he was 3, his mother did take him to his first film, *Snow White*. The people in the picture moved and talked, and he was permanently movie-struck. The small boy ran up to touch the huge figures on the screen, and Nettie had to grab him and drag him back. That really happened, he said, but it's also a parable. You have the fascination with the screen, the mixing up of film and life, and the attempt to escape from the mother into the realm of imagination. He sat watching next to his mother, transported into the magic animation, suddenly, he said, in love with the film's wicked, beautiful stepmother. When the lights came on, he had to go back to the flat with Nettie, where he learned that his life was much better at the movies than at home.

When Allan was 8, his little sister Letty came along, like his own Shirley Temple, to lift his spirits and open up a channel of affection. His primal relationship to her figures powerfully in his life. She brought out the best in him—let him be a good big brother. He found himself looked up to by a lovable little female who thought he was sweet, and that became the pattern of his desire (*pattern of desire*: the way you keep hoping things can and should be). She was a model and a mirror for the right kind of love-object and friend. He could identify with her, teach her things, help her, and see how she admired him. Allen says that in Letty he just got lucky: having a kindred spirit as a little sister was just one of those good things that sometimes happen in life. She idolized him.

What would it mean to love your little sister more than your mother? It might mean that you would always worry about a Letty turning into a Nettie. Later in his movies, one casting decision makes that point graphically. In *Manhattan* (1979), teenage Mariel Hemingway plays the sweet girlfriend of the fortyish Woody Allen character. Twenty years later, in a cameo in *Deconstructing Harry*, she plays a prudish shrew who torments him. In *Crimes and Misdemeanors* (1989), there's a delicate cross-generational relationship between the documentary filmmaker Cliff, played by Woody, and

Cliff's schoolgirl niece, Jenny, that I'm sure grew out of Allan's life. Cliff takes the girl regularly to old movies, which they talk about; they have fun and enjoy each other's company. This companionship, in the midst of the deadly absurdity and moral abominations in the film, carries a seed of hope. Going back to Letty and his boyhood with her looks like the role of a lifetime for Allen.

Like Letty, another girl, his teenage cousin Rita Wishnik, played a lasting role in the making of his psyche and his films. When he was 13, Allan lived in the same house and sometimes shared a room with the 18-year-old Rita. An absolute cinemaniac and lover of show biz, she played Beatrice to his little Flatbush Dante and guided him in the tawdry paradise of movieland. They went to the movies together, and she taught him to love Hollywood glamour and scandal. Woody Allen, you can see in his films and life, identified with Rita and her star-struck dreams. Later he said revealingly:

I remember Rita as a young girl, as the whole country was at the time, just awestruck at Frank Sinatra. . . . He was just the end-all of all there was. He was at the pinnacle of the glamorous world . . . he was simply a god, just simply a god. . . . The thought that in any configuration my dreary little life would somehow connect with his even tangentially was laughable. Here I was . . . living in a tiny little flat in Brooklyn with no one in my family in any remote way in show business or really achieving anything, everybody struggling at these low-class jobs. . . . If someone had said to Rita that the mother of my children would be the ex-wife of this illustrious man, it's so unfathomable she would have thought they were from Mars. (Lax, 82–83)

Those words in the context of Rita's tutelage give you the plot of a Lot-complex wish-fulfillment: the daughterwife of the biggest celebrity of an era becomes the star of his artwork and the mother of his child.

2.
THAT'S ENTERTAINMENT

When he was growing up, the burgeoning entertainment business became a huge new social force. Broadcasts broadened life; moving pictures gave new mobility to imagination. Movies and radio socialized people—for good or bad—by teaching them what life was supposed to be like. Those are great themes that drive Woody Allen's vision, as *Radio Days*, *Crimes and Misdemeanors*, and *The Purple Rose of Cairo* show. The entertainment in-

dustry, combined with the effects of the Depression and World War II, created a popular culture that was secular, assimilationist, and profitable. It
raised the status of performers to new heights. That was big news in Brooklyn. Jews like the Konigsbergs knew that Jews invented and ran the movie
business and also that most of the great comedians who emerged in radio
and films were Jews. They also knew that the funnymen, moguls, and stars
alike often had to change and anglicize their names and tailor their material to please and fit a mostly gentile public: like Lot in Sodom, they might
find it dangerous to seem too Jewish. Jews, so to speak, had a forum in
America in which to make themselves popular and influential, melt the pot
of bigotry, and make a pot too; but at the same time their changing position in society made Jewish identity more problematic. None of this was
lost on the precocious 16-year-old who in 1952 began his career by trying to
get work doing magic tricks in the Catskills (he failed) and writing gags for
New York columnists (he succeeded). That year, he decided to use the name
Woody Allen instead of Allan Konisgsberg.

From the time he became Woody Allen until he and Mia Farrow split
up in 1992, he lived out a fantasy story of success. Being funny for money
was the way for him to rise out of Brooklyn and move on to Manhattan and
the whole pieces-of-silver-screen world. He sold his jokes to journalists,
then to television stars, then directly to audiences as a stand-up comic, a
short-story writer, a screenwriter and actor, a playwright, and finally as a
master filmmaker. But he was after something more than just commercial
success. He put his faith in a comic style and vision as the best way of com-
prehending the world. Over two decades he developed a sympathetic, rue-
ful persona that related to people psychologically and made smart men and
women identify with him as they had with no comedian since Chaplin. This
was the visible Woody Allen, a nebbishy, self-deprecating figure of knowing
wit who mixed candor with a deft mockery of the vanities by which people,
himself included, live. This fast-talking, stammering figure would come
across as brilliant and entertaining, but unthreatening and oddly seductive—a wry but sweetly neurotic genius. Allen moved it from the cabaret
and late-night TV talk shows onto the screen. The implicit message of this
comic persona would seem to be: *I am strong enough and smart enough to
admit and confess the failings and the truths that others have to hide. I don't
need to brag and I don't need the lies and poses that others use to be big.*

Psychological development and complexes depend on the nuances of your historical position and experience. When Allen, an American male born in 1935, was growing up, the Depression and World War II determined life, but they didn't traumatize him or freeze his outlook. For thirty years from the time he was born, the economy got better and better. The country won what everyone saw as a just war against a wicked enemy, and also it kept getting richer. Older people were obsessed with making a livelihood and military victory, but Woody's age group was *of*, but not *in*, the war. Collectively, his generation of males assumed the role of little brother, left at home with females, looking up to those big shapers—through organized violence—of the brave new world.

A boy might take another tack and belittle, even mock, domineering people and pretensions. He might push to make a virtue out of weakness, try for intimacy with women, adopt an anti-heroic stance, be candid, and look to ingratiate himself through humor and intellectual daring. If you weren't a conqueror of men, maybe you could be an ally, a confidante, a mentor, a champion, and also a seducer of women. Maybe, eventually, somehow, you could supplant the macho generation of Humphrey Bogart and Frank Sinatra.

At the beginning of an early Allen film, *Play It Again, Sam* (1972), you get an unexpectedly haunting close-up of Woody, who plays a dweeb eager to score with women. He's sitting in a theater watching the famous ending of *Casablanca* in which Rick (Humphrey Bogart) gives up Ilsa (Ingrid Bergman) for the sake of the higher cause—Allied victory. Allen's rapt face says almost all there is to say about the power of the film medium—the attraction and influence of movies on and in his life and times. But it and what follows have another meaning. Bogart here epitomizes the generation that won the war by putting duty before all else. In *his* film, Allen co-opts and internalizes Bogart as a fantasy big-brother figure who helps him with advice about women and sex. In effect, though Bogart is his ostensible idol and role model, he makes Bogey disappear—the Bogey who takes it upon himself to do all of the heroine's thinking for her and says that "problems of three little people don't amount to a hill of beans." In Allen's world, women matter, sex matters, and the relationships and the problems of individual people matter, because if they don't, there's finally nothing left but force.

In the 1960s and '70s, Allen became the cinematic laureate of trying to get laid and what it all could mean. It meant more than sex. In *Stardust Memories* (1979), a heckler asks director Sandy Bates (Woody Allen) why he can't keep making funny movies like his early comedies (a common critical cliché about post–*Annie Hall* Allen), but another complains that his movies are always psychological, never political. In fact his comedies of those times feature and convey important cultural and political history. Grounded by age, reading, and temperament in the aftermath of the Depression, the war and Holocaust, and in postwar existential philosophy, Allen imagined and filmed, in effect, the rejectionist politics coming out of the Beat Generation of the 1950s, Vietnam, Woodstock, and, later, Nixon's Watergate—what the 1968 French student rebels called the true Marxist revolution "*à la Groucho.*"

He was, in that swinging era, the comic prophet, cheerleader, and analyst of the sexual revolution and the more subtle revolution in the status of middle-class females and in gender relationships generally. You could argue that Allen's generation—both men and women—made the sexual revolution. Sex and love for Woody Allen, the Clauswitz of comedy, could be war, politics, and revolution by other means.

3.
MARRYING LOT'S DAUGHTER, 'STARDUST MEMORIES,' AND FILM

Besides a blooming film career, Allen had two wives before he met Mia Farrow. In the pre–joy-of-sex era of the 1950s, 20-year-old Woody married his first regular girlfriend, Harlene Rosen, a serious, arty, 17-year-old from Brooklyn. An intellectually ambitious (see Alvy Singer's second wife in *Annie Hall*) philosophy student, Harlene graduated from Hunter. She thought Allen should have been a great writer instead of a cheap comic, and she disdained the crudities of show biz. Before they divorced in 1962, while he was struggling to do stand-up routines in nightclubs, he took up with Louise Lasser, an aspiring actress and a manic Lot's daughter. A Brandeis dropout, she was the glamorous Fifth Avenue offspring of a financial wizard father and a self-destructive mother. In an American retrospect, you could see Harlene as a stable, sensible girl of the Eisenhower '50s and Louise as the break-loose daughter of the psychedelic '60s.

Allen says that the Dionysian Louise had a huge impact on him. She gave him times of intense passion and joy in the years when he was making himself into a performer. The only problem, he said, was that "she was crazy as a loon" (Lax, 170). She had a father fixation. Her mother tried to commit suicide, and when Louise saved her life, she was furious (see *Interiors*). In 1964, while Woody was in Europe doing his first movie, *What's New Pussycat?*, the mother did kill herself, shattering the daughter. Louise and her family (like Mia Farrow's) provided Allen with great material and helped make possible the brilliant deconstruction of family relations that would mark his films. They ruefully married in 1966, divorced in 1969, and remained friends. He gave her major roles in three of his early movies, and she directly inspired some of the very best scenes in all his work—the magnificent flashbacks in his portrait of Dorrie in *Stardust Memories*.

In the delicate Dorrie-Louise sequence, Allen touches directly on the Lot complex and suggests an obsessive intimacy that has the feel of reality behind it. Film director Sandy Bates (Woody Allen) both probes and kids Dorrie (Charlotte Rampling) about her intense bond with her father (her mother has been institutionalized). She admits that she flirted with her accomplished Daddy, loved his looks, had a big crush on him, and says they had a special relationship. Sandy jokes about incestuous impulses and the erotic pull of father-daughter closeness. Later, when she falls into a paranoid breakdown, she accuses Sandy of being attracted to her young relative, a 13-year-old girl. She screams at him not to deny it—she knows the look and mood, because she had the same libidinous conspiracy at the same age with her father. Sandy tries to calm her mania, but in retrospect, with Mia Farrow and Soon-Yi Previn in mind, the prophetic nature of the scene is uncanny.

Woody Allen chose to make movies starring women with whom he had erotic relationships, and he sometimes got involved with women whose lives helped him to imagine and create his art, or who resembled figures he'd already put up on the screen (no thoughtful viewer of *Manhattan* would be surprised that Woody at 56 fell in love with a 20-year-old). *Stardust Memories* shows overtly how he wanted to direct the women he loved and love the women he directed—a fact with important cultural and historical, as well as personal, implications. In the late 1960s and the '70s he had notable liaisons with Louise Lasser, then with Diane Keaton, and later with the teenage actress Stacey Nelkin—the major inspiration for Tracy (Mariel Hemingway) in *Manhattan*—none of which he could, or wanted to, make permanent and exclusive. The subject of his sexual interest often became the subject of his art—and sometimes vice versa.

He reveals an important conflict in himself and in many other people when he seems, in the course of his "autobiographical" movies, to fantasize women as both interchangeable and irreplaceable—haunting figures of memory, unique and yet somehow blending into one another, each of whom he does and *does not* wish to transcend. A man may want to hold on forever to a beautiful young woman he has loved, but that desire might lead him to find other young women on whom to focus and preserve his stardust memories—in life and on film.

Both the ruthlessness and creative force of Allen's Lot complex become clear in his treatment of memory, art, and Lasser herself in *Stardust Memories*, for which she functioned as his muse. In an extraordinary scene, the fictional movie director Sandy Bates imagines his best, most lovely memory: the real director Woody Allen focuses the camera on the beautiful face of Charlotte Rampling, and the soundtrack gives us the great music of Louis Armstrong playing and singing "Stardust." Sandy Bates is explicitly dealing with the question of what gives life value—when has he known the joy that makes life seem good? He remembers looking at Dorrie. His male gaze takes her in as she's reading, prone on the floor. The camera shows him in a brief shot idly looking at her. It's a quiet moment in a morning of light. She looks up, catches his eye; contentment plays over her face. She goes back to reading. The camera stays on her, then switches back to the Woody's face, registering a little smile. The focus quickly moves back to Dorrie, who looks up. The music keeps on pushing happiness. The camera stays on her. She moves her leg slightly to the rhythm of the music; a subtle sexuality is starting to flow. Amusement, engagement, and the erotic desire of her director begin to animate her expression. She herself is gazing, taking in the man across the room, taking the lead, putting the shot of the primly eating, erotically hungry little man in perspective, moving before our eyes from objectivity to subjectivity in a glorious view that Allen holds and treasures.

There aren't many minutes of the Dorrie character in the picture, but when you see her, she's fascinating—emotionally vulnerable, *touching*. A character in the film says she's a person who has only two good days a month, but then she's fabulous—precisely how Allen described Lasser in the Eric Lax biography.[5] In an earlier flashback, Allen, with jump-cut close-ups of Dorrie's face and her talk about being institutionalized, had shown her tragically breaking down, with all of beauty's doomed fragility. The film's Dorrie sequences here make the inspiration of Louise Lasser in Allen's art of memory sublime. And yet, in the movie, the narcissistic director Sandy employs as a secretary a dowdy, overweight, aging woman who performs menial duties—a banal figure without a hint of glamour or passion. For the part Allen cast Louise Lasser, turning his stardust reverie into a gross Lot's wife.

4.
PORTRAIT OF THE NEUROTIC ARTIST
MAKING IT BIG

Woody started going to a psychiatrist in 1959 at age 23, because, without apparent cause, he had a wide streak of morbidity (again and again, his films mock death obsessions) and, inexplicably, he suffered from *anhedonia*, the inability to be happy. Through Alvy Singer in *Annie Hall*, Allen memorably defines the mindset of this condition: "Life is full of miserableness, loneliness, and suffering, and it's all over much too quickly." In therapy, he found that psychoanalysis had a special appeal for him. It was a means, quite literally, of clarifying his vision of himself and thus a key to making his pictures. It had a Viennese Jewish heritage, like his mother, and, like her, it had a fatalistic, know-it-all bias towards hard truths. It also asserted the key role of jokes and the sense of humor in personality and life, and with its own built-in institutional absurdities (the couch, primal scenes and screams, the countertransference of the analyst, pretentious jargon, etc.), it provided delicious comic fodder. It was, in its essence, not the righteous, scary faith of Abraham, willing to sacrifice his son, but the faith of "the Lot of Dora," hoping for salvation through the knowledge of young women and empathy with daughters (see Chapter 9).

Allen played the role of Lot's daughter as well as Lot. Like the real and mythical Shirley Temple, he was adept at pleasing powerful older men who could help him. One reason he could create female characters so alive and complex is that he himself knew what it was to have to bedazzle older men in order to get what you needed. Early on in his movie career, he got Arthur Krim, a chief executive of United Artists, to make *the* key decision that made his art possible: Krim signed a deal giving Woody total control and responsibility for what finally appeared in any film written and directed by him. And, fittingly, the older man who first got Woody into the movies was the worldly film producer Charles K. Feldman, who had seen and liked his act. Feldman needed a writer to adapt a farce by a Czech author, Ladislaus Bus-Fekete, about an irresistible Don Juan—an enticing subject for Allen. The producer hired him to do the script and then to play a character role in what became the smash hit *What's New, Pussycat?* (1965). Appropriately the work Woody rewrote as his ticket to screenland power was *Lot's Wife*.

In the following fifteen years, workaholic Allen negotiated skillfully various metaphorical Sodoms: the movie world, professional comedy, Manhattan, theater life, publishing, and the whole greening, keening America of the '60s and '70s. He scribbled and scribbled, creating ideas, characters, situations, and lines that he would rearrange, cannibalize, and feed into his various movies. Starting in 1969, a new Woody Allen movie would appear almost every year. By the time he got to know Mia Farrow in 1980, he had an Oscar (for *Annie Hall*) and status as a top filmmaker who could get the best cinematographers, actors, and editors to work for him whenever he wanted.

In his early comedies through *Annie Hall*, he transferred his comic persona to the screen and sharpened it. This figure was an enlarged version of the neurotic, witty wimp—an iconoclastic, intellectual anti-stud fascinated by gorgeous women whom he improbably gets (that image is still the most common public perception of "Woody Allen" in the movies). Among other things, the character was—and is still—a great sight gag, belittling machismo and making fun of macho sex fantasies: the bespectacled little nerd scoring with glamorous movie stars.

Before *Annie Hall*, in his first six films, all comic, his movie mode is essentially parodic—usually, it's worth noting, parody of male authority and/or men's violence. With *Annie Hall, Manhattan*, and *Stardust Memories*, the masterly trio of dark comedies that follows *Love and Death* (1976), Allen's comedy digs deeper into his (anti-)hero's personality and becomes self-absorbed. These pictures could be collected under the title "Three Portraits of a New York Artist as a Not So Young Man," depicting, respectively, a comic (Alvy Singer), a writer (Ike Davis), and a filmmaker (Sandy Bates) —all, not coincidentally, played by Woody. Allen's art and life here flow into one another, and desire looks the same in what you can see of each: a narcissistic, creative male drawn to women, looking for both a lasting erotic relationship and fresh, serial relationships too, needing love and devotion, afraid of rejection, but afraid of being smothered. He managed to fuse on the screen a little-man comic hero, a self-centered, morally troubled artist, sharp, satirical vision, and psychoanalysis—a marvelous thing to do.

5.

THE 'MANHATTAN' PROJECT

Manhattan particularly shows a revealing pattern in his art. Its predecessor, *Annie Hall*, won the Best Picture Oscar, and one of the most interesting things about it is its gender politics. Alvy Singer (Allen) is a celebrity and a mentor whom Annie (Diane Keaton) looks up to, but when the power equation shifts and she becomes independent, the erotics end. Allen loves the idea of mentoring a lovely young woman, but he's ironically self-aware about it. *Manhattan* expands on that theme with scenes that seem crucial for understanding the later visible life of Woody and Mia Farrow.

A fine, daring film, as outrageous in its way as Nabokov's *Lolita*, it's ultimately even dicier in its morality. It treats the sexual relationship between a middle-age man and a teenager as a potentially beneficial thing for both—about as respectable a theme in born-again America as the blessedness of atheists. This version of the Lot complex features Isaac Davis (Allen), a fortyish, disillusioned TV writer undergoing a midlife crisis. His bisexual ex-wife Jill (Meryl Streep) has left him for "another woman," taking custody of their son, and is writing a book about their marriage, exposing him to the world. (Two decades later life would imitate art when Mia Farrow published her memoir *What Falls Away*, "exposing" Allen.) His best friend Yale, a married Columbia professor, is having an affair with Mary (Diane Keaton), a neurotic, pseudo-intellectual writer. Ike, however, has a tall, beautiful, 17-year-old girlfriend Tracy (Mariel Hemingway), a ravishing romantic fantasy for an aging male. Like a sexually mature Alice, she's the center of innocence and goodness in the movie—a spiritual trophy girl, who also loves to "fool around" and sleep with Ike. He teaches her things—what old movies are good, for instance. Allen, however, projects onto the young woman not only the characteristics of the ideal student, but also those of the good *mother*: uncritically accepting, full of devotion, and happy to mirror his qualities and fantasies.

Woody's relationships with Stacey Nelkin, whom he met making *Annie Hall* in 1976, and with Mariel Hemingway obviously fed the movie. He saw things in them he wanted to get on film. The Nelkin liaison reportedly lasted two years and "wasn't just about the bedroom." She is quoted years later: "I was 17 and he was 41. . . . It was a real relationship and a mature one that was perfectly normal. . . . It was a very moral relationship. There were a lot of wonderful things about it. I learned a lot from Woody about music and film. I was crazy about him."[6] Any Pygmalion would be proud of such testimony. As for Mariel Hemingway, consider what you have here: the Woody Allen figure takes the seed of the greatest ultra-macho author-hero of mid-century America, Ernest Hemingway, and absorbs Papa by making the granddaughter part of his work and life.

On screen, Ike treats Tracy with avuncular tenderness; his plan at first is to give her laughs and experience, have fun, and then send her off to an acting career. But she loves him, and he hurts her badly when he takes up with the older Mary. When Mary dumps him, he decides he loves Tracy after all and runs across town to stop her from going to London. The movie ends ambiguously with her telling him, "Look, you have to have a little faith in people."

Faith, in fact, is the problem in the glib intellectual milieu of this movie. At one point, Ike talks into a tape recorder, and the character and his creator Allen seem to fuse in his quest to believe in something:

"Well, all right, why is life worth living? That's a very good question. Well, there are certain things I guess that make it worthwhile. Uh, like what? Okay. Um, for me, oh, I would say . . . what, Groucho Marx to name one thing . . . uh, and Willie Mays, and, ummm, the second movement of the Jupiter Symphony, and ummm . . . Louie Armstrong's recording of 'Potatohead Blues' . . . um, Swedish movies, naturally . . . *Sentimental Education* by Flaubert . . . uh, Marlon Brando, Frank Sinatra . . . umm, those incredible apples and pears by Cézanne. . . . And Tracy's face of course. . . . "

Analyze that list and you see that it's a profession of *aesthetic* faith. Allen's cinematic art, in other words, turns "Tracy's face"—and/or the real face of Mariel Hemingway, the remembered face of Stacey Nelkin or Louise Lasser, or Diane Keaton, or of some other lovely, bright girl—into an object of faith, a thing that makes life worth living. Relationship, aesthetics, sexual attraction, art, and self merge. It's the Lot complex as male projection—preservation of the seed of civilization through the girl's inspiration, but not through her fertility or agency. It's his progeny, not hers.

Allen's *Manhattan* project of choosing the younger woman over the older animates *Interiors* (1978), the oddly powerful, Bergmanesque movie he made just after *Annie Hall.* This film shows people living lives of quiet desperation without the resources of comic vision, and in it you can see how serious Woody Allen is about exploring the nuanced dysfunctions of family life. It's driven by the idea of intergenerational alliances between father and daughters against a domineering, narcissistic mother. Allen imagines the overthrow of the mother and identifies with the erotics and aesthetic aims of daughters and sisters—a preview of his coming attractions.

In his movie-making so far, Allen had proved himself a comic genius and made remarkable films with scenes and sequences of greatness. But when he began casting and directing Mia Farrow he found he could go much further in projecting his art beyond the visual image of his own probing self-consciousness.

II.
Mia

The history of Mia Farrow reverses Genesis: first you get Lot's daughter, then Lot's wife. She adored her father, who died when she was a teenager. When she was 21, she married Frank Sinatra, thirty years her senior. She took another older man, Andre Previn, away from his wife Dory and married him. She adopted and tried to save afflicted children from all over the world. She formed an intimate relationship with Woody Allen, who was old enough to have a wife before Mia was even 10. She made thirteen movies he directed, had a child with him, and then had to look at the naked, erotic pictures he took of her adopted child Soon-Yi and endure the marriage of that sexagenarian to her estranged daughter. It's a story that could make you believe in the Bible.

1.
THE CHOSEN DAUGHTER

Mia Farrow has lived an extraordinary life. Though her book, *What Falls Away* (1997), downplays her career, her achievement in Allen's films arguably make her one of the major actresses in movie history. She fascinated and won the love of some of the most talented and celebrated men of her era. She has been a dedicated mother and humanitarian nurturer to needy children. Moreover, in an uncanny fashion, she has embodied, symbolized, and been caught up in defining cultural moments and movements in the second half of the twentieth century (rather like Woody's Zelig in the first half). For instance, as Allison Mackenzie in the prime-time TV serial *Peyton Place*, it's she who first made the image, reality, and significance of the "flower child" live for the broad public in the 1960s. Likewise in her movie role as a victim of demonic sexual abuse in *Rosemary's Baby*, she turns out to have been a harbinger of the recovered memory movement and one consequential strain of feminism. And, obviously, her war with Allen brought into focus some of the sorest issues still afflicting and shaping gender relations.

She was born Maria de Villiers Farrow in 1945, a princess of Hollywood royalty. Her Irish mother was the movie star Maureen O'Sullivan, best remembered for her role as Tarzan's Jane. Her charismatic father, John Villiers Farrow, was a successful film director. According to a wild family legend, he was the illegitimate son of Edward VII and a 19-year-old Australian beauty, dead in childbirth. By turns he had been a privileged Australian orphan and South Seas adventurer, a writer, a director, a decorated naval officer, a devout Roman Catholic, a notorious womanizer, and a drunk. Mia, the oldest child of seven, for her first nine years led a golden Beverly Hills life. But Maureen O'Sullivan was always making movies, and, as Mia saw it, didn't provide enough mothering. Both parents also had serious drinking problems. In 1954 Mia suddenly got polio, and had to stay still and recuperate. That experience led to her passion to save and help distressed children. Bedridden, she read many books, but the one she says had a huge effect on her was Charlotte Brontë's *Jane Eyre*. She too would mourn for a lost childhood, look on men as potential Rochesters, and feel the pull of self-regarding righteousness. Read *What Falls Away* and you can often find melodramatic *Jane Eyre* prose: for example, "From a distant fragment somewhere in the mind of God I was shown a different earth, a giant orb howling out its long symphony of pain."[7]

She, the chosen daughter, loved her father, who adored literature but looked down on the film business. He taught her sailing and poetry, Gregorian chants and John Donne, the virtues of the Church and the charm of the libertine. One day when she was 8 or so she rushed into his office and found him with an actress; the two were in a flustered flurry trying to cover up "a little slit" (27) and restore clothing. The woman, it seems, was the second wife of Frank Sinatra, Ava Gardner, with whom her father was having an affair.

When he had time, he and Mia would go on outings, and forty years later she remembered the abject adoration she felt for him: "If he chanced to glance down at me he'd sometimes smile and in those moments I nearly drowned in such almighty happiness and gratitude and love that the only . . .

thing I could think to do was to lay down on the pavement, there at my father's feet, and offer him my entire mortal being" (40–41). Those words, half St. Theresa, half Lot's daughter, convey her sense of the patriarchal romance that shaped her life (and, of course, the lives of many achieving modern women). But that complex, dangerous dedication of the daughter to the father indicates trouble to come. Abjection, though it may be felt as religious and/or erotic ecstasy, is neither a stable condition nor a happy one. It breeds resentment.

After recovering from polio and moving into adolescence, she saw and experienced many different kinds of life. Living and working in England, her father kept on drinking, and her parents' marriage continued to deteriorate. Farrow had Mia sent to a strict Catholic school in Surrey. There she showed dramatic flair, made friends, and found she could survive Spartan conditions. Like many a Catholic girl, she vowed to be a nun, but then found she lacked a vocation. Meanwhile her father, totally demoralized, drank more and more and eventually couldn't get work. Drunk one night, like some Emily Brontë character, he chased after his wife with a carving knife, and Maureen had Mia take her place in her bed, sure he wouldn't stab his own daughter. Soon, only the Jesuits would talk to him.

After graduation, Mia took a few classes in London and then left for Manhattan, where her mother had gone back on the stage to bring in some money. There O'Sullivan took up with the director George Abbot. When the distraught Farrow called one night, suspicious and wanting to talk to his wife, Mia answered, but she felt she just could *not* tell him where her mother was. Later the phone rang again; Mia let it ring and ring. She couldn't pick it up, she says, because she didn't want to lie to her father or betray her mother. That night, she writes, John Farrow died "of a heart attack with the phone in his hand" (64). Even if you didn't have a complex, that might be enough to give you one.

2.

MARRYING FAME
(AND YOUR FATHER'S LOVER'S HUSBAND)

Mia decided to try acting herself to help the family. When she was 15, somebody wanted to screen-test her for *Lolita*, but her father forbade it. Now, with him gone, she started taking drama classes, agent shopping, and table hopping. Maureen told her that her face was serviceable: she could look both pretty and not so pretty. In truth, Mia was a beauty who looked both wholesome and vulnerable. She soon found a part in a Wilde play, and then she got a big role in a new TV series, *Peyton Place*.

For the shooting of the pilot she went back to California and their old home. She writes that when she was done and about to leave, she decided, like a neo-gothic heroine, to enter the shut-up bedroom of her dead father. She found the familiar personal details of his room—writing materials, the poems of Donne, and a crucifix. Carried away, she laid her hands on the initials JVF stitched on the bedspread. The touch of the monogram triggered for her a paternal message from beyond: "Find eternity in this and every instant of your life" (77).

It was a *Jane Eyre* moment. Ecstatic, she lay right down on the bed where her father died and mated with his spirit: "A world familiar as my name burst open streaming pure and painful love, and I accepted; there, finally I embraced the essence of my father, and with him, humanity in its hideousness and its brief quivering beauty" (78). She got up and looked in the medicine cabinet. Nothing remained except a little box that said "Mia." In it she found her baby teeth, which, in love and peace, she carried back into life. No ingratitude sharper than serpent's teeth here, just virgin proof of the father's special favor—sentimentality *dentata*—thank heaven for little pearls.

In 1964, *Peyton Place* made her famous. She played a dreamy nonconformist teenager with long, straight blond hair. Allison—Alice: the hair was like Alice in Wonderland's, except that Mia was a pubescent young woman. She came across as a new kind of girl, an intelligent but spacey free spirit who rejects phoniness and follows an inner light. No one now much remembers this nighttime soap, but millions who saw took in the image Mia projected—a perfect video-girl for the 1960s counterculture. Soon thousands of girls would be ironing their hair and affecting Mia's style. You could be ethereal, naïve, and sexy too, and do what you wanted without bothering either to fit in or to rebel directly.

In the turbulence of the '60s, Mia found—like Woody Allen—that the puritan dam of America had collapsed, and she was swept away. Not surprisingly, given her father fixation, she was stuck on older men (she was close friends, in those years, with Salvidor Dali, a mentor, and Yul Brynner, whom she called "Dad"). What she most needed then was an erotic relationship to replace and make up for the father she hadn't saved, and she found it in a sensational marriage.

Out with her father one day, when she was 11, she met Frank Sinatra. "Pretty girl," he said (80). At the studio eight years later, she saw Sinatra making a movie, and he called her over. She says that just as soon as she looked into his eyes, he lit her up and love sparked. (In her book, right in the middle of a passage describing this meeting, there's a photo section in which a picture of her father in his bedroom is juxtaposed with pictures of Frank and Mia. As anyone can see, John Farrow on his bed is a dead ringer for Sinatra.) Three days later, he sent a plane to fetch her and her cat to his Palm Springs palace. It was an old script for him, but new for her. He embraced her, and "the loneliness, fearfulness, doubt, desire, yearning for closeness and for approbation, for meaning and for miracles, and for truth too, all came together in silence beyond words" (91). Or in the jargon of Sinatra's Rat Pack, "ring-a-ding ding"—she finally answered the father's call.

They became lovers and in 1966, when Mia turned 21, they wed. It was a surprising marriage, to say the least. In one of his houses she found several pictures of Ava Gardner. When Frank spoke about Ava, it distressed him, so Mia kept quiet. Once Ava gushed that Mia was "the child she and Frank never had" (104), and there's a distinct whiff of incest floating around Mia's life of that time. She says her father and Frank used the same after-shave and had "the same identical smell" (128). In bed, Mia literally took the place of her father's lover. Psychologically, she avenged, transcended, and replaced her own mother.

From this distance, it still seems strange that they would marry. For twenty-five years (1940–1965), Sinatra's voice and songs had been the focus and catalyst for the feelings and private yearnings of huge numbers of people, but before she met him, Mia didn't care about his music. It seems she wanted the strong, missing father figure who would love, cherish, take care of, and empower her, and—child of the 1960s—she also wanted to be rid of the taboos of the past. What did he want? It puzzled Frank's mother, Dolly. Her conquering son, the charismatic friend of presidents (and Mafia bosses), had actually wed this rail-thin, otherworldly near-child: "She don't talk, she don't eat. What's she do?" What Mia did was to make him *feel so young.*

Besides *mimetic*, or *triangular*, desire—people wanting and loving what others they wish to be like admire and love—it seems there's a variant: *generational* desire: people may long to possess and attach to themselves what or whom those of another generation most value. That Sinatra would choose to *marry* a girl thirty years younger, with whom he had little in common but who was becoming the symbol of a new era, shows the intimations of mortality and the need for regeneration that might roil in even the most powerful of men. It was a royal wedding of pre- and postwar American generations. Mia was a princess of the free-thinking baby-boomers and hippies; Frank was the brash king of "do-it-my-way" individualism. They loved one another in their fashion, then went their own ways. Sinatra didn't much want her to work, and her career was taking off. She, barely of age, was offered her first starring film role in Roman Polanski's *Rosemary's Baby*, and, much to Frank's displeasure, she accepted. That provoked the end of the marriage. In 1968, he had her get a Mexican divorce. In her memoir, Mia describes how she met and adored Frank's daughters Nancy and Tina, who "became like sisters" (98). The Sinatras were like family, and looking back on it all, she says her relationship with Frank was a bit like "an adoption that I had somehow messed up" (129).

3.

'ROSEMARY'S BABY'

In the saga of Mia and Woody, *Rosemary's Baby* figures in her life in the way *Manhattan* figures in his. People look for stories to internalize and make sense of their lives. Whether they admit it or not, artists of all kinds subsume into their personalities and perceptions the characters, words, subjects, and stories they represent, create, and inhabit. Roles and plots that actors invest so much time and energy on sink into their minds, and the part (the *part* which they *get*) can easily become a part of them.

Rosemary's Baby, still Farrow's best-known film, features a young wife victimized by a careerist show-business husband in league with a powerful male establishment, a coven of witches, and, ultimately, the devil. On the surface, the movie, based on Ira Levin's novel, is a modern, urban gothic—an escapist, supernatural thriller. On a deeper level, however, it's a work that makes visible lurking tensions and fears swirling in the '60s and '70s. It shows a fascination with the occult, with faith, with diabolical plots, mind-altering drugs, sex and sexual fantasy, and with the fluid lines between memory and reality. And the powerful image of young Mia Farrow suffering amid the patronizing forces of evil became a memorable vision of female victimization.

The narrative may sound silly, but it has power as allegory. Unbeknownst to newlywed Rosemary, her actor husband, to get starring roles, secretly makes a Faustian deal with an elderly leader of a satanic cult and arranges for a drugged Rosemary to mate with the devil and bear an infernal son. Unconscious, she undergoes an orgy of rough sex with Satan (standing in for her husband) and gets pregnant. Then, during her term, she discovers the conspiracy, but she can't get anyone to help her. After she gives birth, she learns the truth and means to kill the little fiend, but maternal feeling takes over, and at the close, she casts Madonna eyes on the child.

Oddly enough, the movie had an impact on gender history and feminist politics: is the potential life in a woman before she gives birth ultimately her responsibility or does it finally belong to the patriarchal power that has traditionally ruled culture? Rosemary exists to be used by others and has little say over her own body. She's regarded as a vessel to bear a child. Her essence is her reproductive capacity—her genitalia and womb. Her individuality is almost beside the point, and the feelings of helplessness that Farrow projects make it clear why *choice* would drive the feminist agenda in the last third of the twentieth century. The film and Rosemary-Mia's plight in it also endorse fears of male conspiracies and provide a powerful script stressing the cover-up of male sexual abuse. From a radical perspective, *Rosemary's Baby* can even be seen to subvert Christian eschatology, the incarnation of Jesus Christ in the Virgin Mary (Rosemary), and the whole tradition that makes it the primary function of woman to bring into being and nourish the vain illusion of male immortality and divinity.

But that's not all. From a conservative Christian perspective, the Age of Aquarius had turned into an ungodly orgy of sex, drugs, and rock-throwing roles. *Rosemary's Baby* could touch people wondering what had befallen Jimmy Stewart–Frank Capra America. Why were people desecrating family and religious values? The devil, alive and well in the USA, made them do it. It's not far from *Rosemary's Baby*'s righteous passion to the mass hysterical belief in the prevalence of satanic ritual abuse. As American as apple pie, witch-hunting is countenanced by this movie. *Rosemary's Baby*, in which she acted out a plot of maternal longing, victimized innocence, and the vulnerability of women, surely worked to shape—consciously or unconsciously—Farrow's later reaction to Allen's infidelity.[8]

4.

CELEBRITY FLOWER-CHILD,
MOTHERHOOD, MEETING WOODY

When Mia parted from Sinatra, she moved on to embrace an opulent form of hippiedom. She made love, inhaled, read widely, marched in protests, sought inner peace, and raised her social consciousness. She went to India to study with the Maharishi, a famous guru of the time, and there she frolicked towards transcendence with her fellow pilgrims, the Beatles. When she entered into the Marharishi's cave for private meditation, the venerable one groped her (Lot *is* everywhere). Eventually she found herself in the swinging London of the late '60s, and there she took up with another older man: the brilliant conductor, pianist (jazz and classical), composer, and polymath Andre Previn. Mia says of him, then moving into his forties, "I kept thinking how much my father would have liked and enjoyed him" (156). In 1969, he got her pregnant with twins. His wife, poet and songwriter Dory Previn, deeply resented Mia and contested a divorce, so Mia's first two children were born out of wedlock in 1970; when Previn's divorce came through, they married. Dory, meanwhile, wrote a memorable song about Farrow expressing a modern Lot's wife warning about flower-power: "Beware of young girls who come to the door, wistful and pale, twenty and four, delivering daisies with delicate hands." In light of the future, the irony is perfect: *what goes around comes around, or as ye sow, Soon-Yi shall reap.*

Mia Farrow has two vocations: acting and motherhood. In her eight-year-long marriage to Previn, she found the latter, and she grew up. Though Andre wasn't very keen on her acting career, she appeared in some splashy films, mostly negligible, and acted on the English stage. As for motherhood, she made it her primary concern. By the mid-70s, she'd borne three children and almost died of peritonitis. The experience took her back to her polio days and changed her life. She acted on her "save the children" impulse and started adopting orphans from Asia—including, in 1976, Soon-Yi, a little Korean street urchin. In these years she mixed with the smart set, made friends, and earned money in movies. She and Previn, devoted to his music and always traveling, grew apart. By the end of the decade, Mia had six children, three by Previn and three adopted, was divorced, again amicably, and was living in America, a single mother, and acting on Broadway.

In New York, she saw and loved *Manhattan* and wrote Woody Allen a fan letter. In April 1980, "the day after Jean-Paul Sartre died,"[9] Woody took her to lunch. It lasted into the night. In the movie *Alice* (1989), in which Allen makes visible much about Farrow's personality, there's an extraordinary scene when the normally circumspect Alice, supposedly under the influence of a magic herb, turns the full power of her sex appeal on a man she decides to have an affair with. On screen she opens herself completely to what the man is saying—just flows out to him, then absorbs him. The erotic charm of her focus is overwhelming, and you can see how and why Mia could make the most brilliant men fall in love with her. She and Woody talked music, ideas, writers. He was the most witty and entertaining kind of mentor, and she was the most advanced and fascinating sort of student—mature, receptive, admiring, knowledgeable, *and gorgeous.* And she had the Hollywood life he fantasized over back in Brooklyn. They could learn from each other—even make beautiful movies together.

He was working on *Stardust Memories*, in which a moviemaker flounders among women, unsure of where to take his art. He needed a muse and a leading lady for the future, somebody besides himself to write about and for. She needed support, steady work, and professional direction. Soon, as so often happens in his films, he was showing a beautiful woman the things he loved. They were exchanging books, having dinner, walking, blinking lights at each other across Central Park from their respective flats, and turning Manhattan into their "isle of joy" (Mia in Woody's world: *the great big city's a wondrous toy, just made for a goy and boy.*) Off screen they never actually wed, but on screen their talents and even, at moments, their identities did. For a decade everything seemed to work wonderfully.

III.
Visible Life in Film

When they got together, Allen asked her if she'd like to be in a movie. She startled him by saying she wasn't very good. "In the past," he said, "actresses who have worked with me have tended to come off very well" (Lax, 200). That was what she needed to hear. He was dedicated to the art of film as John Farrow, her father, had never been, and he needed and respected good acting. Mia did whatever he asked of her professionally, and he would later say: "Mia is an extraordinary actress. . . . She . . . can always do it. If you ask her to play that shrinking character in *The Purple Rose of Cairo*, or the silly cigarette girl in *Radio Days,* she does it. If you ask her to play nasty, she does it. If you ask her to play something sexy, she does it. . . . She'll come to the set and quietly do her needlepoint, and then put on her wig and dark glasses, or whatever, and just scream out the lines and stick a knife in your nose—and then go back to sewing with her little orphan children around her" (Farrow, 217).

From 1982 to 1992, Allen made a string of movies with Farrow that constitutes one of the glories of American cinema. Each of the thirteen pictures they made together deserves careful attention (an amazing fact in itself, given the transience of films), but I see their artistic success and the power of their special relationship playing out most clearly in *Zelig* (1983), *Broadway Danny Rose* (1984), *The Purple Rose of Cairo* (1985), *Hannah and Her Sisters* (1986), and *Husbands and Wives* (1992).

1.
'ZELIG'

Allen's films are a technological collage of materials from many different places and times, but Mia became the instrument and anchor of his vision. Take the much praised *Zelig,* the brilliant comedy made in documentary style about a changing little man, "the chameleon man." The movie treats thematically one of the great features of twentieth-century history: conformity to the group. Leonard Zelig (Woody Allen) becomes famous as the ultimate conformist in the 1920s and '30s (with starchy Presidents, he looks like Herbert Hoover; among "Negroes," he turns black; with doctors of the mind, he becomes a psychiatrist; with Hitler, he goes to a Nuremberg rally). The film is complex, but the plot is simple: the love of a good woman redeems a man and the superficiality of life. It's an artwork trying to make visible the spirit of a century that could invent the terms *public relations* and *fitting in,* and in it Mia plays Eudora Fletcher, a bespectacled psychiatrist and eventually Zelig's savior and wife.

Allen projects onto Farrow his desire to see and experience psychotherapy as maternal, rather than patriarchal. But even more telling is his transformation of Mia, the radiant star of the film of F. Scott Fitzgerald's *The Great Gatsby* (Fitzgerald is one of the narrators of *Zelig*) and the gorgeous walking aphrodisiac of Woody's *Midsummer Night's Sex Comedy* (1982), into a spinsterish, plain-looking doctor who looks a lot like himself and Zelig. Farrow the actress and Zelig, like Allen the filmmaker, are vocational chameleons. The film also shows Woody and Mia on the screen giving to the other what they desired of one another off screen: for him, some magic elixir that would combine effective psychotherapy and a woman's devoted love; for her, the chance to do good and important work. Zelig, besides being a sweet guy, turns out to be a promiscuous philanderer and an unfaithful Jew; he breaks ultimate taboos by desecrating family values and becoming a Nazi. Yet his maternal-but-young therapist lover sticks by him and acts out his wildest fantasies of salvation. She will go to any lengths for her man and forgive him anything. Within the culture of shallow celebrity and absurd mutability, only Mia-Eudora's love and integrity last. In this wildly inventive film, it's pretty to think so.

2.
'BROADWAY DANNY ROSE'

In his work, Allen often uses the showbiz milieu to reflect the world and its meaning—just as the religious use the state of the Church and the practice of faith as the index of the human condition. This movie preserves the seed of comic salvation, and Woody, a prophet of comic faith, specifically wrote it for Mia. It's her funniest role and one of his funniest movies. In it, like some Astaire-and-Rogers team of the absurd, they work and play off of each other: a schleppy, fast-talking little loser and a hard, sexy gangster moll wriggling through adventures together and producing a sweet comic gospel. The film is steeped in the modern American hunger for laughs, love-is-the-answer moral redemption, and feel-good news about the entertainment world and the Mafia. It's also steeped in Woody's World versus the Sinatra Nation and an evolving version of Lot's daughter.

Sitting one night in an Italian restaurant, Mia and Woody noticed a tough-looking blonde in dark glasses. Faunish Mia said it would be fun for her to go against type and play a hard-as-nails "broad" (Farrow, 215). She'd spent time among such women—gum-chewers, chain-smokers, midnight shade-wearers. She knew the way "Honey," a Sinatra crony's wife, talked, and she remembered other voices from those old days and nights in Frank's traveling circus. In *Broadway Danny Rose*, Allen would give her, in the raucous part of Tina Vitale, the chance to act out and purge some very complicated feelings from her past. And he would get a chance to play her moral teacher as good, grubby Danny Rose. Talking ethics, Danny spouts out to the cynical Tina, whose philosophical norm is to do the other guy before he does you, his creed: "Acceptance, forgiveness, love. Now that's a philosophy"—lovely words that became sad and ironic for the two.

The way the story is told matters. It's framed by group of real stand-up comedians sitting in a Broadway deli swapping gags and stories about their profession. The talk settles on Danny Rose, a funny little agent for pathetic acts, and his relationship with Tina, a hot Brooklyn Mafia widow and the mistress of Danny's best client Lou Canova. Danny has nursed Lou, a fat, has-been, married Italian singer, back to the edge of success. Long flash-back sequences in which the tale is told flow out of the round-table patter, and that means that Allen imagines the authority within the film about what's real, what's going on, and what people are like belongs to the comedians. They are the priests of Allen's faith that you can regenerate life by turning it into funny material.

Mia called Tina one of the two best roles she ever had, and she just explodes in the part with electric vulgarity—a pent-up urge to mimic the bimbos of her first husband's world. She was out to out-crude the crude and blast through every vestige of dutiful daughterdom. Tina (same name as a Sinatra daughter) was Mia's answer, prompted by Woody, to Dolly's rude question, "What's she do?" *She satirizes you.* Woody too plays partially against type. He still has his persona of what Farrow calls the "lovable nebbish, endlessly and hilariously whining and quacking, questioning moral issues. . . . with his heart and his conscience on his sleeve" (216). (In bitterness, she would later claim Woody was never anything like that.) Danny, however—a booking agent for losers—is not a creative genius in anhedonic angst about selling out, but a ten-per-cent-of-nothing saint and holy fool. The story turns on his betrayal by Lou and Tina and her moral redemption. His fictional sibling isn't some *Woodyish* hotshot, like Alvy or Sandy, but Joyce's Leopold Bloom. Allen himself had dumped his loyal first agent Harry Meltzer and after *Bananas* he stopped writing scripts with his boyhood friend Mickey Rose. So in creating Tina, who convinces Lou to get a sharper agent, he may have been projecting his own guilt on her—and then purging it. The heart of *Danny Rose* is the redemption of Tina, but Tina is a part of Woody as well as a foil for him.

In retrospect, just setting down facts of the plot makes clear how the movie figures in the Farrow-Allen relationship. Tina is enmeshed in an odd love affair with a charismatic, erotic Italian singer whose time has past. At one point Danny tries to impress Tina by showing her a glossy picture on his wall of Frank Sinatra. Tina moves in a milieu where the Mafia and the threat of violence pervade. The mother of an Italian boyfriend insults her. She's a hedonist who develops a conscience through the prodding of a small Jewish man, to whom she transfers her affections. In one scene, when she's taken Lou the singer away from both his wife and his devoted agent, she's haunted by Danny, his goodness, and her cruelty to him. For once in the movie, her shades are off; she sees her beautiful face in the mirror, and soon she leaves Lou, and eventually finds Danny Rose/Woody Allen. The last shot of Tina shows her getting together with Danny in front of the Broadway Carnegie Deli, the temple of comic faith where the gagsters tell her story. She moves from the Italian singer to the Jewish funnyman.

Mia had represented for Allen the fabulous world of Sinatra. Inspired in part by mimetic desire, he wanted Mia, took her, and then, in this movie, saw himself moving her to a kinder, gentler world where she could assume agency and moral responsibility. And in playing Tina, Mia, whom Sinatra hadn't supported in her acting career, found a new freedom and an expansion of her talent. She and Woody mock and transcend the sexism of a generation that classified women by terms like dames, broads, or "real ladies." But notice that Allen in this film has, in effect, replaced Sinatra as the father figure—Danny Rose, the nerd as moral patriarch of comic faith, sires the new Tina. Woody does it *his way*, exorcising Sinatra, but claiming Mia for the heart of his comic vision. Tina here is not a mother, like Mia, but, in the end, still another kind of good but patronized daughter figure.

3.

'THE PURPLE ROSE OF CAIRO'

What *Alice in Wonderland* is to literature, *The Purple Rose of Cairo* is to cinema: a modest little comic fantasy that turns out to be a masterpiece. It's a moving vision of how art works, how it relates to desire, and why an institutionalized fantasy life, though it may be ridiculous, is necessary. It shows how a dominant art form in any given age—say the movies or television in our time—implicates and affects people, and how sad and amusing that fact can be.

Allen has called it his favorite picture, and even in her book denouncing him, Farrow, with all that went wrong, calls her part as Cecelia one of "the best and most rewarding roles I have ever been given" (215). It marks the time of their life together when they were most at one and at their best. If you look at that shot of Woody Allen rapt at the movies, staring at Bogart on the screen in *Play It Again, Sam*, and then at the close-up of Mia Farrow as Cecelia in the last scene watching Fred Astaire, her tear-stained, star-struck face slowly changing from grief to vicarious pleasure, you can see how deeply the director and his own star could merge with one another.

Lewis Carroll looked at Alice Liddell and found that he could inhabit the girl in his imagination, that she was the perfect vehicle for his art and humor, that through her he could organize his fantasy life and give it point. Allen saw he could do the same through Mia. He'd written a short piece, "The Kugelmass Episode," about a professor who magically enters Flaubert's *Madame Bovary*, falls for the heroine, takes her back to New York and checks her into The Plaza hotel, but who also starts showing up in copies of the novel. It's clever, but it's basically a sketch. In *Purple Rose* he took the interpenetration of life and art, his great theme, and focused it in the life of a sympathetic young woman, Cecelia, a sweeter and more worthy Madame Bovary.[10] The quiet, subtle beauty of Farrow's performance conveys a yearning, naive desire for romantic pleasure and idealism in art that gives the film its depth and originality.

It's the grim middle of the 1930s American Depression in a New Jersey mill town, and pretty Cecelia, a gentle, dreamy waitress married to an out-of-work oaf, goes to the movies whenever she can. At work, she keeps gossiping with her sister (Stephanie Farrow, Mia's sister) about Hollywood stars until she gets fired. Her husband Monk beats her and cheats on her; and the town Cecelia walks through looks like a brick slough of despond. She escapes from this "real life" into fantasy at the local cinema, the "Jewel."[11] What's playing, the film-within-a-film, is a ditzy comedy called *The Purple Rose of Cairo* about rich people in their wacky, socialite world. Watching it for the fifth time, Cecelia catches the eye of the movie's dreamboat, Tom Baxter, played by "Gil Shepherd" (Jeff Daniels). Suddenly Tom walks out of the movie into the audience to tell her how he's noticed and admired her. The line between "on screen" and "off screen" is crossed, and a chaotic interplay between imagination and reality results. Symbolically the juxtaposition of the black-and-white world of the movie and the technicolor world of "life" works like beauty shop mirrors on opposite walls that set you adaze in an infinity of reflection. Not only do you have a vision of the American '30s, you also have Allen's brilliant take on late twentieth-century America where an ambitious actor, Ronald Reagan, walked right out of the Hollywood screen talking Capra corn to become a big box-office president and blur forever distinctions between news and entertainment.

Fantastic things happen in *Purple Rose*. Cecelia and Tom, smitten with each other, run off, and the cast in the movie starts bickering and fighting. The characters complain about their fictional lives being disrupted and about their lack of freedom. The movie audience, outraged at the breakdown of illusion, yells at the characters and hassles the management. Tom declares himself in love with Cecelia and refuses to reenter the film. Meanwhile commercial Hollywood must deal with the crisis, and moguls send Gil Shepherd to New Jersey to try to get his character Tom back into the film. Cecelia and Gil meet by chance. They spark, and a triangle develops in which the "real" Gil and the ideal Tom vie for her. Wonders keep on coming: Tom's idealism about women charms a madam (Dianne Wiest) and a band of whores; Gil, Cecelia, and a near-comatose old lady magically revitalized by their singing, make joyous music together; the screen characters begin to assert themselves and become memorable personalities. Tom and Monk meet and fight about Cecelia in a church, and when Cecelia tries to explain God to Tom, he thinks God means Irving Sachs and R. H. Levine, the writers of *Purple Rose*.

Tom, without money, does reenter the film, taking Cecelia on a mad Manhattan whirl of joy. Gil shows up at the theater and tells Cecelia he'll take her back to Hollywood with him. She has to choose between perfect Tom ("He's fictional, but you can't have everything") and Gil, the charming egotist. She opts for Gil because he's "real," goes home to pack, but finds when she returns that Gil, with Tom back safely in the picture, has decamped. She's heartbroken, but the manager tells her a new movie is playing. She slides into a seat, and, as she settles into watching Astaire and Rogers in *Top Hat* dancing "Cheek to Cheek," the film ends.

4.

THREE DIFFERENT ANGLES ON
THE LOT COMPLEX IN 'PURPLE ROSE'

Woody: Not "I Am a Camera," but "I Am a Projector." Movies do make the faith of Woody Allen—movies and jokes. He sees himself as a survivor from the Dead Sea of the Depression, in which his grandfather lost all his money and his mother's spirit turned to salt.[12] Allen has said that his personality is defined by the wish to be somebody else and that one figure he'd love to be is Gigi strolling on the Champs Elysées, a belle époque Parisian girl dressed in stunning purple followed by shoals of admirers. He could see himself also as a purple rose, battered black and blue by the hard world, charmed and fooled by the illusion of perfection, put upon by actors, press agents, executives, and the public, moving in a dark world, longing for endless previews of coming attractions, finding solace from movies. He appropriated the talent, looks, and interpretive skill of Farrow, and, through them, projected Rita and himself into Cecelia.

Allen said that he was stunned by the glamour of Manhattan when he first saw it as a 5-year-old with his father, and that from then on he was in love with New York City and conflated it with the movies: "I love any old film that ever begins or takes place in New York City. To me, people who lived in Manhattan would go from the Copa to the Latin Quarter; they'd hear jazz downtown, they'd go up to Harlem, they'd sit at Lindy's until four in the morning. . . . It was . . . so seductive that I've never really recovered from it" (Lax, 21). The high point for Cecelia—and the radiance on Farrow's face—comes when Tom takes her through the silver screen and Woody projects his own fantasy onto her: a Manhattan baby loving the lullaby of Old Broadway. When little Allan first went to the movies, his mother pulled him back when he tried to walk into the picture. Here in his own movie, through Mia, he can and does go through the screen. He replaces his "Oedipus-Wrecks" mother with a grown-up version of Shirley Temple, a Lottish Little Miss Broadway.

Mia: Preserving Seed; Awakening in the Cave. Why would Mia love this role? One reason is that her husbands hadn't told her, "Mia you're a terrific talent. You must act; it's up to you as an actor to express my vision." That, in effect, is what Allen does in this film. Farrow by this time knows him. She knows what he thinks, what moves him, how slow he is to trust, how much he's projecting into this film, what the movies have meant to him, how much he's invested in Cecelia. He chooses her over everyone else, even himself, to interpret his passion to make cinema his life. What she's wanted most in the world is "a life that would be meaningful" (Farrow, 338). Mia, through Cecelia, is symbolically representing the meaning of *his* life as: (1) a self inseparable from cinema, its history, and its functions, and (2) a being that flows into a living woman's image to preserve the essence of human need. In this particular movie this man can better impersonate his deepest self and desire through her.

But another reason operates. In *Purple Rose* she's acting on her own, her own agent—*not* interacting with Woody. She gets to play a victimized, romantic, pure-hearted woman. This beaten-down, mousy-pretty woman carries the moral weight of the movie. Depression (what a word!) is everywhere, all around her, inside and out. How do you fight depression? You get drunk on the movies, yearning for something perfect, some alternative visionary world of beauty, wit, glamour, or maybe even truth and astonishing intelligence. When Cecelia tells Tom, "People get old and never find perfect love," Mia speaks for both herself and Allen, and at that moment, there's no distance between them. And yet, there is. Allen's dream self may be in her, but he's gone from the screen. She's absorbed him; she's whole.

Deep Purple. Purple Rose lets you see the whole enterprise of modern critical theory as a daughter of Lot. Once upon a time you had art followed by its explanatory, benevolent parasite, criticism—first there were the creative artists sowing their seeds and then came their handmaidens, the critics, the biographers, the historians of culture who dutifully preserved that seed. In the second half of the twentieth century, critics, tired of their satellite "feminized" status, threw off their "daughterly" reverence for patriarchal creation and claimed agency for works of art. They too create the meaning and the unfolding history of works of art

What does all that have to do with *Purple Rose*? Cecelia, whose imagination is sired by the movies, begins as a passive consumer of what's put before her, but the power of her imagination and desire takes the movie over, pulls it to pieces, deconstructs the old order, and exposes this movie, and by extension, any significant artwork, as a huge, complex, amorphous social and psychological process whose effects go on and on. I'm not equating Cecelia with any particular *la vie en rose* Parisian critic (such as Derrida, Foucault, Lacan, Kristeva, Bourdieu, or Cixous), but I am saying that her desire and the primacy of audience need in the film make them her analogical kin.

Allen is a great parodist, and parody, among other things, is creative deconstruction. Freed from its objectified status, imagined by others, *Purple Rose* and its figures transcend their original conception and become fabulous. The shallows deepen. The naïve, passive spectator of life turns out to be not only the reason that art and fantasy exist, but the authorial heart of the matter. Her desire and image focus the jokes, the ideas, the moving pictures. Stereotypical characters become individualized, a head-waiter becomes a great tap-dancer, a haughty countess finds moral elo-quence, the black maid breaks free of subservience, and the artwork becomes a seed of unlimited progeny. One character, observing the black-and-white-characters in the movie quarreling with the technicolor "real" people in the theater, utters as suggestive a remark as you can imagine on the whole institution of literature and drama and the psychological trans-actions it involves: "If they're real they want to be fictional, and if they're fictional, they want to be real." Living people want stories and fantasies to reshape and broaden the sense of their lives and deaths; but when people then look at characters and imagined figures, they reflect on the way those fictional creations convey information about reality.

5.
'HANNAH AND HER SISTERS'

In *Hannah*, the most popular movie Allen and Farrow made together, you can see how her life fed his art. It's a big ensemble picture, flawed and messy, unlike its immediate predecessors, but it's a very funny, very per-sonal, and sometimes moving film that grows directly out of Woody's fas-cination with Mia and her relatives, with secret affairs, intra-familial erot-ics, and the jangly turn-on of tabooed sex. Returning to the three sisters theme of *Interiors* (and Chekov), he takes the personalities and experiences of Mia and her sisters (as well as sisters of other partners in his past) and turns the material into coded confessional comedy.

The film could just as easily be called *Hannah and Her Misters*. It liter-ally has a split personality (his): the three main male figures portray three faces of Woody. The two male leads, the present and past mates of Hannah —the unfaithful, love-driven Elliot (Michael Caine) and the hypochondri-acal, professional funnyman Mickey (Allen)—split the focus of the movie into the lusting, romantic side and the existential, comic-vocation side: Woody half-and-half. But there's also the older man, Frederick, an alien-ated, brooding painter—anhedonic, pessimistic, tormented by the pain and amorality of existence—the lover and mentor of Hannah's younger sister Lee (Barbara Hershey). Played powerfully by Max Von Sydow, Ingmar Bergman's male star, the antisocial Frederick connects with the world only through his art and his liaison with Lee, whom he instructs.

These male figures all want to implant their sense of what's beautiful and good into the minds of younger women—Hannah's sisters. In this comedy (and in most of Allen's Lottish erotic pedagogy) love relationships flourish when a woman opens herself to a man's desire to teach her about value, beauty, and art, and they fade when she closes up to him. Woody Allen represents men using culture to seduce women: Frederick to Lee: "I'm just trying to complete an education I started on you five years ago"; Elliot to Lee: "I'd love to get you this [e. e. cummings poetry]—and maybe—and maybe—we—um—we could discuss it sometime"; Mickey to Holly (leaving a punk band performance to go see the great Bobby Short sing Cole Porter): "Can I take you someplace to hear something nice?" The strategic tack in those lines replicates and can stand for the basic Woody-to-Mia approach: *How would you like to star again and again in my movies? I'll do for you what Fellini and Bergman did for Giulietta Massima and Liv Ullman: make you part of radiant art in terrific films.*

Much of Hannah was filmed in Mia's Central Park West flat with her children around. At this time she and Woody were trying to conceive a child, and the script makes an inside joke of their failure. Woody plays a dissatisfied TV comedy-maker and faith-seeking hypochondriac who was once married to Hannah. He seems to be impotent. Off screen, Mia and Woody were moving towards adoption, but on screen the way for them to have children, which Hannah badly wants, is through sperm donation. That fertility plan works, but the marriage fails. Hannah's present husband Elliot (Michael Caine), even as she wants to have another baby with him, makes love to her sister. In retrospect, the movie is a melange of pieces playing on Allen-Farrow biography and telling not just of what was past and passing, but of what was to come.

Mia's mother Maureen O'Sullivan, cast as Hannah's mother, later felt that *Hannah* was "a complete exposé" of Mia: "She wasn't being anything—she was being Mia" (Fox, 164). Details of her life abound in the film: she has twins; she has adopted children; one of her children, Fletcher, appears as "Fletcher"; she patronizes her younger sister. O'Sullivan saw in the movie Woody washing Farrow dirty linen in public—and no wonder. In a scene with Hannah's mother drunk and in a terrible row with the father, Allen has Hannah say in voice-over, "She was so beautiful at one time, and he was so dashing. Both of them just full of promise and hopes that never materialized. . . . [A]nd blaming each other. It's s-sad. They loved the idea of having us kids, but raising us didn't interest them." That last line reflects sharply on Mia's ambiguous history.

The film was intended, Allen said, as "a romanticized view of Mia" (Fox, 164), and it puts Hannah at the center of a histrionic extended family like Mia's own. A viewer, however, might also see her as a well-meaning but passive-aggressive character dominating everyone—an empress in Bo Peep's clothing. During the filming, neither Allen nor Farrow could make up their minds about Hannah: was she admirable, or a manipulator with a dark will to power—or both? Mia's fine performance conveys the enigmatic reality of ambivalent human nature as well as maddening big-sister competence and superiority.

In the movie, Hannah's husband Elliot falls in love with her younger sister Lee. This semi-incestuous situation doesn't end the marriage, but it shows something about Woody's transgressive libido (see also *Deconstructing Harry* [1997], in which he would make outrageous comic art out of the Farrow sisters' sibling rivalry and sex adventures). Allen had a history of getting involved with sisters of his featured actresses and intimates, namely Diane Keaton, Janet Margolin, and, most notably, Mia Farrow. As Mia intimates in her autobiography and as Kristi Groteke makes clear, there's more than a hint in this picture about his relationship with Mia's sister Steffi (Farrow, 226; Groteke, 184–186).

But suppose Woody did have an erotic affair with Mia's sister and used and transmuted this relationship into *Hannah*. So what—why does it matter? Such behavior and art suggest that he, like men in the Bible's Genesis—in the story of Lot in the cave, or in Jacob's history, for instance—needs to replicate and recharge desire and, subconsciously at least, imagine women as a group of sisters to possess. Such males split the anima of female essence that obsesses and nags at them; they long again and again to experience the potent high of fresh sexuality. Men like that are dangerous, and they are embedded in the history of womankind.

6.

CRUCIAL SCENES

AT THE HOTEL CARLYLE

In *Hannah and Her Sisters*, Mickey goes with Hannah's sister Holly (Dianne Wiest) to the Hotel Carlyle, where Bobby Short is singing and performing. Bobby Short is playing "I'm in Love Again" on the piano; an art deco mural fills the wall behind him. He sings: "Why am I/Just as reckless as a child?/Why am I/Like a racehorse running wild?/Why am I/In a state of ecstasy?/The reason is 'cause something's/Happened to me/I'm in love again/And the spring is comin'/I'm in love again/Hear my heart strings strummin'/I'm in love again/And the hymn they're hummin'/Is those cuddle-up, huddle-up blues/I'm in love again/And I can't rise above it."

Just as Mickey, wanting to impress a woman with whom he's starting up, takes her to see this splendid performer, so Woody, wanting to show his audience something fine, give it pleasure, seduce it into intimacy, and create joie de vivre, puts Cole Porter on his sound track and Bobby Short in his movie. This rendition makes for a stunning, charged scene. It not only comes across as exactly what a perfect date might include, it also expresses, in the sweet knowingness of the lyrics and the drive of the music—what the hope and rush of new love might feel like and be. It expresses what Allen loves—art and erotics fused.

And yet the Carlyle scene ends in farce. The film shows Holly bored by the music and elegance of the Carlyle and resenting Mickey's presumption to know better than she what's good. She seems, in the words of the tune Allen uses as the film's theme, "to have heard that song before," and the date is a total disaster. Love and its discontents are repetitive, and they reverberate back and forth between art and life.

Allen sends Mickey to the Carlyle because he imagines him having taken a woman there before with pleasure, and who would that woman be if not Hannah, Mickey's ex-wife, played by Mia, whom Woody himself had taken to the Carlyle? The location, it seems, figured in their romantic history. But things and people change.

In a scene from life, after the debacle in January 1992 when Mia found out that Woody was cheating with Soon-Yi, the two desperate ex-lovers somehow decided that they would visit the Hotel Carlyle, take a room, and try to recapture that old feeling. As a tryst it was a bigger disaster than Mickey and Holly's movie date. Hostility boiled. Allen said in court that Mia became hysterical, and, instead of making love, threatened to jump out the window. But in his testimony he turned this horror show into a bad comic routine; fortunately, he said, the Carlyle rooms didn't have real windows. Mia and Woody were like restless children, running wild, and the interplay between what went on in his movies and what they did and said is remarkable. Shortly after that aborted, unromantic Carlyle interlude, he said they went back again—with the same results. With Allen and Farrow, life imitates art, art imitates life, life imitates art, art imitates life.

7.

'HUSBANDS AND WIVES'

Husbands and Wives puts the Lot complex in focus and reflects on the whole saga of Mia and Woody. He was shooting a film about an artist played by himself who is secretly involved with a 20-year-old girl and pondering the end his marriage to his wife played by Mia Farrow *at the exact same time* he was really having a secret affair with Soon-Yi, the 20-year-old adopted child of Farrow, and pondering the end of his relationship with Mia, his onetime mate and muse. The film, among other things, is a stark, startling meditation on the fusion of the artist's imagination, work, and experience: dissolve the scene, dissolve the relationship, dissolve the *on-screen, off-screen* boundaries.

This film, of course, transcends Allen's personal life, and it could have been called just as aptly, à la Bergman, *Scenes From Two Marriages* or even *Exes and Ohs* (as in "Oh God, I can't stand this anymore" and/or "Oh, Baby!"). People who say that Allen's movies lack social relevance miss or downplay both the force of psychology and the importance of love and marriage as a subject of, and in, history—especially recent history, when a high percentage of marriages end in divorce and gender roles are in flux. Woody again features transgressive erotic drives, and, more sharply than in any movie since *Manhattan*, he centers on the desire of aging men for younger women. Though he said the screenplay was conceived years before and had "no autobiography in it at all" (Fox, 228), it's obvious the tensions in the movie, in the lives of Woody and Mia, and in the lives of countless "husbands and wives" are intimately related.

What makes a marriage, what holds it together, what breaks it apart? What are the lies—white, silly, treacherous, and/or vicious—that mates tell each other? When husbands and wives reflect on themselves and other married people what do they see? Why didn't Woody Allen marry Mia Farrow? Why did he marry Soon-Yi Previn? Why were President Clinton and White House intern Monica Lewinsky attracted to each other? Why didn't Hillary Rodham Clinton divorce her husband, and what does it all mean?

"What is this thing called love?" as the song on the soundtrack asks while the opening credits run. You can get some good ideas from this film, a work of ruthless honesty.

The movie starts off with novelist and professor Gabe Roth (Woody Allen) telling his wife Judy (Mia Farrow) that he has a very talented girl in his creative writing class who's written a terrific story, "Oral Sex in the Age of Deconstruction." Judy, an art magazine staffer, wants a baby badly, but Gabe, trying to finish a novel, doesn't. The film features the Roths' deteriorating relationship, the post-separation history of their married friends Jack (Sidney Pollock) and Sally (Judy Davis), the infatuation of Gabe with Rain (Juliette Lewis), the precocious writing student, and Judy's developing interest in Michael (Liam Neeson), an editor at her magazine (she fixes him up with Sally, but really wants him for herself).

Allen makes the movie in a dazzling cinema verité style. He sees the camera here taking over the functions of psychoanalyst, confessor, and judge. He's out to show the things husbands and wives keep from one another and often from themselves, and he uses a semi-documentary style. The cave of the dark-room, the cave of therapist's office has become the cave of the screening-room, the den of videotape: the existence of film-life gives people the medium by which they can confess their truths and analyze their experience. The characters speak thoughtfully to an unseen interviewer in long, searching close-ups, but only after the camera records action and dialogue in speedy, jump-cut takes and jerky, hand-held shots. Camera techniques help define the characters and their moods. Different photo methods work to fit and create the mental states and personalities of the figures (racing motion for nervous, domineering Sally; slow, sinuous movement for seductive, confident Rain; calm, still shots for calm Michael).

I'm not digressing here; the cinematography is a big part of the message. This movie shows that husbands and wives imagine themselves in this newly dominant mode of communication, film and videotape. The meaning(s) of life emerge and are determined in the imagined retrospect of an on-camera interview. This film and the subsequent history of Woody and Mia say that pictures and testimony tell the story and viewers interpret that story. Says Roth-Woody to the close-up camera in the interview that ends the picture, "I blew it. . . . Can I go now? Is this over?" That piece of candid camera, if applied to his involvement with Mia and Soon-Yi, would seem as telling as anything he would later say on the subject—in court or out.

A continuing theme for Allen is the fragility of mating: partners get on each other's nerves; sex between them becomes spiceless, then infrequent; men especially are tempted to cheat on their wives. This picture, however, offers a complex critique of the Lot pattern and leaves stereotypes far behind. You see, for example, two different kinds of women, Sally and Judy, threatened with the unfairness of the Lot's wife role, and two different kinds of women playing the Lot's daughter parts. Things are changing. Gabe claims that change is death, which was the truth for Lot's wife, but Judy tells him that change is what makes life. Preconceptions don't always fit in this film.

Jack takes up with Sam (Lysette Anthony), a blonde aerobics instructor a generation younger. He's besotted by youth. He wants to relax with somebody who doesn't tax him mentally—a sunny, flesh-toned somebody he can make do whatever he likes. Cerebral, hyper-intense Sally rages when she sees that mouthing off about independence and amiable separation fit neatly into a con game that men run: trading in old models for new. Played by Judy Davis, she's a great comic creation—a ball-buster and a truth-teller bristling with prickly life. As she screams out her anger, she takes on mythic proportions—the aging woman who resists male duplicity and the dumb force of ignorant daughters. Sam starts out as a soothing cliché for Jack, but he winds up manhandling her in one of the ugliest scenes in all of Allen's films. The point is that Sam is a great piece and an exciting idea for the older man, but not a real person. She's expendable, like one of the daughters in Sodom, and in the end, she just disappears. But Sally, the saltiest of women, doesn't lose her savor, and Jack, having made a fool of himself and a brute too, begs her to take him back. The older woman has an entertaining mind and can say grown-up things.

Allen, in his artist's fascination with Farrow, makes Mia's Judy a variant on the characters she played in *Hannah* and in *Crimes and Misdemeanors* (1989). As in those films, he shows the Mia-figure's gentle streak of selfishness. She quietly does as she pleases, and, better than any other character, she knows how to take care of herself. Judy's ex-husband (Benno Schmidt) calls her passive-aggressive. In the intimate interchanges between Gabe and Judy, you can't help but sense, given the context of Woody and Mia's relationship at the time, that scenes and lines are generated right out of life. Later Farrow and her supporters would come to see Woody's use of her in this film as a mean-spirited betrayal (he had her, in effect, rehearse and enact *on screen* a break-up she didn't see coming). "You use sex to express every emotion except love," she observes.

When Judy wonders whether he's attracted to the girls in his classes and Roth assures her "They don't want an old man," she tersely lays bare a key aspect of *Lot* and a major problem in the life of the species, "I think old men do better than old women." And of course he's lying. Some girls do want an older man. In one "interview" segment, he talks about how often and easily professors—not him, *perish the thought*—sleep with their students. Meanwhile he's carrying on a flirtation with the self-possessed, seductive Rain.

One of Allen's great subjects is the fading of erotic attraction towards those you love or once loved and what results from such change. What stays constant for many is a consistent form of erotic desire, but not for one particular person. That's a hard subject for people, and *Husbands and Wives* probes it. Mia's Judy is being replaced by the younger woman in Gabe's emotional life, though self-censoring Woody partially blurs that shift by making Roth reject an affair with Rain. Still, he shows that Gabe cares more about a melodramatic kiss with Rain than about sex with Judy, and finds Rain's libido more intriguing than Judy's. What's interesting is that Judy, fitted to play the new Lot's wife, refuses the role; she preserves her own love-life, renewing and satisfying her desire elsewhere.

Sex, Allen proclaims through his characters' quips and monologues, is nature's practical joke on pride and dignity—above all, on his own. This film pays special attention to personal patterns of libido. Roth talks about how he goes for "kamikaze women"—women who risk everything, do anything, but crash and destroy you. Gabe had loved a woman named Harriet Harman (the alliteration of first and last names looks suspiciously like that of *Louise Lasser*) who thrilled him by fulfilling all his sex fantasies, but wound up in an institution: "She was sexually carnivorous. We would do it in stalled elevators . . . the bushes, . . . with other women. . . . She was great, but nuts," says Roth.

High culture (Euripides, Genesis, Joyce, and Freud) and popular culture (Groucho, Harpo, Mel Brooks, and Woody) indicate that there's a Dionysus running through human nervous systems longing to take charge, burst out, and restage memories real or false—even, and maybe especially, in balding little middle-aged men. Allen subtly dramatizes this in the comic, but tense and complex, intergenerational erotics between Roth and

Rain. This figure, brilliantly conceived by Allen and acted by Juliette Lewis, is one of the surprises of the film—such a surprise that reviewers had a hard time talking about her at all. In light of the historical drama of the Clintonian fin de siècle to come, Rain, author of "Oral Sex in the Age of Deconstruction," emerges as a prophetic figure. *Husbands and Wives* presents her as a force in the world, like Henry James's Maisie or Lewis Carroll's Alice, but not a force of moral innocence. Rather, she's sophisticated, ambitious, and, by old standards, promiscuous. No sweet Tracy from *Manhattan*, she's hell on what she calls "the mid-life crisis set," for whom she represents, as she says, "lost youth" and "unfulfilled dreams." She's already had as lovers her father's business partner, a friend's father, and her own grizzled psychiatrist. Thus Allen imagines male adepts in the mysteries of commerce, the psyche, and aesthetics—the modern Johnny Appleseeders of civilization—subjecting themselves to the ambitious daughter. Rain wants power over men of power ("all accomplished men," she tells Gabe of her conquests), and she serves as Woody's agent in diminishing the aura of male authority.

For the filmmaker, as well as Gabe Roth, the heady ozone of taboo hangs over this liaison, and he can't help showing Rain going to a New York Knicks game with her middle-aged date, as Soon-Yi did with Woody at the start of their intimacy. Rain's a male projection, of course, but she does illustrate an unfashionable fact of modern life, namely, that well-educated young women who go to bed with older men are often strong, successful people who know what they're doing, what they want, and where they're hoping to go. Rain wants Gabe's professional help. Her writing talent brings out the mentor in him, and her admiration for his craft and work— she's read his fiction—makes him happy. She tells him she loves his work and gives him that most flattering message for a teacher, *you changed my life and made me want to do and be like you.* She wants his attention and approval, but he needs hers, too. Generations can fall in love over a mutual passion for a work of art or a vocation.

But the Rain part of the movie is more comic and satirical than I make it sound. Woody mocks himself and sometimes this ambitious girl who, like the young woman in the old glossy magazine ads, later says of the trouble she causes him, "Well, I'm worth it!" Gabe agrees to lend Rain the manuscript of his new novel, which she tactfully praises but loses in a taxi. And as she talks about it, she, like a good feminist, roasts Woody's Roth for his sexist attitudes. She calls his views of women "disappointing"—"shallow and retrograde." Nothing else in the movie brings him down like that—not even being mistaken for her father. Angry, he whines and mopes because the aging male artist fears, like the plague or impotence, that the up-and-coming generation will brand him as retro and irrelevant.

The Kiss. At her 21st birthday party in her parents' penthouse, there's a romantic thunderstorm, lights go out, and Gabe and Rain find themselves drinking wine, alone in the candlelight. She asks him for a birthday kiss, and he gives her a prim peck. "No, no, not like that—on the mouth," she says. He jokes nervously, saying things like, "You want me to bend your head back and thrust my tongue down to your toes?" "Why is it," he says, "that I'm hearing $50,000 worth of psychotherapy dialing 911?" A good answer could be *because psychoanalysis is ridiculously overpriced*, but a better one is surely *because that's what my portrayer is hearing*.

May and November, these two do kiss provocatively—passion, wide-open mouths, tongues. Lightning flashes, the heavens roar, and the natural fireworks of metaphorical orgasm fill the screen, giving the scene the comic edge it needs to keep it from being embarrassing. Rain offers herself and he's tempted, but he turns her down: "Things would be different if I was younger or you were older" (*after all, this is fiction*).

A passionate, romantic kiss is an odd phenomenon; it's a mutual opening up and prelude to adult sexuality, but it originates in earliest childhood. The kiss, unlike intercourse, would seem to grow out of infantile experience and intergenerational contact. It develops out of sucking and breasts and then moves through touching, oral affection and warm respect between parents and children to the hot stuff. Its history, therefore, is incestuous.

If, like many in our time, you perceive human existence as a social construct and the cultural heritage of humanity as patriarchal, then it follows that sexual relations between older men and younger women likely have a tinge of incest about them. I want to juxtapose that Rain-Roth intergenerational kiss with the one that gives the title to Kathryn Harrison's 1997 incestuous memoir, *The Kiss*. Comparing them raises issues that surface in *Husbands and Wives* and that drove the bitterness of the real-life conflict between Woody and Mia. Harrison, then 20, describes a kiss in an airport with her long-estranged father that changed and marked her life.

With his hand under my chin, my father draws my face toward his own. He touches his lips to mine. I stiffen.

I've seen it before: fathers kissing their daughters on the mouth. A friend of mine's father has kissed her this way for years, and I've watched them, unable to look away, disquieted by what I see. . . .

. . . As I pull away, feeling the resistance of his hand behind my head, how tightly he holds me to him, the kiss changes. It is no longer a chaste, close-lipped kiss.

My father pushes his tongue deep into my mouth: wet, insistent, exploring, then withdrawn. . . .

In years to come, I'll think of the kiss as a kind of transforming sting, like that of a scorpion: a narcotic that spreads from my mouth to my brain. The kiss is the point at which I begin, slowly, inexorably, to fall asleep, to surrender volition, to become paralyzed. It's the drug my father administers in order that he might consume me. That I might desire to be consumed.[13]

These two kisses taken together provoke and focus questions of impropriety, responsibility, and the role of incestuous impulse that arise in older men-younger women liaisons generally and in this movie and the Woody/Mia/Soon-Yi case in particular. Do the kisses really have anything in common? Does the appearance of such kisses in the media signal change and progress in gender relations? If a probing, erotic kiss is initiated by a self-possessed young woman rather than the older man, does that make it all right? Does the scorpion kiss expose the birthday kiss as culturally incestuous and morally contemptible? Can and should we get quit of the Lot complex? Various women and men have different answers to such questions, many of which involve turning them into professional and legal matters, but also into the stuff of vital art. Meanwhile, the thoughtful *Husbands and Wives* seems to show—whatever its maker would later contemplate and do—that wives no longer can or should be traditional daughter-figures, nor husbands father-figures.

IV.
The Visible Life Shatters

In their collaboration, then, Allen and Farrow accomplished great things and showed off their talent and humanity. Both the films and the making of them became a great part of their lives and identities. And nothing that they would do to one another, none of their sorry efforts to abase and defeat each other, can spoil their achievement. Nevertheless, the end of their relationship presents a fearful piece of modern gender history.

Woody and Mia were an acknowledged, if odd, couple. Before and after they fell in love, got together, and established their own brand of mating, Mia took in those needy children from all over the globe. In 1976, with Andre Previn's consent, she adopted that little Seoul street-girl, reportedly the daughter of a prostitute.[14] The child, a true refugee from Sodom and Gomorrah, didn't even know her name, and it was at the orphanage that they started calling her Soon-Yi. By the time Farrow and Allen broke up in 1992, Mia had born four children of her own—three by Previn and one by Allen—and adopted nine others. As for Woody, a self-centered, well-organized creature of work and routine, he had little interest in mixing his life with a family. He told Mia he was committed to her, but leery of marriage (Farrow, 224). They lived separately, he alone and she in her teeming little rainbow coalition.

At least until the birth of Satchel in 1987 (now Seamus) and sporadically after that, she wanted him to marry her and get more involved with the children. And she wanted to have a child with him. He grumbled, finally agreed, and then for two years she couldn't get pregnant. But after she adopted Dylan in 1985 (now Eliza), he found in his growing love for the little girl something old and something new: the reincarnation of his affection for Letty as a child and the missing desire in himself to be a father. And then Satchel, their own son, was born.

They acted together as co-parents to Moses, Dylan, and Satchel, kept up a cordial partnership, worked, talked, and often ate together, but, according to him, their sex life was over. She, however, felt that the "commitment of a decade together . . . had provided us with a permanent, solid base" (252). At the time, she agreed with Eric Lax, writing in 1988: "few married couples seem more married" (253). And she quotes Woody approvingly, "we both have our own developed lives—her with a major family and me with a career" (253). In December 1991, with Mia's blessing while they were shooting *Husbands and Wives*, Allen legally adopted Moses and Dylan. But within a month, she would discover his nude photos of Soon-Yi—seismic proof of sex with her daughter.

Soon-Yi was an outsider even in Mia's motley brood. "She was always so icy cold, even as a child," said Mia later. The girl, it turned out, felt badly patronized by Mia, and so much that fired Charlotte Brontë's imagination

FIGURE 11.1 In 1989, Mia, carrying Satchel, 2, Woody, wheeling Dylan, 4, and, at rear, Soon-Yi, then 17. Dave Parker/Alpha/Globe Photos, Inc.

in Mia's favorite *Jane Eyre* also burns hot in this case—the rage of class, economic, and racial jealousies, the bitterness about female beauty, forbidden erotic strategies and alliances, and the outsider child's need for attention. Soon-Yi never bonded with her legal father, Andre Previn, and for a long time she didn't like Woody. Mia urged him to pay attention to her because she needed a "positive male role model." He refused, but then in 1990, when she was a high school junior, he took her to a basketball game (Farrow, 240). From then on, she developed a crush on him, and eventually they conspired to have sex.

When Mia let herself into Allen's empty apartment and found the sex pictures, the immediate result was an orgy of passion and bitter emotional incoherence for both of them. That first evening she screamed at him—in what reads like a classic Woody Allen line—the basic rule of domestic life: *"You're not supposed to fuck the kids"* (Farrow, 276).

1.

WHAT THE HEART WANTS

How did it all happen? I see the image of Altdorfer's great Lot painting hanging over the Woody/Mia/Soon-Yi episode—the coarse sensual expression of Lot, the look of sly manipulative power on the face of the daughter lying with him, and the distraught angst of the other female at the cave mouth, with the world of the past burning up. Of course the Lot's daughters theme appealed to Woody, as *Manhattan* and *Husbands and Wives* show, but it took three to make this erotic tangle.[15] Somehow, like the fictional Maisie and Lolita, Soon-Yi found herself wanting her mother's amusing partner for herself. The Woody/Mia/Soon-Yi triangle makes clear ambiguity in the Lot myth about the plight of Lot's wife and cultural confusion about the role of young females as both daughters and erotic subjects.

But still, how *do* you explain the odd coupling of Woody and Soon-Yi, thirty-five years his junior, not really beautiful, not a genius—not a stunner in any way? As an erotic motive for an aging man, the chance for arousal with a willing young woman should never be underestimated. Also, in the beginning, the idea (as in *the very idea!*) of intergenerational sex with the misprized Asian daughter of Mamma Mia, the golden goy of goodness, might seem an irresistibly outrageous story. It was, according to Camille Paglia, "an act of defiance against . . . home and mother and everything in morality and custom that enslaves the sex impulse"[16]—and such an act can have its revolutionary appeal.

After Mia found she'd lost Soon-Yi to Woody and Woody to Soon-Yi, she wondered whether the jump from a Seoul world of degradation to a life of wealth and privilege had overwhelmed the girl. According to Kristi Groteke, the nanny, Mia once said that if Soon-Yi had stayed in Asia, working as a factory girl or whore, like her birth mother, she might have understood things and fit into her life with integrity, as she failed to do in America (Groteke, 87). That's devastating, but the rivalry between Soon-Yi and Mia cut deep. Farrow staked much of her life on her project of saving vulnerable children, but when she found the pornographic Polaroids and confronted Soon-Yi, the girl reportedly told her she'd now replaced her unmarried mother-by-adoption: "The person sleeping with the person is the person having the relationship" (Groteke, 101). Soon-Yi, hungry for love, may have been seduced by Allen, or she may have been getting back at Farrow for patronizing her (e.g., *I, Lady Bountiful, prove my worth by succoring the wretched of the earth—even someone like you*). Or she may have been imitating Mia (sincerest form of flattery) in falling for Woody, getting together, using sex, and making pictures with him (*Mia, needing a father-lover, got Sinatra; she got Woody*). Who knows for sure? But the record shows she came to resent Mia deeply.

In an interview, Allen said words that would be widely mocked, "The heart wants what it wants."[17] Of course the heart has its reasons, but such rationalization turns absurd if you imagine him answering the old question, *how did you meet your wife?* As unruly an organ as any, the heart can desire many things—among them, virginal love, erotic variety, Pygmalion erotics, a docile lover centered on yourself, the high of breaking taboo, psychological revenge, dark alliances, the making of sexually explicit pictures—and even the *frisson* of incestuous relationship.

2.

PORNO PICTURES

That Allen would have married Soon-Yi had her mother not found the photos seems improbable. He'd engaged in clandestine affairs with much younger women before, and nothing dire had really happened. He tried hard to downplay the Lottish tinge to the relationship—the mother-daughter connection and the perceived aura of incest. But it was disingenuous for the man in perpetual analysis who made psychoanalytic movies to play dumb about underlying motives. He was, indeed, blasting those false idols in his past: family piety and motherhood. "The pictures," said a revolted Mia, "were a grenade he threw into our home, and no one was unharmed" (Farrow, 283).

In late twentieth-century America, the age of technological reproduction, it was almost inevitable that the existence of the photos would come out. Sex on film, tape, and the Internet not only becomes property, it easily turns into a legal weapon and evidence of moral turpitude. What Farrow saw carried this message for her: *if Woody Allen could do this, he was capable of anything.*

If Alice Liddell's mother found that Charles Dodgson had made dirty pictures of her daughter, if Shirley Temple's mother came upon explicit sex reels of Shirley at MGM, their consternation could not have been greater than Mia's—and the analogy matters for several reasons:

- These mothers, in the interests of themselves and their families, were all making use of the picture-making talents of men involved with their daughters. But a mother has a duty to protect a daughter from harm and exploitation, including most emphatically sexual exploitation, and she usually depends on her mate or the men closest to her for support in so doing.

- Photography is often a way of celebrating, memorializing, and possessing time-doomed physical beauty and noteworthy experience. It can make it seem as if time stands still. To make pictures is to indulge in a kind of virtual reality (a new form of photography)—picture-makers have virtual power and can create highly seductive fantasies of controlling and giving form to the flux of existence. Film can thus become a medium of temptation, and you might have to watch out for people used to directing others in making pictures. Photography is a means of production, and one thing it produces is desire—you may want to have, do, and/or be what you see.

- Photography has been instrumental in producing the uncanny, modern sense of childhood as a special, separate part of life, and yet one that always remains with you. Taking pictures of children is a way of having them constantly available in retrospect, and photography, which developed as the increased focus on childhood developed, is the most child-centered of arts. Fed and formed by such things as photo albums and family videos, modern perception of children offers the illusionary permanence of the child—the projected "inner child" and "child within." People like to believe in the sanctity of childhood, and they can easily become fascinated with such reputed phenomena as "recovered memory," which, for the most part, seems to be an induced condition purporting to show that the child you were not only still lives, but, like a star in the latest studio release, can have new and contemporary experiences sparked by current events. What this paradoxical sense of both a detachable child (*look at the darling I once was in this snapshot*) and a continuous self (*look at this photograph of 6-year-old me with my dog and you can see why I'm a veterinarian*) might lead to understandable temporal confusion. You might ascribe to grown daughters the condition and vulnerability of little girls and to little girls the experience and mental concerns of grown daughters.

- Film teaches people the habits of voyeurism—and of exhibitionism too. In all its forms, photography can be a highly sexual process and activity. It touches, aids, and abets libidinous impulses that develop very early in life. And, of course, movieland—the commercial world of cinema—is built on sex appeal.

- The violation of a pornographic picture for the parent—what could drive you crazy—is that the raw sexual image undeniably says *your* daughter (or son) is being seen as a promiscuous sex object, that there is a market for such a sight, and, further, that the child—*your* child— either was coerced into posing, or, just as scary, *wanted* to do it.

- In 1998, if you looked up *Mia Farrow* on the Internet, you could find a listing for "nude" photos of her. If you clicked on, you could see a frontal shot of her youthful face and bare breasts. Subscribe, it said, and you'd get much more. In her salad days, it may be, Mia had wanted, or agreed, for whatever reasons, to have naked pictures made of herself. Men like to see sexy young women undressed, and it seems quite likely that she, like Soon-Yi, had posed to please a man. So the photos could bring home, at least subliminally, shame, guilt, and disgust at the inability to keep a daughter from being sexually used, at the excesses of her own camera-loving youth, and at the seemingly continuous cycle of the sexual exploitation of interchangeable, replaceable females.

• If what's really going on in Lot's cave can and does present dirty pictures of humanity, that fact needs to be brought to light. If the real scandal and depravity of Sodom and the cities of the plain (that is, *the world*), is the buried, repressed news of fathers' incestuous desire for daughters and the patriarchal insistence on cover stories hiding—figuratively, if not literally—a system of sanctioned abuse of girls, then out of the dark places, out of the caves of shame, can come images, in our new era of electronically visible life, that might lead to social progress.

3.
BREAKING UP UGLY

Farrow and Allen were in turmoil after the discovery. In the aftermath he offered what she had before wanted, marriage, and at one point she even agreed: "Okay. . . . Just promise me you'll never sleep with my daughter again" (Groteke, 83). In the months to come it would be as if they were riotous performers spinning and jerking about in the jump-cut style of *Husbands and Wives*. They spoke of reconciling, but planned a legal separation. Mia worked to turn the children against Woody, but couldn't even cut herself off from him. He kept trying to placate her and avoid confrontation, but he also tried to get her doctors to hospitalize her (Groteke, 106–107). They said anything to each other, contradicted themselves, and often didn't know what they meant or felt. Each thought the other was crazy. Both were into heavy therapy and so were some of the children. Allen wanted to avoid public disgrace; Mia raged, cried, grieved, and even threatened suicide. They called each other sick. But they kept seeing each other. She told him to stop meeting Soon-Yi, and he said if she'd give the Polaroids back or burn them, he'd break off with her daughter. But she didn't and he didn't.

Like most betrayed spouses, she had huge mood swings between abjection and outrage. In her bitter bewilderment, she felt the twin pillars of her identity had crumbled—inspired Mother Mia to the Soon-Yis of the world and Movie Star Mia, the featured, trusted consort in Allen's movie realm. It was horrible to think that Woody could possibly choose Soon-Yi over her. But what was worse—what she had to struggle to repress and deny—was the idea (it turned out to be true) that, for whatever reason,

Soon-Yi loved Allen more than she loved her mother-by-adoption and, just as disturbing, that Woody loved Soon-Yi more than Mia herself did.

To fight depression, rebuild self-esteem, and get a grip on the future, she would have to reassert her maternal role as a child protector and vent her anger. To break free of Woody, she needed to demonize him—and it wouldn't be hard for the star of *Rosemary's Baby*. Shaken and appalled by what she failed to see developing in Soon-Yi's life, Mia wondered what else she missed. She settled on Woody's strong feelings for their adopted daughter, 7-year-old Dylan. She had been worried for years, she later said, about Woody's relationship with Dylan. After the Soon-Yi pictures, Mia, caught up in the gender issues of the decade, began to see his affection and love for the child in a new light: *perverse sexuality and child abuse.*

In her days of rejection trauma, she talked to intimates—including Casey Pascal, Dylan's godmother and her close friend from convent school days. Casey, tuned into the late 1980s' furor over sex abuse, fed Mia's fire. She told Mia that Woody's behavior with Dylan had been inappropriate—too attentive, too uninhibited. Kristi Groteke, Dylan's nanny, was soon wondering at Mia's desire to find that Woody had committed some kind of some incident of molestation (Groteke, 128).[18]

When Allen came to celebrate Dylan's birthday that 1992 summer, a distraught Mia left a note for him: "CHILD MOLESTER. MOLDED THEN ABUSED ONE SISTER. NOW FOCUSED ON YOUNGEST SISTER" (Groteke, 121). It would be a war, and that charge would be her A-bomb.

4.

THE PASSION TO
LIGHT UP THE CAVE

I want to put this seemingly bizarre case in context of the history of Lot and Lot complexes as they unfold in modern times. The Lot-Scripture had daringly suggested that civilization and the future—the father's seed—would be preserved through the agency of daughters; women could and would take responsibility for saving and continuing the world. But that story was compromised by illicit sexuality and the revulsion of incest. The Victorians, as you can see in Chapters 2 and 8, tried to salvage and use the great potential of Lot's daughters by purging the story of sex and imagining innocent young girls as the agents of salvation; these pretty children would appeal to the best side of human nature and make a world where hope, decency, and beauty could bloom. That idealization led, culturally, to an intensified focus on girls, to closer bonding and identification between daughters and fathers, and thus to new, developing opportunities for female agency and progress. But for women, it also produced serious contradictions and problems.

Featuring daughters and promoting their ambitions might provoke cross-generational rivalries and have the effect of turning mothers and older women into metaphorical Lot's wives. Aging women, for instance, might see husbands leaving them for the younger women whom they met through work. And, in younger women, competitive feelings and their drive for worldly success might come to foster a sense of guilt—guilt that would demand displacement and sublimation—about rejecting and leaving behind an older female generation.

Also, if little girls were supposed to be pure and sacred, what about their abuse by men? If men—if the *world of the fathers*—paid lip service to sugar-and-spice girl icons but countenanced or overlooked for millennia incidents of violence, sexual misconduct, and mental cruelty against females, that patriarchal hypocrisy would generate social and psychological fury. The nightmare of the Victorian Lot paradigm—the ultimate ironic horror—would be if daughters were infantilized as little girls, but their relationships with the father were incestuous and sexual. The nineteenth-century ideology of faith in children had sought to remove the stain of sexuality, but then Freud came along with his sex psychology. A religious heritage that proclaimed the corrupt nature of sex combined with a so-called science that stressed the predominance of the sex drive in shaping human life to promote a prurient consciousness that could and would find sexual misconduct everywhere—cradle to grave.

This heritage of Lot's daughters drove a strong cultural consensus to expose one of history's nastiest practices: the abuse of children—especially girls. The late twentieth-century feminist movement was exploring and publicizing a whole history of sexism and violence against females. Strategically and politically, if the society were, for whatever reasons, invested in the idea of daughterly purity, then allegations about sexual abuse against girls, especially if provided *by* girls, would offer credible evidence in outing male predators and hidden patterns of exploitation.

From 1985 to 1992, during Dylan's lifetime , the subject of female child abuse became a feminist rallying point and a significant field of vocation (and income) in psychology, law, law enforcement, medicine, sociology, and education. In the 1980s alleged cases of sexual abuse of children, rarely reported or discussed at the beginning of the 1970s, jumped by more than 2,000%. There was an explosion of such charges against divorcing and divorced fathers and stepfathers. Child abuse would more and more often be seen and defined as sexual abuse.

That was the trouble. The sin of predatory sex or incestuous sex with children did not threaten the individual consciences of most grown-ups—in fact, it could work to soothe them. Most adults cannot help, at times, indulging in behavior that can surely be defined as abusive towards children, but they refrain from—and are repelled by—direct sexual abuse. Sexual abuse of children, physical pedophilia, is thus an easy target, and it can serve as a scapegoat and screen from the infinitely larger problems of general child abuse and parental failure: neglect, inadequate care, abandonment, corporal punishment, insensitivity, irresponsibility, and cruelty (mental and verbal as well as physical). Lighting up Lot's cave became a necessary goal and a strategy in women's liberation, but it also could and did lead to false allegations, mental health malpractice, unconscionable pressuring of small children to say what their parents wanted, irrational credulity, and irresponsible fanaticism.[19]

5.

MIA'S REVENGE

In early August, Farrow moved to charge Allen with molestation of Dylan. She turned her videocamera on the child: questioning and taping her over some days, she produced a "chilling" little noir documentary.[20] In it, among other things, the girl indicated that Woody had improperly touched her "privates" and taken her up into an attic, with the heads of dead people lying around, to fondle her sexually. If Woody could make pornographic photos of Soon-Yi, Mia could make a film that would show *his* true obscenity. If, in *Husbands and Wives*, he could get her in her pain and confusion to utter the truth of their life and relationship in lines of his own devising, she could get Dylan to talk about her relationship to her father as her mother had come to see it. Usurping Allen's role as the director, Farrow ran this show.

Novelist Philip Roth writes, "Nothing so big in people and nothing so small, nothing so audaciously creative as the working of revenge," and, for Farrow, nothing so irresistible and imitative of the methods of the film-making object of her revenge: *So you like younger women, Woody? And, you men, you like sporting with Amaryllis in the cave while your old lady gets petrified? Well, Mr. Funnyman Fellini, Mr. Lecherous Lot, how do you like my little daughter in* my *film exposing you as the lacivious household bully and incestuous reprobate you've been since the beginning of time?*

Mia took Dylan to her physician to be examined. The results showed no sexual abuse, but the doctor was required by law to notify Connecticut authorities of the allegation. The case thus became a matter for the police as well as social workers. When Dr. Coates, the family therapist, found out, she informed Allen and the New York authorities. He was as frantic and angry about the accusation as Mia was when she found out about Soon-Yi. It would be hard to imagine anything much more damaging—unless it would be losing your mate to your daughter.

In this scandal, they lost all sense of proportion and made themselves small. She formally filed dubious criminal abuse charges that, in the popular imagination, branded him with both incest and child molesting. She apparently did want it to be true that he *had*, rather than *had not*, abused Dylan. And he, calling her an unstable, unfit mother, sued to take Dylan, Satchel, and Moses away from her (*what's wrong with this picture—Woody Allen fighting for custody of children?*). He also gave those out-of-focus interviews in which, having taken up with the legal sister of his children and adopted daughter of his longtime mate, he blithely opined that it was all just fine. The man who made *Alice* honoring Mia's concern for children now made her out to be a cruel mother; the woman who played loyal Dr. Fletcher standing by Zelig in the storm of perverse publicity now called Woody a pervert. In the wake of Freud, Joyce, Nabokov, Shirley Temple, and feminism, they were engaged, as they had often been in their movies, in the messy, necessary late twentieth-century enterprise of deconstructing Lot.

Legal deconstruction was played out on two fronts, the custody case in the New York Family Court and the Connecticut investigation on the criminal accusations regarding Dylan. Allen had the nearly impossible job of trying to prove a negative (*I did not touch my adopted girl's "privates" improperly, and I am not an incestuous freak*), and the ambitious Connecticut

state attorneys were avid to indict and put him on trial. To show his innocence, he agreed to take a lie detector test. The polygraph administrator
bared Allen's flesh, hooked him up, put sordid questions to him, and, based
on the overall interpretation of the produced polygrams, concluded that
"the physiological responses recorded for the relevant questions were consistent with responses indicative of truthful answers." Woody passed—a
bedraggled feather in the genius director's cap. Mia did not choose to take
a lie detector test.

Meanwhile the matter had been referred to the Yale–New Haven Hospital Child Abuse Evaluation Clinic that evaluated more than 1,500 such
cases (and usually sustained charges). After a thorough, professional investigation, the investigators concluded that Dylan's allegations, videotaped by
Mia, "were made up by an emotionally vulnerable child who was caught up
in a disturbed family and who was responding to the stresses in the family"; moreover, it seemed likely that she was "coached or influenced by her
mother."[21]

This de facto exoneration of the abuse charge came when the custody
trial was going on, and Allen thought it would help him to win. But it didn't
matter. In the popular mind, the Soon-Yi affair made him look like a guilty
moral cretin; his broken relationships, betrayals, and taboo-breaking love
life caught up with him. Elliott Wilk, the hostile, controversial Family Court
judge, castigated him as "self-absorbed, untrustworthy, and insensitive" and
without proper "parenting skills" (Farrow, 325, 322) and awarded the children to Mia. New focus on the victimization of women meant that his case
was lost, no matter how far-fetched the accusations against him were.

In historical perspective, Mia's attitude and action in going after Woody
for child abuse might be rationalized thus: when a man loses erotic interest
in his mate and transfers it to younger women, he may feel that it's just nature and can't be helped, but the inevitable result of such infidelity is that,
one way or another, it damages and violates not just his spouse and older
women in general, but little girls and their future as well. When a man lav-
ishes affection on a small daughter and idealizes her, when he shows more
love for her than her mother, in effect, he really does molest and stunt the
potential development of females and prey upon their spirit and the future
well-being. The pattern can turn daughters into habitual father-lovers and
their minds into areas of obsessive, claustrophobic, life-with-father psycho-
dramas, as Mia Farrow knew full well from her own experience. She, like

many people, felt that even if Woody's sex with her legal-age daughter was not officially a crime, it was disgustingly immoral—evil. And since sexual behavior with an underage daughter *is* criminal, and since Mia believed that Allen, no matter what he professed, couldn't help thinking of female beings as sex objects, and since she knew that sexual and psychological abuse against small daughters was going on all over the world, she charged him with molesting Dylan. In so doing, she was convinced she was standing up for victimized girls—*and women.*

6.
"LOVE THAT DARE NOT
SPEAK ITS NAME"?

How, though, could *he* rationalize bringing his case into court? No doubt, in his own mind, he felt sapped by the blackjack of false accusation, and he also saw himself on the side of daughters against manipulative, irresponsible mothers. But a more illuminating, though oblique, way to answer the question is to see how the no-holds-barred Woody Allen–Mia Farrow custody trial at the end of the twentieth century meshes with the famous case of Oscar Wilde and London's Gay 'Nineties sexual politics a century before. These trials would signify for many on different sides the opening up and coming out of various closets, hotel rooms, family rooms, attics, support-group halls, and even Oval Office anterooms. The parallels between them are remarkable. Two of the greatest wits of their times, both masters of cerebral comedy and darlings of the cognescenti, were mangled by sexual scandal. Tawdry on the surface, both cases raised profound social issues. The two men found themselves in the spotlight for breaking erotic taboos and assaulting "family values." And just as the vulnerable Wilde skewered himself by suing the Marquis of Queensbury for libel over allegations of his homosexuality, so the vulnerable Allen opened himself to scorn and loss by suing Mia for custody of the children. Both featured, in Wilde's memorable if misleading phrase (he and Allen both were anything but tongue-tied), "love that dare not speak its name"—homosexuality in the 1890s, Lot's-daughters love (older man–younger woman) in the 1990s. What was on trial was an egregious flaunting of sexual decorum and social convention. And in both instances, it was the apparent disregard of children that provoked the greatest public wrath.

Here is the famous and still moving speech in which Wilde defended himself and defined his terms more than a century ago:

The "Love that dare not speak its name" in this century is such a great affection of an elder for a younger man as there was between David and Jonathan, such as Plato made the very basis of his philosophy, and such as you find in the sonnets of Michelangelo and Shakespeare. It is that deep, spiritual affection that is as pure as it is perfect. It dictates and pervades great works of art like those of Shakespeare and Michelangelo, and those two letters of mine, such as they are. It is in this century misunderstood, so much misunderstood that it may be described as the "Love that dare not speak its name," and on account of it I am placed where I am now. It is beautiful, it is fine, it is the noblest form of affection. There is nothing unnatural about it. It is intellectual, and it repeatedly exists between an elder and a younger man, when the elder man has intellect, and the younger man has all the joy, hope and glamour of life before him. That it should be so the world does not understand. The world mocks at it and sometimes puts one in the pillory for it.[22]

The tenor of Wilde's defense here no longer offends most people. If you're reading this, you probably can and do sympathize with the emotional drama and anguish behind Wilde's words, no matter how self-serving and disingenuous they seem, because they express a desire and need for tolerance, kindness, and sexual liberation that ultimately connects with—indeed, may be inseparable from—human freedom. Time has softened the threat to public morality that Wilde represented and the anger at the pain and upheaval that his erotic life caused to his wife, his sons, and his mother. What remains is a plea for understanding and recognition of erotic desire that has generated art, beauty, and love in the world.

But if you change the language a bit, suspend disbelief, and imagine Woody speaking it, you can find the grounds for outrage that put both Wilde and Allen in the dock of disgrace. And beyond that you can see the ambivalent challenge and the rationalized drive that has made Lot so important in modern history:

The "Love that dare not speak its name" is such a great affection of an elder male for a younger woman as there was between Boaz and Ruth, between the Lord God and Mary, such as Freud made the very basis of his philosophy, and such as you find in the writings of James Joyce, as well as Shakespeare. It is in this century misunderstood, so much misunderstood that on account of it I am placed where I am now. It is beautiful, it is fine, it is a lovely form of affection. There is nothing unnatural about it. It is intellectual as well as physical, and it repeatedly exists between an older man and a younger female, when the elder man has power, intellect, accomplishment, wit, lust, and a time-menaced creative drive, and the younger female has all the joy, hope, ambition, and glamour of life before her. That it should be so the world does not understand. The world mocks at it and sometimes puts one in the pillory for it.

On the face of it, that speech transposed to Woody and Soon-Yi (and Lot relationships in general) can ring ridiculously hollow and false because it leaves out bodies, money, the oppression of females, and the ruthless will to sate desire—the libido of the elder, the power and status differential between age and youth, the ambitious hunger of the younger, and the potential prostitution in the encounter. Nevertheless I want to claim that the spirit that animates the words and their implications about intergenerational love and relationship not only bear on Allen and Farrow, but also on modern gender and social history. They certainly express the vision of *Manhattan* and the essence of Allen's *apologia*.[23] Allowing for the different idiom, his defense of his involvement with Soon-Yi parallels Wilde's sentimental passion for Queensbury's son, "Bosie" Douglas, different as the origins and class of their young loves might be: "There's no logic to those things. You meet someone and you fall in love and that's that. . . . She's a wonderful person, you know, completely open and honest, direct and unspoiled. For the first seven years of her life, she was eating out of garbage pails, living in the streets. Then she was adopted into a very unhappy situation for her. But she's great—up and funny and has a wonderful sense of humor."[24] "It's a fully dimensional relationship," he said (Isaacson, *Time*, 62). Of course the cases are utterly different, but that language has essentially the same mixture of candor and self-deluded idealism, of hypocritical self-justification and truth, that you find in Wilde. And in each case, you find erotic drama born from the ambiguous, world-historical mythology represented by the various Sodom residents in Genesis 19.

V.
Aftermath

Mia Farrow held onto her family, adopted more children in the years following the split, and sought to foster them all. Her relationship with Philip

Roth in the '90s (with whom Allen has much in common—including a geezer badboy image) proved she could still draw brilliant, distinguished men to her, but she wanted to be more than a star companion to clever patriarchs. She was determined to escape the hard irrelevance of the old Lot's wife role. She conceived, wrote, and published with pride her memoir, *What Falls Away* (1995), motivated by the will to get even with Allen and to put her Lot's daughter history in perspective. And she threw herself into the humanitarian work of ending polio and other diseases that prey on children. She has apparently sought a new solidarity with women and new equanimity in her outlook. She does a bit of acting, lives independently, and wraps her life into the vital flow and animation of her progeny, the seed, finally, of her own charity and nurturing will. As for the man who sacrificed her in lying with her daughter, she still regards him as fit for Dead Sea damnation.

And yet, there's a revealing passage in her memoir getting at the true ambivalence in her life with Woody—and in the Lot story. Mia is recounting some of Allen's worst failings, but then she describes how she went back to the *Husbands and Wives* set to shoot the few scenes she had left after the postponement during the big blow-up in January 1992. Woody's behavior, she says right in the middle of one of her more spiteful passages, was "gentle, apologetic, and caring" (283). She performed the tortured scenes of her break-up with him in that dazzling film with subtle, riveting skill that conveys depth, power, and end-of-the-affair honesty, despite her ravaged condition. So they *did* make beautiful movies together.

Woody Allen kept on with Soon-Yi and married her in 1997 (lately, like Mia, they have been adopted babies). Sleeping with her sank his popularity, but still he kept turning out distinguished movies. Two of his best, *Deconstructing Harry* (1997) and *Sweet and Lowdown* (1999), feature highly talented men of doubtful morality who make wonderful art, but cheat and betray women who love them. Both are comic masterpieces of mea culpa psychology and how it relates to art. You sense in them Allen using and probing his own guilt towards Mia and finding ways to turn it into a complex moral and aesthetic vision.

But no film is more revealing about Allen's Lot complex than the documentary Barbara Kopple made about him, *Wild Man Blues* (1998). It features the European tour of the New Orleans style jazz ensemble in which he plays clarinet. Soon-Yi, his wife-to be, travels with him, and her calm and concern obviously help keep this aging, nervous man going. She acts as the daughter-wife who mothers him—a caring, sensible woman with a practical sense of reality. Sometimes, though, she plays the spoiled girl who can tease him into liveliness. Tellingly, his sister Letty is also on the tour, ministering to him. She and Soon-Yi pamper this man in his sunset years. But when he's on stage, performing, he's transformed, years falling away. Throwing everything into his music, he shows the passion and drive of a dedicated artist. You can see that the same single-minded focus, joy, striving, and commitment he shows as an amateur reed-man is exactly what he brings as a professional to the making of his movies. And you can also see Soon-Yi somehow preserving, along with Letty, the seed of his creativity.

The film ends with Woody, Soon-Yi, and Letty back in New York having lunch with his mother and father. Nettie disparages Woody's career, his resentment of her, and his choice of Soon-Yi, an Asian woman. "Truly, the lunch from Hell," he says, escaping from the old woman's verbal fire and brimstone, now accompanied by her younger replacements from the beginning and end of his life. It was an old story for him.

part iii

Lot's Daughters at the Millennium:
Potomac Testaments

Chapter 12

Complex Darkness

CAROLIVIA HERRON AND
'THEREAFTER JOHNNIE'

I n the last decade of the second millennium in Washington, D.C., capital of the most powerful nation on earth and a city obsessed with
power, the flowing Lot complex and myth could be seen to make news,
shape history, change the political landscape, and form minds for the future. I want to look at two very different Lot testaments from along the Potomac that can sum up and recapitulate the force and historical significance
of the unfolding story of Lot's daughters. This chapter shows both the sexual anarchy and the apocalyptic potential of the story; the final chapter
shows it being transformed in a way that might mean progress for women
and for society as a whole.

I.
'Thereafter Johnnie' and Lot

In 1991, Carolivia Herron, a writer and mythologist from Washington, D.C.,
published *Thereafter Johnnie*, an oracular novel about an African-American
family she had worked on for twenty years. It sensationally features father-
daughter incest, and it's consciously based on the Lot myth, which Herron
represents as crucial for understanding social and personal experience in
the United States. The novel explicitly politicizes the Lot story by tying it
both to the American heritage of slavery and to the broad feminist movement, but it also represents a complexity of incestuous desire that resists
and mocks any simplistic notion of group identity or "political correct-

ness" (including Herron's own). It can be read as history, all right, but history with both the full force of individual psychology and the anthropological sweep that makes the reality of life so complex and, in every sense of the word, awful.

Thereafter Johnnie caused a stir when it first appeared, but, by 2004, according to Herron's website, it was out of print and in danger of being forgotten. That's a shame, because, like Toni Morrison's *Beloved* or J. M. Coetzee's *Disgrace*, it provocatively imagines a disturbed and disturbing vision of what is past, passing, and to come in the entwined matters of race, gender, sexuality, faith, and ethnic history. It portrays some of the most graphic and hauntingly provocative scenes of father-daughter incest ever written, and it needs to be better known. I hope that by quoting liberally from it I an encourage more people to read it.

This tale of incest insists upon the continuing power of myth both to form and explain inner and outer reality, and it narrates in particular how the living matter of Lot figures indelibly in both private and national life. Herron tells a messy story about the terrible fate of a family on the eve of the new millennium. Its members are inescapably wired into Lot. She wants to show how people somehow, whether they know it or not, do live in, and perceive through, evolving versions of myths—those controlling scripts they inevitably follow and rewrite.

She proclaims and shows not only that the Lot story lives, but why it lives: its dark narrative of disaster, sin, and displacement holds the epic possibilities of an enigmatic future. Even in its cataclysmic crisis, it features the creation of new and mysterious generations. For Herron, the Lot family proves that the birth of illicit children of outsiders may lead to an apocalyptic future. Here, she is following both the spirit and the letter of the Bible, where the Lot story really does end with the climax of the Christian Scripture, Revelation. There Jesus, "the root and offspring" of Lot (through David: Rev. 21:16), in the words of his prophet John, reveals the bloody, glorious triumph of the Heavenly Kingdom in the future. From the sexually wayward and damned might come the spiritual light that could possess the world—or incinerate it. And, crucially for Herron, the light that shines in the end is now that of a black *daughter*—"Johnnie," not John.

Categorically, here is what makes Herron's testament important for my study:

- She ties the *Lot* story of incestuous sex and its heritage of outsiders' progeny becoming the light of the world to African-American experience and to a third-world, 9/11-type mood of apocalypse.
- She renews James Joyce's decision to put Lot at the center of twentieth-century art and life, and she absorbs, adapts, and uses his Irish version of Lot at the end of *Finnegans Wake* to try to imagine on American soil the regeneration of life through daughters, to memorialize the passing mother, to structure her own dreams and nightmares of American life, and, ultimately, to find and render the unity of psychological, historical, material, geographic, and mystical existence.
- She dramatizes fully what has been a main concern in much African-American writing generally, and—even more broadly—in the expanse of modern literature by women: the frustrated desire for the love and strength of the missing, misbehaving, or alienated father figure.
- She represents with skill and candor the terrible force, tension, and complexity of sexual attraction and incestuous impulse that can both animate and destroy family structures.
- She features the developing agency of daughters, imagines without flinching a young woman's conscious, willful seduction of a father, and revamps the Lot myth to make its illustrious progeny female, rather than male.
- She renders and doesn't repress—as is often done in serious literature—the direct appeal and full force of tabooed sexual experience.
- She, in a powerful feminist text, imagines and doesn't minimize what a contemporary patriarch has to offer that daughters might want and need; and she also shows how much a father longs to be part of his daughters' ongoing life.
- She struggles to conceive of an apocalyptic, "happy" ending for her modern Lot family myth, but the suffering and evil in her version and the pain in her vision overwhelm her, leaving her with only an indistinct, messianic light from a new Sodom's burning (a nuclear flash?) at the end of the long cave of history.

But I don't want to reduce this daring writer and her stunning novel, with its sometimes confusing parables and allegories, to such a cold academic outline. *Thereafter Johnnie*, like a Dickens novel, is a literary cathedral featuring wonderful stained glass, gargoyles, vaults, and buttresses that don't exactly mesh. The book is a shocking work about uncontrollable love and sex, and it has as much subversive force as any portrait of Lot's daughters since Altdorfer's. Herron, in this strange book, represents the hypnotic force of incestuous desire as almost no one else ever has.

As the Bonnie Raitt lyric goes, she gets "into it / Down where it's tangled and dark." She renders in detail the daughter's desire for the father and his sexual touch, and she imagines the sexually adept, accursed father succumbing in ecstasy to his lust for the daughter. That is a terrible and dangerous thing for a writer to do. Like its original in Genesis 19, this story is so unsettling that it invites soothing misrepresentation or selective forgetting, as many of the reviews and the critical study it has had bear out.[1] Herron, with her last-page judgment of postmodern America as irredeemable and her allegorical castigation of the sins of patriarchal racial violence and exploitation by cruel white men, does provide some fuel for the tanks of political correctness. She wrote the book over two decades, so naturally she had different purposes in mind at different times, but her feel and respect for the unique contingencies of individual life transcend conventional attitudes and intentions. The book is not easily assimilated into any conventional wisdom or easy political formulations. She outrageously features the full sensuous intoxication of the father-daughter intercourse, and by doing so she stresses what the Bible renders in Lot's daughters: the amoral sexual basis of life and the powerful erotics of intergenerational relationship. She brings to life this old story that must find sublimation and emotional antidotes if civilization is to exist.

Everything in the story of *Thereafter Johnnie* carries allegorical, symbolic, and mythic meaning because, according to Herron, that's how life works. You may know little or nothing of Christian theology or the Lot family, for example, and even doubt that there really is such a thing as the Lot complex, but that doesn't mean they aren't somehow a part of you and your life. Herron's novel, like anyone's mind, is a chaotic stew of intersecting literary tags, philological puns, old and new stories, folklore, song lyrics, epic and scriptural allusions—what James Joyce calls "messes of mottage" and "quashed quotatoes."[2] Real people and memories, like fictional characters, are shaped by language—its immortal, various history and usage, its innumerable narrative forms. That's a big reason why human psychology can be so anarchic and why Herron, a scholar of myths that she feels to be alive and wants to hang on to and use, creates such overdetermined characters and such an anarchic novel. It would be hard to analyze or touch on all—or even a fraction—of her mythic allusions, but focusing on her use of Lot's daughters does get at the special quality of her art.

II.
Daughters Seeking Transcendence

The novel begins and ends with "Johnnie," who has become the mystic light of a fallen world at closing time for "the American Century." What Herron seems to imagine in her—and it isn't always clear—can be understood as the potential, if dubious, triumph of female agency whose history began with Lot's daughters. Johnnie, in Herron's mythology, follows and subsumes Jesus Christ (and her father and her mother's father, John *Christopher* Snowdon), ending the patriarchal era and mindset symbolized by the masculine terms for the monotheistic Christian deity, "God the Father" and "God the Son." Johnnie says her mother, Patricia, named her "Kristen Dolores, meaning 'she before whom Christ sorrowed,' that is to say, Johnnie."[3] I take it that this complex allusion to a trinity of Johns (John the Baptist, John the loving disciple and Gospel-maker, and John the seer of Revelation on the eve of destruction and the Second Coming) foretells the replacement of the divine Christ by this transcendent daughter who supernaturally takes upon herself all the sins and suffering of the world. Thus, by Herron's light pointing "thereafter," you can see the seed of gender revolution implicit in the Lot story come to full mystical bloom in Johnnie.

In the literal chronicle of a "black intelligentsia" family, Johnnie is the daughter of John Christopher Snowdon, a skillful Washington heart surgeon, and his own daughter Patricia. John Christopher and his wife Camille have three gifted daughters, Cynthia Jane, Patricia, and Eva. But the favorite, the beloved, "the pet, the prize of the ages," the "singer of songs," the knower of languages, is Patricia, whose name "is derived from the word for father, *pater, patria, patrician*—father and nation" (187). And this ultimate Daddy's girl is nicknamed "patPat," after the heartbeat of her father's vocation. She falls in love with the father, seduces him, and, against his will, though not his desire, he becomes her lover. She wants to have his baby and does, though he wants her to abort it. Then he tries to stay away from her and the child. When he pays Patricia to leave town, she moves in nearby with a lesbian woman, Diotima, who cares for her (and who turns out to be a teller of the tale). Johnnie, who as an infant witnessed and remembered her mother having ecstatic sex with her "grandfatherfather," speaks her first word, "Daddy," at 14. Then when her mother tells her she is cursed and won't tell her who her father is, she shows that she can write too, scrawling on the wall the ultimate in a Lot-complex daughter's *ressentiment*, "I HATE YOU MOMMY I HATE YOU MOMMY I HATE YOU MOMMY" (146).

"Pretty Pat," the incestuous daughter and sistermother, always longs for her father's touch, but after seventeen years, she sees that she cannot have him—cannot have the permanent physical union with him that is her obsession. She walks into the Potomac River and, longing to diffuse and dissolve her separate being, drowns. With her mother gone, Johnnie takes action, visiting her aunts, her "grandfatherfather," and her grandmother to learn the story of her being. By the book's end, the nation is in crisis. Black people have left the city for mountain conclaves; third-world nations, out to blow up America, have made a separate pact with African-Americans not to bomb them; the Potomac is a traveling little lady who stops to watch a black girl and a decrepit old white man having a dream about white fathers and sons impregnating black mothers and then having sex with their own daughters. In the end, the Washington Monument has become, in the backward glance of the new millennium, a pillar of salt, and Johnnie has become pure, eternal light—the ambiguous light of the future in the final chapter "Matin" (mo[u]rning-time in America?). The incest shatters the family, destroys the bonds of the sisterhood, and somehow leaves the city of Washington an abandoned ruin. It even causes the American landscape in the end to become the setting and the container of a broken nation's evil memories, motley legends, and apocalyptic prophecies. And if all this sounds like the opium dream of a psychotic analyst, a mullah terrorist, or an unhinged student of *Finnegans Wake*, I'm still oversimplifying the novel.

III.
John Chris and Lot:
A Devil's Tale

Herron uses the fate of Lot to predetermine the fate of the father, John Christopher, and she uses this black doctor, who holds the material heart sacred, to show the enduring force of the Lot-Scripture. As a boy, John Chris remembers a Sunday sermon about God being mad and burning up a city. The preacher preached about different kinds of love in the Bible: eros, philos, and agape: "Now the first word that means love means carnal love, you all know what I'm talking about, I'm talking about sex, I'm talking about lust after the body, I'm talking about those perverted sins for which the great God in Zion, Almighty Jehovah rained down fire and brimstone on those ancient cities of iniquity, Sodom and Gomorrah, leaving only Lot and his daughters alive" (79–80). Then the preacher tells of agape, divine love, and says Christ's beloved disciple John had it. He didn't die like the other disciples, but "got to see the holy city of the heavenly Jerusalem before he died and the end of all earthly things, the Apocalypse, was revealed to him when he was chained to the island of Patmos, yes . . . Jesus Christ himself came back for him" (80).

But all this scares and confuses the boy, who meets a vagabond in the Georgia countryside: "I have to find an island of Pat but I'm afraid of the island I'm afraid . . . please don't burn me up like those cities. . . . don't chain me to an island. Please don't burn me, let me be saved like Lot and his daughters" (82). This evil tramp is the devil, equally at home in the American South, in Hawthorne's New England, or in Herron's Washington, and he makes his wicked bargain:

"I don't know, maybe you ought to burn up. You ain't nothin' but a little black boy, maybe you ought to die! . . . I'll wait until you're grown up and you think you're happy and I'll come and burn you up then."

"No, no, please don't burn me, I want to be saved from the fire like Lot was saved."

"Like Lot? You're sure?"

"Yes."

"You're a fool but ok, it's a deal." (82–83)

Herron is using Scripture, parable, and story here as the mythic mode is always used—namely to claim authority, explain the inexplicable, and make acceptable the unacceptable.[4] Both the irony of human wishes and the greatly underestimated role of word magic in shaping destiny come out here (notice that the chance "isle of Pat" becomes a part of this character's verbal program—and life history). But what also stands out are the mysterious and inevitable effects of unfathomable moral fables and lessons, represented here by the Scripture. Again and again in Herron's use and variations of *Lot*, she returns to the subject of how mythic visions and language get integrated into individual lives and histories. It seems that, like the Snowdons, people get caught up in stories and teachings of the past and must live in that awkward interplay between old, confusing verbal formulas and what's appropriate for their own reality. No one can be free of what is told and retold, but the stories you make your own in childhood can burn you and others up.

IV.

Daddy, I Hate You/Daddy, I Love You

Herron goes deepest into the ambivalence of mythic knowledge and power with Patricia, whose passion for mythologizing she warily shares. Johnnie's aunt says of Patricia after her death: "And she still believed in her myths, she actually quoted Lot's daughters to me, 'Come, let us make our father drink wine, and we will lie with him, that we may preserve seed of our father,' as if we lived at the end of the world" (206–207). That name Patricia, derived from the words for father and nation, can take you into Herron's Lot story and why it so rivets her: "The Soul of Patricia. The Soul of the Daughter of the Father," says Cynthia Jane. "A name like that fit right into the myth she spun for herself and felt compelled to act out in her body" (187). Herron is compelled to imagine and sexualize the "Soul of the Daughter of the Father" in the body of a contemporary black woman. She wants to identify and focus on that woman, and she wants to show you now, in the American world, the pity-and-terror-arousing tragedy that that figure can provoke who finds and mythologizes her being in love for the father—for, in one sense, mindless *patriotism*. Patricia's journal gets at the mystical desire—and frustration—of the modern daughter dedicated to the father and all he has signified:

You are the father who gave me being. Whom should I desire but you? Whom should I possess? You will return with me to the other world of light and joy where we may live at ease among the gods where I shall sit beside you, the queen of heaven as you are the king, and I will be your darling and your daughter forever, although in this world you have deserted me whom once you thought so lovely. Blessed is she whom thou has desired never. Cursed be she who has been loved of the Lord. (34–35)

That passage is an abstract of both the feminine desire and male projection inherent in the incest of Lot's daughters and in the Christian theology featuring Mary—daughter, bride, and mother of God. It is also a definitive statement of both unconditional female love for the father and disillusion with patriarchy's failure to fulfill its spiritual promise to women.

But it is not in abstraction that Herron best conveys the full impact of such concepts as "The Soul of the Daughter of the Father," "preserving the father's seed," and the spiritual bond of daughters and fathers in the world. It is in the extraordinary sex between them. Herron writes powerfully of sexual experience. It's hard to think of a novelist who does it better—though it's so blatant and raw that you can see how readers, needing defenses, might find the scenes disgusting or even ridiculous. With her unselfconscious precision at describing sex, her skill in finding its rhythms and making it intimately pornographic (not *obscene*), it can provoke the sort of revolting fascination and painful embarrassment you might feel if you were watching the ecstatic incest of real people you cared about. She pushes you to imagine the power in history of the daughter's love for the father and the father's desire for the daughter—the power, that is, of the Lot complex.

For this novelist that complex and Lot's daughters are more than the academic hot air of Freudian psychology and cultural studies. They signal something in the desperate saga of human nature that got out of control, warped gender relationships, turned destructive, and now demands shocking erotic cries and images to help the truth batter through the complacency of conventional thought. Herron is out to show that incestuous impulses—the daughter's urge to seduce the father, the father's to touch the girl's body, the complex of feelings and guilty fantasy life that surround the daughter's impossible desire to possess the father's sex, to be one with him—have epic consequences. Patricia's intercourse with her father is Herron's way of making you see and feel the whole historical, cultural dynamic of the father as a bitter aphrodisiac for the daughter.

This scene brings into focus the subject and end of my study, and I quote from it at length. It opens up the forbidden sexual drama and the force of erotic intoxication in Lot's cave—that mainline hit—and it renders the voice of an articulate daughter of Lot speaking and summing up at the end of the millennium not just her own passion but the almost unspeakably conflicted desire, resentment, rage, and need of countless daughters over centuries. Here, with her nod to Sylvia Plath's "Daddy" poem and

Yeats's "Sailing to Byzantium," is how Herron imagines in Patricia and her father what the myths of incest might mean, how they now reflect the manic schizoid eroticism that patriarchy has fostered, how deep they run, and how and why they are now being transformed:

And she almost rejects him entirely right then except she oddly changes her mind as a strangeness begins its slow circles within her and she opens herself above him, suddenly panting as she moves her leg over him, kneeling above him, she grasps him in her hand and sits upon him, squeezing and massaging him with her tightness, pulling him into herself, with warm liquid oozing down upon him, dripping down his thigh.

Pain holds her away from him for a while but she eases herself down, then the slow riding begins, raising her hips and then down, rotating her hips away and then closing deep around him, lifting herself each time more slowly more deeply down against him and lifting her arms high above her. . . . He holds her hips so tightly she lifts him from the bed each time she rises. And her circle of passion sweeps out in a circle to the edge of her body, every pore opens for the conclusion, it comes to her edges, her knees, her ankles, she twists into the final heat but especially her hands, explodes from the center to culminate in the fingertips of her right hand which she lifts alone into the air and she looks down upon her father and calls him, "Daddy, Daddy!" He sees the flush rise in her as the moment comes, and she begins to fall, and quickly he turns her beneath him, pushing into her and holding himself there, and then he is no longer her god, nor her king, nor her lover, nor her father, but he is an erected penis urging itself into a female hole, only that, he is a penis with a female hole to enter, and does enter it, expending itself himself within live female flesh, pushing and pushing and pushing in, without will or hope, only a risen penis inside a live female. It expends itself, John Christopher's penis in Patricia his daughter, with climax swirling outward from the center, turning and turning, passion and possession sweeping them out and away gyring, widening as liquids mingle between their legs, they are swept into silence. Caught in that sensual music, caught, the golden bird, caught by a touch, Patricia, prettyPat, patPat, patPat, whispering possessed in her forgotten baby voice as her father sleeps, "I don't like you, stop hurting me, don't you hurt me any more, you're mean to me, if you hurt me any more I'm going to kill you when I grow up, what are you doing to me Daddy, that hurts me, is it a fire Daddy? . . . is it a fire you put on me Daddy, I don't like you Daddy, you're mean to me Daddy, don't hurt me anymore Daddy, Daddy my hands and my feet don't feel good, what did you put on me Daddy, I hate you Daddy, please hold me, Daddy I'm scared lying here shaking and trembling, I hate you Daddy please hold me, I hate you Daddy please hold me, I hate you Daddy please hold me, please hold me, please stop my hands and my feet from trembling, please calm the fire you touched onto me, Daddy, Daddy, Daddy, please hold me Daddy I hate you, please hold me Daddy, please love me Daddy, please touch me Daddy, Daddy, Daddy, stop hurting me Daddy, don't touch me anymore, I hate you, I love you, please hold me Daddy, Daddy, Daddy, I hate you Daddy, I love you. I love you Daddy, Daddy, Daddy, I love you." Whispering the words she had no words for in the beginning . . . as he sleeps . . . she whispers possessed by the words she did not have at the beginning, "Daddy, Daddy, Daddy. I hate you, I love you, I hate you, I love you, I hate you, I love you, I love you, I love you, Daddy, Daddy, Daddy." (119–121)

Anyone who reads that version of Lot's daughter with any care will likely have strong reactions to it. Two things that come through for me are the way a young woman can seek and find a real, if momentary, democracy of the flesh in sex and the way the entitled male can lose the conscious burden of selfhood, time, and responsibility in erotic ecstasy. Their bodies do not remain their separate possessions, nor do they seem whole without the other. But what's left after the mutual paternal and filial orgasms is the woman as child—infantilized, helpless, obsessed, abject, and mad about her need to live within the embrace of Daddy-love. Getting the seed of your father here might make you a mother, but it keeps you, in one way or another, beneath the father and still a little girl. Herron's text is wailing this old, patriarchal news from a modern daughter's fictional nowhere.

But now I, like other readers of Herron's work, or like biblical commentators on Genesis 19, am finding moral detergents to scrub away a dirty text. There is a part of Herron, like another of her spiritual mentors, Emily Brontë, that rebels against such moralizing and remains, even against her conscious aim, of the party of Dionysian eros. What seems to attract Herron and her doomed Patricia to the idea of physical incest is that it breaks down the generational and gender barriers that can make everyday life seem a jail of custard piety. Defending her incest to her sister, the nun Cynthia Jane, Patricia says, "I will have god and only god as my love" (208). When Janie tells her "God is a spirit," she replies in an updated *Wuthering Heights* vein:

I've known that god all my life, the sexless god of everything. . . . I've already stood at the top of heaven, Janie. . . . It bores me, the eternity of god is trite and dull and so painfully easy. . . . What is hard, Janie, is to get your body laid, to be somebody's bitch. If I were in heaven I would break myself. I would be Satana and carry with me my third part of heaven. Eternity is long to have only your mind and nothing else." (208)

V.
The King of Hearts

The daughters in the novel conspire in and with poetry, but Herron's new Lot is a man of science. At its best, the book is a testament of wonder, and one of its most powerful sections, the consecutive chapters "Three Witches" and "The King of Hearts" (42–71), features the reaction of the rational, well-meaning father watching his grown girls cavort together. Totally oblivious to him, they sing out black poetry, wanting, manically, to fly away on the wings of Negro spirituals. He feels excluded from the lives he sired. They dance in a circle together that he wants to break. He fears and envies their bonding in a sisterhood of poetic knowledge. He's proud of them, but he worries, as a father might, that his girls, more and more self-sufficient, don't love him. And, worse, it puts him in "hell, it was hell" (51)—he fears the sex drive that they stir in him. Watching them dancing together, in their ecstasy, involuntary desire brings "this stirring of the fire upon [his] thigh."

Herron describes him here as an almost a conventionally ideal modern African-American father, dedicated to his medical vocation, a good provider, a man who gives his wife a greenhouse and "the finer things," his daughters a pool, summer camp, education, and whatever he thinks can enrich and empower them: "you took good care of them, you watched each one as she was growing up so you could be there tearing down barriers whether it was some racist teacher at school or if they needed more money or clothes in a different style" (45). The novel is getting at a form of paternalism you see working every day: "you made them high and precious and they were all you wanted and you wanted to be like that too . . . and then they left you out . . . and since you could not be with them you would try to overpower them" (53–54).

That desire leads to the amazing "The King of Hearts" chapter in which the father, writes Herron, tries to awe and "turn them, with your surgical magic" (54). He, wanting to impress his daughters, arranges for them to watch him operate. He takes the heart out of a sick dog, gives it to his daughters to hold, then puts it back in the "bitch," who recovers. "The King of Hearts" is a monologue by John Christopher, but it hearkens back to Renaissance dialogues between Self and Soul and makes vivid the present-day controversies in cognitive studies over the nature of intelligence and humanity. The doctor presents his side of the dialogue between science and poetry, but Herron shows the dependence of each on the other. Says the father to the daughters:

You read too much poetry. And you believe the wrong things about poetry. Poetry doesn't come from outer space. Poetry doesn't descend from heaven. Give life a chance. Life is stronger than the interpretation of life. . . . Do you want to learn to believe in life? Come and see. Watch. A golden bird you say. A sick rose. A forbidden apple. Poetry. Yeats. Blake. Milton. That's all you talk about. It took blood and a flesh heart to imagine the golden bird to interpret the sick rose to envision the fruit. (57–58)

"The soul," he says, in language hailing the imperium of his scientific vocation, "is nothing but light that feeds the heart that pumps the blood that feeds the brain that talks to the heart that moves you" (60).

Then the feminist Herron, through him, offers a surprising apologia and rationalization for the history of patriarchy and its civilizing sublimations (though she mocks the jargon of vocational self-importance too). His arrogant but eloquent words make the case that the developing female agency of the last two centuries has been nurtured, not hindered, by an evolving patriarchy's organization of knowledge and professions. Female agency—daughters' intellectual liberation—depends on the scientific revolution, the fathers' intellectual seed:

[A]nd where do you think your equal rights came from anyway? They came from the progress of medicine—much more than any progress of poetry! Do you want to know what enslaved you? It wasn't somebody's idea! It wasn't intentional male chauvinist pigism! It was massive pulmonary embolus, it was complications of coronary artery disease resulting in ventricular septal defects mitral insufficiency ventricular aneurysm and sudden death. It was stenosis of the paten arteriosus coarctation of the aorta vascular rings atrial septal defects tetralogy of Fallot it was transposition of the great vessels, tricuspid atresia aortic pulmonary window ruptured aneurysm of sinus valsalva it was illness of the body. It was misconfigurations of electrons and protons. Magnetic misattractions.

And do you want to know who freed you? Shall I let you know who freed you? *WE* freed you, damn it, *we* freed you! Medicine! Doctors! We gave you the life than none of your poets could give you. We gave your thoughts a chance! We gave people a chance! Do you think we could afford to let females read poetry or write it or go to school if we needed babies! If we needed babies because the population was being wiped out in childbirth and disease! Your freedom is a luxury

I give you, medicine has given you the right to your own life, your own body—
I came that you might have life and that you might have it more abundantly.

 . . . This and this only is the Kingdom of Heaven. This is the multi-foliate
rose you keep talking about in your poetry. The Heart. (70–71)

But even celibate popes and cardinals know the rose is also the opening
of the female sex. Remember in *Beloved* how Morrison describes Paul D,
seduced by the ghost-daughter, "when he reached the inside part he was
saying, 'Red heart. Red heart'" (117), and Herron may be in dialogue here
with one of her mentors. The doctor is a desperate sublimator, trying with
science and medicine to keep from obsessing on that other "inside part"
and literally crying "Red heart. Red heart. Red heart." That, for Herron, is
the problem with males: the vital organs of women sooner or later turn out
to be the sexual parts.

Her novel here is also in subtle dialogue with Toni Morrison's *The
Bluest Eye* and with Alice Walker's *The Color Purple* and its despicable older
men. There the father-figure is, for all intents and purposes, a monstrous,
incestuous oppressor-rapist, and the move towards freedom means getting
away from male power, influence, and sex. In Herron's novel it's not so simple. One thing she's getting at in Dr. Snowdon's obsessive paternal lecture
and his "surgical magic" demonstration is the seductive force of professional competence and meaningful work. Like many other feminists at the
end of the twentieth century, she sees that science as a male enterprise has
meant a distortion. Says the King of Hearts, "My daughters mock my science, they tease my knowledge, they call me names, dream forestaller, inter-
rupter, destroyer of the temple, Daddy, Daddy, Daddy" (62). That holds the
gist of one part of Alice Walker's meaning. The more important point of
Snowdon's monologue, though, surely puts forth the view of what has been
implicit in much of my book: *in the great, unfolding modern Lot story, the
most important kind of intercourse between father and daughter is vocational,
not sexual*. The father, in his medical speech, is a mind-fucker, but even in
its intellectual brutality, that kind of intercourse can generate hope as well
as destruction. Within the narrative, the effect of the "King of Hearts" may
be to break sisterly solidarity, but its larger meaning for women is surely
(like the lyric from *A Chorus Line*) "I can do that! I can do that!" and for the
modern culture in general a proud "My daughter—the doctor!" The father's seed has impregnated the daughter's life with the appeal of the career
open to talent, regardless of gender.

VI.
Carolivia Plurabelle

Before she wrote *Thereafter Johnnie,* Herron changed her given name Carol to Carolivia. It would be fitting if she took her name to honor and identify with Joyce's Anna Livia Plurabelle in *Finnegans Wake.* Anna Livia stands for the Liffey River that flows out to sea through the Irish capital Dublin, for woman as the source of flowing life, and for multivoiced, multifaceted, beautiful and weeping female humanity. A sister says of Patricia that she "acted out . . . a mythological narration of incest and national identity" (188), which is true of Herron's writing, but, as I indicated in Chapter 2, is also true of the last Anna Livia Plurabelle's passage in the *Wake.* There the voice of the mother looking back blends into the voice of the daughter. In her own ending, Herron is influenced, I think, by the end of Joyce's Irish epic and world compendium of myths and languages, in which the mother and daughter fuse in the personified river and the ongoing circulation of water that makes and irrigates the earth. She even seems to have adopted Joyce's conception of *Finnegans Wake* as the dream of an old man dying by the side of the Liffey.

Herron tries to merge Patricia's personal story of incest and her drowning in the Potomac into a loose allegory of Patricia as a figure who both suffers and represents the corruption and demise of an enslaved America—a Lot's wife as well as a Lot's daughter. At least that's how I read the jumbled mythic narrative at the end. Patricia, diffused in the Potomac, seems to reappear in the last chapter, somehow metamorphosed into the river that has become an old mother making her way from the mountains to the ocean through a nation doomed by its basis in the system of slavery. Inherent in that patriarchal system was a racist, sexist concubinage that debauched the American heritage. The hope is literally that woman-become-river (Mother Potomac) can wash away the sins of the world. That would leave the light of the daughter, Johnnie.

Conceptually, the last chapter of the novel is blurry and chaotic. The ambitious fusions of the novel in the end remain dubious and don't quite come off, either logically or aesthetically, as Herron seems to know when she writes about Patricia's spaced-out mythologizing that destroys her ability to focus (see 187–188). But, like Joyce, what Herron is looking for is a way of showing what she has realized and come to in using the Lot myth.

She wants to remember and immortalize the abandoned mother, Lot's wife, who redeems the present by facing the truth of what has to be left behind. She wants to encompass all of national history. And above all, she wants to feminize the idea of the nation, to show that nations are produced by the interactions between fathers and daughters, and to stress that a country is not synonymous with parents—not a fatherland or a motherland—but a daughterland. The future of the nation—the future of the world—means for her, as for Joyce, the coming to life of the daughter's voice. In the largest sense, this signals a feminist politics. To love your country would be to think of it as a daughterland.

VII.
Desperately Seeking Daughterland

In this book of African-American life, Herron shows that as yet there can be no real black equivalent for the sugary white solution of the Lot complex in the sacralized girlchild—Alice in Wonderland, Maisie, Shirley Temple, and so forth. John Christopher Snowdon, with all the "advantages" he could provide, tried that formula. The daughter Johnnie, trying to piece out the meaning of her motherless, crazy life in a city, nation, and world beset by race war, indicates why history made it hard to make Shirley Temples of black girls:

What happened? Slavery happened. Africans came into bondage to Europeans in a new promised land. And males with light, bright, white skin slept with the black females who had nursed them, and slept with their sisters, and slept with their daughters and nieces and cousins and begot children—and thus began a great crime of these contending peoples of one nation. (174)

With such knowledge and such an inheritance, the desexualizing of daughters flies against a wall of history. And yet for Herron, like Morrison and Walker, the need to enunciate and find hope and innocent possibilities for daughters is not just a symbolic desire, but an urgent necessity in building a future and sustaining faith in African-American life.

Before there can be hope for the daughterland and the daughterworld, however, the Lot myth must be modified, as Herron imagines. She makes two key changes in the old story: (1) instead of giving birth to sons, the daughter gives birth to a daughter—that is, the seed of the father, which Lot's daughters preserve so that it can produce sons, here is transmuted into female issue; (2) Camille, the new Lot's wife, is not only remembered, but reanimated, and the incestuous progeny of her daughter is reconciled to her.

The concept of the daughter rather than the son issuing from the apocalyptic incest is key, but in the story Johnnie, the figure at issue, often seems amorphous—the promising "light" lost in a fog. "Alight" in the last word of the novel, she nevertheless remains for the most part a vague presence. That's my skeptical reading, and, like Herron herself, whose writing (like most important authors) can seem at war with her conscious intentions, or like Patricia, I suppose I'm at times of the party of Satana. For me, the daughterly light, life, and promise rest with the three older sisters, the legitimate daughters of this novel's Lot. Their depicted triumph is to conspire and, like their author, to revel in the eerie, wonderful, abnormal normality of their subjective perceptions and language.

When I look for evidence in this woeful tale that might carry faith, hope, and charity into a developing daughterland, I find it primarily in the intellectual curiosity and the capacity for joy of the "three sisters" generally—specifically in the sexual sensuousness and the passion for mythology of Patricia, the moral responsibility and religious concern of Cynthia Jane, and the prophetic, oracular sensibility of Eva—all of which the prose represents brilliantly.

Also, belying my put-down of Johnnie, there is one earlier, visionary image of her moving as a light through an abandoned library in Washington, the city now depopulated under threat of war. She moves through reading rooms, past card catalogs, past the map room, past stacks where they kept Milton, kept the Bible, kept prophecies of fate: Johnnie, in something like a hallucinatory trance, identifies herself with "this little light of mine" from the old spiritual. Somehow here, she is the lonely daughter, seeker, and source of illumination in a time of crisis trying to use and preserve the fragile means of enlightenment threatened by fiery destruction. For a moment, Herron can make you see and feel the mysterious daughter as the vague little light trying to preserve culture in an age of darkness—"I'm gonna make it shine."

VIII.
Rehabilitating Lot's Wife

In the rehabilitation of Lot's wife, Herron devotes four chapters to Camille —John Christopher's wife and the girls' mother. Here the active role of the grandmother in Black American lore and life becomes the means to imagine the cast-aside wife and mother of the Lot complex revitalized. Camille loves her man "Johnny-Chris" with a passionate, loving sexuality; she loves flowers ("She sows a green garden in her mind" [224]); she loves to play and touch the piano. She embraces, takes in, and protects her granddaughter of shame, the spawn of her rival, the daughter who took away the love of her life. Herron imagines a reversal in which Camille, Lot's wife, leaves Washington for the mountains. There, she writes to Johnnie, asking her to join the war refugees: "Our race could die. A catastrophe could leave isolated pockets of black folk all over the Alleghenies without interconnection. I would be a pillar of salt trying to look back toward you" (228).

But with Camille, the backward look of Lot's wife is the forward look of a woman seeking to preserve the daughter-seed of the future. Herron imagines precisely Camille's abilities to love a man with passionate sexuality; to see, feel, and hear the beauty as well as the tears of things; and to know the hellishness of life without hating it and getting her mind stuck, futureless, in the tragedy of what's happened. As so often with Herron, she unflinchingly gets at the hard truth driving the terrible, enduring myth of Lot. Camille contemplates the incest of beloved husband and daughter, and, mulling over many possible causes for it, identifies a heartbreaking reason that animates the faithless erotic history of older men turning to young women: "It's because I love him and he doesn't love me."

Herron has turned the story of Lot's wife on its head. "Remember Lot's wife" had meant the driving need to break with the past. But remembering Camille, remembering Lot's wife in *Thereafter Johnnie*, means remembering a figure that sets herself against disjunction. Even in the betrayal and horror of her experience, she looks to join with new generations of her race. Herron imagines Camille in the end giving up the status of being defined as a wife (Johnny-Chris has died and been cremated) and packing up and leaving her house, but this development—it's very murky—is rendered as an acknowledgement, not a rejection, of her historical past. In the penultimate chapter, the aging woman, rather than the father-fixated daughter or the daughter-drunk father, lives on into the new era. The idea, if not the execution in the novel's end, is clear: Lot's wife must be seen as a pillar of the potential daughterland "of the millennium" (241).

And if that's the progressive moral of the story, it does not lessen the emotional force of the novel's explicit sex. The powerful, morally ambiguous effects of the rendered incest do not harmonize the disjunctions or settle the erotic conflicts in the human soul—or, to use John Christopher Snowdon's term, "the heart." Herron, in her erotic descriptions, is a lyrical singer of sex, and yet its irresistible power and its history, epitomized for her by the affair of Lot's cave, plunges her into apocalyptic despair.

Her last half page sends the story into nihilism and chaos. After composing a folk tale in which the Potomac, both a little old lady and a river, bears away "the tormented sand" of Johnnie's "village" (Washington) and ends her "father's dream," Herron imagines an immortal Johnnie blessing the people, wishing them a "Happy New Millennium" (242). "But," says the narrator, "it came not to pass." The book concludes with the city and presumably all Northern America "eliminated by strange fire." Johnnie has become pure light, but that might well be the final light of a hydrogen holocaust.

So Herron's last vision, like so many of those who feel dispossessed, like Lot's wife, is given over to fire and brimstone. Her fixation on incest and its appalling hold on the imagination burns through her art—just like the sexual fire in John Christopher burns through his science and civility. And after imagining the flame of patriarchal incest burning up Patricia until it takes a river to quench her fire, Herron finally cannot pardon her fictional world. After such knowledge as the Lot story brings her, what forgiveness?

IX.
Herron's Recovered Memories

There is a problem in the critical discussion of Herron's work, and D. H. Lawrence's advice to readers applies: "Trust the tale and not the teller." Despite the notoriety that flared up in the early 1990s around Herron, what matters most about her is surely the power and depth of her writing. But the problem exists, and it's this: by the time she finished and published *Thereafter Johnnie*, her life had taken a turn that would bring her a sensational, if short-lived, celebrity, but would also work to keep her novel from getting the serious, continuing attention it deserves. In 1989, with the book essentially done, she began a heavy regime of psychotherapy. Though she was a successful 41-year-old professor and writer, her visionary mental life seemed strange and painful to her, and to understand why, she sought help. She put herself in the hands of a militant therapeutic community that championed and advocated the truth and explanatory power of recovered memories of childhood sexual abuse to account for adult women's troubles.[5] And when her book came out in 1991, Herron went public with a series of astounding charges of sexual and criminal abuse in her childhood.

At first, she was a media star for the recovered memory movement, but then, as journalists probed more deeply into her life and background and even interviewed "law-abiding" relatives she'd accused, many of her "memories" seemed outlandish. For example, under therapeutic authority (and very likely implicit pressure, including drug-induced "flashbacks"), she reported clear recovered memories of being raped ninety-one times before she turned 12. She said that her own aunt prostituted her as a child in a tourist home, where a man she called "Big White Daddy" often had sex with her, that she was forced to watch several murders of children by "Big White Daddy" and others, that an uncle was a cruel rapist, that her grandparents acquiesced in her debauching—and on and on in accelerating horror. None of this was corroborated. Some family members told interviewers that Carolivia had been a genius, but weird from the beginning. The overall effect of this controversy was, in the short run at least, to undermine her authority and detract from her work.

But to judge the quality of *Thereafter Johnnie* by visions, delusions, dreams, or false memories of Herron makes no more sense than to judge the quality of Blake's or Yeats's poetry by their hallucinatory supernatural encounters. The more subtle difficulty is that the phenomenon of the recovered memory movement, like her novel, is part of the ongoing history of the Lot complex. What you have (or had) in the recovered memory movement is, in part, a conspiracy of daughters trying to get out of their caves of private crisis and get free of the seductions and projections of patriarchy (see Chapter 11). And at the same time you also have the symbolic backward look of a Lot's wife at her girlhood trying to account for the devastation of the present.

Psychologist Janice Haaken, trying to account for the impossible-to-believe, fantastic nature of so many recovered memories and the larger, valid social truth she thinks they can convey, calls the process "transformative remembering."[6] Of course that's one way to define fiction and the way it's made. But if recovered memories are fiction, they're fiction with a purpose. This revised Lot story screams that patriarchy, as usual, lusts after daughters, except now the daughters are children. As you can see in Chapters 10 and 11, in the wake of "maiden tributes" such a development was predictable and, like so much in the history of Lot's daughters, all of a piece in chronicling the desire of women to move from being physical and symbolic objects to active subjects. This Lot story, however, to which Carolivia subscribed, led to intellectual backsliding, and seemed at times, like the worst of Calvin and Freud mixed up and dumbed down: the wanton, vicious sexuality of men dooms the poor girlchild to a predetermined fall into miserable womanhood. The point I mean to stress is that neither the Victorian image of the pristine girl nor the reverse image of the evil "Big White Daddy" (they are surely linked) has the depth, the analogic truth, or the explanatory power of Herron's novel.

X.
The Color Purple
versus Chiaroscuro

Obviously *Thereafter Johnnie* is not a simple story, but a complex one. *Lot* is much more than a transparent cover story for female victimization and men's sexual desires projected onto daughter figures. Herron's book pulses with lyrical, suggestive language and imagery that can expand and shake your mind and flood it with the varied, contradictory lights and darks playing over a range of possible meanings in the historical Lot syndrome. One way of symbolizing the contrast between Herron's recovered memory story and her novel—the difference in what they express—is by juxtaposing her color schemes for each: the single, solid color purple of her life against the chiaroscuro of her art.

Like Patricia, Herron seems to live in and by her personal myths, and one would seem to be an emotional identification with the sexually and culturally victimized fictional females (Celie, Nettie, Shug) of Alice Walker's *The Color Purple*. Purple in that novel is a sign of "womanish" faith in the natural wonder and beauty of creation (and implicitly, the beautiful color of embodied female sex) and thus the passionate force of oppressed women's indomitable nature and mutual love. And so it was for Herron.

Donna Britt reported (in *The Washington Post*), "From the moment she was allowed to choose her own clothes, she dressed in as much purple as she could lay hands on—today she wears a purple velvet cape, a dashiki dress the color of fresh-cut irises, violet shoes, even." The reason for this, she maintained, is that when she was a little child, in front of her grand-parents' house, there "was a large lilac bush"—underneath which Herron hid, she says now, from her rapist. . . . Even today, she explains, "the plant's lavender color represents safety, a haven." Purple, a flamboyant color and the proverbial hue of royal authority, in Herron's personal memory pro-claims and stands for the one overriding reality of the daughter's life: a reign of incestuous male sexual oppression that must be overthrown by fe-male agency bringing such abuse to light.

But in her novel, she sets against that monochrome "color purple" her "Chiaroscuro," a haunting chapter featuring Johnnie moving forward through family traumas and insanity amid striations of dark and light into new life and a mysterious, shadowed enlightenment in, of, and for the fu-ture. "I am subject to dreams and fantastic visions" (171), says this sibylline Lot's daughter at the end of the twentieth century. And chiaroscuro, "the technique of using both light and dark in representation," is the way Her-ron shows you Johnnie's outlook, which is both literal and allegorical:

Light—the marble, the ice, the fields, the rooftops. *Dark*—the sidewalks, the streets, the trees, the water. "And the towers. The towers of St. Matthew's Cathe-dral . . . the towers of the Throne of the Third Heaven, the tower of the Old Post Office Pavilion . . . the towers of the National Cathedral—all light, and the tower obelisk of George Washington. What happened? It was slavery. And white and black are so close. And dark and light are so close" (173).

Reading this phallic edifice complex description you can find a chilling, Revelation-Johnnielike prophecy in the wake of 9/11 and the destruction and massacre of the Twin Towers. This chapter shows the progeny and cri-sis of the future emerging from the sexual, racial, political, and religious contingencies of the present and from the warped, complicated psychology of an individual's childhood. More broadly, chiaroscuro typifies the mode and feeling of the whole book in which contradictions abound, black and white flicker, lights and shadows play, and amazing illuminations—sometimes contradictory—alternate with horrible darkness.

Even purple appears in a different light in the novel. When Patricia walks into the water to drown herself, her purple-loving, purple-dressed creator makes Johnnie's incestuous mother dress in the precise lavender, purple, and gold of the deadly Whore of Babylon in Revelation. There are many ways of looking at things, and the meaning of how they appear may take different shapes and colors in art. Everything can be relative (as you might expect in a novel named for the offspring of incest). The Lot complex is the source of death and fertility, bad faith and hope, obscenity and erotic ecstasy.

Big questions come out of *Thereafter Johnnie*: Is the daughter an agent in the Lot syndrome or is she simply a programmed victim? Is sex just something done to an impassive girl? Is human life inevitably warped by the often perverse biological glitch of raw male libido? What's revealing is that Herron leaves these questions up in the air, floating both "yes" and "no" answers. In the most disturbing and explicit sex scene in the novel, when Johnnie is a baby, lovesick Patricia asks her father to come to her Hilton Hotel room. For their final sexual encounter (Herron calls the chapter "The Last Time"), she puts on her mother's wedding nightgown, and when John Christopher Snowdon arrives, he has her take off all her clothes and do what he tells her. "Are you going to make love to me again? I'm afraid of you, Daddy. I don't know what you're going to do. . . . Will you make love to me again? I want you to make love to me. I don't trust you" (15). But they do not fuck. In front of the infant Johnnie, who somehow registers it all, he manually brings Patricia to orgasm. The point of view is magically articulated from the baby's perspective, apparently a traumatic "rememory" of a strange, allegorical "primal scene." But what is the allegory? With respect to physical sex, response, and anatomy, you have a woman's point of view. You don't have male gratification. There is no phallus, no climax of male seed, no rendered sexual experience except the woman's; she's seduced into the pleasure and physical high of sex through the expertise of the father.

It's finally an ambiguous chapter and an absolutely bizarre passage—an extraordinary condemnation of sexual patriarchy and a detailed rendering (even a covert celebration) of female orgasm under morally appalling, cities-of-the-plain conditions:

[T]he merciless father . . . pulls the lips of her sex together and pulls in rhythmic motions toward the curly dark pubic hair of my mother so that the soft inner flesh massages his daughter's my mother's vagina and then moves up in insistent soft patterns to the tender flesh just above her vagina right there and farther warm to the base of her clitoris my mother's where he presses the sides together slightly, still not touching his daughter's clitoris directly but urging with his brown fingers on the reddish flesh of her sex. . . . He urges his daughter's sex softly . . . palpitating steamy tenderness in which her clitoris trembles and. . . .

She does not strive or struggle because he is taking her there in his hand . . . and his five fingers coax her desire and lift her up. . . .

"Daddy. Daddy. Oh, Daddy!"

As it was in the beginning.

"PrettyPat, my darling."

"Daddy."

As it was in the beginning, is now, and evermore shall be.

"Yes, come to me my darling. Come."

"Daddy, Daddy."

"Yes."

Swirled without end, Amen. (15–17)

The contradiction is that sex is shown and condemned here as insidious paternal manipulation, and yet the controlling vision of sexual experience and pleasure has become female. The spirit and flesh of the passage, masked by the patriarch's outrageous command and control, suggest lesbian sex.

Within the logic of the unfolding narrative, the father's visit and action here doesn't make much sense. Later, you learn that he's in agony, drowning in guilt, damned and staying away from the daughter's reiterated pleas to sin again. Portrayed earlier in the story's chronology ("Three Witches," "The King of Hearts," and even "The First Time") as a conscientious, if flawed, character of talent caught up in a tragedy, here he seems to turn into a freaky, autocratic degenerate—the doctor behaving like a boss pimp reclaiming his property. But the scene is consistent with a short interpolated passage from later in the book, offering a "pat" explanation of the original sin in Patricia's craving for the father. Herron, at some point in composing the novel, decided that she needed to provide a pious moral escape clause for Patricia's incestuous passion and allow her to be read not only as daughter-seducer, but also as a helpless victim of infantile sexual abuse. When I quoted Patricia's long "Daddy" speech after their first incestuous intercourse, I omitted this significant authorial intrusion:

Shaking and trembling and no one to hold her as she shakes and trembles in her first orgasm, not this time but the first time, the first time, hidden, forgotten, violated by the touch of her father's fingers upon her two-year-old clitoris, "is it a fire you put on me Daddy . . . " (120)

So "the last time" repeats and gives closure to "the first time," which is simply an act of child molestation.

There's great difficulty about taking this "recovered memory" literally: (1) the incident is inconsistent with the character and description of Snowdon and his relations to his young daughters that Herron takes pains to imagine and show; (2) if you see the memory as realism, then this story—since few fathers are deliberate sexual abusers of their own babies—is merely the case of a nasty pervert indulging in a sordid, "bad touch" assault on an infant and therefore easy to distance from ordinary life and psychology (see Chapter 11); (3) the idea that the father's sexual molestation programs Patricia to seek him as a lover is a highly doubtful one, at best.

If, however, you read the recovered memory (and most of the incestuous sex) allegorically, look what follows: the symbolic touch of the father early on shapes the daughter's passion and she longs to be at one with him in all that he achieves, loves, and wants. She wants him and his world and shuts out the rest of life and reality. And she offers all her beauty, all her imagination, all her adoration to him in order to find identity and power in him. Such is one complex, reactionary pattern of the Lot complex that has driven life and history.

The story says that the incestuous catastrophe of the book transcends the personal, that social structure and sexuality cannot be kept apart, that we live, as a child lives, under the threat of crisis and invasion. But the female issue of the father and this daughter is a different kind of being from Patricia. Johnnie says, "I am subject to dreams and fantastic visions," the material out of which Herron, her creator, makes her art. Snowdon, with Patricia, looks at his new daughter, the little girl Johnnie.

"Why does she look at me like that?"

"It's because she's so black, and her eyes are white."

Lot's daughters: chiaroscuro.

Chapter 13

The Impeachment of Lot

THE CLINTONS,
LEWINSKY, AND TRIPP

The most famous and notorious modern instance of the Lot complex is the President Clinton–Monica Lewinsky scandal that erupted at the end of the twentieth century to make and alter American history (for instance, it helped make George W. Bush president). A tawdry affair made into a huge political affair and then flowing into cultural memory, it offers a good example of how the Lot pattern lasts and how deeply it continues to inform experience and consciousness. Though, as usual with Lot stories, people (often the very politicos and scribes who owe their position and status to the fact that it happened) try to downplay its importance, the case still provokes wonder. Moreover, as a source for books, "treatments," movies, and videos—not to mention countless jokes —it will continue to shape the imagination of the future and have an impact on relationships between older men and younger women. For one thing, it shows dramatically how the meaning of the Lot narrative can evolve. It makes clear how the story's focus on the erotic and reproductive agency of women has developed, and it features the new Lot plot in which women push to transform sexual/reproductive power into vocational and political authority. What you see when you set Clinton-Lewinsky in the context of *Lot* is a world in which gender roles become more fluid and where women's relationship to power is changing. It is, to adapt Toni Morrison's famous words at the end of *Beloved*, "not a story to pass on"—that is, it is an offensive story that might seem best kept hidden or forgotten, but actually one that ought not to be omitted, passed over, or neglected because it represents that which has shaped and does shape the history of the world and its people.

I.
The Stuff of Living Myth

The figures in the case—even and especially in their banal interactions—carry important typological significance, and already the episode has become the stuff of living myth. *Exposure* is a big part of that myth's meaning and the drama of the relationships in it I want to explore. That's why the full Lot text moved from relative obscurity into new prominence in the twentieth century. "Oral Sex in the Age of Deconstruction," Woody Allen's prophetic line from *Husbands and Wives,* not only makes a wicked epithet for the Clinton administration, it provides a capsule summary of the Lot syndrome at the end of a millennium.

Oral Sex. People are talking about what used to be hidden in the cave, the old-as-the-hills sexual behavior of various Lots and their girls. The scandal that brought on an impeachment ties right into *The Scarlet Letter,* that basic American text about a father's hidden sexual guilt, the vulnerability and redeeming power of daughters, the put-upon, long-suffering mother, and the obsessive, puritanical urge to dwell on and condemn extramarital sex. Now, however, political structure replaces religious structure as the primary medium of power and authority. Sex turns into the wagging tongues of politics, and its complex language speaks in several voices deconstructing old structures, including *Lot.*

1.
REVIEWING THE CASE

President William Jefferson Clinton (born 1946), husband and father, engaged in "inappropriate and intimate contact"[1] (oral sex and genital stimulation) in the recesses of the Oval Office with governmental intern and employee Monica Lewinsky (born 1973), a woman young enough to be his daughter. They saw one another alone on at least nineteen occasions and talked freely on the phone more than fifty times over a two-year period (though some of these conversations involved phone sex, most did not). The president could easily have broken off contact with her after two or three months (as he meant to), but he didn't. They not only aroused each other sexually, they also liked one another. They had an emotional connection, common interests, and a bizarre companionship. Both were sexually adventurous and seductive; both, love-hungry and overweight, had moved through childhood, puberty, and the life that followed driven by their sensual appetites. Both behaved outrageously for the fun of it sometimes, relishing that what they did made a farce of propriety and public decorum.

She meant different things to him. He talked to her and treated her like a friend, a confidante, a sex object, a daughter, a personified bad habit, a phone-sex voice, a problem to get rid of, a lover, and a member of the up-and-coming new generation he wanted to be part of. He wanted erotic fun and release, but he also wanted to mentor her, advance her interests, point her towards a good life, and then dump her. As for Lewinsky, it's easy to see that for a daughter who "always wanted to *be* Daddy's little girl,"[2] the point was the drive for intimacy in body and spirit with the most charismatic American Daddy of them all. Also, however, she wanted to mother the "little-boy" in him (Morton, 70). So these flawed people, caught in flagrant indecency, show as well as anybody can the bent of the Lot complex to erase generation lines.

Commentators on the affair seemed compelled to mention that Clinton had sex with a young woman hardly older than his teenage daughter Chelsea (born 1980). People were always bringing her up: "What must poor Chelsea think?" They weren't, however, looking for a real answer, which, intensely personal, would have been that the daughter was sorry for her mother, confused about her father's sex life, but still full of love and regard for him. The actual girl worried about her parents' marriage and wanted to keep them together. But the smug question conveyed another—in effect, "Where have you gone, Shirley Temple?"—and it was meant to make the daughter into that popular symbol of faith, the pure and virtuous young female. "What must Chelsea think?" reduced her from a thinking person a metaphorical seed of innocence. "Chelsea" became a term of implicit moral rhetoric to castigate her father and "Monica" (Figure 13.1). It was important that the shameful, sinning president be seen (like Lot) to be involved with two daughter figures.

In popular imagination, an older man's sex with a younger woman often gets confounded, consciously or unconsciously, with incestuous meaning, desire, and threat. If there is a "patriarchy" (that is, a patriarchal system and structure involving social responsibilities and organization, and not just a collection of men who, physically stronger than women, habitually

FIGURE 13.1 Monica Lewinsky with President Clinton in the Chief of Staff's office in 1995. AP/Wide World Photos.

push them around for selfish reasons), then, in the intercourse of a "patriarch" with a much younger woman, there logically must always be a trace of incest and guilty conflict. The plotter Linda Tripp (born 1950), Lewinsky's ruthless confidante, mused on the tapes of her phone conversations with Monica: "I wonder if he ever reflects on the fact that here he is having a fling with someone that is close to his daughter's age. And I have to say in answer to my own question, I believe a lot he's thought about that, because I think that's a great big part."[3]

Tripp, that bitter pillar of salt in the story, also wonders if he "considered someone doing this to his daughter." It's very hard for lots of people not to think of young adult women as girls and daughters. And even sophisticated moderns can still tend, at some level, to split images of young females into, on one side, nice daughters who deserve and need paternal protection and, on the other, easy-lay, disposable hotties who serve as moral warnings about bad parenting and the evils of libido. But the very fact of this split-screen focus in the full glow of postmodern publicity also works to superimpose the good-girl, bad-girl daughter figures back onto each other.

Pop psychology, according to Hillary Rodham Clinton's biographer, Gail Sheehy, tells you that "[m]en of fifty are especially vulnerable to having affairs or to starting new families when an adored daughter departs."[4] Chelsea, when her father took up with Monica, was an adolescent growing up and getting ready to go to college. Sheehy says the prospective loss of this adorable daughter was hard on him: "For years Chelsea had been his Saturday-night 'date' for dinner on the many weekends when Hillary [born 1947] was out of town" (312). "A mental health professional," Sheehy writes, "takes the Chelsea connection even deeper." Such reporting, meant to describe a particular situation, gets at a turn-of-the-century mythology that not only glorifies the blooming daughter, but makes her into the object of a continuing male quest.

On one phone tape, Tripp urges Monica to remind the president that she is scarcely older than his daughter: "In fact, that's a question you might want to ask him," Tripp counsels. "I mean, he would die rather than let this happen to Chelsea, but you're supposed to be a stoic soldier." Replies Monica: "I thought the same thing" ("Tripp Tape Excerpts," AP, 1998). They flare with resentment here at the old good-girl, bad-girl pattern. What both felt being defied and defiled was some real, if vague, new image of justice and equality for young women.

Intellectually, the case does work to break down stereotypes. The fusion of these two daughters, Monica and Chelsea, and what it might mean, does in fact signal the reshaping of gender consciousness and imagination that I'm mapping. For example, maybe "bimbos" and immaculate daughters are really sisters who need and want vocations; or maybe "bimbos" and immaculate daughters are paternalistic projections turning into mythical creatures of the past—extinct distinctions. One feature of the Lot-Scripture that gives it imaginative life is the unity of sisters. "Preserving the father's seed" as a goal for daughters could turn into a drive to realize an independent future, but now that future might no longer be synonymous with sex, babies, and motherhood. It might be more various—closer to the potential freedom of men who can choose their work.

And, as the whole episode plays out, it offers another historic fusion and variation on the *Lot* text: the regeneration of Lot's wife (Hillary) as a daughter of ambition, a survivor, and a reanimated pillar of the community. In this case, not only does the erotic daughter-figure not replace the dead wife, the wife moves to replace the husband in authority. What was the father's germ of political power can become the mother's. He may be immobilized and transfixed in the past, but she might be animated to move forward into territory where the imperative of preserving and transforming the *mother's* seed could mean hope and the chance of progress for lucky daughters.

2.

CLINTON AS LOT

When the scandal broke, people thought of the Bible and fallible patriarchs. The Reverend Jesse Jackson, civil rights leader and an adulterer himself, soothed Chelsea and Hillary by comparing Bill to King David and Samson, sacred heroes who couldn't resist sexual temptation (Sheehy, 311). And—almost too pat to be true—Clinton, feeling persecuted, brought up the Lot chapter himself and "had a very interesting analysis of the sinners of Sodom" (Sheehy, 316). He was the first, then, to bring up Lot analogies to himself, and they abound. Gregarious, an effective leader, good at persuading people, warm-hearted, brilliant, sometimes a big liar, the president was actually an outsider in the culture of Washington, D.C., the new political Sodom. He lived and prospered by cunning ability, luck, hard work, ambition, and shrewdness, but many Capitol "insiders" wanted him driven out and destroyed.

Clinton, like Lot and *not* like Abraham (no Isaac), was—and is—defined by his relationship to women, not men. Apparently a posthumous child, he never knew his father. His mother's husband, William Jefferson Blythe, a philandering traveling salesman, staggered into a ditch and drowned months before the boy's birth.[5] Two strong women, his rigid grandmother Cassidy and his flamboyant, four-times married mother Virginia, a moneymaking practical nurse, raised him. His stepfather, Roger Clinton, proved to be a feckless alcoholic whom Bill, as an adolescent, faced down to protect his mother. The boy grew up in the wide-open little city of the plain, Hot Springs, Arkansas, where gambling, prostitution, and his mother flourished.

The big trauma of his early life came when Virginia left him with his grandmother and went off to earn a nursing degree and support herself. He felt abandoned. When she returned, this high-living daughter fought her own mother in a nasty custody battle for Bill. The daughter won. Virginia came back to claim and love her boy, go to work, and prevail in her own unconventional way (in her practice she treated, among others patients, the whores of the town). She loved him, and he knew it, but the turbulence around his early life left him with compulsive hungers (like Monica). The growing son saw the daughter replacing her mother as the source of authority, saw Virginia as both a career woman and a flashy siren, and saw the advantages of having plenty of women—and different kinds of women—to take care of him. When he married, he chose Hillary Rodham, a highly intelligent, tough, stable, and ambitious woman, and she became a pillar of strength in his life.

Lot is at his equivocal worst when he offers to sacrifice his daughters to the Sodomites. The comparable Clinton moment came when the Monica story was breaking and he blurted to the media, "I did not have sexual relations with that woman—Ms. Lewinsky." Clinton, a habitual womanizer, shows how the sacrifice of Lot's daughters can stand symbolically for the use of women to feed the needs of powerful men. He met thousands of women, mentally undressed hundreds of them, hit upon (or was propositioned by) scores. But in Washington, he lived under constant media scrutiny, working at the so-called toughest job in the world. His wife was completely immersed with him in the duties of governing. The president, says Lewinsky, told her, "I have an empty life except for my work, and it's a [word deleted] obsession" (AP, 1998). She says, as if she were a modern version of the elder daughter who must minister to the father for the public good, "Every president, every [word deleted] president we have ever had has always had lovers because the pressure of the job is too much."[6]

Nearly 50, running to fat, hair turning gray, hearing and sight getting poorer, his twitchy erotic drive curtailed by marriage and the nature of his office, Clinton finds himself skulking about in a shameful cave with Monica, having and hiding forbidden sex. Momentarily, he occupies a squalid refuge from power politics and life-and-death decisions. Outside, the world is too hot and too cold, people always wanting things—his wife included—always asking or telling him what to do. Inside his head, he sometimes feels that he's running on empty, a hypocritical fool in an absurd play. Monica intoxicates him with her blatant sexual come-on. He loves sensual pleasure, and he needs to feel that he is absolutely lovable. She offers him the outrageous high of breaking taboos. Life is hard but she's easy.

These people are not the blessed or the righteous. The groping, furtive fellatio in the Oval Office bathroom, hallway, and private study, the late night masturbatory phone sex, give you a sorry Lot contorted in darkness, dignity lost. In both the ancient and modern cases, the literal accounts make the young woman the instigator. Lot, befuddled in the cave by his girls, is a hapless figure on the brink of obscurity. He doesn't even know for sure that he's had sex. And the Lot analogy with Clinton's bumbling effort to explain to others—and himself—why, in his own mind and by the letter of the law, he really did *not* have a sexual relationship with Monica, is remarkable. In retrospect, one of the most puzzling things about the president's affair with her was his refusal to have intercourse. Much to her annoyance, he even tried to keep from ejaculating. He seemed to love the thrill of dark sex; she was willing and eager to give him anything he wanted —so why no fornication? The reason seems to be that he had promised religious authorities, his wife, legal counselors, friends, and, no doubt, some internalized moral authority that he would refrain from adultery (as defined in some strange, legalistic fashion). Linda Tripp, an obsessive Clinton watcher, said of him, "He's a compulsive sexomaniac," but he needed to deny it or compartmentalize it in some psychological cavern (AP, 1998). Like Lot he was an equivocator with real, if odd, scruples, and some shaky imperative was telling him not to spill his seed wantonly—especially not in a semi-incestuous womb.

So: no presidential, patriarchal gene preservation in Lewinsky. That's one very big, *then*-and-*now* difference between the Bible story and the Clinton story, and it gets at a radical change in Lot-complex history. In their rabid prurience, the president's hostile investigators insisted on making public the most salacious material of their probe. The Starr Report details the fact that the president inserted a cigar in Lewinsky's vagina, and then tasted it. Sometimes (Freud again) a cigar is just a cigar, but sometimes, it seems, it turns into a slapstick contraceptive device. The point of the Lot's daughters passage in Genesis is a perceived necessity for the father's seed to impregnate the daughters in order to repopulate a world short of people. The point of Clinton's physical relationship with Monica was sex that would *avoid* pregnancy.

Though he wanted to be "in touch" with a member of the younger generation, Clinton as Lot, not his wife, was now the one looking back. In testimony about the case, it came up several times how much Lewinsky reminded Bill of his mother, Virginia, that rebel daughter who loved him and reclaimed him from *her* strict, stiff mother. The pull on him from different sides by those two, the "proper" woman and her fun-loving daughter, made for the conflicts and needs that would define his life as a man. That daughter was the first woman whom Clinton loved and who loved him. This mother of his, who raised him in Hope and Hot Springs (the names read like allegorical towns in a modern *Pilgrim's Progress*), made him know that sex and the love of women made all the difference and much of the joy in life. He told Monica, "You're full of piss and vinegar, just like her," and "she would have liked you. . . . You are very much alike" (Morton, 83, 87).

In the Oval Office a concupiscent, mouthy young woman was ready for fun. She also seemed soft and completely accepting. Monica wanted Clinton, planned to get him, went after him, and never said otherwise. And she didn't seem to ask for much. He had many such girls in his time, but not lately, not in the White House, where his own beloved daughter was growing up. Clinton's candid conversation with Lewinsky has a truly besotted Lottish quality: "They talked about when they had lost their virginity, about her combat boots—'Just like Chelsea's,' he noted—referring to his teenage daughter" (Morton, 72). He'd been a good and loving father to his daughter, he felt, and he wanted Monica to know about that close relationship with Chelsea.

Of course, he spoke to Monica in the time-dishonored language of the married man of affairs to the younger, "other" woman, telling her how lonely he was and how he cherished the time they spent together. But he seems, like so many husbands, to have been telling the truth. It was soothing to drop the defenses of leadership, communicate honestly about sex, about childhood, about self-doubt, about this young girl's love-life, and about—say—the awful weight of committing troops to combat. When he looked down into Lewinsky's eyes, he could see the man he loved. Even after he tried to end the relationship in 1996 and they didn't see one another alone for almost a year, he still would call her late at night to talk about life and sex. The smart thing would have been to drop her like a hot tomato. Their compulsive behavior in the White House cave would have remained hidden. But something about her intoxicated him, and she fed the need for fresh intimacy that Linda Tripp told her drove him—as it did so many men.

3.

MONICA AS LOT'S DAUGHTER

Monica Lewinsky, in the history of the Lot syndrome, may not cut an impressive figure, but for several reasons she and her case carry great social significance.

- she demonstrates that a modern young woman's assertive drive for sexual freedom can have the force and consequence of a man's;
- she shows the critical dilemma for a daughter who comes to define her identity and worth by her ability to satisfy male sexual desire;
- she stars in a melodrama about girls stuck on finding substitutes for missing fathers and father-love;
- she makes clear the need for daughters to have realistic vocational plans and options to survive in the modern world;
- through a sublime piece of farce, she makes a world-historical mockery of the whole idea of preserving the father's seed.

A bright but scattered girl, she craved the attention of older guys. As a rich and privileged child, she longed for the love and approval of her father, Dr. Bernard Lewinsky, a Beverly Hills oncologist. She wore a pink t-shirt that said "Daddy's Little Girl," and, according to her mother Marcia, that's what she "so wanted to be" (Morton, 26). But that wasn't the father's way; he tended to be distant and hard to please (like Hilary Clinton's father). When she was a high school freshman, her parents divorced. Marcia told her that her father was having an affair with a nurse at work, and Monica was devastated. Her mother got custody, but the girl fell apart. She went on compulsive eating binges, got fat, felt a mess, couldn't get a real boyfriend, botched her schoolwork, and found herself at 16 talking to therapists.

At Beverly Hills High, 17-year-old Monica first saw 25-year-old Andy Bleiler, the new "technician" in the drama department. He was no Rochester or Monsieur Heger, but he liked to flirt. Though he married an older woman in her 30s, he had affairs with students. He and Monica got involved. Her relationship with her father just then was at a low point, and she fell in love with this married man. After Andy's wife got pregnant, Monica began having sex with him, and her erotic life with him continued for years. She kept seeing him even after she went away to college. Eventually, during her last year at Lewis and Clark, he moved with his family to Portland. She made friends with his wife and babysat for the children, but still she kept having sex with him. It was an odd, addictive liaison for her, but, besides a recurrent sense of being used, she somehow got pleasure and power out of it.

It's hard to discuss the sustaining emotional payoff that compulsive sex has for some people, because, rationally considered, its joys seem so fleeting, so personal (even solipsistic), so unquantifiable and disconnected from the usual discourse and calculation of daily life. Yet the cave has its mysterious boons. Monica found worth in her very ability to give and feel deep sexual pleasure. And she felt that common, if shameful, surge of exhilaration that comes from feeling and holding—if only for the moment—the full erotic passion of someone who supposedly belongs to somebody else. Running with the married man specializing in drama, she was in dress rehearsal for the White House.

What's so striking about the 22-year-old Lewinsky's encounter with the president is her bold, conscious use of sex to get close to him—her deliberate provocation of his lust. Through her mother's influence, Monica was appointed a White House intern in summer 1995. She first saw Clinton at an outdoor reception with his wife, and there she felt his "sexual energy" (Morton, 57). She kept lining up at White House ceremonies until she met his eyes, squeezed his hand, made him aware of her D.C. groupie ardor and, in her words, "shared an intense but brief sexual exchange" (Morton, 58). The next day, his 49th birthday, she kept exchanging steamy looks with him at a White House lawn party. He gave her, she says, a full, *strip-naked* look and brushed his arm against her breast. That night she went home and read the autobiography of Gennifer Flowers, Clinton's onetime lover.

She got a job in the White House and began work on November 15. Right away she did everything she could to get the president to have sex with her. A budget fight with Congress had left only a skeleton staff in the White House, so junior employees and volunteers mixed that day with the most powerful figures in the administration, including Clinton. As she saw him walk by, she made it a point to mime "Hi." Later at a party for a staffer, the president paid lots of attention to Monica. He went into the inner office of the Chief of Staff, and when he came out, she pulled up her jacket and flashed her thong underwear for him to see. Still later, alone with him for the first time in an aide's office, she told him she had a big crush on him. They soon were kissing passionately. She tried to make clear to him that she knew the rules for affairs with married men and could be, in a sense, his secret service girl. After they went back to work, he found a way to get her alone again, and they began that history of oral sex that helped deconstruct an era.

In her biography, Lewinsky flaunts her pleasure in this first infamous tryst with Clinton and also asserts her sexual independence. She realized that he was a sexual soulmate, a fellow erotic adventurer. And she, the daughter, was surely the sexual provocateur in their relationship. Later, even when he let her down, she refused to whine about him as a sexual predator. Her flouting of public morality and dignity in the White House of course turned people against her, but maybe even more damaging was her refusal to put the blame on Clinton. She alienated those who yearned for faith in daughterly innocence (girls as cultured pearls of virtue), and she choked off potential sympathy from various political groups (feminists, Republicans, the religious right) because she would not play the sexual harassment victim.

In early 1996, Monica and the president got to know one another in the recesses of the Oval Office and during his late-night phone calls to her. She realized she could give him pleasure and erotic thrills he couldn't get from his wife. He made Monica feel that he respected her, that they had a strong emotional bond. Cynics might snigger—especially since in February, trying to end things, he told her he wanted to work on his marriage and spare his daughter and wife. But he couldn't stop calling her, seeing her, kissing her, letting her touch him—until his office managers had her transferred to the Pentagon. And still he kept up intimate phone communication with her through the rest of the election year. He told her that after the election he would bring her back to a White House job. "Why," he whined with a potentate's hypocrisy, "did they have to take you away from me?" (81).

For Monica, absence was an aphrodisiac. She at first had seen the affair as a lark, but then, especially after her exile to the Pentagon, she had time to think about it. She had severe up-and-down mood swings. He was great, she thought, and his regard made her feel lovable and important as she never before had. But as the weeks passed, in that old pattern of "the other woman," her emotional life was on hold, and, waiting for his calls, she felt deprived and empty. She was locked into her Lot complex. She began, in that time of exile, another affair with another older man, but it ended disastrously with him seeing other women and Monica stuck with an unwanted pregnancy. She had an abortion. By the end of November, sunk in depression, she went back into therapy. In December she also went to bed one last time with Andy in Portland to prove she could still enjoy—and provoke—sex. And, more ominously, she had started confiding in her friend, Linda Tripp.

4.

LINDA TRIPP AND
MAKING SEX ORAL

From the beginning of the relationship in late 1995, Monica had talked (cryptically at first, then directly) to her friends, her mother, and her aunt about Clinton. Over the eighteen months of the affair, she always meant to keep things secret, but she just couldn't. Celebrity is a public matter, and what's the point of loving and being loved by a celebrity if no one knows about it? In the Potomac wilderness does a thong snap or a sliding presidential zipper resonate if no one hears? If your compulsive drive is to be close to male power, you somehow want it known when you succeed beyond your wildest dreams. But those closest to her, when they took in the news, told her to get out of what was obviously a hopeless, dangerous liaison.

That definitely was not what she wanted to hear. Eventually she made a new friend, Linda Tripp, who sympathized with her, drew her out, and encouraged her in her romantic hopes. They had much in common. Linda, old enough to be Monica's mother, was a fellow exile from the White House, a co-worker at the Pentagon, and a binge eater. Fascinated by Clinton, she had a big picture of him on her desk and loved talking about him. After six months of friendship, Lewinsky finally told her everything, and for a year Linda became her confidante and ruinous alter ego. The fateful, compulsive conversations of these two—especially the ones that Tripp secretly taped—became the oral sex that deconstructed an administration.

Tripp stands out as a highly significant, if repulsive, figure who makes clear what a nightmarish dead end the Lot complex and myth can become for modern women. That myth, in the complexes it figures, points up, besides the possibilities for sisterly cooperation and new survival strategies, the potential for intense rivalry among conspiratorial women wanting to have and keep for themselves the father and his power. Monica, confused, longing for the president, but shut out and lonely, made Tripp into a trusted big sister. According to Lewinsky, Linda, in a perverse folie à deux, stoked her desire to prolong the affair and live out the dream. Tripp, the contemporary of both Hillary Rodham Clinton and Marcia Lewis (Monica's mother), figured not only as a bad big sister, but also as a jealous, vengeful stepmother. Displaced sibling and maternal identities and rivalries figure in this relationship. At one point on the tapes, Monica blurts out to her, "I almost called you mom." "Whew," says Linda, "this is a weird movie" (AP, 1998). It was a weirdness that she herself plotted and recorded, but such generational confusions go back to the Bible.

Tripp, embittered by a hard childhood, a troubled relationship with her father, difficulties with her own daughter, and a rocky divorce, was nonetheless a smart woman with excellent practical skills and sharp psychological insight. She had made a career for herself as one of that mid-level class of highly competent, over-qualified female office workers who keep Washington—and the world—running. She first got a job as an army secretary and then worked for the secret Delta Force, where she developed an aptitude for "insider" intrigue. Eventually she landed a job in the White House Press Office, where, working from 1990 to 1994 for Bush and Clinton, she used her talents to get into other people's business, sniff out sensational gossip, and make the contacts that would turn her into a world-class snitch.

The corridors of power (and especially its caves and tunnels of love) sparked a sensibility already smoldering with *ressentiment*. Tripp allegedly spread stories about the first President Bush and a reputed mistress and about Mrs. Clinton and Vince Foster, the White House counsel who had been Hillary's colleague and close friend (Tripp is supposedly the last person to see him alive before his suicide). In the month Monica started talking to her, the desire to capitalize on Clinton's promiscuity by using Monica took over Tripp's life.

About Bill Clinton, she felt both sexual fascination and prurient indignation—that love-hate, "scarlet-letter" potion that can drive Americans wild. According to Lewinsky, Linda had a real crush on him, and only later did she realize how jealous the older woman was. Tripp projected wildly (Monica's mother called her delusional): Hillary Clinton was jealous of *Linda* and thought *she* might be having an affair with Bill; that's why they got *her* out of the White House. Nevertheless, Linda told Lewinsky what she most wanted to hear, flattering her, playing the wise female mentor, sharing interests and intimacies—all in all, like some lumpy python, slithering her way into the girl's confidence.

She knew Clinton, she said, *knew the kind of girl he liked, and Monica was perfect for him*: "Oh, he would go crazy for you" (Morton, 96). Listening to the love-struck girl, conspiring with her, trying to get at her deepest thoughts and manipulate her, Tripp, it seemed, wanted to transcend her own identity, live through Monica, put herself at the center of things, shape events, and revenge herself on the kind of people who had made her life so hard. She was out to exploit Lewinsky, make money and news, pull the adulterous president down, and have a life of importance.

Just after the 1996 election, Monica broke down and told Linda that she'd had a real affair with the president, but now he rejected her and never called. Tripp told her she knew he would, and when he did, Monica began to put great faith in Linda's thinking. The Clinton-Lewinsky phone calls had never entirely stopped, but at the end of 1996 and the beginning of 1997, the two, in one way or another, were seeing each other again. At the beginning of the New Year it looked as if, from her conversations with Clinton, she would get a White House job. But then nothing happened. In the days and months that followed, Lewinsky says Tripp became a combination seer, controller, and endlessly patient friend, talking over every word, interaction, and nuance of feeling that went into her relationship with Clinton. Linda, for the obsessive Monica, had turned into a second self, a human diary, and—worst of all—an authority figure whose approval she desperately needed.

5.

THE END OF THE AFFAIR

On February 28, 1997, Monica found herself alone with Bill in the Oval Office for the first time in ten months. They were both feeling erotic. As they began to kiss, he warned her they had to be very cautious. He told her he didn't want to be "addicted" to her (the word betrays his Lottish intoxication). She told him how much he meant to her and how much she wanted, for the first time, to bring him to climax. He finally agreed, and she felt he was close to consummating the love between them. Later, at home, she found semen marks on the blue dress. She told Tripp everything in those days, and Linda saw it as invaluable evidence of presidential corruption.

Things deteriorated. Unbeknownst to her, Tripp was conspiring with journalists and enemies of Clinton, and some of this intrigue got back to the White House. Linda in these days was always pushing at Monica and playing on her sense of injustice. When Clinton next met her alone late in May, he told her their affair had to end. The scene was highly emotional, and they both wept. He said that in his personal life he had been a promiscuous marital cheat, and it filled him with self-loathing. A decade before he decided it would be "better for *his beloved daughter* if he and Hillary stayed together and worked on their marriage" (Morton, 114; emphasis mine). He tried to be faithful, but sometimes he backslid; he cared for Monica deeply, which made it hard for him. But he made clear he was choosing Chelsea over her, and again she was devastated.

By that May meeting, Clinton knew plots menaced him and he was trying to protect himself from a deluge of political brimstone. Clinton, after his re-election and with the nation prosperous and at peace, had maneuvered himself and his party into a formidable position, and the best way—maybe the only way—for his enemies to bring him down, was to exploit his sexual behavior and expose him as an incorrigible sinner. Monica, feeling shut out, sent him an articulate note, with one sentence composed by Tripp that could speak for both of them to the cosmos: "I feel disposable, used, and insignificant."[7] And, advised by Linda, she also wrote an impassioned, "stream-of-consciousness" letter, whose message was essentially that she had followed her heart and would give him one last chance (unwritten, but easy to infer, was "or else"). Betty Currie, the president's secretary, soon phoned to arrange a meeting in his office on Independence Day. He was harshly paternal with her at first, accusing her of threatening the President of the United States. And he called her ungrateful. Coached by Linda, she reproached him for not getting her back to the White House. But when she started crying, he took her in his arms and comforted her. He said they were like one another in their passionate temperament, and they had to watch out.

Suddenly the Fourth of July was a great day for her. He said he wished he could see her more, and he told her then he might be alone in three years after this term was over. She definitely wanted to replace his wife, but she also wanted to be his daughter, as her words show. She told him that his wife had cold eyes and went on to identify with her ultimate rival: "You seem to need so much nurturing and the only person you seem to have worth for is your daughter. You are a very loving person and you need that, and I think you deserve it" (Morton, 122). That not uncommon fantasy to be both daughter and a wife more loving than the mother was again making history.

But the mood at their meetings from then on was different. Though he still cared for Monica, he had been told that Tripp was her unnamed friend, and he asked her if Linda could be trusted. *Absolutely*, said Linda's beguiled dupe. For most of the rest of 1997, Monica was an unwitting spy being run by a master control, Tripp. Linda, in the last half of 1997, involved herself in a conspiracy with literary agent and Clinton foe Lucianne Goldberg, reporter Michael Isikoff, and the lawyers in both the Paula Jones case and Kenneth Starr's independent counsel investigation. (In the fall, an anonymous woman, alleged to be Tripp, tipped off the Paula Jones lawyers that they should subpoena Lewinsky, thus instigating the whole impeachment saga.)

On October 3, 1996, Tripp began illegally taping Monica's phone conversations, and in their talks she sought to provoke and record a candid Lewinsky talking about her secret relationship with Clinton. The goal, apparently, was to use the girl to build a case against the president. The tapes make a remarkable, if depressing, document—a debased *fin-de-siècle* electronic combination of *Les Liaisons Dangereuses* and La Rochefoucauld—with Tripp as a crude, treacherous *philosophe*, Monica as the clueless, cast-aside mistress, and both women as gossipy, demotic neo-courtiers in the D.C. power structure. Tripp, who talks on the tapes of "the void," couldn't help but reveal herself in all her conflicted acidity and foul-mouthed rage. About Clinton (and the whole phenomenon of male promiscuity), she blurts out, "I want to kick him in the nuts so that they flatten into little pancakes and he can never use them again."[8] That may not be Jane Austen, but it does get at a common, heartfelt, but often repressed and displaced twentieth-century response to the Lots, King Davids, Henry VIIIs, Lord Byrons, Kennedys, and Clintons of the world and the kind of gender relations such figures symbolize. And yet, ultimately, Tripp played the game of power-hungry *men*. She keeps referring to Clinton's daughter ("he would die rather than let this happen to Chelsea"), driving that painful comparison home to Monica. And then, like the worst kind of male sexist pig, she mocks the teenager's gawky adolescent looks in order to flatter Monica, "Well, who would want to with her?"

Though it's not always easy to take other people's romantic lives seriously, Lewinsky really did love Clinton, and the slow process of losing him for good brought her great anguish—crying fits, unstable moments, and the desperate moves of a discarded lover. During those three months of taped conversation, Monica was trying to hang on, always scheming to see Clinton, wanting his kind words, waiting for his calls, looking for his help in getting her a job in New York (the help came, but she realized she didn't much care then about any office or enterprise where he didn't work). In order to help destroy the president, Tripp betrayed Monica to people who wanted to expose the girl and make her a criminal. Linda even wore a wire so that agents could record what her friend told her, and she finally lured Monica into a trap where the isolated girl could be threatened, bullied, and harassed by Starr's zealots. She served Lewinsky up to Clinton's enemies and the media like a succulent rump roast, and they ate her alive.

6.

THE RAPE OF THE FROCK

For the historical record, the most important thing on the tapes is the talk about the semen-stained dress. Monica, giving clothes to a slimmed-down Linda in September, had shown her the infamous blue dress. In a call before Thanksgiving, Lewinsky mentioned that she had got her weight down so she could once again wear the dress, and therefore she was sending it to the cleaners. Tripp desperately objected, saying Monica didn't know what was going to happen and she had to protect herself by keeping such evidence. Why? "It's just this nagging, awful feeling I have," said Tripp, and so Monica did stow, for safekeeping, the presidential stain of honor.[9] It was the sorry, silly, crucial piece of evidence that made the impeachment of the president possible.

If you now set these figures, Tripp and Lewinsky, next to the original daughters of Lot, you get a wild, postmodern vision of both foolish consistency and epochal change. In the Bible, the first-born says to the younger "we will lie with him, that we may preserve seed of our father." The wording, keeping in mind Clinton's dried semen DNA, seems ridiculously, marvelously literal: "preserve seed"—the joke of some perverse deity. It's the perfect instance of Marx's famous line, "all great, world-historical facts and personages occur, as it were, twice. . . . the first time as tragedy, the second as farce."[10] Thinking of these two sets of paired women, I would add a corollary that world-historical figures appear over and over in the patterns and contents of people's minds down the centuries, and, in shifting perspectives, they *always* can be seen to preserve both tragic and farcical seeds. In crisis, Lot's daughters thought wrongly that their father was the only man in the world. In a way that's what Lewinsky and Tripp thought about

Clinton, and these two would lose themselves in him entirely, overwhelmed
—a cautionary tale—by the magnet of power.

In themselves, then, these two come across here as parasites lacking independent purpose and autonomy in a man's world. Abandoned by their
own fathers, both of them became utilitarian objects for other, harsh patriarchal authorities. Monica erupted into public consciousness as the ultimate roundheel in American history. For agreeing to testify in full about
her relationship with Clinton, she got legal "immunity" from the men who
persecuted her. No one, however, could give her immunity from misogy-
nistic scorn that plagues her to this day.

Linda Tripp, ironically finding the celebrity she hoped for, lived (for a
time) in infamy, a Judas of feminism. Once the scope of her betrayal became obvious, she sought refuge in proclaiming patriotism. Few believed
her, but, etymologically she had a point. As Carolivia Herron makes clear
in *Thereafter Johnnie*, the word in which she wrapped her motive, "patriotic" (deriving from the Latin *pater* and *patria*, "father," "fatherland") is
telling. On the surface, Tripp ended up serving the interests of very conservative men and forces calling themselves patriotic, but defining the nature
of patriotism narrowly. In doing the bidding of Republican strategists and
the smut-raking Office of the Independent Counsel (Kenneth Starr), Linda,
the self-proclaimed foe of patriarchal piggery, abased herself to the strictest
of fathers—politically partisan men wielding the might of the state and en-
forcing the law as they asserted it. And Tripp, as the woman who sold out
her girlfriend, became an easy scapegoat in proceedings that were sleazy
and unpopular.

Tripp took the fall for many conniving men, several of them hypocritical fathers with adulterous pasts. She meant, she said, to do her duty and
protect young women, but the legal process she joined resulted in a revealing series of images that could be hung in a misogynist hall of fame: terrified Monica cornered and trapped like a bewildered panda by bulb-flashing
papparazzi; stubborn Clinton friend Susan McDougall, reluctant Starr witness, in orange prison garb, shackled like a cop-killer for claiming fifth
amendment rights; Paula Jones, the pawn of the conspiracy and sexual harassment suit against Clinton (paid off and cut loose), in money trouble,
boxing professionally on Pay TV, absorbing punches from another tabloid
daughter, the disgraced ice-skater Tanya Harding; gross Linda herself, in
"before" and "after" professional makeover pictures; Chelsea Clinton walk-

ing between her parents towards a helicopter, desperately holding hands with each, as if to keep them from flying off in separate directions. If this is what comes of patriotism, it looks like the last refuge of women-bashing.

This whole case is marked by the symbiotic relationship between Monica and Linda, each fascinated by Clinton and moved to sexualize his aura of power. Without them together—without Lewinsky's unrestrained sexuality and without Tripp's obsession with authority and her will to politicize and punish male promiscuity—there would have been no impeachment, with all that it could and would mean for the politics of gender and American history. The literal need to "preserve seed" of the older man for the sake of her plot drove the "first-born" Tripp to use and deceive her young dupe, but the goal had changed from having sex and progeny with the patriarch to showing up the corrupt nature of patriarchal sex, getting even with men, and getting ahead personally. As for Monica, she had fantasized the giving of sex as something that could regenerate her spirit by taking in an ideal father's seed, and now here was reality—as scummy a saga as you could imagine. She snapped her thong and pretty soon she'd been coerced her into grand jury testimony about dried semen in her wardrobe. The two women are a part of history, of course, and that history may seem degraded when scientific perception can dissolve the symbolic seed of mankind into literal old cum. And yet mutual preservation of the patriarchal semen by Lewinsky and Tripp was, in fact, an act of immense significance because, paradoxically, it shows what a sterile and ridiculous idea preserving the father's seed could become.

7.
REVISING
"THE SAME OLD STORY"

Is there, after all, any special or deep understanding to be gained by comparing the Clinton-Lewinsky case—and specifically Monica and Linda—to the Lot story? My "yes" depends on this rationale: what seems inexplicable in one instance can appear comprehensible and even logical when you find and compare various examples of similar behavior over time and see the patterns and literary precedents from which they emerge. A desperate hunger and competition for love and power—and potential female outrage at the ruses of deceiving fathers—poured into the stream of consciousness from ancient caves, and its flow, shaping the landscape of culture, runs through language and literature into the offices, homes, and courtrooms of the present. Why did Tripp behave with such ruthlessness? What really made her decide to savage both a girlfriend who trusted her and the greatest man she'd ever known—each of whom she "had a crush on"? She had many reasons, but most relate to resentments figuring in the Lot myth.

Among the pageant of Lot's daughters, you have several examples of startling cruelty (even sadism) that even now leave audiences puzzling with wonder. In *King Lear*, what makes Goneril and Regan behave so viciously to their father, their sister Cordelia, and to each other? What motivated Emily Brontë to write Heathcliff's words about the innocuous characters he plots against, "I have no pity! I have no pity! The more the worms writhe, the more I yearn to crush out their entrails! It's a moral teething, and I grind with greater energy, in proportion to the increase of pain" (118)? Why did Charlotte Brontë in *Jane Eyre* make Rochester's wife a mad beast, burn her up, and blind and scar her aging hero in deadly fire, before he comes, in the end, to impregnate a young woman half his age? In Dickens's *Great Expectations* why does Miss Havisham plot to destroy children's love and hope, and why does the fixated old woman finally have to burn to death? Why did Freud's Dora so despise her mother or seek revenge on the doctor who thought he was trying to help her? Why did Mia Farrow accuse Woody Allen of child molestation? Why did Herron turn a good father into a monster? And why did Linda Tripp toy with Monica like a cat with a mouse? Set against *Lot* and one another, these questions are as easy to figure out as the destiny of hot lava in a volcano.

When a man with two (or more) daughters is intoxicated by the charms of one, imagine what the other feels. Think what it can be like for an aging woman to be obliterated in a man's regard and replaced by younger women. Or imagine the surge of idealistic disdain when a father-identified girl sees an ambitious, worldly older woman exploiting a husband whom she doesn't love or care for. Explosions will happen, and the social terrain will change. You can see why Monica and Linda, the Tweedledeepthroats of the Oval Office follies, have, in fact, made history.

The truth would seem to be—despite the partisan irresponsibility and immoral, anti-democratic forces that Clinton's impeaching enemies set loose with "Monicagate"—that, in the kaleidoscope of time, Lewinsky's plight represents as benighted and unjust a social condition as the feudal droit du seigneur, and Tripp's anger and righteous pose are, in some sense, fully justified. Ironically, by setting such bad examples, these two did help spawn a progeny of hope and progress for women and gender relations: things should and could be better and fairer. I quote Marx again, changing his word "men" to "women" and applying the statement to Lewinsky and Tripp: "[Women] make their own history, but they do not make it just as they please; they do not make it under circumstances chosen by themselves, but under circumstances directly found, given and transmitted from the past" (595).

II.
Hilary and Chelsea Clinton:
The Wife's Quest for Authority;
The Redeeming Daughter

How can humanity's Lot complex be resolved? As long as family structure and natural reproduction persist, it can be resolved only through the muck of people working through their individual lives. Piously and pedantically, perhaps, but accurately, it seems possible to say and see that a successful resolution of the historical Lot complex has, does, and will depend upon finding ways

- for women to lead lives that make them more than bearers of their fathers' lives and values into the future—more, that is, than creatures merely relative to men;
- for fathers to honor daughters and respect, support, and take joy in their independence and potential accomplishments;
- for aging women to find the means to power, relevance, and fulfillment in the world and in their own minds in order not to get petrified in and by the past;
- for daughters to reconcile their quest for agency with the lives of their mothers.

Predicting the future, of course, is like analyzing the fog, but I do see positive aspects in the Clinton impeachment fallout and, through and beyond that, hope for the Lot story as it moves into the twenty-first century. "Every limit is a beginning as well as an ending," says George Eliot, and the former president's wife Hillary and daughter Chelsea, in aspects of their visible lives, can stand, at the limit of the millennium, as signal figures in the evolving epic. They are, of course, living people, not characters or figures fixed in language or history, and no one can really know for sure the deep psychology, the moral worth, or the ultimate significance of the Clintons (or any living celebrities). But the visible life of public figures (what you can see and read) does count, does have real meaning, because it reflects, projects, and symbolizes strong social currents and desires churning in the world.

1.
THE WIFE

Like Lot's wife, Hillary is known by her husband's name and, for most of her adult life, by her relationship to him. She has had her own Lot complex to resolve. She internalized her father's iron will, his work ethic, his drive to succeed, and his passion to exercise authority. A tough man, difficult to please, Hugh Rodham trained Hillary to compete hard, not to whine, to be a doer and excel in life. From him, a conservative Republican, she first got her interest in politics (a Goldwater Republican in 1964, she did not become a liberal until the late '60s). He taught her to be strong, made her believe that her efforts mattered, and imbued her with a sense of her own special talents. He was a demanding father, not given to praise his children, but he made her feel that she must (and could) attract and then stand up to the male gaze that would become crucial for smart girls in the last third of the twentieth century—not the gaze fixing them as desirable sexual objects, but the one evaluating them for vocational promise and ability. People remarked all through her adolescence, youth, and into her middle age that Hillary just didn't much care how she looked, and the reason was that what mattered to her, like her father, was what you knew, what you could do, and how well you did it—not whether you looked pretty.

Her father's sense of competition, which he passed on to her, seems to have included her. Somehow, in his closed-mindedness, he saw her, his most capable child and the one most like him, as a rival—and a female one at that. Hillary resented her father's autocratic manner, but the lesson she absorbed from him was that power was good. To get authority, she learned from living with this man, you had to attach yourself to authority.

She now lauds her mother, Dorothy Rodham, but it's clear that growing up she was father-identified and wanted to outstrip both her mother and her two younger brothers.[11] And when she realized how hard it was to get her father's approval, she wanted to beat him too. What she got from her mother was love and the permission—indeed an implicit plea—to make her own life better than her mother's. Dorothy had been an emotionally battered child of divorce, and she taught Hillary that marital breakup was disaster: the woman must keep things together and hold on to her husband at almost any cost. The lesson obviously sank in.

Different roads to power and modes of power fascinated her. As a teenager, she let herself come under both the liberal influence of a socially conscious young Christian minister and the conservative sway of a zealous, right-wing history teacher. She was interested in what both men had to teach about their different realms of historically male-dominated authority—moral faith and political struggle—and she basked in their approval.

Her academic ability got her to a prestigious women's college, Wellesley. There she became a leader among ambitious daughters in a time bursting with feminist aspiration. Besides a burgeoning women's movement, the era featured the rebellious "greening of America" with its historic Vietnam, racial, and sexual protests. To be conservative and Republican was not the way to power for youth in this time of change, and Hillary changed.

She made a brilliant record in college. Eventually she won her class presidency, and, as the first student in college history to speak at the formal graduation ceremony, she gave a rousing, radical farewell to Wellesley. From there she went to Yale Law School, following a common American road to power. There she excelled, and there also she met Bill Clinton and fell in love with his erotic and political charisma.

She knew Clinton was aiming very high—the top. He would try to get it by winning elections, and his immense ambition and charm moved her. She felt that he would be extraordinarily successful and that they complemented each other: she was organized, he was spontaneous; she could control her emotions; he had heart and fire; both of them were strong-willed, brilliant, hard-working, and eager to run things, and they loved each other and respected their mutual hunger for power.

Hillary began her career as a formidable young Washington attorney (she quickly proved herself an effective advocate for children's welfare), but, against the advice of friends and colleagues, she followed Clinton to Arkansas and married him. She loved him and bet on him as her best means to fulfillment. People warned her about both Bill's sexual hustling and the drawbacks of an alien, backwater culture. But she tied her future to the man's and even took his name.[12] Power, she felt, still usually came through the male. And this one, she judged, was a rising star who would make her a full partner in his political ascent.

He trusted her, they strategized together, and it all worked out. She had her own successful legal career and, beyond that, exercised political authority, though not, strictly speaking, in her own name. They even managed to have a daughter who brought them joy. This team, then, with lots of ups and downs and bumps and grinds, turned their hopes to reality in Arkansas, and, just as they planned, they used the governorship as a rocket booster to the Clinton presidency ("You get two for one," said Bill in 1992).

Clinton, however, had always lied to her about sex with other women. His philandering was notorious, but most of it she didn't know about—or ignored. And when he went into abject bouts of repentance over cheating she did find out about, she would somehow manage, sooner or later, to forgive him. She said during the 1992 presidential campaign that she was no Tammy Wynette (performer of "Stand by Your Man"), but she was. Why didn't this strong, capable woman end the marriage in the 1980s, as she thought about doing? One reason was that she loved her husband and another was that she had built her ambitions for power into their relationship. Also he loved and needed her, told her so, and made her believe it. Moreover, this warm man had given her the kind of effusive esteem she craved but did not get from her father, *and* Clinton was also what her father most valued: a winner. Chelsea, their daughter, undoubtedly was a major reason why she stuck it out. Her mother and her own experience convinced her that a girl, to reach her full potential, needed bonding with both father and mother—two parents who can stay together and care for the child.

The Monica explosion, however, came as a catastrophe and threatened to ruin their lives. Her partnership with Bill had lasted, she thought, into settled middle age and achieved for them extraordinary power and success, but suddenly it looked hopelessly compromised. The president's infidelity and Starr's decision to publicize to the high heavens the sexual details of the Clinton-Lewinsky affair threatened to turn her into a real Lot's wife, wedded to the past and left behind. She had attacked the Starr probe as a right-wing vendetta and, until the semen stain made his lie palpable, defended her husband passionately. People felt sorry for her, but the media commentary talked of her in tones of patronizing superiority: *she was an*

enabler; she should have divorced the creep years ago; she made a devil's bar-
gain; she needs our prayers in the wreckage of her marriage; this is what hap-
pens when women put career before marriage; this is what happens when
women don't put career before marriage—and so on.

What she chose to do and did marks a key point in the story of Lot's daughters. This woman and wife determined not to get paralyzed by and in the past. She knew that if she simply stayed in the White House playing the stand-by-your-man role for rest of the term, or if she somehow cut herself off from public life and lived in a cocoon of pity and virtue, she would still be defining herself by her relationship to her husband and his behavior. She needed to act positively on her own and move forward. After the successful defense against the impeachment efforts, she made her major decision: she would run for senator in New York, a place where neither she nor Bill had ever lived. With all the practical effects of that choice, I want to stress its symbolic significance as both a remembrance and a transcendence of Lot's wife.

Hillary's move surprised people. She was severely criticized: she was a carpet-bagger who couldn't win; a chilly, arrogant, unfeminine politico trading on both the treacly sentiment for a so-called wronged woman and her husband's famous name; she was using the electoral process for both psychotherapy and revenge; she should wait and run in either Illinois (her father's state) or Arkansas (her husband's state), where seats would open up a few years later. All that, however, missed the big picture for women's history: this very prominent, mature woman was not looking back in a time of crisis but taking the lead. She could, with her political vocation, outlast and defeat the sex-obsessed Clinton haters and make her acquiescent, contrite husband a part of *her* future career.

I want to repeat my major theme, which is not about whether Hilary Clinton is good or bad or whether she proves to be a memorable or trivial political figure. It is this: in the massive volume of rolling social history from biblical times to the present, her example serves as a parable for the idea that a woman needs to and can find ways of increasing her power and gaining great authority in the world by developing and using special vocational talents even while aging and losing those ancient sources of feminine power: reproductive capacity, sex, and the physical attractiveness of youth. She could move beyond both the necessary, earlier dependence on men for career opportunities and the public and private obsessing about sex and gender matters that hovers around ambitious women's lives and fate. History and modern American life were opening up hopes of power and agency for professional female politicians, and Hillary had been a model for the potential fulfillment of those hopes. New York was new territory, not old—neither her father's nor her husband's state. In retrospect, it was just the right place for her to run and win—a place where her liberalism and feminist bent could best help her. It turned out that she could take the patriarchal seeds in her life—the father's tough will, her longing for the vocation of politics, her husband's position, connections, support, and the sympathetic victim's role in which his adultery cast her—and make them hers.

Hillary, a Lot's daughter buoyed by the history of Lot's daughters, did not turn into a Lot's wife, and that fact becomes a big part of the whole problematic, disturbing, but progressive Lot story. Implicit in Lot-complex history lies unease with women's status and a quest for better and more honest gender and generational relationships on which to sustain faith and civil society. The tension between the Lot-Scripture and the fundamental patriarchal scripture of Abraham's willingness to sacrifice Isaac (females as well as males make the key decisions) and between the Lot myth and Oedipus myth (destiny is with daughters as well as sons) belongs to the same long human epic as the tension through which a humiliated older woman takes power and bonds with an ambitious daughter.

2.

THE DAUGHTER

The image of Chelsea is of a young woman who grew up having a strong, loving relationship with both her father and mother. The Clintons hoped to raise her without the distortions that celebrity brings, but they also wanted their child to learn about the concerns and values of the public life they had chosen. They shielded her from media glare, but they didn't hide her away from the family business. Hillary, a feminist with a professional interest in child-rearing issues, took seriously the education of the girl, and Bill found in Chelsea a cherished being for mentoring and camaraderie. All accounts stress her closeness to him and his delight in her. Since she was his only child and he had no son, he could get free of much of the gender-stereotype projections that fathers often inflict on their children. In his dealings with her, he could be warm and responsible, and he didn't have to be seductive or a liar; he could resolve the contradictions about females that churned his mind.

When the Monica crisis came, he could find a new integrity in his relationship with his daughter and put in stark perspective the needy lechery that marked his feelings about women. The appeal of the real daughter came, for a while, to overshadow the appeal of other younger women. The daughter—and this is a positive side of the Lot myth—could lead him "away from the city of destruction" (temporarily, anyway). As for her, she had to see her father as a flawed human being, not a symbol of authority, and to realize her own independence from his authority, a very difficult thing for a daughter to do.

This father-daughter relationship exists in a rich cultural context of redemptive Lot's daughters. In it, you can see and project, for example, the sweetness and promise, amid painful family turbulence, of the father-daughter reconciliations in the later Shakespeare plays, and you can find signs of moral redemption similar to what you get with *The Scarlet Letter*'s sinning hero acknowledging his daughter. Like the Brontë sisters, she can see and identify with her father's vocational goals and ideals, but without enmity towards the interests of other women. And like Carolivia Herron's figures in *Thereafter Johnnie*, her developing sense of self and life are bound up with both her father's disgrace and the revived sense of apocalyptic possibility that the 9/11 attack brought home.

While the Monica scandal was brewing and breaking, Chelsea Clinton was living a supposedly "normal" life at Stanford in the guise of a regular student, privacy protected. She attended classes, read texts, wrote papers, passed courses, mixed with the other students, made friends, and sought out professors in their office hours—all with secret service agents discretely watching out for her. She studied, among other subjects, Dante, the Bible, Shakespeare, the Brontës, and the history of FDR. She dated, went to parties, but, as a daughter of famous, brainy, work-obsessed parents, she knew she was expected to find and have her own vocation. People speculated: would she go to medical school, law school, or, like her father to Oxford for post-graduate work? Would she would try to redeem the father she loved by following him and her mother into a political vocation. She lived with the pressure to achieve.

I don't wish to sentimentalize Chelsea Clinton or predict a happy future for her (she certainly might get stuck looking back at the wrong time). The biblical rain of fire and brimstone makes terribly clear the uncertainty—and the treachery—of the future. And bathed in privilege, she is by no means a typical young woman. But neither were Lot's girls, and I do mean to call her, in her visible life, a new Lot's daughter. She makes clear the potential in this vital myth. A jogger like her father, she would often run in the hills above Stanford, but she would not be running alone. A second woman, just a little older, would run with her, and at the waist of her companion's sweatsuit, you could see a bulging holster. This woman was protecting the daughter. Until the late twentieth century, the second runner would not have been female, and the daughter would not have been running like her father. The symbolic vision I see here is of a long history of women moving from the conspiracy of the cave to running where they want.

Let me now put in a very positive light the image of Chelsea in which I before saw a daughter desperately coping: the news photo of her between her parents, holding hands with each, heading off on a "family vacation" during the height of the scandal. She is not choosing between them, but making a public demonstration of her love for both. She is the main figure of action in the picture, and, revising the Lot complex, she does not replace the mother in joining the father, but joins with them both to preserve the hope and good spirits of the past into a new time. She is much more than an icon of wholesome innocence or an objectified relic of family values. She looks to be taking responsibility for the future. She is here the redeeming daughter trying to keep things going, but she is neither idealized nor sexualized. Thinking of Hillary Clinton's book about the plight of children in the modern world, *It Takes a Village*, you could say it takes the history of Lot's Daughters to raise the Chelsea of this photograph (Figure 13.2).

She gave a revealing interview shortly after the 9/11 Manhattan cataclysm to *Talk* magazine and its editor Tina Brown. Chelsea was in New York the day when the struck towers burned and fell, and she reflects on how the disaster razed the security and peace of mind that she, like so many, had taken for granted. In confessing fear, she sounds a little like a postmodern cities-of-the-plain refugee, "I do not think it is out of place to divide my life into before and after the 11th."[13] Her father was in Australia, and when he returned, "*she* was anxious to bring him to Manhattan, *knowing* 'he would want to connect with everyone who was confused and suffering, *including*

FIGURE 13.2 Chelsea Clinton holding her parents together in 1998. AP/Wide World Photos.

his daughter.'" That sentiment conveys the bond between them, and it can stand for a continuity of benevolence in the private, familial relationship on which a public culture depends.

This daughter, in the interview, also referred to another key transference in resolving the Lot complex: the ability to move beyond the equation and identity of power with the father. In the wake of the killing, she paid tribute to Hillary Rodham Clinton. In the modern resolution of the Lot syndrome, no words are more pregnant or imply more than these: "I thanked God my mother was a senator representing New York." The daughter of a powerful father could put faith ("I thanked God") in her mother's leadership in a time of crisis. The working through of female ambitions, disillusions, and agency, and of paternal ambivalence, weaknesses, desires, and positive sublimation makes the story of Lot's daughters live in language, in personal life, and in the continual remaking of the world.

Notes

Preface

1. Bill Clinton, *My Life* (New York: Knopf, 2004), 182.

Chapter 1

1. Martin Luther, *Lectures on Genesis: Chapters 15–20*, vol. 3, *Luther's Works*, ed. Jaroslav Pelikan (St. Louis: Concordia, 1955), 305.

2. For reference purposes, see Appendix for Genesis 19, the Lot chapter as it reads in the King James translation of the Bible.

3. The early Christian Origen records a fantastic allegorical interpretation that reads Lot as God and his two daughters as the Old and New Testaments. See Origen, *Homilies on Genesis and Exodus*, trans. R. E. Heine (Washington, D.C.: Catholic Univ. of America Press, 1982), 120: "But I know that some, so far as the story pertains to allegory, have referred to the person of the Lord and his daughters to the Two Testaments. But I do not know if anyone freely accepts these views who know what the Scripture says about the Ammonites and Moabites who descend from Lot's race (Deut. 23:3; Exod. 34:7). . . . We pass no judgment on those who have been able to perceive something more sacred from this text."

4. Some of this material appears in my article, "The Lot Complex, Joyce, and the End of *Finnegans Wake.*" *The Recorder: The Journal of the American Irish Historical Society*, 7, no. 2 (1994): 58–77.

5. Immediately after "Remember Lot's wife," Jesus says, "Whosoever shall seek to save his life shall lose it; and whosoever shall lose his life shall preserve it" (Luke 17:33). In the very next chapter, he says, "Suffer little children to come unto me, and forbid them not: for of such is the kingdom of God. Verily I say unto

you, Whosoever shall not receive the kingdom of God as a little child shall in no wise enter therein" (Luke 18:16–17).

6. My focus is on Lot's daughters, not Sodom's sons or Gomorrah's daughters, worthy subjects from Genesis 19 that also call for study—and are getting it. Nor do I center this book primarily and definitively on Lot's wife, though the subject of the daughters' relationship with the mother figure is crucial and inseparable from any serious consideration of young women.

7. For provocative discussion of the father-daughter relationship, see Sandra Gilbert, "Life's Empty Pack: Notes toward a Literary Daughteronomy," *Critical Inquiry* 11, no. 3 (1985): 355–384; Paula Marantz Cohen, *The Daughter's Dilemma: Family Process and the Nineteenth-Century Novel* (Ann Arbor: Univ. of Michigan Press, 1991); Lynda Boose and Betty S. Flowers, eds., *Daughters and Fathers* (Baltimore: Johns Hopkins Univ. Press, 1989); Judith Lewis Herman, with Lisa Hirschman, *Father-Daughter Incest* (Cambridge, MA: Harvard Univ. Press, 1981).

8. To adapt a phrase of Eric Auerbach, "it's fraught with background" and history. See Ilana Pardes, *Countertraditions in the Bible: A Feminist Approach* (Cambridge, MA: Harvard Univ. Press, 1992); and Harold Frisch, "Ruth and the Structure of Covenant History," *Vetus Testamentum* 32, no. 4 (1982): 425–437.

9. The putative female fantasy projections of the violent death of the mother in the so-called Electra complex, psychoanalysis's terminologically and conceptually impaired offshoot of Oedipus, seem very dubious. Electra seeks to avenge her *dead* father, a very different familial configuration from the much more basic, common Lot complex I'm illustrating.

Chapter 2

1. *Finnegans Wake* scholar Adaline Glasheen (*Third Census of Finnegans Wake* [Berkeley: Univ. of California Press, 1977]) writes, "in FW almost any 'Lot' or 'Blotto' or 'Lout' may refer to Lot" (173).

2. Ezra Pound apparently sparked Joyce's interest in the Lot story. In 1920, when Joyce was thinking about what he would write after *Ulysses*, Pound gave him his own new book, *Instigations*, which features a disparaging but important reference to the Lot material in Genesis. What grabbed Joyce's attention was Pound's claim for the superlative interest of the story: if Pound, Joyce's mentor in worldly matters at this time, said the Lot story was the most extraordinary thing recorded in the ancient past, then it must really be worth looking into.

3. See Carol Loeb Shloss, *Lucia Joyce: To Dance in the Wake* (New York: Farrar, Straus & Giroux, 2003).

4. James Joyce, *Finnegans Wake* (New York: Penguin, 1967).

5. See Margaret Anne Doody, *Frances Burney: The Life in the Works* (New Brunswick, NJ: Rutgers Univ. Press, 1988), 35–36.

6. Frances Burney, *The Wanderer; or, Female Difficulties* (London: Pandora, 1988), xxi–xxii.

7. Fanny Burney, *Evelina; or, The History of a Young Lady's Entrance into the World* (London: Oxford Univ. Press, 1968), 1.

8. George Eliot, *Silas Marner: The Weaver of Raveloe*, ed. Terence Cave (Oxford: Oxford Univ. Press, 1996), 190–191.

9. Nathaniel Hawthorne, *The Scarlet Letter*, 3rd ed. (New York: Norton, 1988).

10. For instance, in *The Old Curiosity Shop*, the abused little servant girl called "the Marchioness," replacing her apparent mother Sally in the life of equivocal Dick Swiveller and turning into the agent of his moral salvation, grows up as his ward to marry him; and in *Little Dorrit*, Amy, eclipsing bad Mrs. Clenham and silly Flora Finching (based on the first woman Dickens tried to marry, Maria Beadnell, whom he found ridiculous in middle age) revives Arthur Clenham. So it goes in most of Dickens. He inscribed what he had found in himself: a moralized, constructive Lot complex, under control, more or less purged of genital libido.

11. See my "The Favorite Child: *David Copperfield* and the Scriptural Issue of Child-Wives," in *Homes and Homelessness in the Victorian Imagination*, ed. Murray Baumgarten and H. M. Daleski (New York: AMS Press, 1998).

12. See Hilary M. Schor, *Dickens and the Daughter of the House* (Cambridge: Cambridge Univ. Press, 1999) for illuminating, perceptive discussion of Dickens's imagination of females in his fiction.

13. Fred Kaplan, *Dickens: A Biography* (New York: Morrow, 1988), 378; see also Claire Tomalin, *The Invisible Woman: The Story of Nelly Ternan and Charles Dickens* (London: Viking, 1991), 108.

14. Charles Dickens, *Great Expectations*, ed. Angus Calder (London: Penguin, 1985), 322.

15. For discussion of aging women in Dickens, see Carolyn Dever, *Death and the Mother from Dickens to Freud: Victorian Fiction and the Anxiety of Origins* (Cambridge: Cambridge Univ. Press, 1998).

16. Henry James, *What Maisie Knew*, ed. Paul Theroux (London: Penguin, 1985), 118.

17. Some of this discussion of erotic pedagogy appears in my "A Jamesian Sentimental Education: *What Maisie Knew*: French Literature and Sacred History," in *The Erotics of Instruction*, eds. Regina Barreca and Deborah Morse (Hanover, NH: Univ. Press of New England, 1997), 116–126. For more discussion on the subject see also Julie Rivkin, "Undoing the Oedipal Family in *What Maisie Knew*," in *The Turn of the Screw and What Maisie Knew: A Casebook*, eds. Neil Cornwell and Maggie Maline (New York: St. Martin's, 1998), 194–219. Especially

helpful is Neil Hertz, "Dora's Secrets, Freud's Techniques," Chapter 7 in *The End of the Line: Essays on Psychoanalysis and the Sublime* (New York: Columbia University Press, 1985).

18. Sigmund Freud, "Some Psychical Consequences of the Anatomical Distinction Between the Sexes," *The Freud Reader*, ed. Peter Gay (New York: Norton, 1989), 673.

19. Breuer, Joseph, and Sigmund Freud, *Studies on Hysteria*, ed. and trans. James Strachey, with Anna Freud (New York: Basic Books, 2000), 40–41.

20. *The Freud Reader*, 76n7.

21. Elisabeth Young-Bruehl, *Anna Freud* (New York: Simon and Schuster, 1988), 15.

22. James Joyce, *Ulysses: The Corrected Text*, ed. Hans Walter Gabler with Wolfhard Steppe and Claus Melchior (New York: Random House, 1986), 50.

23. Virginia Woolf, *Moments of Being*, 2nd ed., ed. Jeanne Schulkind (London: Hogarth Press, 1985), 108.

24. Vladimir Nabokov, *The Annotated Lolita*, ed. Alfred Appel, Jr. (New York: McGraw-Hill, 1970), 327n6.

25. Toni Morrison, *Beloved* (New York: Penguin, 1988), 116–117.

26. I will explore this subject at length in discussing Carolivia Herron and her extraordinary novel *Thereafter Johnnie* in Chapter 12.

27. Joyce Lore-Lawson, "The 'Real' Lessons of Sodom and Gomorrah," Open Forum, *San Francisco Chronicle*, sec. 1, September 2, 1993.

Chapter 3

1. See J. A. Loader, *A Tale of Two Cities: Sodom and Gomorrah in the Old Testament, early Jewish and early Christian Traditions* (Kampen, Netherlands: J. H. Kok, 1990), 140:

> All the contributors to the perpetuating of the tradition are united in that they share a common heritage. But their varying religious, philosophical, theological and historical backgrounds made varying demands upon their abilities to use the heritage. For this very purpose, however, these settings within which they worked also provided them with the interpretative perspectives on the tradition. That is how the reception and re-creation of traditions work. That is how they are kept alive.

Add "biographical," "psychological," and "sexual" to his list of "backgrounds," and Loader gives you here a fine summary of how the study and transmission of literature, art, and, indeed, the human imagination in general works.

2. Joshua Benjamin Kind, *The Drunken Lot and His Daughters: An Icono-*

graphical Study in the Uses of This Theme in the Visual Arts from 1500–1650 (PhD diss., Columbia University, 1967), 34.

3. Robert Davidson, *Genesis 12–50* (Cambridge: Cambridge Univ. Press, 1979), 78. See also Claus Westermann, *The Promises to the Fathers: Studies on the Patriarchal Narratives*, trans. David E. Green (Philadelphia: Fortress Press, 1980).

4. See, for example, *The JPS Torah Commentary*, ed. Nahum M. Sarna (Philadelphia: Jewish Publication Society, 1989), 134; and Davidson, *Genesis 12–50*, 78.

5. Origen, *An Exhortation to Martyrdom, Prayer, First Principles: Book IV, Prologue to the Commentary on the Song of Songs, Homily XXVII on Numbers*, trans. Rowan A. Greer (New York: Paulist, 1979), 180.

6. Origen says, almost wistfuly, "As we have been able, we have carved out these explanations according to the allegorical understanding of Lot and his wife and daughters. We pass no judgment on those who have been able to perceive something more sacred from this text. *Homilies on Genesis and Exodus*, trans. Ronald E. Heine, The Fathers of the Church 71 (Washington, D.C.: Catholic Univ. of America Press, 1982), 120.

7. J. Martin Mulder, "Sodom and Gomorrah," vol. 6, *The Anchor Bible Dictionary*, ed. David Noel Freedman (New York: Doubleday, 1992), 102.

8. For example, in the apocryphal Wisdom of Solomon, Lot is a good man, but in the Book of Jubilees, "Lot is severely judged as the arch-example of incest" (Loader, 78); "Philo thinks he was unreliable, rebellious and moody" (90); but Josephus extols the virtue of Lot and says that the daughters "thought the whole of humanity was dead and that they therefore acted in good faith to preserve the human race," and besides, "Lot knew nothing of what was happening" (103).

9. *Genesis Rabbah: The Judaic Commentary to the Book of Genesis*, vol. 2, trans. Jacob Neusner, (Atlanta: Scholars Press, 1985), 229.

10. In Paul Hallam, *The Book of Sodom* (London: Verso, 1993), 105–108, *Selections from The Talmud: Being Specimens of the Contents of That Ancient Book, Its Commentaries, Teachings, Poetry and Legends*, trans. H. Polano (Philadelphia: Claxton, Remsen and Haffelfinger, 1876).

11. Mulder quotes the *Targum Pseudo-Jonathan* in "Sodom and Gomorrah," 102.

12. See Anne Michele Tapp, "An Ideology of Expendability: Virgin Daughter Sacrifice in Genesis 19:1–11, Judges 11.30–39 and 19.22–26," in *Anti-Covenant: Counter-Reading Women's Lives in the Hebrew Bible*, ed. Mieke Bal (Sheffield: Almond Press, 1989); Phyllis Trible, *Texts of Terror: Literary-Feminist Readings of Biblical Narratives* (Philadelphia: Fortress Press, 1984); and Mieke Bal, *The Politics of Coherence in the Book of Judges* (Chicago: University of Chicago Press,

1986). See also Sharon Pace Jeansonne, *The Women of Genesis: From Sarah to Potiphar's Wife* (Minneapolis: Fortress Press, 1990)

13. Augustine, *Contra Faustum*, *A Select Library of the Nicene and Post-Nicene Fathers of the Christian Church*, vol. 4, ed. P. Schaff (Buffalo: Christian Literature, 1887). See Kind, *The Drunken Lot*, 55.

14. Anne W. Lowenthal, *Joachim Wtewael and Dutch Mannerism* (Doorn-spijk, Netherlands: Davaco, 1986), 92.

15. Lowell Gallagher, "Lot's Wife and the Perversions of Cultural Memory" (Faculty Working Paper, University of California, Los Angeles, n.d.)

16. In Hallam, *The Book of Sodom*, 195, from "A Strain of Sodom," *The Writings of Quintus Sept. Flor. Terullianus*, vol. 3, trans. Rev. S. Thelwall (Edinburgh: Clark, 1870). See also J. P. Migne, *Patrologiae cursus completes*, vol. 2, Series Latina (Paris: L. Migne), 1101–1106. The poem is actually a later pseudo-Tertullian text that tells the story of Lot and the destruction of Sodom. The poet is following and embellishing motifs from the Jewish tradition, "especially in terms reminiscent of Josephus." See Loader, *A Tale of Two Cities*, 131–132.

17. Joyce, *Finnegans Wake* (New York: Penguin, 1967), 212.16.

18. Regarding the matter of survival for Abraham and Lot: "In both cases the continued existence of the family is in jeopardy, but in the case of Abraham the matter is resolved by divine intervention while Lot's daughters take matters into their own hands" (Loader, 44). See also L. R. Helyer, "The Separation of Abram and Lot: Its Significance in The Patriarchal Narrative," *Journal for the Study of the Old Testament* 26 (1983): 77–83.

19. *Genesis Rabbah*, 228–229.

20. All subsequent Christian commentary follows this teaching, e.g., Clement of Rome, Jerome, Augustine, Martin Luther, and Jean Calvin. See Loader, *A Tale of Two Cities*, 72.

21. The passage continues: " . . . They did not begin again, they did not desire again. In all this, is one able to convict them of sinful abandon, of criminal incest?" In Kind, *The Drunken Lot*, 48–49.

22. Augustine, *De Civitate Dei*, trans. David S. Wiesaen, vol. 3, Loeb Classical Library (Cambridge, MA: Harvard Univ. Press, 1968), 280–281.

23. See Georgiana Donavin, *Incest Narratives and the Structure of Gower's Confessio Amantis* (Victoria, B.C.: English Literary Studies, 1993), 76, who quotes this passage from Augustine's commentary, *In Psalmum LXXXVII*.

24. It's worth noting how this emphasis on the drunken Lot would preserves a seed of knowledge right down into our sociological age about what a huge role alcohol plays in family abuse and incest.

25. Luther, *Lectures on Genesis*, 308.

26. How ironic that this anti-Semite would turn out to be a spiritual father of Freud.

27. Jean Calvin, *The Book of Genesis*, vol. 1, *Commentaries on the Old Testament*, trans. A. Malet, P. Marcel, and M. Reveillaud (Geneva: 1961), 305.

28. For a discussion of Calvin's commentary and Lot paintings, see Lowenthal, *Joachim Wtewael*, 92.

Chapter 4

1. See Lowenthal, *Joachim Wtewael*, for discussion of iconographic symbolism in *Lot* painting, especially pages 92 and 108.

2. Martin Luther, *Lectures on Genesis: Chapters 15–20*, vol. 3, *Luther's Works*, ed. Jaroslav Pelikan (St. Louis: Concordia), 282, 310.

3. "In the biblical account of Lot and His Daughters there is no hint of eroticism, thus Christian exegetes could exonerate father and daughters of the sin of lust. In contrast, illustrations more often than not exploited the erotic potential of the subject with displays of nudity and intimacy and suggestive accoutrements, such as the vegetable. The slung-leg motif, a classic sign of sexual union, is pervasive" (92).

4. Kind says, "Undeniably, the Altdorfer remains the most remarkable of the drunken Lot representations which were done during the first portion of the sixteenth century" in Joshua Benjamin Kind, *The Drunken Lot and His Daughters: An Iconographical Study in the Uses of This Theme in the Visual Arts* (PhD diss., Columbia University, 1967), 154–155.

5. The cross in the wine goblet is hard to see in most reproductions, but easy to see in the original.

6. "This erotic subject was infrequently treated in the Middle Ages but was considerably more popular with artists from the Renaissance onwards. It was often paired with Susanna and the Elders, both subjects affording a pretext for the depiction of attractive female nudes." R. A. D'Hulst and M. Vandenven, *Rubens: The Old Testament*, trans. P. S. Falla (London: Harvey Miller, 1989).

7. D. Stephen Pepper, *Guido Reni: A Complete Catalogue of His Works with an Introductory Text* (Oxford: Phaidon, 1984), 35–36.

Chapter 5

1. See *Cleanness*, *The Complete Works of the Pearl Poet*, trans. Casey Finch (Berkeley: Univ. of California Press, 1993), 771–1072.

2. William Shakespeare, *Pericles: Prince of Tyre*, ed. Stepehn Orgel (New

York: Penguin, 2001), 1.1.67–70. Otto Rank quotes these lines as the epigraph to Chapter 11, "The Relationship between Father and Daughter in Myth, Folktales, Legends, Literature, Life, and Neurosis," in his important and still useful study, *The Incest Theme in Literature and Legend: Fundamentals of a Psychology of Literary Creation*, trans. Gregory C. Richter (Baltimore: Johns Hopkins Univ. Press, 1992).

3. Georgiana Donavin, *Incest Narratives and the Structure of Gower's* Confessio Amantis (Victoria, B.C.: English Literary Studies, 1993), 7.

4. John Gower, *Confessio Amantis*, vol.1, bk. 8, ed. Russell A. Peck (Kalamazoo, MI: Medieval Institute, 2000), 239–240.

5. For an interesting and important discussion of the father-daughter relationship in *Pericles*, see Deanne Williams, "Papa Don't Preach: The Power of Prolixity in Pericles," University of Toronto Quarterly 71, no. 2 (Spring 2002): 595–622.

6. Sigmund Freud, *The Standard Edition of the Complete Psychological Works of Sigmund Freud*, vol. 12, ed. James Strachey (London: Hogarth Press, 1995), 301.

7. Louis Menand, *The Metaphysical Club* (New York: Farrar, Straus and Giroux, 2001), 314.

8. See Jane Addams, "A Modern Lear," *Survey* 29 (1912): 131–137.

9. See Susan Strehle, "The Daughter's Subversion in Jane Smiley's *A Thousand Acres*," *Critique* 41, no. 3 (2000): 211–226.

10. William Riley Parker, *Milton: A Biography*, vol. 1 (Oxford: Clarendon Press, 1968), 585.

Chapter 6

1. Jane Austen, *Persuasion*, vol. 5, *The Novels of Jane Austen*, 3rd ed., ed. R. W. Chapman (Oxford: Oxford Univ. Press), 82.

2. *Mansfield Park*, a work of immense consequence, points the way to, and suggests an agenda for, major Victorian fiction (for instance, Charlotte Brontë's *Jane Eyre* and *Villette*, Dickens's *Bleak House*, and Thackeray's *Vanity Fair*).

3. Jane Austen, *Mansfield Park*, vol. 3, *The Novels of Jane Austen*, 3rd ed., ed. R. W. Chapman (Oxford: Oxford Univ. Press).

4. See Edmund Heward, *Lord Mansfield* (London: Barry Rose, 1979); Gretchen Gerzina, *Black England: Life before Emancipation* (London: J. Murray, 1995); and James Oldham, *The Mansfield Manuscripts and the Growth of English Law in the Eighteenth Century* (Chapel Hill: Univ. of North Carolina Press, 1992).

5. For discussion of the subject and speculation on its role in the novel, see Brian Southam, "The Silence of the Bertrams: Slavery and the Chronology of *Mansfield Park*," *Times Literary Supplement*, February 17, 1995; Edward W. Said,

Culture and Imperialism (London: Vintage, 1995); Robin Blackburn, *The Overthrow of Colonial Slavery 1776–1848* (London: Verso, 1988); Thomas Clarkson, *The History of the Rise, Progress and Accomplishment of the Abolition of the African Slave-Trade, by the British Parliament,* (London, 1808); and Katherine Sutherland, "Introduction," *Mansfield Park* (London: Penguin, 1996). It seems quite clear, however, from the conversation between Fanny and Edmund Bertram in chapter 2, volume 2, that Austen does not imagine Sir Thomas as a foe of abolition.

6. Lionel Trilling, *The Opposing Self* (New York: Harcourt Brace Jovanovich, 1955), 185.

7. See Linda Troost and Sayre Greenfield, "The Mouse that Roared: Patricia Rozema's *Mansfield Park*," in *Jane Austen in Hollywood*, eds. Linda Troost and Sayre Greenfield (Lexington, KY: Univ. Press of Kentucky, 2001).

8. For discussion of *Mathilda*, see Ranita Chatterjee, "*Mathilda*: Mary Shelley, William Godwin, and the Ideologies of Incest," in *Iconoclastic Departures: Mary Shelley after Frankenstein: Essays in Honor of the Bicentary of Mary Shelley's Birth*, eds. Syndy M. Conger, Frederick S. Frank, and Gregory O'Dea (Madison, NJ: Fairleigh Dickinson Univ. Press, 1997), 130–149; Margaret Davenport Garrett, "Writing and Re-Writing Incest in Mary Shelley's *Mathilda*," *Keats-Shelley Journal* 45 (1996): 44–60; Susan M. Bernardo, "Seductive Confession in Mary Shelley's *Mathilda*," in *Gender Reconstructions: Pornography and Perversions in Literature and Culture*, eds. Cindy L. Carlson, Robert L. Mazzola, and Susan M. Bernardo (Aldershot, England: Ashgate, 2002), 42–52.

9. See Katherine C. Hill-Miller, *My Hideous Progeny: Mary Shelley, William Godwin, and the Father-Daughter Relationship* (Newark: Univ. of Delaware Press, 1995).

10. Mary Shelley to Maria Reveley Gisborne, 30 October, 1834, in *The Letters of Mary Wollstonecraft Shelley*, ed. Betty T. Bennett (Baltimore: Johns Hopkins Univ. Press, 1983), 2:215.

11. Anne Mellor, *Mary Shelley: Her Life, Her Fiction, Her Monsters* (New York: Methuen, 1988), 22. My discussion of Mary Shelley and *Mathilda* owes much to Mellor's perceptive and provocative work.

12. *Shelley and Mary*, ed. Lady Jane Shelley (London: privately printed, 1882), 2:410A.

13. She chose the name of her heroine from several sources that feature a "Mathilda" as the subject of improper, illegitimate love. In the first English gothic novel, Horace Walpole's *The Castle of Otranto* (1764), the villainous father, wanting to get rid of his wife, replace his dead son, and marry his nubile daughter-in-law, offers his own daughter Mathilda to the girl's father. Mathilda is also the name of the hellish sexual temptress in Matthew Lewis's gothic blockbuster, *The*

Monk (1796), and the fiendish female protagonist of Percy's own 1810 Gothic tale *Zastrozzi, A Romance*.

14. Mary Shelley, *Mathilda*, in *The Mary Shelley Reader*, eds. Betty T. Bennett and Charles E. Robinson (New York: Oxford Univ. Press, 1990), 180.

15. Mary was still in dialogue with Percy here. In 1819, before she started *Mathilda*, the Shelleys had been reading Dante. Matilda is the woman the poet last sees—his last temptation—before radiant Beatrice comes to take him to paradise (on earth, the boy Dante had fallen in love with Beatrice when she was 9 years old). In effect, Matilda can be seen as the sweet woman as love-object that the God-seeking male may find it convenient to forget and leave behind. A woman, feeling emotionally abandoned, could easily read her as a sacrificed woman whose own story gets typically, if unwittingly, suppressed by a great poet. Percy's leading lady is named Beatrice. Mary chose Mathilda.

16. See Mellor, *Mary Shelley*, 255n27, for *Mathilda*'s succinct publishing history.

17. Jane Austen, *Northanger Abbey*, vol. 5, *The Novels of Jane Austen*, 3rd ed., ed. R. W. Chapman (Oxford: Oxford Univ. Press), 160.

Chapter 7

1. See Elizabeth Gaskell, *The Life of Charlotte Brontë* (London: Penguin, 1985); *The Brontës: Their Lives, Friendships and Correspondence*, 4 vols., eds. T. J. Wise and J. A. Symington (Oxford: Blackwell, 1932); John Lock and W. T. Dixon, *A Man of Sorrow: The Life, Letters and Times of the Rev. Patrick Brontë, 1777–1861* (London: Thomas Nelson, 1965); Juliet Barker, *The Brontës: A Life in Letters* (New York: St. Martin's, 1995); Rebecca Fraser, *The Brontës: Charlotte Brontë and Her Family* (New York: Crown, 1988); Winifred Gérin, *Emily Brontë: A Biography* (Oxford: Clarendon Press, 1971); Lucasta Miller, *The Brontë Myth* (New York: Knopf, 2003).

2. See Barker, *The Brontës*, 3.

3. Lock and Dixon, *A Man of Sorrow*, 34.

4. Ibid., 96.

5. He could get no one but his conscientious, unmemorable sister-in-law Elizabeth, "Aunt Branwell," to live with the family. This spinster, a strict, rather dour Christian, did noble and selfless duty by the children, teaching the girls domestic skills and religious precepts, but she didn't inspire the children or give them much maternal love or guidance.

6. Gaskell, *Life of Charlotte Brontë*, 94.

7. Branwell, alleged father of a bastard child, notoriously cared too much

about bodies—or at least sensual being. His father and Charlotte later believed and insisted that Branwell's life went to hell, drink, and opium because a Mrs. Robinson, the sexy, rich, adulterous mother of the boy whose tutor he was, had seduced him, led him on, then jilted him when her husband died and she was free to marry.

8. Christine Alexander, ed., *An Edition of the Early Writing of Charlotte Brontë*, vol. 1 (Oxford: Blackwell, 1987).

9. Matthew Arnold, *The Letters of Matthew Arnold: Volume 1, 1829–1859*, ed. Cecil Y. Lang (Charlottesville: Univ. Press of Virginia, 1996), 262.

10. Irene Tayler, *Holy Ghosts: The Male Muses of Emily and Charlotte Brontë* (New York: Columbia University Press, 1990), 149.

11. Gaskell, *Life of Charlotte Brontë*, 172–173.

12. Ibid., 174–175.

13. See Alexander, *Early Writing of Charlotte Brontë*.

14. One, from Ellen Nussey's brother Henry, who matter-of-factly wrote her that *as a curate he had to have a wife to teach the parish children, and as someone else had turned him down, would she marry him?*, would figure in her creation of St. John Rivers in *Jane Eyre*.

15. Kathleen Tillotson, *Novels of the Eighteen-Forties* (Oxford: Oxford Univ. Press, 1967), 278.

16. Gérin, *Emily Brontë*, 292.

17. Charlotte Brontë, *Jane Eyre*, 2nd ed., ed. Richard J. Dunn (New York: Norton, 1987).

18. Virginia Woolf, "*Jane Eyre* and *Wuthering Heights*," *The Common Reader* (New York: Harcourt Brace, 1925), reprinted in Dunn, *Jane Eyre*, 456.

19. Adrienne Rich, *On Lies, Secrets, and Silence: Selected Prose, 1966–1978* (New York: Norton, 1979), reprinted in Dunn, *Jane Eyre*.

20. Sandra M. Gilbert and Susan Gubar, *The Madwoman in the Attic* (New Haven: Yale Univ. Press, 1979), reprinted in Dunn, *Jane Eyre*.

21. For instance, represented *desire* in this novel suggests why after writing *The Vindication*, Wollstonecraft could still try to kill herself out of blind love for a caddish older man, and why Victorian scandalmongers, when Charlotte Brontë dedicated *Jane Eyre* to William Thackeray (he had put away a mad wife of his own), might put it about that she was his mistress.

22. In *Jane Eyre*, says Adrienne Rich, "we find an alternative to the stereotypical rivalry of women" (op. cit.) but, though that might be true, for instance, of the brief bonding of Jane and the Rivers sisters at Marsh End, it's actually like saying in *Oedipus Rex* we find an alternative to the stereotypical rivalry of men. Jane is the real alternative and rebel against the status quo—not Bertha.

23. Helene Moglen, *Charlotte Brontë: The Self-Conceived* (New York: Norton, 1976), 126.

24. Two particular aspects of the rendering of the madwoman open her to interpretations that would fit the changing uses and needs of future readers: (1) Brontë marginalizes her. Bertha comes from an alien "Indian" race, and English Jane Eyre's view towards her is like one of the chosen people looking down on cities-of-the-plain heathens or the pagan tribes of Moab and Ammon. That cultural vision, could, should, and would be reversed, as Jean Rhys, for example, proves. (2) By rendering Bertha's character and history through the voice of Rochester, Brontë provides later commentators with deniability: in effect, *this is the way misogynists may think about such women, but the story of Bertha might really be otherwise.*

25. Emily Bronte, *Wuthering Heights*, 3rd ed., eds. William M. Sale, Jr. and Richard J. Dunn (New York: Norton, 1990).

26. Barker, *The Brontës*, 392.

27. Writes Stevie Davies in *Emily Brontë: Heretic* (London: Women's Press, 1994), "My intuition is that *Wuthering Heights* is not a heterosexual's book. Its intense pledging of itself to the idea of likeness implies to me a lesbian consciousness: but I cannot prove this and indeed it is not necessary to consent to such a proposition to see how powerfully the gyandrous or androgynous sensibility dominates the work."

28. "Editor's Preface to the New Edition of *Wuthering Heights* (1850)," in *Wuthering Heights: Authoritative Text, Backgrounds, Criticism*, 3rd ed., eds. William M. Sale, Jr. and Richard J. Dunn (New York: Norton, 1990), 322.

29. "Biographical Notice of Ellis and Acton Bell (1850)," in *Wuthering Heights*, 319.

30. Barker, *The Brontës*, 534.

31. Gérin, *Emily Brontë*, 148.

32. "Poems from the 1850 *Wuthering Heights*," in *Wuthering Heights*, 267.

33. Edward Chitham, *A Life of Emily Brontë* (Oxford: Blackwell, 1987), 243, quotes "Mr. Frank Peel of Heckmondwike."

34. Gérin, *Emily Brontë*, 165.

35. "Emily Brontë's Diary," 26 June 1837, in *Wuthering Heights*, 296.

36. Chitham, *Life of Emily Brontë*, 26; see also page 81.

37. Barker, *The Brontës*, 389.

38. Ibid., 388–389.

39. Letter, *New York Times Book Review*, October 29, 1995.

40. Letter, *New York Times Book Review*, December 3, 1995.

41. Chitham, *Life of Emily Brontë*, 159.

Chapter 8

1. For a fascinating study of the relationship between nineteenth-century British writers and the idea of girls in literature see Catherine Robson, *Men in Wonderland: The Lost Girlhood of the Victorian Gentleman* (Princeton: Princeton Univ. Press, 2001). For a brilliant, controversial, indispensable study of the child in Victorian culture and the relationship between childhood and love, see James R. Kincaid, *Child-Loving: The Erotic Child and Victorian Culture* (New York: Routledge, 1992). See also Deborah Gorham, *The Victorian Girl and the Feminine Ideal* (Bloomington: Indiana Univ. Press, 1982).

2. W. T. Stead, "The Maiden Tribute of Modern Babylon," pts. 1–4, *Pall Mall Gazette*, July 6, 7, 8, 10, 1885.

3. W. T. Stead, "Notice to Our Readers," *Pall Mall Gazette*, July 4, 1885.

4. Stead, "The Maiden Tribute," pt. 1.

5. Ibid., pt. 1.

6. Ibid, pt. 3. "Freud alerts us to the ways in which we have been educated into thinking that children are pure, asexual, and innocent, and to how 'anyone who describes them otherwise can be charged with being an infamous blasphemer against the tender and sacred feelings of mankind'" Carol Mavor, *Pleasures Taken: Performances of Sexuality and Loss in Victorian Photographs* (Durham: Duke Univ. Press, 1995), 11.

7. Charles Terrot, *The Maiden Tribute: A Study of the White Slave Traffic of the Nineteenth Century* (London: Frederick Muller, 1959), 35.

8. Terrot also says, "Stead, between the years 1884 and 1888, came nearer to governing Great Britain than any other one man in the kingdom" (142).

9. Michael Pearson, *The Age of Consent: Victorian Prostitution and Its Enemies* (Newton Abbot, Devon: David and Charles, 1972), 125.

10. F. W. Whyte, *The Life of W. T. Stead*, vol. 2 (London: Jonathan Cape, 1925) 341–342.

11. Walkowitz's *City of Dreadful Delight* (Chicago: Univ. of Chicago Press, 1992) devotes chapters 3 and 4 to "The Maiden Tribute of Modern Babylon." See also Deborah Gorham, "The 'Maiden Tribute of Modern Babylon' Re-Examined: Child Prostitution and the Idea of Childhood in Late Victorian England," *Victorian Studies* 21 (1978): 353–379; Raymond L. Schults, *Crusader in Babylon: W. T. Stead and the Pall Mall Gazette* (Lincoln, NE: Univ. of Nebraska Press, 1972).

12. *Pall Mall Gazette*, July 6, pp. 1–2.

13. Carroll to Lord Salisbury, 7 July 1885, *The Selected Letters of Lewis Carroll*, 2nd ed., ed. Morton N. Cohen (London: Macmillan, 1989).

14. Derek Hudson, *Lewis Carroll: An Illustrated Biography* (New York: C. N. Potter, 1977).

15. *St. James's Gazette*, July 22, 1885, 6.

16. Morton N. Cohen, *Lewis Carroll: A Biography* (New York: Knopf, 1995), 203.

17. See, for example, Mavor, *Pleasures Taken*. The nude picture of Evelyn Hatch is egregious, but such pictures as those of Irene Macdonald and Alice Liddell in beggar's rags, as well as many others, also might interest a Minotaur.

18. Vladimir Nabokov, *The Annotated Lolita* (New York: Vintage, 1991), 377.

19. Paul Taylor, *The Independent*, November 8, 1994.

20. Louise Doughty, review of "Alice's Adventures Under Ground" by Christopher Hampton.

21. See Kincaid, *Child-Loving*, for a wonderfully perceptive discussion of the subject.

22. Jackie Wullschlager, *Financial Times*, October 31, 1994, 15.

23. Lewis Carroll, *Alice in Wonderland*, 2nd ed., ed. Donald J. Gray (New York: Norton, 1992), 118.

Chapter 9

1. Sigmund Freud, *Dora: An Analysis of a Case of Hysteria*, ed. Philip Rieff (New York: Simon and Schuster, 1997), 56. See also Sigmund Freud, *Fragment of an Analysis of a Case of Hysteria*, in vol. 7 of *The Standard Edition of the Complete Psychological Works of Sigmund Freud*, trans. and ed. James Strachey (London: Hogarth Press, 1995).

2. For the factual context and background of *Dora*, see Charles Bernheimer and Claire Kahane, eds., *In Dora's Case: Freud—Hysteria—Feminism*, 2nd ed. (New York: Columbia University Press, 1990); Hannah S. Decker, *Freud, Dora, and Vienna 1900* (New York: Free Press, 1991); and Lisa Appignanesi and John Forrester, *Freud's Women* (New York: Basic Books, 1992). For a helpful and provocative reading of Freud's *Interpretation of Dreams* that bears on the reading of Dora here, see Alexander Welsh, *Freud's Wishful Dream Book* (Princeton, N. J.: Princeton University Press, 1994). See also Peter Brooks and Alex Woloch, eds., *Whose Freud?: The Place of Psychoanalysis in Contemporary Culture* (New Haven: Yale University Press, 2000). For an account of Freud's place in history and culture now, see Eli Zaretsky, *Secrets of the Soul: A Social and Cultural History of Psychoanalysis* (New York: Knopf, 2004).

3. See Rieff, "Introduction," *Dora*, vii, for the context of Freud's remark in his letter to Fliess of October, 14, 1900; and J. M. Masson, ed., *The Complete Letters of Sigmund Freud to Wihelm Fliess, 1887–1904* (Cambridge, Mass.: Harvard Univ. Press, 1984).

4. See Felix Deutsch, "A Footnote to Freud's 'Fragment of an Analysis of a Case of Hysteria,'" in Bernheimer and Kahane, *In Dora's Case*, 35–43.

5. Sigmund Freud, *An Autobiographical Study*, in vol. 20 of Strachey, *The Standard Edition of the Complete Psychological Works*, 34; emphasis mine.

6. James Joyce, *Ulysses*, 288.

7. In what must be the most egregious example of the Lot complex in first-generation psychoanalysis, the talented analyst Sandor Ferenczi, Freud's brilliant disciple, colleague, and friend, treated Ella, the daughter of his mistress Frau G., and then married the girl.

8. Joan Acocella, in "The Empty Couch," *The New Yorker*, May 8, 2000, 116, pinpoints one reason for women's continuing interest in psychoanalysis: "For many people of my generation, especially women, psychotherapy is not so much an issue as a history, a language in which they learned to speak of themselves, and of life."

9. Elizabeth Young-Bruehl, *Anna Freud* (New York: Summit Books, 1988), 81.

10. Kahane notes that for many feminists reading *Dora*, "Freud's interpretive strategies were critically determined by his inability to deal with the feminine" (27). Jacqueline Rose sums up this line of criticism, "Quite simply, the case of Dora is seen to fail because Dora is repressed as a woman by psychoanalysis ("Dora: Fragment of an Analysis," in Bernheimer and Kahane, 129). Hélène Cixous says of Dora, "It is she who is the victim, but the others come out of it in shreds" (Hélène Cixous and Catherine Clément, "The Untenable," in Bernheimer and Kahane, 280). See also Robin Tolmach Lakoff and James C. Coyne, *Father Knows Best: The Use and Abuse of Power in Freud's Case of 'Dora'* (New York: Teachers College Press, 1993).

11. See Shloss, *Lucia Joyce*.

12. James Joyce, *Finnegan's Wake* (New York: Penguin, 1967), 115.21–35.

Chapter 10

1. Fitzgerald to Zelda Fitzgerald, 29 July, 1940, in *Correspondence of F. Scott Fitzgerald*, eds. Matthew J. Bruccoli and Margaret M. Duggan (New York: Random House, 1980), 602.

2. Shirley Temple Black, *Child Star: An Autobiography* (New York: McGraw-Hill, 1988), 59. I am deeply indebted to this fine, well-written, always entertaining, and important autobiography for much of the information in this chapter. Anyone who reads *Child Star* will likely be struck by its candor, its transcendence of the platitudinous nature of conventional "show biz" biographies and impressed by the largeness, openness, and good humor of its author and subject.

3. See Robert Windeler, *The Films of Shirley Temple* (Secaucus, NJ: Citadel Press, 1978), 13.

4. For another view of the cinematic relationship between Temple and Robinson, see Karen Orr Vered, "White and Black in Black and White: Management of Race and Sexuality in the Coupling of Child-Star Shirley Temple and Bill Robinson," *The Velvet Light Trap* 39 (1997): 52–65.

5. This scene is cut in some videotape versions.

6. She continues about her mother, "[S]he merits and receives my lifelong adoration, deep and indestructible" (179).

7. The accompanying caption in *Child Star* reads, "Caged by J. Edgar Hoover, like a skunk, Yosemite Valley, 1938."

Chapter 11

1. *The New York Times*, sec. 4, October 1, 1995.

2. Woody Allen, *Side Effects* (New York: Ballantine Books, 1981), 186.

3. Lloyd Rose, "Humor and Nothingness: Woody Allen," *The Atlantic*, May 1985.

4. Eric Lax, *Woody Allen: A Biography* (New York: Vintage Books, 1992), 19.

5. "[T]he two days are almost worth it because two good days a month with Louise were better than a good year with most other people": Lax, *Woody Allen*, 170).

6. Quoted in Tim Carroll, "Woody the Secret Womaniser," *Daily Mail*, November 20, 1993, 45.

7. Mia Farrow, *What Falls Away: A Memoir* (New York: Doubleday, 1997), 7. Kathryn Harrison, herself the author of a memoir about incest with her father—*The Kiss* (New York: Random House, 1997)—in reviewing *What Falls Away* called Mia a "waif-woman fascinated with the never-never land of childhood" ("Intimate Strangers," *The New York Times*, sec. 7, February 23, 1997).

8. Specifically, *Rosemary's Baby*'s popular success spread interest and belief in the existence of satanic cults and was surely in part responsible—directly or indirectly—for the book by Michelle Smith and Lawrence Pazder, *Michelle Remembers* (New York: Congdon & Lattes, 1980). Historians of the recovered memory movement have shown that a key factor in the satanic ritual abuse craze of the 1980s and early '90s and the related epidemic of sexual child-abuse accusations was the widespread, diffusive influence of this sensational, if irresponsible, and now discounted memoir. This account by Smith and her psychiatrist (later her husband), Dr. Lawrence Pazder, purports to describe the recovered memories, retrieved in trance therapy, of Michelle's horrendous experience before the age of 5 in a satanic cult that had tortured her, sodomized her, and

abused her in countless horrific ways. Its popularity led to a slew of women, under sympathetic therapists' hypnosis, drugs, and suggestion, remembering abuse, incest, devilment, and satanic mistreatment. That, in turn, led to such excesses as the witch-hunt daycare scandals of the 1980s. By the time the domestic affinities of Mia and Woody exploded, people, including Mia, would be primed to believe the worst. For discussion of this social history, see Richard Ofshe and Ethan Waters, *Making Monsters: False Memories, Psychotherapy, and Sexual Hysteria* (New York: Scribner, 1994); Lawrence Wright, *Remembering Satan* (New York: Knopf, 1994); Debbie Nathan and Michael Snedeker, *Satan's Silence: Ritual Abuse and the Making of a Modern American Witch Hunt* (New York: Basic Books, 1995); Elizabeth Loftus and Katerine Ketcham, *The Myth of Repressed Memory: False Memories and Allegations of Sexual Abuse* (New York: St. Martin's, 1991); Frederick Crews et al., *The Memory Wars: Freud's Legacy in Dispute* (London: Granta Books, 1997); Janice Haaken, *Pillar of Salt: Gender, Memory, and the Perils of Looking Back* (New Brunswick, NJ: Rutgers Univ. Press, 1998). See especially Mark Pendergrast, *Victims of Memory: Incest, Accusation, and Shattered Lives* (Hinesburg, VT: Upper Access Books, 1995), 47–48.

9. See Kristi Groteke, *Mia and Woody: Love and Betrayal*, with Marjorie Rosen (New York: Carroll & Graf, 1994), 59.

10. The film's interplay between fictional and "real" characters, of course, has many precedents and analogues: for example, Lewis Carroll's *Through the Looking-Glass*, Pirandello's *Six Characters in Search of an Author*, Buster Keaton's *Sherlock, Jr.*, Flann O'Brien's *At Swim-Two-Birds*, Jean Cocteau's *Orphée*, and Allen's own *Zelig*.

11. Woody actually shot the "Jewel" scenes at his old neighborhood theater in Brooklyn, the Kent, "one of the great, meaningful places of my boyhood" (Lax, 25).

12. Lax, *Woody Allen*, 28.

13. Harrison, *The Kiss*, 67–70.

14. Peter Shard, *Daily Mail*, December 26, 1997.

15. Although Mia and her camp accused Allen of seducing Soon-Yi, Mia's lawyer Eleanor Alter, long after the custody case, mused, "You know, I think she came after him."

16. Camille Paglia, "The Dangers of the Gay Agenda," *Salon*, October 28, 1998 (writing as "Camille").

17. Walter Isaacson, "The Heart Wants What It Wants," *Time*, August 31, 1992.

18. Two points would later make Farrow's post-Soon-Yi assertions about her pre-Polaroid concern that Woody was an abuser of Dylan look dubious: first, her support the previous December for his legal adoption of the girl, and, second, Allen's continuing support of independent, professional therapy for Dylan,

beginning more than a year before (therapists were legally bound to report any suspected child abuse). Since he favored Dylan talking to professionals to whom she was free say anything about him, and since they had to inform authorities of sexual abuse, it would seem he had no qualms or guilty anxiety about what the girl might say. In 1991 Mia and Woody talked about Dylan and they decided to have her evaluated by Satchel's therapist, Dr. Susan Coates. As a result, in April 1991, the girl started going to Dr. Nancy Schultz, a psychiatrist who saw her until Mia fired her after the smash-up in August 1992. Neither Dr. Coates nor Dr. Schultz believed or corroborated the charges of sexual abuse against Allen.

19. For compelling accounts of this turn of events, see Pendergrast, *Victims of Memory*; Nathan and Snedeker, *Satan's Silence*; and Moira Johnston, *Spectral Evidence, the Ramona Case: Incest, Memory, and the Truth on Trial in Napa Valley* (Boston: Houghton Mifflin, 1997).

20. Kristi Groteke, Mia's erstwhile friend and supporter, calls the videotape "chilling," but adds that some people say it looks rehearsed, as if Dylan were acting. She says the girl is melodramatic, "manic and distracted" when answering Mia's questions about where Allen touched her, but she doubts that Mia coached Dylan as to specific words or details. Woody argued that the tape was doctored; and, according to Groteke, it "had undeniably . . . been stopped and restarted several times" and also spliced (127).

21. Bill Zehme, "So You're the Great Woody Allen?" *Esquire*, October 1994.

22. See Richard Ellmann, *Oscar Wilde* (New York: Knopf, 1988), 463, for a description of the trial.

23. Ironically, 21-year-old Mia Farrow said when she married Frank Sinatra, "There is nothing wrong with an older man marrying a younger woman" (315). See Marion Meade, *The Unruly Life of Woody Allen: A Biography* (New York: Scribner, 2000).

24. Ira Berkow, "Woody Allen Goes From Defense to Offense," *New York Times*, November 2, 1995.

Chapter 12

1. For critical discussion of *Thereafter Johnnie*, see Arlene R. Keizer, "The Geography of the Apocalypse: Incest, Mythology, and the Fall of Washington City in Carolivia Herron's *Thereafter Johnnie, American Literature* 72, no. 2 (2000): 387–416; Elizabeth Breau, "Incest and Intertextuality in Carolivia Herron's *Thereafter Johnnie, African American Review* 31 (1997): 91–103; Brenda O. Daly, "Whose Daughter Is *Johnnie*? Revisionary Myth-Making in Carolivia Herron's *Thereafter Johnnie*," *Callaloo* 18, no. 2 (1995): 472–91; Barbara Christian, "Epic Achievement," *Women's Review of Books*, Oct. 1991: 6–7.

2. James Joyce, *Finnegan's Wake* (New York: Penguin, 1967), 183.22–23.

3. Carolivia Herron, *Thereafter Johnnie* (New York: Random House, 1991), 133.

4. Amy Johnson, "*Thereafter Johnnie*/Carolivia Herron" (working paper, Department of English, Stanford University, 1997).

5. See Donna Britt, "The Author, the Relative, and a Question of Incest; Carolivia Herron's Disputed Tale of Childhood Horror," *The Washington Post*, June 25, 1991.

6. See Janice Haaken, *Pillar of Salt: Gender, Memory, and the Perils of Looking Back* (New Brunswick, NJ: Rutgers University Press, 1998), for a helpful, informative analysis of recovered memory in recent psychological and social history. Like me (see "The Lot Complex, Joyce, and the End of *Finnegans Wake*," *The Recorder* 7, no. 2 [Fall 1994]: 58–77), Haaken uses Lot's wife and other Lot material in Genesis 19 as a rich metaphorical frame to focus on her subject.

Chapter 13

1. Phil Kuntz, ed., *The Starr Report: The Evidence* (New York: Pocket Books, 1998), 355.

2. Andrew Morton, *Monica's Story*, (New York: St. Martin's, 1999), 26. I am very much indebted to this readable, extremely useful biography of Lewinsky. It convincingly presents her perception of the case.

3. "Tripp Tape Excerpts," Associated Press, *The Washingon Post*, October 2, 1998. These excerpts are from the edited transcripts of the Lewinsky–Tripp phone conversations released by the House Judiciary Committee. Tripp made the tapes between October 3 and December 22, 1997. The material is on line in the archives search section of www.washingtonpost.com.

4. Gail Sheehy, *Hillary's Choice* (New York: Ballantine Books, 2000), 312.

5. There is some question, however, whether Blythe really was the father. See Sheehy, *Hillary's Choice*, 94–95.

6. "Tripp Tape Excerpts." Like Dora's father and Herr K. in Freud, the chief executive reportedly told Monica he got little or nothing from his wife ("he was unhappy in his marriage" [Morton, 114]). Hillary Clinton seemed to Lewinsky (and others) to be hard, not soft or giving. A late-fortyish woman (she suffered from endrometriosis, which had made it difficult for her to conceive, and then, after bearing Chelsea, impossible), his wife, whom he loved, could make Clinton feel the claustrophobia of aging. He told Lewinsky that when he was no longer president, he might very well be single. During Kenneth Starr's investigation, it turned out that Clinton had given her a book of poetry by Walt Whitman. Later, it came out that he had given the same book to Hillary years before. The repeat gift, some said, proved his total cynicism, but it looks more like an effort to hold

off time and retrieve from the past the identity—momentarily at least—of the romantic wooer.

7. Monica Lewinsky to President Clinton, 29 June 1997, in *The Starr Report: The Evidence*, ed. Phil Kuntz (New York: Pocket Books, 1998), 427.

8. Ruth Marcus and Joan Biskupic, "Democrats Find New Ammunition," *Washington Post*, October 3, 1998.

9. David Finkel, "How It Came to This: The Scandal in 13 Acts," *Washington Post Magazine*, December 13, 1998. Five years later, on the HBO television special, "Monica in Black and White" (2002), when asked why she preserved the dress with the presidential stain, she answered that she kept it just as you might keep as a souvenir the sweaty T-shirt of a rock star.

10. Karl Marx, "The Eighteenth Brumaire of Louis Bonaparte," *The Marx-Engels Reader*, 2nd ed., ed. Robert C. Tucker (New York: Norton, 1978), 594.

11. See Hillary Rodham Clinton, *Living History* (New York: Simon and Schuster, 2003).

12. When it seemed necessary to help Clinton win in the socially conservative South, Hillary changed her name from Hillary Rodham to Hillary Rodham Clinton.

13. *Washington Post*, "Chelsea Clinton Speaks about Sept. 11 Terror Attacks," November 11, 2001.

Index